The Dynamics of Care

"Wolstenholme and McKelvie bring two lifetimes of award-winning experience in applying system dynamics to health and care dynamics to the creation of this new book. In spite of amazing advances in all areas of medical science with associated increases in our ability to diagnose and treat complex medical problems, our medical system as a whole is facing multiple crises. These problems arise not from how we diagnose and treat patients on a one-on-one basis, rather from how components of care are organised (or more often not organised) into a coherent overall system of care. Our current dysfunctional system of care is the target of Wolstenholme and McKelvie's insightful analysis. Focused on **flows** and **throughput** as key analytic concepts, this new book condenses and focuses insights from over 80 empirical studies within a coherent analytical frame. All of us interested in and concerned about the cost and quality of maintaining a health population need to read and come to grips with the points that they are making in this important new book."

—David F. Andersen, *O'Leary Distinguished Service Professor, Emeritus, Nelson A. Rockefeller College of Public Affairs and Policy, University at Albany, State University of New York, Albany, New York*

"This very welcome book offers the hope of sound and sustainable solutions to persistent and serious problems that not only cause untold misery to millions but also impose considerable costs in many societies. The exceptional work it reports on illustrates that a fundamental new capability has been reached—it is now both technically and practically feasible to *simulate* most management and policy challenges we face. This is as true for small, local issues as it is for large problems of wide scope. These working, quantified simulations are powerful because they mimic the observable behaviour of the systems we want to better manage, not just the performance outcomes of concern, but everything else of significance. They therefore allow us to experiment, boldly and at trivial cost, with software facsimiles of the real world, rather than (as we have always done until now) on the real world itself. This potential is now recognised in the UK government report 'Computational modelling: Blackett review', which makes clear that every executive, advisor and policy-maker, in every field of endeavour, should understand what such simulations can do and know how to implement and exploit them."

—Kim Warren, *Managing Director Strategy Dynamics, London, UK*

Since its inception more than seven decades ago, the NHS has become one of the great unchanging features of the British landscape. The flip side of such permanence is its inability to move with the times in the way that has revolutionised other industries.

In this timely book, Eric and Douglas peel back the mystique around care delivery. They introduce two key concepts, feedback and flow, and show why any attempt to modernise delivery will fail without carefully responding to these underlying principles.

The strength of this book is the weight of examples culled over many years of practical experience. It is a call to learn to build a better care system and it provides some powerful clues as to how to change care delivery for the better, and in an affordable way.

Happy reading!

—Terry Young, *Professor Emeritus of Health Care Systems, Brunel University, London and Director, Datchet Consulting* (https://datchet.consulting/)

"A recent report in the *British Medical Journal (Global Health)* addressed the issue of health system modelling research, emphasising that models should capture the dynamic interactions between the main health system components and acknowledge constraints. This new book by Eric Wolstenholme and Douglas McKelvie describes a methodology (system dynamics) which eminently satisfies that call. Through a number of examples distilled from their extensive consultancy roles in health and social care, they urge a move away from considering specific departments, to a consideration of coupled health systems which transcend organisational boundaries, where inter-connections, inter-dependencies, flows and stocks become the new perspective instead. Those involved in planning for improved service delivery in health and social care can now learn how to rehearse their ideas in silico by deploying simulations which capture the nuances of health systems and can leverage counter-intuitive policy responses."

—Brian Dangerfield, *School of Management, University of Bristol, UK*

Eric Wolstenholme · Douglas McKelvie

The Dynamics of Care

Understanding People *Flows* in Health and Social Care

Springer

Eric Wolstenholme
Symmetric Scenarios
Edinburgh, UK

Douglas McKelvie
Symmetric Scenarios
Edinburgh, UK

ISBN 978-3-030-21880-5   ISBN 978-3-030-21878-2 (eBook)
https://doi.org/10.1007/978-3-030-21878-2

© Springer Nature Switzerland AG 2019

This work is subject to copyright. All rights are reserved by the Publisher, whether the whole or part of the material is concerned, specifically the rights of translation, reprinting, reuse of illustrations, recitation, broadcasting, reproduction on microfilms or in any other physical way, and transmission or information storage and retrieval, electronic adaptation, computer software, or by similar or dissimilar methodology now known or hereafter developed.

The use of general descriptive names, registered names, trademarks, service marks, etc. in this publication does not imply, even in the absence of a specific statement, that such names are exempt from the relevant protective laws and regulations and therefore free for general use.

The publisher, the authors and the editors are safe to assume that the advice and information in this book are believed to be true and accurate at the date of publication. Neither the publisher nor the authors or the editors give a warranty, expressed or implied, with respect to the material contained herein or for any errors or omissions that may have been made. The publisher remains neutral with regard to jurisdictional claims in published maps and institutional affiliations.

This Springer imprint is published by the registered company Springer Nature Switzerland AG
The registered company address is: Gewerbestrasse 11, 6330 Cham, Switzerland

Foreword

This new book by Eric Wolstenholme and Douglas McKelvie is a very welcome addition and should find a wide audience. Both authors are well known in the field of system dynamics simulation modelling and have been leaders of our field and its UK contingent for many years.

Eric started his academic career in 1976 and taught at several universities (Bradford, Stirling, where he was Professor and Head of the Department of Management Science, Leeds Beckett University and London South Bank). He has published two books before this one and many articles, and was Founding Editor of the *System Dynamics Review* journal, President of the International System Dynamics Society and winner of the Society's highest honour, the Forrester Award, in 2004. He has also been a system dynamics consultant since 1994. With Douglas, as well as David Monk, he formed the consultancy, SymmetricSD, in 2005 to focus on issues of health and social care.

Douglas started as a social worker in his home country of Scotland, serving 12 years on the front lines and 10 years in senior regulatory roles. He joined the consultancy OLM in 2002, where he met Eric and David, and started his study of system dynamics. By 2012, he had won the Gleave Prize for best real-world application of system dynamics in the UK (on alcohol harm), and in 2016 and 2017, he assumed leadership positions in the System Dynamics Society in the UK and internationally.

It is fortunate for us that these two modellers and consultants, with complementary backgrounds and some 16 years working together on more than 80 projects, have gathered those experiences together in writing this book (Some of this work has been published previously, but most has not.). Their broad theme is how health and social care systems—despite good intentions all around—are prone to behave sub-optimally, providing less benefit and allowing more harm than they should, due to perverse incentives or conflicting goals within or between organisations. Douglas is not the first Scot to remind us that "The best laid schemes o' mice an' men/Gang aft agley".

The authors describe how this theme plays out in two UK contexts they know well, hospital care and mental health care. In both cases, persistent or "wicked" problems have been made worse and harder to handle due to ageing of the population. With regard to hospital care, the wicked problem is delayed hospital discharges. A discharge does not take place in the UK until an appropriate post-discharge destination is located that can provide the right level of continuing health and social care. In the USA, the lack of such a destination might result in the patient simply being sent home to fend for themselves. In the UK, the result is instead a delayed discharge, which ties up capacity and increases the risk of a hospital-acquired infection. Numerous attempts to solve such bottlenecking at the hospital level have failed. The authors conclude that a more integrated approach is needed in which social care spending is put in the proper balance with that of hospitals. The need for such rebalancing is becoming even greater with population ageing because of the more complicated post-discharge needs of the elderly.

With regard to mental health care, the wicked problem is lack of access to needed specialty services, such as those for depression, dementia and alcoholism. Long waiting times for such specialty services have persisted despite an understanding that "stepped care", employing intermediate resources for less complicated cases, is the right solution. Although most agree on this desired end state, what has proved challenging is the implementation problem—how to get from here to there. How, during a period of transition, should one deal with existing and transitional backlogs of patients, and how should funding be gradually reallocated from specialty to non-specialty practitioners? These are not easy questions to answer without a model, and trying to muddle through without a model is prone to "Gang aft agley".

There is something universal in an approach to problems that boils things down to flows, capacities and backlogs, and that identifies how attempts to deal with backlogs will prove ineffective or counterproductive if the underlying cause is not addressed. Operations researchers and system dynamics modellers have approached many problems this way since the 1950s. Eric and Douglas are not the first to adopt such a "flow perspective" (to borrow Eric's term), but they surely have been the most persistent and successful during their 16 years together in exploring its many manifestations in the area of health and social care.

You should read this book whether or not you are familiar with system dynamics or with care dynamics specifically. You will find rich description based on real-world cases, logical structuring of the issue and clear presentation of the results. You will also find a general introduction to the concepts of system dynamics as applied to typical care variables such as admissions, discharges and length of stay. Plentiful diagrams and behaviour-over-time graphs are used as needed to help tell the various stories in this book, but no higher mathematics is employed. This is the wisdom gained from hard work by a dedicated team plying the care-modelling trade for 16 years together, and there is much to be learned here.

Barrytown, New York
August 2018

Jack Homer

Preface

Unlike many collected works, this book is not an assembly of previously published papers although some elements of some chapters have been published before. Neither, like many systems and system dynamics texts, is it based on applications spread across many disciplines and industries.

It is a focused story of practical consultancy projects[1] in system dynamics modelling by the authors applied to one significant and topical domain: health and social care. The motivation in writing it comes from a desire to reinforce a whole system perspective to the worldwide debate on this topic and to bring the power of dynamic modelling to a wider range of healthcare and social care professionals. To this end, it has to balance the need to be sufficiently technical and rigorous with the need to be sufficiently issue-driven and insightful.

This is achieved by dividing the book into parts. Part I describes simple but rich generic modelling structures which are both important in their own right and providing a glimpse of what is under the bonnet of later project models. While introducing some elements of the languages used to map and describe models, quantitative and mathematical skills are kept to a minimum. It is recommended that all readers assimilated as much of Part I as possible to appreciate the workings of the later project models and to appreciate the helpfulness of even simple models to complex issues.

All our projects in the book are based on models, and it is worth an early comment on this much misunderstood word for those unfamiliar with modelling methods.

We would claim that everyone is a modeller without realising it, but that we do it openly. Whenever people are faced with choice (which is all the time), we all try our best to project and imagine the alternative futures involved. Our ability to think through time, into the past and future, and to create internal simulations is perhaps unique to our species, and our decisions are often based on such ponderings. What we do in this book is to bring managers together around issues of concern to share their implicit mental models and convert them into explicit models. This involves

---

[1] Hence, some of the chapters contain few references.

them surfacing assumptions and agreeing their different perspectives on how the world around them works and, where ever possible, quantifying it. The aim is to improve understanding and learning, rather than to achieve prediction, and often models still contain judgements. Explicit models may still be difficult to validate but are considerably clearer than mental ones which are almost never subjected to validation (Epstein 2008[2]).

Most models in the book have been created by a facilitation process, and in the course of doing this, we have developed our own understanding of the topics covered. So, a few of our chapters contain models which grew out of projects but were developed out of our own interest. It goes without saying that all views, insights and conclusions are quoted throughout the book and are those of the authors and not any particular organisations or clients.

Like most system-based work, the book will appeal more to people who think visually, spatially and temporally rather than in words. This is because it is hard to see a system or describe it in a sequence of words, and diagrams are an essential aid in helping to make systems and feedback visible. Diagrams provide an invaluable "structure" on which to hang data which is missing in many formal statistical models and from most mental models. Mismatches between structure and data provide an important check on the validity of data, and learning from models comes from understanding mismatches between how people think a structure will behave over time and how it really behaves when subjected to computer simulation. System dynamics models are a very inexpensive approach to policy analysis compared with experimenting on real organisations, and hence, the value added can be huge.

In many ways in a digital age where models can be brought to life on computer screens, it might seem a clumsy and perhaps backward step to write a book about them. We agree that there is no real substitute for "playing" with models. The power and impact of digital models and resultant learning can only really be appreciated by personally experimenting with alternative structures and policies and watching output graphs unfold while you watch. However, it is also important to understand the place of models in the world which is what we try to do here.

We know a few people who say that they simply ignore diagrams and graphs (or anything mathematical) when they occur in texts. Well they have an opportunity here to flip past over 100 such figures. However, we would recommend that they pause a while on some of them and try to understand the rewarding language of stocks and flows and causal maps underpinning them. And for those other who wonder about the relevance of mathematics to everyday life, it is important to point out that, although they do not need to know it, the modelling we do is actually a numerical approach to calculus.

Some of the models from the book and elsewhere are available to run on Web browsers, and these can be accessed via www.symmetriclab.com/models. We cannot provide every model in the book because some models are covered by client confidentiality, some are too big to run in a browser, and several were built using earlier versions of the software that either no longer run or cannot readily be

---

[2] Epstein JM (2008), Journal of Artificial Societies and Social Simulation vol. 11, no. 4 12.

converted to a browser-based version. Additionally, our axiom has been that any project model represents only the perspective of the modelling team at the time of the project. We provide training and consultancy for professionals wishing to develop their own models.

Finally, the problem with good system modelling is that when it is carried out well, its insights appear retrospectively obvious. In fact, obviousness is our measure of success. However, to pre-empt such insights is often impossible, which makes applying system thinking a journey of abiding discovery and surprise, but often one which is underrated. Likewise, when good system thinking is implemented, it is largely invisible since little goes wrong. A little like taking pain away, solutions are not instantly perceived. When it comes to asking the question have we created benefits, the answer is undoubtable yes in respect of both efficacy and finance. However, quantifying this would involve knowing what would have been incurred without our interventions.

Edinburgh, UK
January 2019

Eric Wolstenholme
Douglas McKelvie

Acknowledgements

Acknowledgements by Eric Wolstenholme

I wish to thank many people for their help in developing my interest in dynamic modelling.

Firstly, I would like to thank my colleagues in the International System Dynamics Society and in its UK Chapter. I am proud to have help found these institutions and to have been Inaugural Editor of the Society journal the *System Dynamics Review*. I am indebted to Geoff Coyle for introducing me to system dynamics at the Bradford University System Dynamics Research Group in the mid-1970s and to Brian Dangerfield, Associate of the group, with whom I shared a lot of learning. I am also indebted to Richard Stevenson with whom I created the management consultancy, Cognitus, which focused on applying system dynamics across a wide range of industries. The Cognitus team of, among others, David Corben, Russell Parsons and Paul Gisborne were all influential in developing my approach to the subject.

I have particularly found memories of my early exchanges with the system dynamic group at the Massachusetts Institute of Technology in the 1980s and 1990s. My encounters with Jay Forrester changed my life, and many students from that time have been influential in my work ever since. A short, but not exhaustive, list would include John Sterman, David Andersen, John Morecroft, Khalid Saeed, Peter Senge, George Richardson, Jack Homer and Barry Richmond, all of whom progressed to become figures of great influence in the field.

My interest in bringing my knowledge of modelling to health and social care started with publications in the late 1990s and arose from discussions with my wife Liz Wolstenholme CBE, Economist, working at the time for Bradford Social Services in the UK. After busy weeks, we would escape from our three children on a Saturday morning to our local village bakery and discuss the links in our careers over breakfast. The outcomes were rewarding. Liz went on to work in health and serve on the first support force to try to bring health and social care closer together before becoming responsible for producing guidelines on the contentious boundary between health and social care at the Department of Health in London. Our discussions still continue despite her problems with Parkinson's over the last 25 years. I wish to thank her for these contributions. It is interesting and ironic that the healthcare and social care issues she worked on 25 years ago still remain high on the agenda today and are at the heart of this book.

My interest in healthcare and social care modelling deepened through my links with Symmetric, a consultancy company created to develop system modelling work in this area.

In particular, I would like to thank David Monk for his leadership in the procurement and execution of many of the projects described in this book. David has many years of experience in the NHS and has worked extensively with the UK Department of Health and with Chief Executive, Mental Health Networks. Without David, much of the body of work described here would have not existed. I am also grateful to Symmetric colleagues David Todd, now Managing Director of the health consultancy, Synergia, in Australasia, and Steve Arnold, originally one of Symmetric's clients in London. Steve has had an extensive career with one of the former London Health Authorities and played a major role in the projects reported here on alcohol harm, predictive risk, dementia and workforce planning. David Todd helped to procure and execute many mental health projects and in particular the work described here on improving access to psychological therapies. I also wish to thank David Monk and Steve Arnold for their time to read and comment on aspects of the book.

It goes almost without saying that I would like to pay tribute to my colleague and co-author Douglas McKelvie who has over 20 years of experience in social work and social work education. Without doubt, Douglas has taken my original healthcare and social care modelling to new heights and is responsible for most of the detailed models described in this book.

Acknowledgements by Douglas McKelvie

This has been an interesting journey.

My first career was in social work. I qualified in 1980 and worked for 12 years in a generic area team (i.e. including child protection, adult care, supervising offenders on probation and training new social workers) covering one of the most deprived parts of Edinburgh, my home city. In the 1990s, I worked at national level, in social work education and training, regulation and workforce development. I also embarked on part-time study, where I encountered operations research, including modelling and simulation, but not system dynamics. My job included a remit for "workforce planning", which nobody actually believed to be possible (as we describe in the book) and armed only with a spreadsheet and Roger Knox, a database expert, we set out to prove them wrong. Roger was the first person I met who could make the lines on a spreadsheet graph move by clicking on a spinner button.

Acknowledgements

In 2002, having become fascinated with the idea of using computer models (then, I knew mostly spreadsheets), I serendipitously met Gill Smith and David Monk, then of OLM. They recruited me as a consultant, joining a team that newly included Eric Wolstenholme. We are all indebted to Peter O' Hara, Head of OLM, for being so open to employ such a diverse range of people. Meeting Eric was my first encounter with system dynamics and well worth the wait.

I then had the enormous privilege of learning how to build system dynamics models by being, effectively, Eric's apprentice, a role I still occupy. Model building is in many respects a craft; working alongside one of the giants of the field, a wise teacher and effective communicator, has been a joy. It is impossible to have a conversation with Eric without learning something new or gaining a fresh insight.

System dynamics is all about making connections. Learning from Eric, in a UK context, the major preoccupation was, and remains, taking a strategic approach to balancing capacity across complex care pathways to reduce bottlenecks and facilitate service integration. Meeting colleagues in the international society, especially Jack Homer and Gary Hirsch, I was initially surprised to see that their models looked very different, with more representation of epidemiology and disease progression. Comparing the UK and US health systems, this difference in emphasis makes perfect sense. I have tried to combine both strands (service bottlenecks and the dynamics of illness), wherever a project brief required this.

Eric, of course, introduced me to the wider system dynamics community, and over the years, I have worked on projects with Pål Davidsen, Kim Warren, Sion Cave and David Exelby among others. I have been an active member of the SD Society UK Chapter and Healthcare Policy Special Interest Group.

Like Eric, I am indebted to Symmetric colleagues. David Monk and Steve Arnold managed to communicate the benefits of system dynamics modelling to their peers in the health sector. David Todd brought energy, business acumen and a cutting edge to the modelling approach. Angèle Pieters, from the Netherlands, worked with us for a spell and brought some welcome fresh perspectives. Sarah Nield kept us firmly and kindly on track.

More recently, I have been joined by Donald Scott, who lasted the course in social work and has now become captivated by the potential of system dynamics. Donny is another valuable interpreter, translator and connector, and now an indispensable co-worker. We have been fortunate to work with Sarah Wylie (Boyar), who is doing visionary work using system dynamics in the public sector in Northern Ireland. Expect to hear more about this before long.

Fortunately, my wife, Cathy Sharp, who works as Action Researcher in the same field (public services), empathetically knows and lives the challenges one faces when working on a range of projects using a knowledge base and skill set that are not widely understood, to help dedicated public servants tackle complex problems. We seem to manage literally to walk through most issues when either of us gets stuck, and I would be lost without her.

Joint Acknowledgements

We both hugely value isee systems, whose iThink/STELLA software powers most of our work. Until the mid-1980s, system dynamics modelling was a tedious and time-consuming activity. At that time, Barry Richmond established isee systems and developed the STELLA and iThink system dynamics software working on Apple Mac computers using the first windows, icons, menus, pointer/mouse (WIMPS) interface. This was many years before the advent of Microsoft Windows software and for the first time allowed the development of models from stock-flow structures drawn directly on a computer screen. The STELLA Architect software used in this book is a direct descendent of this original software.

Additionally, both of us wish to acknowledge the help and cooperation from many healthcare and social care clinicians and managers who contributed to the studies reported in this book and would like to thank Springer and our editors for the opportunity to publish this material.

The results reported and views expressed throughout the book are entirely those of the authors and are not necessarily the views of the organisations involved.

Contents

1	**The Challenges Facing Health and Social Care and the Relevance of Dynamic Models**	1
1.1	Overview	1
1.2	Case Study—Mrs. Jones	2
1.3	The Challenge	3
1.4	What to Do?	3
1.5	A Way Forward—From Mrs. Jones to Dynamic Models	4
1.6	The Scope and Insights	5
1.7	System Dynamics	6
1.8	Systems Thinking	8
1.9	Systemic Versus Systematic Thinking	9
1.10	Systems Messages	9
1.11	The State of Health and Social Care Worldwide	10
1.12	The Restructuring Cycles of Health and Social Care	11
1.13	Wicked Problems in Health and Social Care	13
1.14	Delayed Hospital Discharges	13
1.15	Access to Mental Health Services	14
1.16	A Word on Software, Modelling, Access to Models and Mathematics	15
1.17	Overview of the Book	16
	References	18

Part I Elements of System Dynamics Important to Health and Social Care Modelling

2	**The Dynamics of Treatment and Capacity**	25
2.1	A Simple One-Stock Map of a Hospital Treatment Pathway	25
2.2	An Exercise in Thinking Through Time with Stocks and Flows	27

xv

	2.3	A Two-Stock Hospital Model with a Capacity Constraint	27
	2.4	Simulation Experiments on the Two-Stock Hospital Model	30
	2.5	Redesigning Policies	32
	2.6	Systems Notes	33
	2.7	Changes to the Length of Treatment	34
	2.8	The Importance of the Two-Stock Hospital Model	35
	2.9	Different Types of Capacity	36
	2.10	A Word on Variation and Costs	42
	2.11	Concluding Remarks	42
		Appendix: The Answer to the Exercise in Fig. 2.2	43
		References	44
3	**Performance Measurement—The Fallacy of Waiting Time Targets**		45
	3.1	The Relationship Between Capacity and Waiting Times	45
	3.2	The Two-Stock Hospital Model	47
	3.3	Other Implications	53
	3.4	The Arbitrariness of Waiting Times	54
	3.5	The Infeasibility of Implementing a Relationship Between Capacity and Waiting	55
	3.6	Conclusions	58
		References	58
4	**The Shape of Illness and the Impact of Interventions**		59
	4.1	Introduction	59
	4.2	Population Dynamics (Ageing Chain)	60
	4.3	Health Condition Dynamics (What Shape Is the Condition?)	61
	4.4	Combining Population Ageing Dynamics and Health Condition Dynamics	67
	4.5	Models that Are Not Condition-Based	70
	4.6	The Purpose, Nature and Intended Impact of Interventions	71
	4.7	Towards a Taxonomy?	84
	4.8	Conclusions	87
		References	87
5	**Feedback Dynamics**		89
	5.1	Feedback	89
	5.2	Reinforcing and Balancing Feedback Loops	90
	5.3	Revealing Feedback Loops on a Stock-Flow Map	91
	5.4	Causal Loop Maps	93
	5.5	Summary of the Rules for Drawing Feedback Loops	95
	5.6	Multiple Feedback Loops, Unintended Consequences and System Archetypes	96

5.7	Problem Archetypes	97
5.8	Solution Archetypes	98
5.9	The Four Problem/Solution Archetypes	98
5.10	Underachievement Archetype	99
5.11	An Example of the Underachievement Archetype in Health and Social Care	100
5.12	Out-of-Control Archetype	101
5.13	Examples of the Out-of-Control Archetype in Health and Social Care	103
5.14	Conclusions	104
	References	105

6 Applying System Dynamics ... 107
 6.1 An Overview of the Process of Building and Validating System Dynamics Models ... 107
 6.2 The Author's Approach to Group Model Building and Modelling as Learning ... 109
 6.3 Other Modelling Approaches ... 112
 6.4 Other Approaches to Health and Social Care Analysis ... 113
 6.5 The Authors' Positioning of System Dynamics for Health and Social Care Modelling ... 115
 6.6 Big Data ... 115
 6.7 System Dynamics Software ... 116
 References ... 116

Part II Projects for Dynamically Balancing Health and Social Care Capacities

7 Hospital Delayed Transfer of Care (Delayed Discharges) ... 121
 7.1 The Issue ... 121
 7.2 A Two-Capacity Patient Pathway Model ... 124
 7.3 The 2004 National Model of Delayed Hospital Discharge ... 130
 7.4 Conclusions from the 2004 Delayed Hospital Discharge Model ... 134
 References ... 138

8 Integrated Care ... 141
 8.1 Integrated Care ... 141
 8.2 Modelling Integrated Care (the 'Balance of Care') ... 143
 8.3 Running the Integrated Care Model ... 147
 8.4 Conclusions ... 154
 Appendix: The Challenge of Modelling Integrated Care—Transparency, Allocation and Alternative Pathways ... 155
 References ... 158

9	**Implementation of a Stepped Care Approach to Depression Services**	**159**
9.1	Introduction	159
9.2	The NICE Guidelines for Depression and Implementation Issues	160
9.3	Using a System Dynamics Modelling Approach to Avoid Unintended Consequences in the Implementation of Stepped Care for Depression Services	161
9.4	Description of the Model	162
9.5	What the Model Enabled	164
9.6	Using the Model to Support Implementation of the Guidelines—Running a Series of Model-Supported Collaborative Workshops	167
9.7	Factors Emerging from the Collaborative Process	168
9.8	Conclusions	169
	References	170
10	**Towards a Dynamic Theory of How Hospitals Cope in Times of High Demand**	**171**
10.1	Introduction	171
10.2	An Overview of Hospital Patient Pathways	173
10.3	The Coping Strategies	173
10.4	Unintended Consequences of the Coping Strategies for Patients	176
10.5	The Coping Strategy Archetypes	177
10.6	Unintended Consequences of the Coping Strategies on the Performance of Hospitals	181
10.7	Identifying Solutions	183
10.8	Concluding Remarks	185
	References	186

Part III From Cost Benefit Analysis to Dynamic Impact Assessment as a Means of Understanding Complexity

11	**Dynamic Impact Analysis for Mental Health Reform**	**193**
11.1	Introduction	193
11.2	The Original Cost Benefit Hypothesis	194
11.3	The Enhanced Cost Benefit Analysis	195
11.4	The System Dynamics Model	195
11.5	Issues Raised in the Treatment and Recovery Sector	197
11.6	Issues Raised in the Labour Market Sector	197
11.7	Issues Raised in the Therapist's Sector	198
11.8	Model Experiments	199
11.9	Results from Running Experiments to Show the Benefits of the 'Fully Operational' CBT Programme	199

11.10	A Mixed Programme	200
11.11	Summary of First Insights from the System Dynamics Model	201
11.12	Results from Running Experiments to Show the Benefits of a Phased Build up to Full Operation of the CBT Programme Over 7 Years	202
11.13	Summary of Further Insights from the System Dynamics Model	205
11.14	Sensitivity Results	206
11.15	Conclusions on the Content of the CBA	206
11.16	Conclusions on the Use of System Dynamics to Supplement CBA	206
References		207

12 Planning Investment in Alcohol Services ... 209

12.1	Context and Client	210
12.2	The Problem	210
12.3	Method	212
12.4	Description of Model	213
12.5	Typical Model Behaviour	219
12.6	Making Sense of the Findings	224
12.7	Wider Applications	225
12.8	Making the Model Usable	227
12.9	Conclusion	227
References		228

13 The Impact of Diagnosis Targets for Long-Term Conditions: Dementia ... 229

13.1	Introduction	230
13.2	Prevalence and Incidence—A Simple Model Structure	231
13.3	Developing the 'Condition Flow Chain' and Triangulating Missing Data	233
13.4	Diagnosis and Diagnostic Capacity	235
13.5	Broader Impact on the Social Care System	242
13.6	Conclusions	243
13.7	Footnote	243
References		243

14 Making Predictive Risk Assessment 'Dynamic': The Underlying Churn Effect ... 245

14.1	Introduction	245
14.2	The Problem—Lack of Impact of Local Implementation of Case Management to Identify Those at Risk of Hospital Readmission	247

14.3	The Model		248
14.4	Population Module		248
14.5	Service Module 1—Use of Hospital		252
14.6	Service Module 2—New Case Management Service		253
14.7	Finance Module		254
14.8	Model Findings		255
14.9	Conclusions/Summary		259
References			260

Part IV Health and Social Care Workforce Projects

15 Classic Workforce Projects 263
    15.1   Introduction (UK Perspective) 263
    15.2   Basic Workforce Model 265
    15.3   Elaborations on the Simple Workforce Model 267
    15.4   Developing a New Profession 268
    15.5   Modelling a Trainer Workforce 270
    15.6   Workforce Model for One Type of Occupation Including Progression and Ageing 273
    15.7   Conclusions 277
    References 278

16 Using a Control Theory Approach to Workforce Planning 279
    16.1   A Control Theory Workforce Model 279
    16.2   Staffing a Start-up Organisation 283
    16.3   Conclusions 284

17 Workforce Projects to Assist Health and Social Care Integration 285
    17.1   Model 1—Modelling Health and Social Care Integration Workforce Change 285
    17.2   Model 2—Care Workforce in the Context of the Wider Economy 289
    17.3   Conclusions 294
    Reference 294

18 A Summary of Systems Messages and Insights 295
    18.1   Summary of the Book 295
    18.2   Concluding Messages 297
    18.3   A Final Word 305

Glossary 307

About the Authors

Eric Wolstenholme began his career in engineering in which he holds a first degree and doctorate. Following a master's degree in operational research, he worked in the Operational Research Executive and Purchasing Department of British Coal before becoming an academic in Management Science at the Bradford School of Management. He has held full professorial posts at, Stirling, Leeds Beckett and London South Bank Universities in Management Science and Business Learning as well as helping to establish and direct two management consultancies—Cognitus and Symmetric. He has written two previous books and a wide range of peer-reviewed research articles. He has an international reputation for his academic and consulting work in the application of system thinking and system dynamics and has been President of both the International Systems Dynamics Society and its UK Chapter. He was Founding Editor of the *System Dynamics Review* and in 2004 received the prestigious Jay Wright Forrester Award for his contribution to system dynamics. In 2019 he received an Outstanding Contribution award from the UK Chapter of the System Dynamics Society.

Douglas McKelvie Prior to joining Symmetric, Douglas worked for over 20 years in social work and social work education, including 10 years as a professional adviser for a national regulatory body. He has developed system dynamics models in healthcare and social care services and for the criminal justice system. He works with policy analysts, public health experts, service commissioners and workforce planners, covering adult and children services, including mental health. He is Member of the Policy Council of the UK Chapter of the System Dynamics Society and was President in 2016.

Chapter 1
The Challenges Facing Health and Social Care and the Relevance of Dynamic Models

Chapter Summary
This Chapter outlines the challenges facing health and social care in many countries and the approach and scope of the methods used by the authors to address these issues. The background to and appropriateness of system dynamics models is discussed along with the current state of health and social care worldwide, with a focus on problems which habitually reoccur despite best efforts to contain them.

The Chapter provides an overview of the book, from the early Chapters designed to familiarise readers of the approach by presenting simple but insightful models to issues such as performance measurement; to later Chapters selected from over 80 projects undertaken by the authors. These chapters cover hospital delayed transfer of care (delayed discharges) and the move towards integrated health and social care; a potential theory of how hospitals cope in times of crisis; implementing stepped care for depression; expanding cognitive behavioural treatment capacity; alcohol harm reduction; planning diagnosis capacity in dementia services; enhancing predictive risk tools and developing workforce strategies. Each chapter might be considered as a taster of what is possible by adding flow dynamics to conventional thinking in these areas.

The projects described were carried out in the UK but many of the messages and conclusions are applicable to a wide international audience, particularly those with state provided services.

1.1 Overview

Health and Social Care are vast social, economic and political global industries with multiple, autonomous stakeholders, many millions of customers and both public and private responsibilities.

So, it is little wonder that these industries have more than their fair share of serious issues.

The methods of System Dynamics and its associated Systems Thinking used in this book are very apposite to health and social care situations since they are most useful when:

- issues are strategic, complex, fragmented and persistent over long periods of time
- the devil is in the *interconnections* not the *detail*
- issues are made worse by the use of adaptive, unilateral, informal, short-term solutions by powerful players
- obvious solutions are likely to have severe unintended consequences
- good solutions are likely to be counterintuitive and separated in time and space from the symptoms of an issue—and usually on someone else's patch
- it is vital to generate shared learning and understanding between multiple owners of issues
- policy testing needs to be carried out quantitatively by multiple-agency teams in a risk-free environment
- it is required to identify balanced, high leverage interventions as a precursor to applying more tactical tool sets.

1.2 Case Study—Mrs. Jones

We all know Mrs. Jones. Now in her 80s, Mrs. Jones lives on her own in North-East England. She was diagnosed with a long term neurological health condition over 20 years ago, although in retrospect she could see that there was evidence of this much earlier in her life. This condition had taken a turn for the worse over recent years and her situation had not been helped by the sudden death her husband and carer and the development of a muscle wastage condition. However, with help from a range of health and social care services and medication she had gained some stability in the recent past. Her situation became more of an issue 6 months ago when the muscle problem began to progress much more rapidly. Three months ago, she became an emergency admission to hospital.

Unfortunately for her, this personal crisis coincided with a winter admissions crisis at her local hospital. She encountered a long wait for an ambulance and a long wait in the ambulance at hospital. When eventually taken into the emergency department at the hospital she spent a full day on a trolley in a busy corridor, due to bed shortages. She was amazed to find that, over the 2 days it took to be admitted to a ward, she had developed very unpleasant pressure sores. Further, her admission was not to an appropriate medical ward, but to an overcrowded surgical ward, where she arrived without her medical notes. By the time her medical team locating her, the medication regime vital to her condition had been severely disrupted and she and her family were understandably distraught and very confused.

What should have been a 3-day length of stay to assess her and adjust medication had already reached 6 days when she acquiring a hospital infection. Finally, due to her worsening condition she encountered trouble finding a suitable post hospital care package apposite to her needs and affordable and acceptable to her family. Even when all this was sorted she underwent further discharge delays resulting from pharmacy provision and transport problems. Her total length of stay in hospital turned into 20 days, in other words she became a very long stay patient—or 'super stranded' to use the jargon of the day.

1.3 The Challenge

It may seem an exaggeration, but the story of Mrs. Jones is only too typical of the experiences of many older people with multiple conditions needing emergency hospital treatment (Healthwatch UK 2017) and follow-up care. Despite the best intentions to provide the best treatment, in recent years many emergency patients have had to wait in ambulances outside hospitals and in corridors before being accepted into hospital. At the same time many other, particularly frail older people with co-morbidities, have been admitted to inappropriate wards and suffered severe delays in discharge and their problems complicated by infections.

So, it is a challenging time for health and social care services, facing;

- An ageing population, living with multiple long-term conditions and growing levels of complex need
- Growing levels of expectation about service access and provision
- Reduced levels of informal carer support, putting more pressure on formal services
- A background of increasing financial pressures.

These challenges manifest themselves in growing hospital waiting lists, delayed hospital discharges and failure to meet waiting time targets in accident and emergency (A&E); and in poor quality experiences for service users and their families.

1.4 What to Do?

Some would pursue more rationing as an option and much work has been done to look at methods (Maybin and Klein 2012). Rationing means using eligibility criteria to match the level of need to the level of service and is applied worldwide, including insurance-based systems. For example, in USA people have different levels of coverage, and the question is 'will my health plan pay for this type of treatment?'. Some would seek to press for more funding. In the UK the NHS no longer meets the European % GDP average spend and, since the 2008 crisis, Local

Authorities have been dealing with significant cuts in resources (Bounds 2017). So, there would seem to be a good case for allocating additional funding. In the UK additional money has been promised for health in England in the 2019 NHS Long Term Plan (www.longtermplan.nhs.uk). However, many people feel this to be totally inadequate and doing little to address the imbalance between health and social care (Stoye 2018; Rawnsley 2018; Rajeev and Campbell 2018; Campbell 2018). Further, it is estimated that about a quarter of this additional money would be necessary to just pay off current accrued deficits (Campbell 2019).

1.5 A Way Forward—From Mrs. Jones to Dynamic Models

At its basic, balancing growing levels of predictable demand with available resources is not a new proposition for any health and care services. Whilst perhaps currently the pressures are more acutely felt, they are not new and perhaps we can learn from prior experience.

This book describes work we have undertaken over the course of more than 80 projects in Health and Social Care in the UK, to examine the aggregate consequences of individual journeys like that of Mrs. Jones as she navigates her way through the pathways of health and social care services.

We have used an approach that recognises the subtlety of the relationships within and across the services and so employs a whole system perspective. It also takes account of broader changes over time. Working with front line staff, managers and academics we have been able to take the basic experience of using the service —the *flow* through the service—and construct computer-based models to represent them. We can then simulate changes—population, dependency, demand or perhaps the impact of introducing new approaches—and look at the net results within the models.

The models are constructed using System Dynamics (SD) and its associated Systems Thinking (ST) principles. These allow for some of the complexity, interdependence and change over time that, regardless of resources, will always challenge health and social care systems. Running the models using real data enables local, regional or even national conclusions to be drawn.

Each project has been specific to its brief, but, in general we have used modelling to;

- Better understand the potential impact of service change without having to wait for the results of its implementation
- Make more informed cases to improve services—understanding the cost of making those changes and of not making them
- Understand the impact of change across the system, and so avoid cost shunting
- Use the process of developing the model as a way of improving mutual understanding of the system amongst its key actors.

1.5 A Way Forward—From Mrs. Jones to Dynamic Models

The work reported is focused on increasing the visibility of patient flows at a relatively strategic level across the many different domestic, departmental and agency boundaries.

Patient flow and congestion is a growing area of study in health and social care (Rutherford et al. 2017; Karakusevic 2016) and we build on this by taking a *systemic* and *dynamic* perspective of flows to identify the best levers or intervention and improvement.

Unlike industrial systems, where materials mostly flow in one direction, in health and social care people flows are complex and people move in multiple directions, miss out some stages and perhaps repeat others. The same service capacity might be used for different purposes; for example, an 'intermediate care' service which has a single capacity, might be used both as an alternative to hospital admission and to facilitate hospital discharge. In the same system, some people might be waiting in hospital to be discharged to an intermediate care setting at the same time as other people in an intermediate care setting now need hospital admission, perhaps because their condition has deteriorated. Alternatively, people might be admitted to hospital having been users of a home care package, losing that package on or shortly after admission, then, several weeks later, cannot be discharged from hospital until another, identical or more intensive, home care package can be procured. Such eventualities are not only possible, but common.

The work also relates closely to productivity enhancement (Appleby et al. 2014), the many quality and efficiency improvement initiatives being taken in health worldwide (The Health Foundation 2016) and the moves towards Integrated Care between Health and Social Care (Ham 2018).

The projects described were carried out in the UK but many of the messages and conclusions are applicable to a wide international audience.

1.6 The Scope and Insights

The book covers a wide range of example modelling projects. These range from improving basic understanding of the fundamental relationships between variables in treatment and condition pathways to delayed hospital discharges and integrated care. They continue through the coping strategies employed by hospitals in periods of high demand to improving mental health provision, to alcohol-related harm, to dementia, to workforce planning and predictive risk. Whilst many of the projects focus on treatment some do impinge on prevention and complement other work in this latter area in the USA (Jones et al. 2006; Hirsch et al. 2014; Homer et al. 2007, 2016; Milstein et al. 2010, 2011).

Many insights are derived and, because of the systems nature of the work across whole patient pathways, they are generic to many of the topics covered. These insights are listed as a set of messages in the conclusions. Like all good systems messages they are reassuringly obvious in hindsight but elusive to remember and apply to new problems.

Perhaps the most important single message is that much more emphasis needs to be placed on *flows* and *flow data*. It is suggested that improving *throughput* rather than *capacity* is the dominant way to improving the performance of health treatment, whereas increasing *capacities* rather than *throughput* is the dominant way to improve the performance of social care by retaining independent living. Further, that balancing health and social care capacity is a win-win scenario for both and better for patients, staff and costs than not doing so. This is because it eliminates the many risky and costly fire-fighting strategies hospitals have to undertake when faced with high demands.

Perhaps the key meaning in the last paragraph is that much-needed systemic solutions and whole system thinking can never be successfully implemented until organisations are recognised as complex entities and are allowed to articulate and dismantle their most extreme and costly coping strategies and return to working within best practice capacities. This is the ultimate new way of working. Such elimination releases hospitals to realise the full potential of investment and innovation and to enable them to manage the increase in longevity their success creates. However, before such a state can be truly realised money must be found for situations in which large debts have accrued from long periods of not coping. Not understanding this would result in it appearing that future balanced spending was not succeeding.

These messages are followed very closely by the messages that the performance of health services is dependent on better understanding of the dynamics of population ageing, the dynamics of health conditions, particularly the bi-direction of patient flows between different states of heath conditions.

A better understanding of strategic patient flows can also assist with designing information systems and the targeting and realism of more operational performance improvement techniques and health economics studies. It can also assist with highlighting the arbitrariness of many performance targets.

We do not claim that using a systems perspective and dynamic modelling can create more resource; but, time and again, our work has shown that it will help maximise the impact of all resources across the Health and Care system.

1.7 System Dynamics

System dynamics combines two familiar words that are already used extensively in social care, sometimes in combination (for example, when describing the interconnections underpinning family dynamics), and uses them in a particular way. System dynamics in the context here describes a specific approach to dynamic modelling that originated in the 1950s, invented by JW Forrester, an engineer and pioneer of digital computing, at the Massachusetts Institute of Technology (MIT). It can best be described as a way of applying ideas from control engineering to socio-economic and management systems.

1.7 System Dynamics

Jay pioneered his ideas in industry (Forrester 1961, 1969) and most prominently by his development of world models for the Club of Rome (Meadows et al. 1972, 2004). He was one of the first people to explore the finite nature of the planet and question the implications of the growth of the human footprint. His models demonstrated the major issues of population growth, resource depletion and pollution being borne out today.

In health and social care, System Dynamics is a means of translating mental models of patient flows into computer simulation models using the language of stocks (accumulations) and flows. This notation allows patient pathways to be visualised for the purpose of sharing and communicating how existing pathways work and to redesign new ones. The pathways can then be modelled and their behaviour over time studied in a risk-free laboratory environment, rather than by disrupting the real activity.

Simulation has become an established tool of research, investigation and training for environments where experimenting with the real situation is difficult and risky. It has applications ranging from space exploration to pilot training to managerial and climate policy testing. System dynamics is applicable to any dynamic system characterised by interdependence, information feedback and circular causality (System Dynamics Society Website 2018) and is in use across a wide range of disciplines.

The importance of computer simulation lies in the benefits it brings to thinking.

Humans excel at innovation and action but are not at all well adapted to thinking about the outcomes and consequences of their actions over time. Our internal simulation competence is very limited even in the simplest situations and those people who aspire to prominent positions are often the ones most adept at temporal processing. Computers are the opposite. They are morons but as such have an amazing ability to carry out boring and repetitive calculations without complaint.

The right mix of people-based ideas and computer-based interpretation over time is a powerful combination and software to bring a simulation dimension to more of us is improving all the time. Forrester perceived this nearly 70 years ago and was his motivation for helping to develop digital computer technology. Today we have the capability to capture the essence of complex systems and, when calibrated with the best data, to emulate their behaviour over time. Note the use of the word emulate here—not to mimic or copy but to match or even out do. The quantitative nature of system dynamics ensures a degree of rigour to minimise ambiguity and focusses attention on the laws of physics underlying many of today's problems which many fields of analysis ignore.

For major texts on system dynamics, see Sterman (2000), Vennix (1996), Maani and Cavana (2007), Ford (2009), Morecroft (1994, 2007), Wolstenholme (1990), Warren (2008) and Richardson and Pugh (1981), Richardson (1999, 1996).

For worldwide review texts on system dynamics in health see Homer and Hirsch (2006), Hirsch et al. (2015), Hirsch and Homer (2016), Wolstenholme (2015) and Dangerfield (1999).

For selected specific papers on health projects see Homer (2012, 2017) for the USA, Todd (2018) and McDonnell (2018) for Australasia and Wolstenholme

(1993, 1996, 2008), Dangerfield et al. (2001), Lane et al. (2000), McKelvie (2018) and Lacy (2018) for the UK. A comprehensive bibliography of system dynamics publications across all fields is available on the System Dynamics Society website (www.systemdynamics.org) and on the UK Chapter of the System Dynamics Society website (http://systemdynamics.org.uk).

1.8 Systems Thinking

There are many schools of *Systems Thinking* (Checkland 1981; Checkland and Scholes 1990/1999; Flood and Jackson 1991; Beer 1989; Richardson1999; Lane and Jackson 1995; Senge 1990; Sherwood 2002; Stroth 2015).

Systems thinking as used here is a means of analysing the feedback structures at the heart of system dynamics models. It can assist with conceptualising models and with understanding and communicating their insights. Feedback loops exist when actions travel through a system and eventually return to their origins to influence future action. If the tendency of the loop is to reinforce the original action, the loop is referred to as a positive or reinforcing feedback loop. If the tendency is to oppose the initial action the loop is referred to as a negative or balancing feedback loop. The sign (positive or negative) of the loop is called its polarity. When feedback loops of different polarities work in combination they give rise to many interesting modes of behaviour over time.

Specific combinations of loops responsible for specific types of system behaviour over time are referred to as system archetypes (Senge 1990). These are made up of intended consequence loops and unintended consequences loops (Wolstenholme 2003). They explain how intended actions often fail due to the fact they encounter or trigger reactions which counter them. The consequences usually only become apparent after significant time delays. Also, they can be hidden from consciousness by natural or organisational boundaries. Their appearance can take us by surprise and cause us to react further. Good systems thinking is about anticipating unintended consequences and taking them into account when designing intended actions.

The side effects of treatments and medications are specific examples of the unintended consequences of well-meaning actions and it is well understood in health that the side effects of treatments can be worse that the disease itself. It is perhaps less well understood that the side effects of clinical and management health policies can also be worse that the problems they are intended to solve.

Systems thinking is a powerful method of visualising feedback in systems. However, on its own it is essentially qualitative and where ever possible feedback structures should be quantified and tested using computer simulation.

1.9 Systemic Versus Systematic Thinking

The emphasis in system dynamics and system thinking is on the word *systemic*, which is not to be confused with the word *systematic*, although clearly there is a stepwise sequence involved in applying them.

The power of system dynamics and systems thinking are that they attempt to examine organisations as a whole to help communication, learning and understanding of the real causes of apparently complex issues. They emphasise the notion that the root causes of problems are often contained within the system itself. Of particular interest in health and social care are the interactions between patient pathways and the structure and boundaries of autonomous agencies which operate them.

Being *systemic* requires the definition of an appropriate view of patient pathways in both *space* and *time* and this is determined by the agreed purpose of a study. Spatially, the movement of every individual patient could be modelled and at the other extreme the aggregate of all patients. Temporally, we could model in time increments and over horizons from minutes to years.

In practice, both perspectives must be sufficient aggregate to help simplify complex situations, whilst being sufficiently detailed to be meaningful. Being systemic is finding a useful balance between a 'complete world' view and a 'reductionist' view. The aim is to reduce detailed complexity (the number of elements in a situation) whilst retaining dynamic complexity (the number of interconnections in a situation). In practice, finding the right perspective for a model generally requires starting at a reasonably high level of abstraction followed by some expansion and contraction. This might be summed up by saying that we need to see the situation of interest as a composite whole, since 'wholes have integrity'.

1.10 Systems Messages

There are many important systems messages arising from many modelling studies across many disciplines and these are very appropriate to the situation health and social care find themselves in across the world.

Despite valiant attempts at transformations to make health and social care more joined-up, one prime characteristic of health and social care delivery is that it is remains very fragmented. There are cultural, budgetary and information system boundaries between primary, secondary and community-based health services and between these and social care services. Patient flows across such boundaries are fraught with difficulties.

Further, many transformations are often reactions which have unintended consequences and lead to many of today's problems being yesterday's imperfect solutions, since 'fixing' a problem to satisfy short-term needs does not make a problem go away in the long-term. A major issue inhibiting our thinking over time is that cause and effect are not closely related in either time or space and that the best levers for problem interventions can be well away from the symptoms of the problem—and often on someone else's patch. As a result, identifying the most appropriate levers for change in any given situation can often be very counter intuitive.

Appropriate change in complex systems is also made difficult by the presence of having non-linear components and the fact that they are self-organising and adaptive. This means that they can always give the appearance of coping by creating and implementing informal strategies to cover the cracks, but at a cost.

However, some good news is that small changes can often cause big results and good levers are worth finding. There are times when it is possible to create win-win situations and so have cake and eat it. Investing ahead of time beyond the minimum necessary to initiate an intended action can avoid later side effects that might well cost more than spending sufficient to apply the real cure now.

Such messages will be highlighted as they emerge throughout the book and drawn together in the concluding Chapter.

1.11 The State of Health and Social Care Worldwide

Health and Social care is a complex multi-faceted industry and the prevention of ill health and the mode of delivery of health and social care varies widely across the globe.

There is a broad split between the USA, where private health provision dominates, and the rest of the world where public health provision dominates, public health care being subsidised to varying degrees by governments from tax income. The overwhelming rationale for public control is to make the services as widely accessible to all as possible. Generally social care, which provides home and residential care for adults and a wide range of services for children, is highly privatised and much less subsidised than health care. It is also funded from different sources. Usually, central governments fund health whilst regional/local governments fund social care. A major issue with these arrangements is that regional/local governments have many responsibilities other than health and, particularly in times of austerity, have many conflicting demands on their budgets.

However, despite the best efforts to the contrary, it is no exaggeration to say that in most western countries health and social care is at a crisis point.

The demand for health and social care services are at an all-time high and the nature of that demand is growing in complexity—based on the needs of an increasingly ageing population and a rise in the prevalence of long-term conditions. This is compounded by an increasing incidence of mental health conditions, cancers and diabetes and life style factors associated with smoking, poor diet, inadequate exercise, substance abuse (recreational and prescription) and unprotected sex.

To some extent health services are also a victim of their own success as successful health interventions prolong life expectancy. This not only adds to demand during the period of extended life but also has the effect of delaying the onset of some conditions and producing latent demand, which when realised can be misinterpreted as new demand. Demand is also stimulated by an increasing aversion to risk which takes many forms but centres on the fear of litigation and the fear of tabloid newspaper headlines. Risk aversion is often seen as a negative consequence of rigorous pursuit of defining targets and performance measurement. Also, in the UK it is claimed that the 111 (non-emergency) telephone advice service is sending growing numbers of people to A&E or calling an ambulance because staff are too risk averse (Campbell 2017).

The supply of public health and social care has seen little real-term growth in resources since the financial crash of 2008 to cope with the demand surges experienced. Increasingly, primary care services have been overwhelmed and hospitals have been caught between high demand for admissions and slow discharges due to adult social care problems. The result has been increased lengths of stay or treatments, infection risks and excessive waits for both emergency and elective treatments. Many have been forced to resort to coping strategies which put patients at risk. Both health and social care organisations are also suffering from the associated problems of staff recruitment and rising staff turnover. On top of all these logistical considerations, health delivery is also beset by the growing problem of antibiotic resistance (Homer et al. 2000).

Despite all the problems, the dedication and motivation of health professional remains high and productivity increases are evident. These have arisen mainly from significant reductions in treatment times associated with shifts of procedures away from hospital to primary and community settings, the use of day-care treatments and the deployment of more and more sophisticated technologies and tele-medicine. Such measures have resulted in a continuous reduction in acute beds in most countries. Also, many measures have been taken to make services more available and to shift imbalances. For example, in mental health significant investment has been made in increasing access to psychological therapies.

The major challenges lie in coping with an ageing population and containing heart disease, dementia, cancer and long term neurological conditions as well as dealing with growing mental health issues across all age groups.

1.12 The Restructuring Cycles of Health and Social Care

Whilst demand and supply issues are the major determinants of congested flows through patient pathways, an additional component of disruption is associated with top down restructuring in health systems funded by governments.

Top down restructuring is very common in the private sectors of industry and one of the few tools available to owners of enterprises to exert influence on their businesses, perhaps to change direction, reduce costs, drive efficiency gains or to justify a downsize in the workforce. Whilst often necessary, many restructures are good examples of seeking to solve problems without a full appreciation of the effect on operational processes.

There is usually an element of centralisation and decentralisation in restructurings, where organisations typically cycle over time between a desire to be small enough to be close to customers and a desire to be large enough to achieve economies of scale. Corporate memories can be quite short and organisational learning is poor. The time between restructuring can be significantly large for managers to have changed or to have forgotten that this is a cyclic occurrence or to convince themselves it will be different this time round. In the meantime, service delivery suffers and these cycles are particularly inefficient to the workforce. Centralisation usually means reducing capacity by downsizing. This effectively discards people together with their knowledge and learning. Although costs may be diminished, workloads are not and great productivity increases are demanded from the remaining workforce.

When subsequent decentralisation and upsizing takes place, capacity is again needed, but this reversal is usually sufficiently later for people to have moved on. There is then a shortage of the right people and organisations have to spend heavily on recruitment and training, all of which takes time. Whilst some flux and change may be good for progress, too many and too much change of this type puts organisations in a constant state of transition and in a continual state of crisis management.

This description of restructuring and its cycles and consequences is also applicable to public organisations. Where health and social care is under government control, politicians inevitably try to mould services towards their particular ideologies and to cut costs to tax payers by changing organisational boundaries and budgets. However, such changes often ignore the consequences to patient pathways and patient flows. The reality is that they can be in a state of flux and chaos for a long time with the costs of disruption potentially outweighing the intended benefits.

The NHS has a very chequered history or reorganisation (Nuffield Trust 2018). For example, ignoring changes to regional bodies and hospitals, since 1996 the government in the UK has restructured health services in England 4 times and there have been periods during which some parts of the country had not completed one restructuring when the next one came along.

In 1996 there were 100 District Health Authorities (DHAs) largely controlling population-based budgets. Between 2002 and 2012 DHAs were replaced by 300 Primary Care Trusts who were to become commissioners to create choice and competition between suppliers, using payments-by-results, rather than block contracts. In 2006 these were reduced to 152 and to 50 in 2009 as a precursor for introducing 210 GP-based Primary Care Clinical Commissioning Groups - many of which are now being amalgamated!

In 2014 the government categorically stated there would be no further top down restructurings, but in 2018 are in the process of establishing Integrated Care Systems (ICS's), Integrated Care Partnerships (ICP's) and Accountable Care Organisations (ACO's). The latter not to be confused with the use of the term in the US and intended to be a means of delivering care rather than funding it (Ham 2018).

This latest initiative is an extension of thinking described in the NHS Five Year Forward View (NHS England 2017). It recognises the need to move away from a hospital-based model of care to one of providing more care in people's homes and in the community and in breaking down barriers between services. Whilst, not dissimilar to a return to community-based budgets, it promises for the first time a much-needed move towards a more systemic view of health and social care and a reduction in fragmentation.

If this were achieved it would be very welcome and in line with the recommendations from many of our projects over the past 15 years, where we have long suggested that from a systems point of view, cooperation and integration, rather than competition, between organisations along patient pathways would be beneficial to improve patient flow.

1.13 Wicked Problems in Health and Social Care

A wicked problem denotes a problem that is resistant to solution (Churchman 1967). Of the many problems facing health and social care, two of the most persistent will be discussed a little further since they are the at the focus of this book and have been the ones we have been asked to provide a systems perspective on most often. These are:

1. delayed hospital discharges (and its link to general patient pathway congestion and hospital capacity planning)
2. access to mental health services for depression.

Wicked problems are defined here as meaning they are policy resistant (Sterman 2000) which is the tendency, despite best efforts, for interventions to be delayed, diluted or defeated by the response of the system to the intervention itself. It arises because we do not often understand the full range of feedbacks operating in the system, particularly the unintended consequences of our actions.

1.14 Delayed Hospital Discharges

Delayed transfer of care is an issue which can be traced back to the closure of traditional convalescent homes but has been most in the news since the early 1990s. It occurs wherever hospital discharge is constrained by agencies providing services required by those being discharged. In systems terms, it is a problem of a single patient pathway passing through different organisations and having inevitable boundary issues.

The issue centres on patients occupying hospital beds although they have been declared as "medically fit" for discharge. This situation can happen in such cases as mental health patients waiting for housing but is most prevalent in the case of older people in hospital waiting for places in adult social care and continuing health care. It is basically an artefact of a caring society where care places are subsidised to try to ensure everyone is looked after post-hospital discharge.

Although small in number compared with the total of hospital patients, delayed discharges constitute significant loss of hospital capacity for crucial elective procedures, significant risk of infection associated with longer hospital stays and increased cost. They contribute significantly to hospitals running well beyond their design capacity and the use of expensive coping strategies to maintain patient flows.

Delayed hospital discharge is a particularly resistant problem despite numerous attempts to solve it. These have ranged from increasing hospital beds, to fining social care, to developing joint health and social care budgets to stepping patients down from acute beds to intermediate care and home for assessment of ongoing needs. Whilst making an impact on costs none of these measures to date have been very effective.

System dynamics models have the ability to address bottlenecks such as delayed discharges by determining the capacity (and hence the spending allocation) needed at each point in patient pathways, taking into account demand, proportions of people involved, length of stays and supply capacities. All of the work reported on this topic in this book points to the need to return hospitals to working within normal design capacities without coping strategies and to then keep adult social care spending in line with hospital spending.

1.15 Access to Mental Health Services

Access to mental health services is another problem which has proved elusive to solve.

Traditionally, people in many countries presenting with a variety of mental health conditions have found themselves with long waits for specialist services. An almost all or nothing approach to service delivery. In the UK since the turn of the century this issue has been addressed with the publication of the National Institute for Health and Care Excellence (NICE) guidelines for 'stepped care'—a range of easily access intermediate services between primary and specialist care and by a major programme for Improving Access to Psychological Therapies (IAPT) by NHS England.

System dynamics models have been used extensively by the authors to support both of these initiatives.

Guidelines are excellent at specifying the services to be delivered but are weaker on how to implement them. It is left to local groups to assess who would need them in the local population, the likely flows of people into and out of them and the capacity planning of each service. Here, modelling has been used not so much to assist with where to intervene in patient flows but to assist with these implementation issues. In particular, how to redistribute funding from specialist services across intermediate services and how to deal with accrued backlogs of demand. As

1.15 Access to Mental Health Services 15

in delayed hospital discharges, the benefits of the modelling centered on improving understanding of patient flows over time as a basis for service planning and delivery.

1.16 A Word on Software, Modelling, Access to Models and Mathematics

In a digital age it seems a little ironic that we are describing dynamic models through words. Good models are experiential learning tools which encourage users to experiment and play with their own ideas and parameters.

The models in our studies are all built using generally available purpose-built software—STELLA Architect (isee systems 2018) which is one of a number of proprietary software products on the market for system dynamics simulation. The authors have been associated with this software since the mid 1980s when it was first available on the Apple Macintosh platform before the advent of 'windows' software. This type of software enables system maps to be built on-screen and a key component is that model building should be led and owned by groups of problem owners not modellers and models should be an extension of the shared mental models of the group. This process facilitates models as learning devices.

Also, current software enables models to be constructed as 'microworlds' with model interfaces or dashboards and story boards, all of which allow people easy access and experimentation. Figure 1.1 shows an example of such a dashboard.

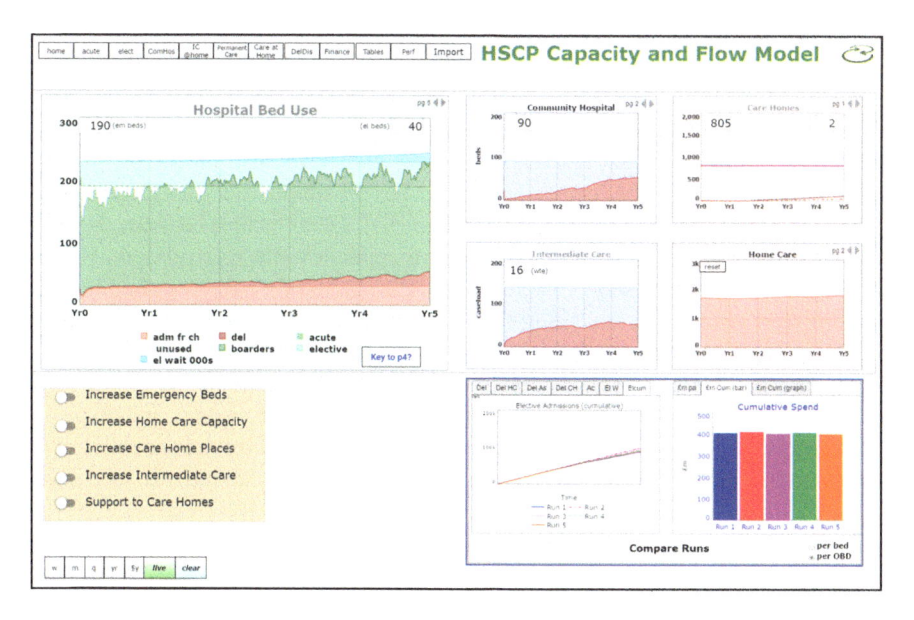

Fig. 1.1 A typical model dashboard

Many of our models are made available to clients in this way and can be operated on their own computers or increasingly via the internet. Some of the models in the book are also available on our Symmetriclab website (www.symmetriclab.com).

System dynamics models are an attempt to get away from models as 'black-box' devices hidden away in a back room and only operated by highly trained analysts. The idea is to create models which are transparent and to embed modelling as an everyday tool to share and enhance thinking. It should always be remembered that a model is only ever built for a purpose and not to model the system for its own sake. Further, like mental perceptions, all models are 'wrong' and are just providing deeper steps on the thinking journey. In many industries modelling is confined to single management disciplines or departments and, for example, can result in very detailed production models and very simple marketing models which are never linked together. So, our aim is also to keep models relatively simple and integrated across organisations. A comparison of system dynamics models with other types of modelling and a description of the iterative nature of model construction is provided in Chap. 6.

The book describes system dynamics with a minimum of mathematics and that included is not of a high level, using only text, graphs and simple algebra to explain formulations.

1.17 Overview of the Book

Part I (Chaps. 2–6) presents the fundamental building blocks involved in creating system dynamics models to help readers appreciate the power of the underlying concepts. It is recommended that knowledge of these structures can significantly improve understanding of the more complex project models described in Chaps. 7–17, as well as improving understanding of health service delivery per se.

Chapter 2 introduces the language of stocks and flows as a means of mapping and modelling patient pathways and describes a simple but insightful model explaining the often misunderstood, fundamental relationships between 7 major hospital variables; bed occupancy, bed capacity, patient waits, referrals, admissions, discharges and length of stay. Chapter 3 uses the model of Chap. 2 to shed light on the arbitrariness of hospital waiting time targets. Chapter 4 examines what we call the *shape of illness*—that is the many ways in which the dynamics of population ageing and health conditions combine with treatments to produce complex pathways. Chapter 5 explains the importance of feedback and system archetypes in understanding dynamics and Chap. 6 the process of modelling and learning with management teams and the conversion of individual mental models to explicit shared models.

Part II (Chaps. 7–10) describe projects undertaken for dynamically balancing health and social care capacities.

Chapter 7 presents two examples of models to shed light on the persistent and costly problem of delayed hospital discharges (delayed transfers of care). This is the

1.17 Overview of the Book

situation where patients who are clinically ready to leave hospital are unable to do so due to waiting for post-hospital health and social care services. The work dispels some obvious solutions to the problem and points to the need to balance social care spending with health care spending to sustain good patient flow.

Chapter 8 describes a model which contains some aspects of integrated health and social care and its effects on delayed hospital discharges. The works show that there are small changes which can make a difference but that ultimately it is difficult to avoid the underlying problem of lack of social care capacity.

Chapter 9 outlines one of a number of projects to support local mental health communities in implementation of the National Institute for Health and Care Excellence in the UK (NICE) guidelines for a stepped care approach to depression. Here modelling helps by allowing analysis of alternative allocations of finance to balance capacity across each step of the new system.

Chapter 10 builds on the delayed hospital discharge work to develop a systems hypothesis of how hospitals handle excessive demand by employing numerous coping strategies at many points along patient pathways. System archetypes are used to describe the coping strategies and their unintended consequences. It is suggested that inadequate social care capacity is again a major determinant of all coping strategies and that coping strategies could lead to more risks and costs to patients and staff than balancing health and social care capacities in the first place. Also important is recognising the symptoms of coping early and taking steps to return to working within best practice capacities are essential for effective operation.

Part III (Chaps. 11–14) describe projects for dynamic impact analysis in health and social care. Dynamic Impact Analysis is a phrase coined by the authors to describe a dynamic approach to cost benefit analysis.

Chapter 11 is a modelling project to support a major programme for Improving Access to Psychological Therapies (IAPT) by NHS England. A planned expansion of cognitive behavioural therapy by recruiting large numbers of additional therapists in the UK was underpinned by impact assessment of the numbers of people who might benefit over time.

Chapter 12 describes a nationally developed model to enable local NHS commissioners (using their own data) to assess the impact of interventions to reduce Alcohol-Related harm for their populations and alcohol-related admissions to hospital. The contribution of modelling was to take into account the two-way movement over time of people between different states of alcohol dependence.

Chapter 13 addresses the impact and relevance of targets for the diagnosis of Dementia. The model highlights the need to know incidence, mortality and progression (*flows*) as well as prevalence (*stock*) of the condition and understand the resulting dynamics when designing dementia diagnosis (and treatment) capacity and challenges the arbitrary nature of current performance targets.

Chapter 14 relates a study to explore why a particular preventive intervention, targeted on people assessed as 'at high risk' based on their predictive-risk score, failed to produce the hoped-for reduction in hospital admissions. Modelling this problem highlighted the importance of recognising flows of people into and out of each risk category.

Part IV (Chaps. 15–17) describe projects to study health and social care workforce dynamics, incorporating recruitment and training delays, target staff in training and in posts, drop outs and retirement flows.

Chapter 15 covers what might be described as 'classic' workforce issues. The first model involved developing a new profession from scratch. The second model involved establishing a trainer workforce from existing employees to train new recruits and the third the strategies for maintaining a workforce of paediatric consultants in the light of implementation of the European Working Time Directive.

Chapter 16 describes a control theory model to design recruitment policies for workforce planning and comments in general on the idea of using control theory solutions in health and social care modelling.

Chapter 17 covers workforce projects to assist health and social care integration. The first model here focusses on examining alternative strategies for adapting the mix of skills and qualifications necessary to create a more flexible workforce. The second examines the relationship between the home care workforce and the people who need and get care. This is a comprehensive model aimed at understanding the impact of care workers on the dynamics of the service, particularly their effect on reducing delayed hospital discharges.

Chapter 18 presents overall conclusions in terms of a number of key messages and insights arising from the projects.

References

Appleby, J., Galea, A., & Murray, M. (2014). *The NHS productivity challenge—Experience from the front line*. London, UK: The King's Fund.
Beer, S. (1989). The viable system model: Its provenance, development, methodology and pathology. In R. Espejo & R. Harnden (Eds.), *The viable system model—Interpretations and applications of Stafford Beer's VSM* (pp. 11–37). Chichester, UK p: Wiley.
Bounds, A. (2017). https://www.ft.com/content/9c6b5284-6000-11e7-91a7-502f7ee26895.
Campbell, D. (2017). *Guardian newspaper*. Retrieved February 22, 2017.
Campbell, D. (2018). *Guardian newspaper*. Retrieved December 6, 2018.
Campbell, D. (2019). *Guardian newspaper*. Retrieved December 18, 2019.
Churchman, C. W. (1967). *Wicked Problems Management Science 14(4)*. https://doi.org/10.1287/mnsc.14.4.b141.
Checkland, P. B. (1981). Systems *thinking, systems practice*. Wiley, Chichester, UK, 330 pp. ISBN 0 471 27911 0 (republished 1999 in paperback, with a 30-year retrospective).
Checkland, P. B., & Scholes, J. (1990/1999). *Soft systems methodology in action*. Wiley: Chicester.
Dangerfield, B. C. (1999). System dynamics applications to European health care issues. *Journal of the Operational Research Society 50*(4), 345–353.
Dangerfield, B. C., Roberts, C. A., & Fang, Y. (2001). Model-based scenarios for the epidemiology of HIV/AIDS: The consequences of highly active antiretroviral therapy. *System Dynamics Review, 17*(2), 119–150.
Dynamics Series, Pegasus Communications Cambridge MA.

References

Flood, R. L., & Jackson, M. C. (1991). *Critical systems thinking*. Wiley: Chichester.
Ford, A. (2009). *Modeling the environment*. Washington, DC: Island Press.
Forrester, J. W. (1961). *Industrial dynamics Cambridge, MA: The MIT Press*. Waltham, MA: Reprinted by Pegasus Communications.
Forrester, J. W. (1969). *Urban dynamics*. Cambridge, MA: The MIT Press. Reprinted by Pegasus Communications, Waltham, MA.
Health Foundation. (2016). Acute hospital productivity, Health Foundation analysis of acute hospital productivity from 2009/10–2014/15.
Healthwatch UK. (2017). What happens when people leave hospital and other care settings? Hospital and other care settings? Findings from the Healthwatch network October 2017.
Hirsch, G., Homer, J. (2016). System dynamics applications to health care in the United States. In R. Meyers (Ed.) *Encyclopaedia of complexity and system science*. Springer: Berlin, Germany. ISBN 978-0-387-75888-6.
Hirsch, G., Homer, J., Wile, K., Trogdon, J. G., & Orenstein, D. (2014). Using simulation to compare 4 categories of intervention for reducing cardiovascular disease risks. *American Journal of Public Health, 104*(7), 1187–1195.
Hirsch, G., Homer, J., & Tomoaia-Cotisel, A. (Eds.). System dynamics applications to Health and Health Care (15 previously published articles with new introduction and extended bibliography). Virtual Issue of *System Dynamics Review*. Retrieved January 2015, from http://onlinelibrary.wiley.com/journal/10.1002/(ISSN)1099-1727/homepage/VirtualIssuesPage.html.
Homer, J., Ritchie-Dunham, J., Rabbino, H., Puente, L., Jorgensen, J., & Hendricks, K. (2000). Toward a dynamic theory of antibiotic resistance. *System Dynamics Review, 16*(4), 287–319.
Homer, J., & Hirsch, G. (2006). System dynamics modeling for public health: Background and opportunities. *American Journal of Public Health, 96*(3), 452–458.
Homer, J., Hirsch, G., & Milstein, B. (2007). Chronic illness in a complex health economy: The perils and promises of downstream and upstream reforms. *System Dynamics Review, 23*(2/3), 313–343.
Homer, J. B. (2012). *Models that matter*. Barrytown, New York: Grapeseed Press.
Homer, J., Milstein, B., Hirsch, G. B., & Fisher, E. S. (2016). Combined regional investments could substantially enhance health system performance and be financially affordable. *Health Affairs, 35*(8), 1435–1443.
Homer, J. B. (2017). *More models that matter*. Barrytown, New York: Grapeseed Press.
Ham, C. (2018). *Making sense of integrated care systems, integrated care partnerships and accountable care organisations in the NHS in England*. https://www.kingsfund.org.uk/publications/making-sense-integrated-care-systems.
Jones, A., Homer, J., Murphy, D., Essien, J., Milstein, B., & Seville, D. (2006). Understanding diabetes population dynamics through simulation modeling and experimentation. *American Journal of Public Health, 96*(3), 488–494.
Karakusevic, S. (2016). *Understanding patient flow in hospitals*. Nuffield Trust.
Lacy, P. (2018). *The whole system partnership*. www.thewholesystem.co.uk/.
Lane, D. C., Monefeldt, C., & Rosenhead, J. V. (2000). Looking in the wrong place for healthcare improvements: A system dynamics study of an A&E department. *Journal of the Operational Research Society, 51*(5), 518–531.
Lane, D. C., & Jackson, M. C. (1995). Only connect! An annotated bibliography reflecting the breadth and diversity of systems thinking. *Systems Research, 12*(3), 217–228.
Maani, K. E., & Cavana, R. Y. (2007). *Systems thinking, system dynamics: Understanding change and complexity*. Prentice Hall: Aukland.
Maybin, J., & Klein, R. (2012). 'Thinking about rationing'. King's Fund.
McKelvie, D. (2018). www.symmetriclab.com.
Meadows, D. H., Meadows, D. L., Randers, J., & Behrens, W., III. (1972). *The limits to growth; a report for the club of Rome's project on the predicament of mankind*. New York: Universe Books.
Meadows, D. H., Randers, J., & Meadows, D. L. (2004). *The limits to growth: The 30-year update*. Vermont USA: Chelsea Green Publishing Company.

McDonnell. (2018). https://insightmaker.com/tag/Patient-Flow and https://insightmaker.com/insight/3517/Health-Systems-and-Data-Science-Course.

Milstein, B., Homer, J., Briss, P., Burton, D., & Pechacek, T. (2011). Why behavioral and environmental interventions are needed to improve health at lower cost. *Health Affairs, 30*(5). https://doi.org/10.1377/hlthaff.2010.1116.

Milstein, B., Homer, J., & Hirsch, G. (2010). Analyzing national health reform strategies with a dynamic simulation model. *American Journal of Public Health, 100*(5), 811–819.

Morecroft, J. D. W. (2007). Strategic modeling and business dynamics: A feedback systems approach. In J. D. W. Morecroft, & J. D. Sterman (Eds.) (1994) *Modeling for learning organizations system.* Wiley: Chichester.

NHS England. (2017). Next steps on the NHS five year forward view. https://www.england.nhs.uk/five-year-forward-view/next-steps-on-the-nhs-five-year-forward-view/.

Nuffield Trust. (2018). *The history of NHS reform.* time.line@nuffieldtrust.org.uk.

Rajeev, S., & Campbell, D. (2018). *Guardian UK report of interview with national audit office comptroller.* Amyas Morse.

Rawnsley, A. (2018). *Guardian newspaper comment.* Retrieved from June 24, 2018.

Richardson, G. P. (1999). *Feedback thought in social science and systems theory Philadelphia: University of Pennsylvania Press.* Waltham, MA: Pegasus Communications.

Richardson, G. P. (Ed.). (1996). *Modelling for management: Simulation in support of systems thinking. International library of management.* Aldershot, UK: Dartmouth Publishing Company.

Richardson, G. P., & Pugh, A. L., III. (1981). *Introduction to system dynamics modeling with DYNAMO.* MA Reprinted by Pegasus Communications, Waltham, MA: The MIT Press Cambridge.

Rutherford, P. A., Provost, L. P., Kotagal, U. R., Luther, K., & Anderson, A. (2017). Achieving hospital-wide patient flow. IHI White Paper. Cambridge, Massachusetts: Institute for Healthcare Improvement. www.ihi.org.

Stoye, G. (2018). *What does the NHS funding announcement mean for health spending in England.* Institute of Fiscal Studies Observation, Economic and Social research Council, London.

Senge, P. M. (1990). *The fifth discipline: The art and practice of the learning organization.* New York: Doubleday/Currency.

Sherwood, D. (2002). *Seeing the forest for the trees: A manager's guide to applying systems thinking.* London: Nicholas Brearley.

Sterman, J. D. (2000). *Business dynamics: Systems thinking and modelling for a complex world.* Boston: Irwin McGraw-Hill.

Stroth, P. L. (2015). *Systems thinking for social change.* White River Junction, Vermont, USA: Chelsea Green Publishing.

Todd, D. (2018). Synergia.co.nz.

Vennix, J. A. M. (1996). *Group model building: Facilitating team learning using system dynamics.* Chichester: Wiley.

Warren, K. (2008). *Strategic management dynamics.* Chichester: Wiley.

Wolstenholme, E. F. (1990). System enquiry: A system dynamics approach. John Wiley & Sons, Ltd.: Chichester.

Wolstenholme, E. F., (1993). A case study in community care using systems thinking. *Journal of the Operational Research Society, 44*(9), 925–934.

Wolstenholme, E. F. (1996). A patient flow perspective of UK health services. *System Dynamics Review, 15*(3), 253–273.

Wolstenholme, E. F. (2003). Towards the definition and use of a core set of archetypal structures in system dynamics. *System Dynamics Review, 19*(1), 7–26.

References

Wolstenholme, E. F. (2008). Influencing and interpreting health and social care policy in the UK. In H. Qudrat-Ullah, M. J. Spector, & P. I. Davidsen (Eds.), *Complex decision making: Theory and practice* (pp. 155–185). Springer, US (with Monk D and McKelvie D).

Wolstenholme, E. (2015). Health care in the United Kingdom and Europe, system dynamics applications to. In R. Meyers (Ed.), *Encyclopaedia of complexity and systems science*. Heidelberg: Springer, Berlin.

Part I
Elements of System Dynamics Important to Health and Social Care Modelling

Chapters 2–5

Overview of Part I

Part I presents five chapters describing the elements of system dynamics underpinning the project models described in Parts II, III and IV.

Chapter 2 introduces the language of stocks and flows as a means of mapping and modelling patient pathways and describes a simple but insightful treatment model explaining the often misunderstood, fundamental relationships between seven major hospital variables: bed occupancy, bed capacity, patient waits, referrals, admissions, discharges and length of stay.

Chapter 3 uses the model of Chap. 2 to shed light on the use of waiting time targets in hospital performance measurement.

Chapter 4 examines what we call the *shape of illness*—that is, the many ways in which population ageing and health conditions combine with treatments to produce complex pathways and patient flows.

Chapter 5 introduces the role of information feedback and system archetypes and how these concepts relate to the behaviour of the world and system dynamics models, and Chap. 6 describes the steps in applying system dynamics models with management and clinical teams.

It is suggested that knowledge of the elements and structures introduced can significantly improve understanding of the more complex project models as well as improving understanding of health service delivery per se.

Chapter 2
The Dynamics of Treatment and Capacity

Chapter Summary

All the case studies in this book are based on system dynamic models representing patient pathways as stock-flow (or 'bathtub') systems. This chapter will introduce these fundamental building blocks and their use in a simple, but insightful, model of a hospital relating 7 key performance variables. This model lies at the heart of many of the project models described in the book.

An exercise is presented using a one-stock hospital model to demonstrate the difficulties encountered by the human brain in thinking about flows over time in even the simplest situations. A two-stock hospital model with a capacity constraint is then described. This structure lies at the heart of all the treatment models in this book and relates 7 major hospital related variables; bed occupancy, bed capacity, referrals, admissions, discharges, length of stay and people waiting. The results of simulating this model are presented to demonstrate the effects of alternative admissions policies on capacity utilisation. The importance of this structural building block is that it can dispel common misconceptions about how the variables are linked together. Its relationships can be used as check on the consistency of data and in Chap. 3 we will describe its relevance to the setting of targets for waiting times.

2.1 A Simple One-Stock Map of a Hospital Treatment Pathway

System dynamics models are constructed in terms of the language of stocks and flows. This is a unique and concise language by which flows (in this case of people, or more precisely patients), can be described along any pathway. Stocks and flows are a means of making systems *visible* to facilitate discussion on how they work.

Moreover, unlike many other ways of describing flow each variable has a defined role and a defined causal *interconnection* with all other variables in the pathway.

Figure 2.1 shows a simple stock-flow map of a hospital treatment pathway. The representation shows people being admitted to hospital from an infinite pool of people (a cloud source) at a certain flow per day and cumulating into a stock of inpatients before being discharged, again into infinite pool (a cloud sink). The analogy is with water flow through a pipe system and the stock can be thought of as a reservoir or bathtub, in which people reside for a period of time.

Such bathtubs are essentially accumulations of resources in the world and are ubiquitous. Deposits in the bank or greenhouse gases in the atmosphere are bathtubs of money and carbon dioxide respectively. In this book, the predominant concern is with resources and stocks of people. In general, accumulations will be referred to using the more formal word 'stocks', but to emphasise the water analogy readers might find it always useful to think of *'bathtubs'*. Those with an engineering background might also like to think of stocks as *'state'* variables as used in control engineering. The origin of system dynamics is actually in this subject and many useful control rules can be transferred from this domain to help policy design in health. Some of these will be highlighted throughout the book.

Stocks occur where we dam or delay a flow for a purpose and are recognisable by being independent of time. In Fig. 2.1 the units of inpatients are just 'people'. If we could take an picture of a hospital only stocks would be seen. For example, the numbers present in each ward (and corridor) at that particular time.

By contrast flow variables, such as admissions and discharges are time dependent with units of 'people/day'. Flows are considered instantaneous and hence can only be measured by averaging them over some period of time.

Flow variables act as taps or control valves on the pipe and change in two distinct ways. They either operate in response to natural laws or to human actions. In Health and Social Care, the latter means the actions defined by the policies of clinicians and managers.

The case when input and output flows to a stock are equal defines a state of sustainability, where the accumulated stock remains in dynamic equilibrium at a fixed level. So as long as inputs and outputs remain constant and equal a stock will stay at whatever value it starts at. This has important repercussions when we start later to think about a stock as a wait list for patients and much more will be said about the importance of dynamic equilibrium in later models.

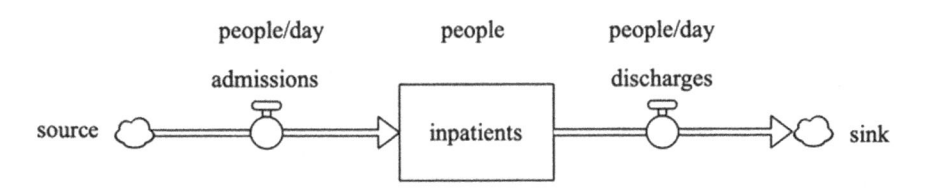

Fig. 2.1 A simple dynamic map of a hospital treatment pathway

2.1 A Simple One-Stock Map of a Hospital Treatment Pathway 27

The importance of distinguishing between stocks and flows cannot be emphasised enough, especially when used politically. For example, the government might claim that they are currently recruiting more nurses than ever. But recruitment is a flow and the stock of nurses will only increase if recruitment exceeds the flow of nurses leaving the profession.

The importance of the distinction between stocks and flows is particularly pertinent to thinking about patient pathway flows through health services. This is because increasing flow variables (such as hospital admissions and discharges) rather than increasing stock variables (such as beds) is the most effective way of improving patient throughput. Increasing the number of beds is a costly option and simply expands the system, which quickly fills up again.

2.2 An Exercise in Thinking Through Time[1] with Stocks and Flows

In order to experience the difficulties our brains have in understanding dynamic situations and the concept of stocks and flows, readers are encouraged to try the problem shown in Fig. 2.2. This is quite a simple dynamical issue. It just requires a little intuition. The 'answer' is given at the end of the Chapter in the Appendix.

2.3 A Two-Stock Hospital Model with a Capacity Constraint

Figure 2.3 shows a more realistic hospital model, where referrals are made to a waiting list prior to admission. The stock-flow chain of Fig. 2.3 is applicable both to elective and emergency pathways. Obviously elective waits are significant, whereas emergency waits are more transitory, perhaps, ambulance, trolley and corridor-waits.

When we link a number of stocks and flows together in series we create what we refer to as a *stock-flow chain* or *flow chain* for short. It should be remembered that the resource flowing through the chain is patients and any chain can only be a flow of only one such resource. It is a rule that we cannot mix apples and oranges and that if we wished to model other resources such as staff or cash, we would need separate flow chains for these which would interact with the patient flows. It should also be pointed out that patients flow from the source to the sink of a flow chain and it is often important in discussing insights to distinguish between upstream variables (those nearest the source) and downstream variables (those nearest the sink).

---

[1]This exercise is a modified version of one posed in 'All Models are Wrong: Reflections on becoming a Systems Scientist' (Sterman 2002) and is used with the permission of Wiley Publishing.

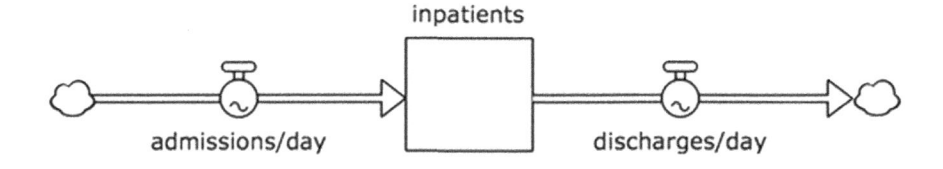

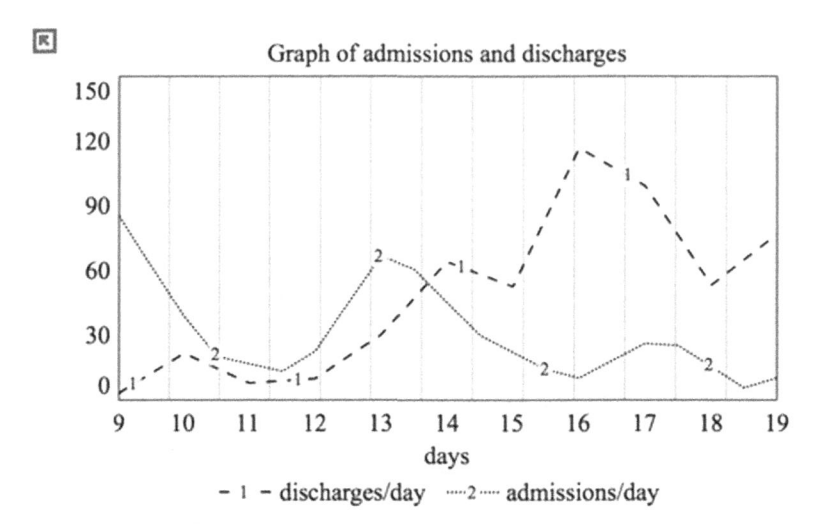

28   2 The Dynamics of Treatment and Capacity

Fig. 2.2 An exercise in thinking through time with stocks and flows

The graph above shows people being admitted to and being discharged from hospital per day over the a 10 day period. Please answer the following questions:
1. During which day did most people get admitted?
2. During which day did most people get discharged?
3. During which day were there most people in the hospital?
4. During which day were there fewest people in the hospital?

It is a rule of the stock-flow language that stock levels can only be changed by changing their inflows and outflows and the key to understanding the behaviour over time of a flow chain is to formulate how the flows work and then to simulate the resultant model.

In the previous exercise Fig. 2.2 the admissions inflow and discharges outflow were simply driven by time series and we had the unrealistic situation of a hospital without capacity limits, which did not seem to mind low utilisation! In reality admissions and discharges are determined by other factors and in true dynamic form are usually based on factors within the 'system'. This type of internal policy structure actually creates information feedback loops which will be explored further in Chap. 5.

2.3 A Two-Stock Hospital Model with a Capacity Constraint

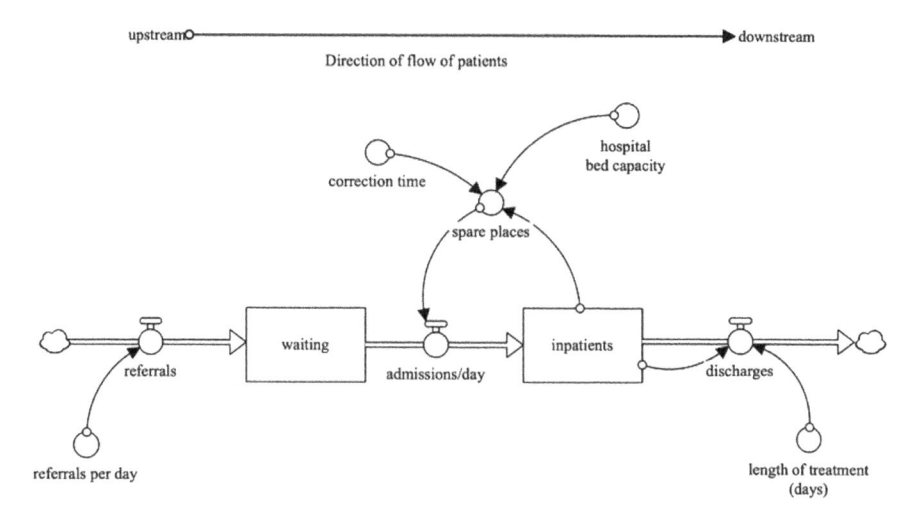

Fig. 2.3 A more realistic two-stock hospital model

In Fig. 2.3, admissions and discharges are driven by the stock of inpatients, the hospital bed capacity and the length of treatment, by taking information as shown by the single arrow links or 'information connectors' in the Figure. Connectors often use intermediate variables known as 'convertors' (small circles) to break the policy development down into easy stages (for example, 'spare places').

Admissions, is a policy variable and the assumption used in Fig. 2.3 is that admissions will be made as long as there are spare places in the hospital. Spare places are calculated by taking the difference between the hospital bed capacity and inpatients (assuming one person per bed!), subject to there being anyone waiting. It is important to note that the dimensions of 'spare places' is 'people' and that to convert this to 'admissions' it is necessary to divide it by a time factor ('correction time'). Such factors are important since they not simply ensure dimensional correctness, but because they have a real meaning. There are always delays involved in measuring and acting on information and delays have a bearing on system behaviour. Here the 'correction time' captures a delay. There are of course implications in this for how we obtain information and its accuracy and timeliness, which in turn has implications for the dependency of policies on good information systems.

On the other hand, discharges in Fig. 2.3 are defined as a natural consequence of patients having spent a certain average treatment time as an inpatient. The discharge rate is formulated as inpatients/average length of treatment. So, the more inpatients the greater the discharges and without admissions the stock of inpatients would decline exponentially to zero. This type of formulation is common to many dynamical systems. It is referred to as a stock draining or exponential decay process and is a true copy of many natural phenomena. For example, it is the way coffee cools to room temperature with a cooling constant analogous to the hospital length of stay—fast at first, but slower and slower as heat drains from the stock. The connectors linking inpatients and length of treatment to the discharge rate are not so much information links as natural influences.

Referrals in Fig. 2.3 are not linked to other elements of the stock-flow chain and are considered here as outside the influence of the hospital system and defined to be an *exogeneous* variable. It is always possible to expand a model to bring such variables into the model and Chap. 4 deals with how flow chains of ageing and health conditions can be constructed as drivers of referrals. One of the most important cornerstones of system dynamics is to try to view a system as *endogenously* as possible since systems are very often the cause of their own problems, rather than the victim of outside effects. It is also important to simulate and test structures before they become too complicated.

The total combined stock/flow/information feedback/policy map of the hospital shown in Fig. 2.3 is referred to as the *structure* of our mental hypothesis about how we view the hospital system and how the hospital operates. It is analogous to a test bed in a laboratory on which experiments can be carried out and is sometimes referred to as the *'physics'* of the hospital because, although virtual, it is an explicit map of the physical elements at play which make the flow work.

2.4 Simulation Experiments on the Two-Stock Hospital Model

We are now in a position to simulate the behaviour over time of the model and to see if our assumptions about its policies are proven by experimentation. However, before we can we must specify a number of factors:

- The initial states of the two stocks. For clarity of demonstration we shall assume that we start with an empty hospital and no one waiting.
- The time units of the variables. We shall stick to the use of days as shown on the earlier figures.
- The time horizon over which we wish to examine the model behaviour. This is specified as 1 year or 365 days.
- The referral rate, which is 20 people per day
- The length of treatment, which is 5 days.

It is always important before running a simulation experiment is to try to anticipated what behaviour might be expected. That is, to test our own mental models and try our own mental simulation capacity. In the case here, we might legitimately imagine (using our mental models and own internal simulators) is that the hospital simply fills to capacity, at which time waiting occurs.

Figure 2.4 shows the resulting behaviour over time of the hospital bed capacity and the inpatient and waiting stocks and this is perhaps not what we were expecting.

2.4 Simulation Experiments on the Two-Stock Hospital Model

behaviour over time of stocks

——— inpatients   – · – hospital bed capacity
········ waiting

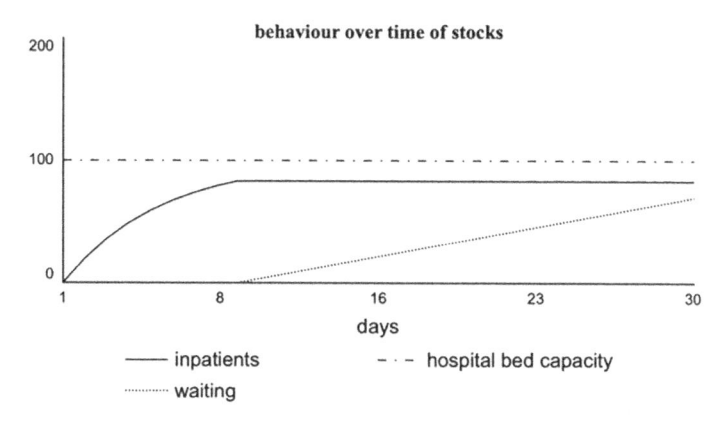

Fig. 2.4 The behaviour of the stocks over time for the model in Fig. 2.3

The number of inpatients never reaches the hospital capacity but reaches a plateau at a point below this. The waiting stock starts to climb when the plateau is achieved.

So here we have our first simple example of a computer simulation result exposing that our mental models about the structure of the hospital we have created is somehow wrong. Working out why this result occurs is our first step to improving our mental model.

The secret lies in examining our assumptions. Assumptions are very important and made extensively in both scientific and social settings. It is good to keep track of them and we were once impressed by working for an organisation which had a post of 'custodian of assumptions' to whom we could turn for the official list. In particular, it is useful to examine a graph of the flows of the model. The model reaches equilibrium when the admissions and discharges are equal (Fig. 2.5), but this does not occur when the hospital is full. It occurs at a lower point.

This lower point can in fact be calculated as follows from the parameter values used in the model:

At equilibrium:
Admissions = discharges
(hospital capacity–inpatients) = inpatients/length of treatment
(100–inpatients) = inpatients/5
500–(5 * inpatients) = inpatients
6* inpatients = 500
inpatients = 83

So, the equilibrium point for this model is 83 inpatients, which is 100–83 or 16.5 below hospital capacity. Interestingly, at equilibrium, the admissions and discharge rates are also 16.5 people per day (83/5). In other words, the inpatients level reached is always one day's worth of admissions less than capacity. This clue suggests revising the admissions policy to allow for this amount might be useful.

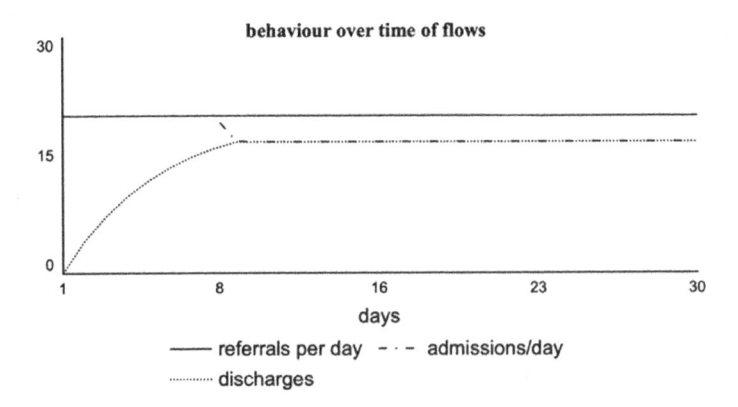

```
                behaviour over time of flows
30

15

 0
   1         8            16          23          30
                         days
            ——— referrals per day   – · – admissions/day
            ············ discharges
```

Fig. 2.5 The behaviour over time of the flows for the model in Fig. 2.3

What we have committed is the cardinal sin for this type of system of not accounting for people leaving when designing arriving policies.

2.5 Redesigning Policies

Figure 2.6 shows a revised model and its behaviour, where the hospital admissions rate is based not only on spare places, but on adding to this the average discharge rate (remember that rates must be averaged before we can measure them). This is both intuitively and theoretically correct. However, we have come across many instances where hospital congestion in accident and emergency rooms has been put down to a lack of beds for admission, rather than taking a whole pathway view and understanding that hospital discharges are also key to this situation. This is particularly true of work in modelling delayed hospital discharges reported in Chap. 7.

In the current climate of hospitals working at or near capacity for much of the time, recognition of the importance of discharge is growing and most hospitals collect discharge information to plan admissions and employ discharge coordinators. When a hospital is working at capacity, *replacement* (one-in, one-out) provides the only space for manoeuvre. However, in the event of hospitals working below capacity it is also necessary to apply a *stock correction* for spare places when deciding admissions to achieve full bed utilisation.

Note that target hospital bed capacity as defined in this model might not be the full number of beds available, but what might be considered a safe level below this. Also note that although hospital capacity is defined here as beds, it could easily be defined as the beds capable of being supported by staffing and clinical teams which might again be less than the actual number of beds available.

It will be seen from Fig. 2.6 that this policy adjustment corrects the behaviour of the model and the full hospital capacity available is realised.

2.6 Systems Notes

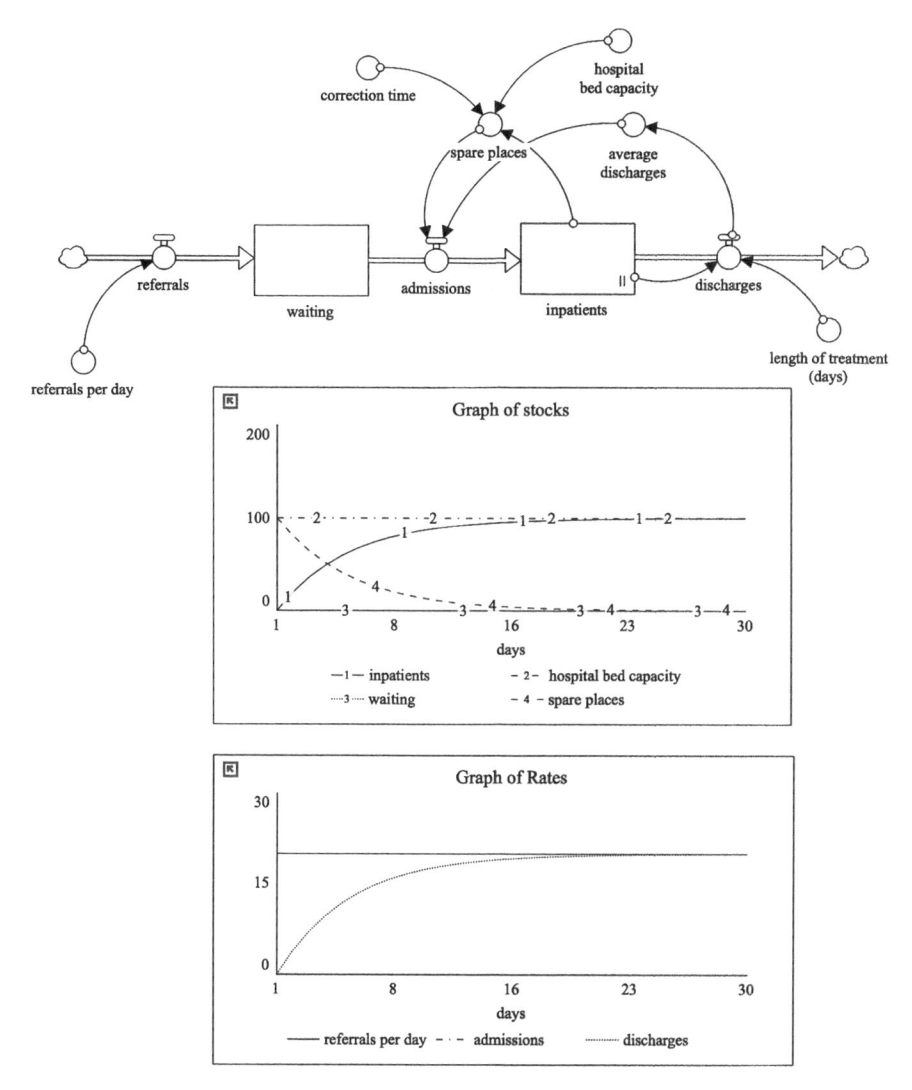

Fig. 2.6 The model structure and behaviour for the two-stock hospital model with a replacement plus stock correction admission policy

2.6 Systems Notes

What is described here as a hospital structure is actually a much more general structure applicable to a number of different flow (supply) chains. Further, there are well known rules of control theory and stock control that govern such systems. These maintain that, to maintain inventory, inflows to every stock in the chain should be corrected for any discrepancy between target and actual levels (known as stock correction), as well as for all average outputs from stocks, including planned and unplanned, such as leakage or drop-outs, (known as replacement). It also quite well known that such rules sometimes are not recognised or forgotten, particular when built into fully automated stock control software. It is not too long ago that a major car manufacturer omitted to include outflow replacement in its reordering algorithms with disastrous consequences.

It is also useful at this point to distinguish between two types of stocks. These are:

- a *time-dependent* stock where a resource passes through the stock over an average period of time and the outflow is a function of the level of the stock. In this book we generally define the outflow of a stock as the level in the stock divided by the average time spent in the stock (delay). For a stock with no inflow this gives, as indicated earlier, an output which mimics many natural processes and causes an exponential distribution of the outflow as the level of the stock declines.
- a *buffer* stock where the inflows and the outflows do not directly relate to the size of the stock which can only be changed indirectly through other parts of the chain in which it resides. Buffers generally act as a means of delaying and dampening a fluctuating inflow into a smoother outflow. Sometimes deliberately large buffers are needed in contrast to just-in-time manufacturing where buffers are kept to a minimum requiring flexible manufacturing rates to track incoming order rates.

'Inpatients' in the two-stock hospital model is a *time-dependent* type of stock where patients reside for the average treatment time, whereas '*waiting*' is a *buffer* type stock separating fluctuating referrals from steady, capacity constrained hospital admissions. The importance of perceiving waiting as a buffer stock will become more apparent when treatment waiting time is discussed as a performance measure in Chap. 3.

2.7 Changes to the Length of Treatment

So far, we have assumed that the average length of treatment in hospital is a fix parameter. However, with increasing skill, productivity and technological innovation, length of treatment is in practice reducing. Length of treatment is actually a proxy for capacity and Fig. 2.7 shows that our original model is capable of demonstrating this relationship. Here the length of treatment has been reduced to 4 days which allows for referrals to be increased from 20 to 25 per day without any effect on performance.

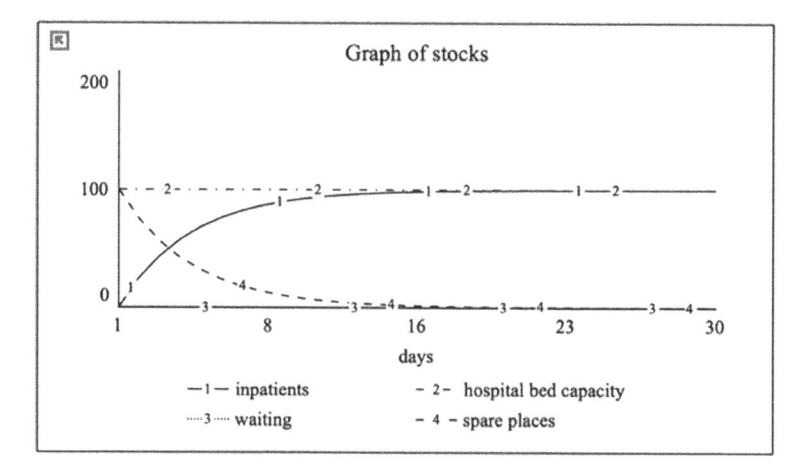

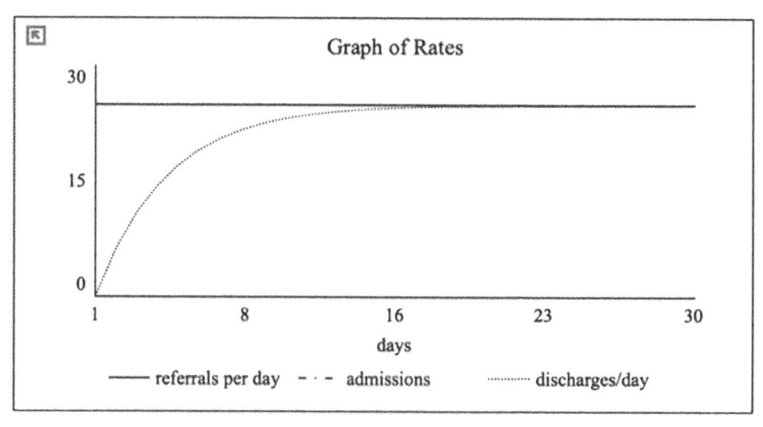

Fig. 2.7 Model structure and behaviour for the two-stock hospital model with reduced length of stay and increased admissions

2.8 The Importance of the Two-Stock Hospital Model

Although relatively simple, the two-stock hospital model of Fig. 2.6 has been at the heart of our modelling projects for many years (Wolstenholme 1996) and is fundamental to the modelling projects described in this book.

The equations defined for the model provide a simple, but comprehensive set of relationships between 7 important variables involved in the movement of patients through any hospital pathway. These are referrals, admissions, discharges, hospital capacity, length of treatment, inpatients and numbers waiting. Experience in using the model in workshops has shown that even people familiar with the workings of hospitals are often confused about how these variables relate to one another over time and have found it useful to see them illustrated in this way.

One example of the use of the model in its own right is in the understanding of the link between hospital waiting time and hospital capacity, the implications of which provide an important challenge to the use of waiting time targets at the heart of hospital performance management. This use of the model will be explored at length in Chap. 3.

Another use of the model is in testing hospital data for consistency. The two-stock hospital model and data consistency which will be addressed here.

On occasions we have collected data which appears totally at odds with the relationships in the model and this has enabled us to query their provenance. For example, there have been instances of hospitals claiming an average length of treatment of 2 days when working with a capacity of 100 beds and average admissions and discharges of 20 per day. According to our modelling relationships, if this where true, discharges would actually be 50 per day (100/2) rather than 20 and the hospital would quickly empty! Whilst there will always be a tendency to understate lengths of treatment and stays and particularly to perhaps exclude long stay patients when compiling average lengths of stay statistics, such figures quoted are usually worthy of further investigation.

This type of 'triangulation' thinking can also be used to infer the magnitude of any missing data items and is used in Chap. 13 on similar formulations for modelling the relationship between the incidence (flow) and prevalence (stock) of dementia.

2.9 Different Types of Capacity

Beds

So far capacity has been defined in terms of beds and an assumption made that there are sufficient staff and medical teams to support those beds. Several other types of capacity exist in health and social care, and we list here some of the most common.

Other Place-Type Capacities

Many other services operate with a simple limit (places) on the number of people who can use a service. For example, residential or nursing home care is also bed-based. However, there may be some flexibility because the main constraint may be 'the number of care home beds that a local authority can afford to purchase' as a bigger constraint than the actual number of places. Day care is slightly more complicated. A day service will almost certainly have a fixed number of places, but some flexibility in how these are used (some people attend for one day per week,

2.9 Different Types of Capacity

others for two or more) means that the capacity calculation for places would be (assuming a five-day week)

capacity = places × average days per user/5

Caseload

Some services, such as social services, operate on a relatively simple concept of a 'maximum number of cases per worker', although usually with some kind of weighting applied to acknowledge that some types of case are more demanding than others. These services are characterised by a relatively low rate of turnover of cases. In this case

capacity = number of staff × maximum cases per person

Time-Based Caseload Capacity

Sometimes it is better to think in terms of the 'maximum caseload of a team' rather a single worker. For example, care at home is a service where one staff member spends small amounts of time with several service users in the course of a day, sometimes in units as low as 15 min chunks. In order to work out the total number of people who can be looked after by an average worker, we therefore must factor in a wide range of variables (number of working hours in the day, average amount of contact time needed per service user, time spent travelling or being trained, other non-contact time, annual leave entitlement, typical sick leave). From a very detailed calculation, it is possible to derive a realistic ratio of 'service users per whole time worker'.[2]

Appointments (Slot-Based Capacity)

This kind of capacity describes how many clinics operate, often working half-day sessions, where there is a fixed number of appointment slots available at each session (note also that the clinic might be staffed by more than one person, and by more than one type of staff, and quite possibly 'running the clinic' is only a fraction of what each worker does). We give a rather more detailed explanation of how we model this (Fig. 2.8).

---

[2]Probably just over 3, in fact.

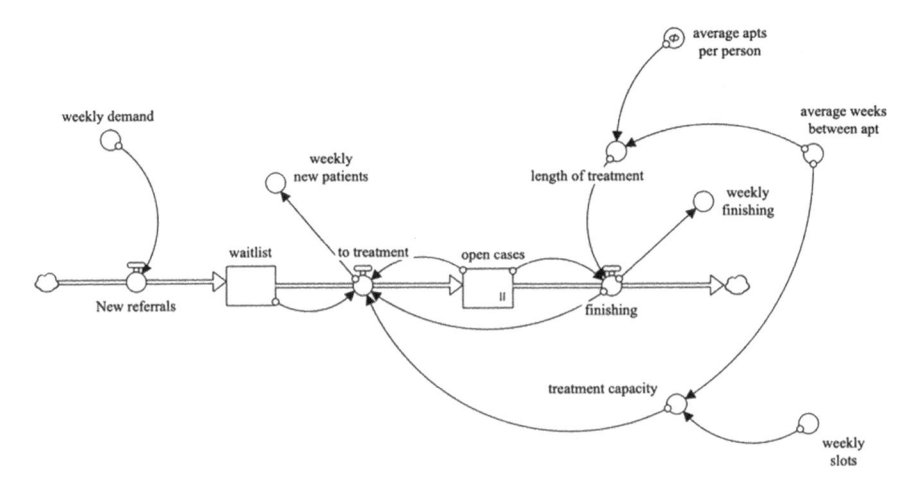

Fig. 2.8 A treatment slots capacity model

The structure will be seen to have many similarities to the hospital model described earlier in this chapter. 'To treatment' is equivalent to 'admissions' a function of the gap between 'open cases' and 'treatment capacity' and (of course) 'finishing'. 'Finishing' is equivalent to 'discharges' and is the 'open cases' divided by the 'length of treatment'.

The main differences between this model and those encountered before are the definition of capacity and length of treatment. Rather than beds, capacity here is the product of the number of slots available per week and the average time between appointments. The number of slots might be a function of the staff and time allocated to clinics. If there are 30 slots per week and patients need appointments every 3 weeks, then 90 is the maximum number of patients who can be on the clinic's case load.

Length of treatment is the product of the average appointments per person and the average weeks between appointments. (If patients need 5 appointments in total and an appointment every 3 weeks, then each patient's treatment lasts for 15 weeks).

Interestingly the average weeks between appointments affects both the capacity and the length of treatment. In this type of out-patient situation with many time dependent factors it is very easy for the human brain to get confused about which variables will have what effect on throughput and the role of a simple model is at a premium.

Figure 2.9 shows the output from the slots model in equilibrium with a demand of 10 people per week. The other parameters for the model are as described earlier and also shown on the slider bars beneath the graph which form a control panel that users can manipulate to experiment with the model. The run button allows the model to be run and the clear button allows all graphs to be cleared and parameters

2.9 Different Types of Capacity

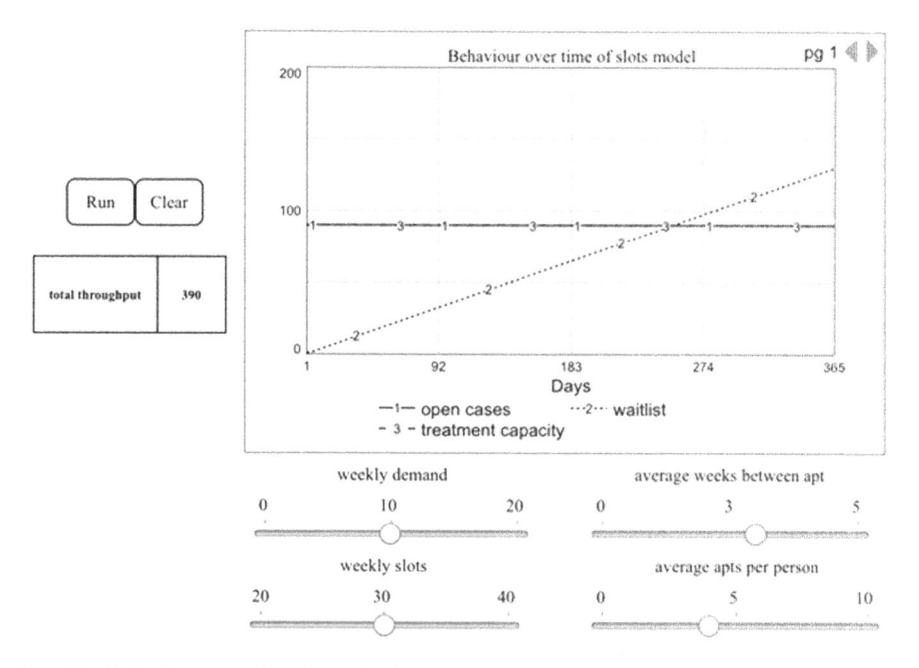

Fig. 2.9 Behaviour over time from the slots model

restored at the beginning of each experiment. The 'total throughput' displayed is the cumulative patients treated over the whole experimental run of the model.

The number of open cases is set equal to the capacity (90), but since the rate of new referrals (10) is greater than the number of cases finishing (30/15 = 2) the waitlist rises.

Figure 2.10 shows what happens if the average weeks between appointments is increased to 4 weeks after six months and Fig. 2.11 shows a similar increase in the number of slots per week made available. It may again be a good exercise to try to think through the effect of these changes before consulting the output graphs.

In both cases capacity rises and the waitlist briefly falls, but as soon as the capacity fills up the waiting rises once more. However, Fig. 2.10 shows no increase in throughput, whereas Fig. 2.11 does!

Raising the number of slots per week gives a direct increase in capacity and hence throughput. However, raising the time between appointments increases capacity allowing more cases to be taken on, BUT makes treatment last longer, reducing the number of cases finishing and not effecting throughput.

It is commonly thought that increasing the average time between appointments is a good way to treat more people. It does in that it increases the number of open cases, but the cases are open longer and total throughput unaffected. In systems

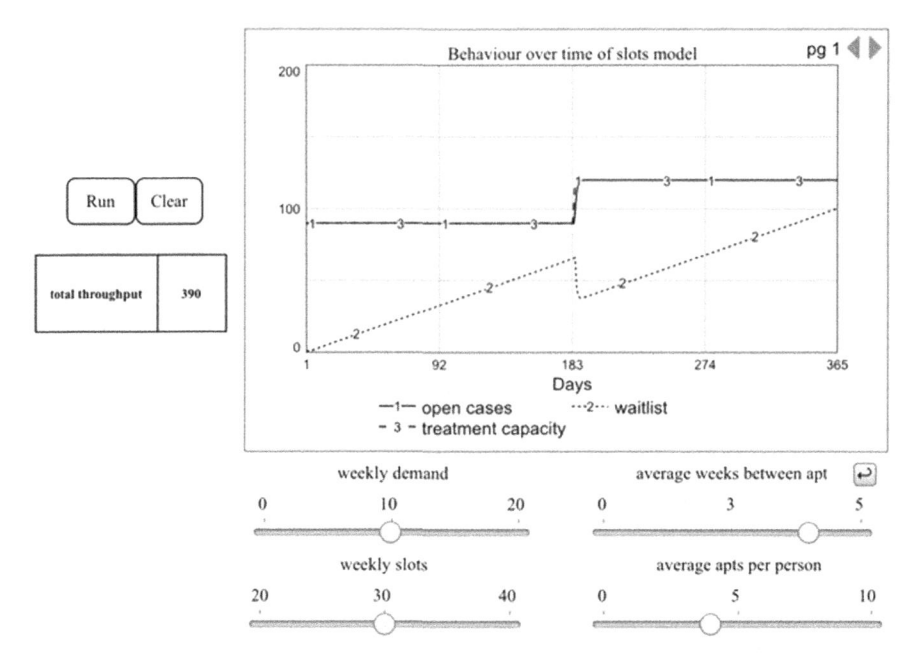

Fig. 2.10 Results from an experiment to increase the average time between appointments

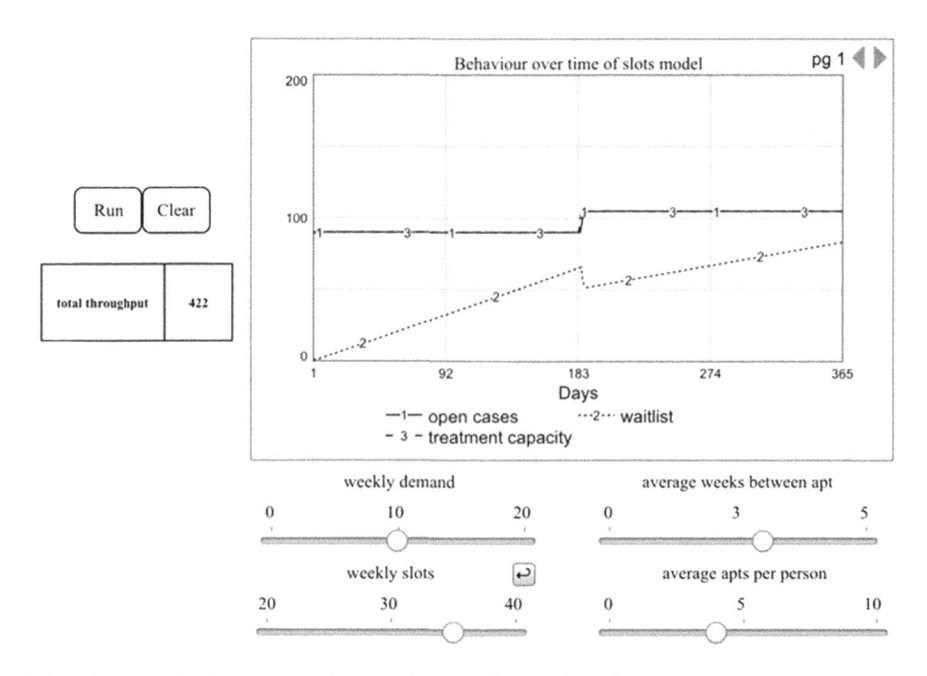

Fig. 2.11 Results from an experiment to increase the number of slots per week

2.9 Different Types of Capacity

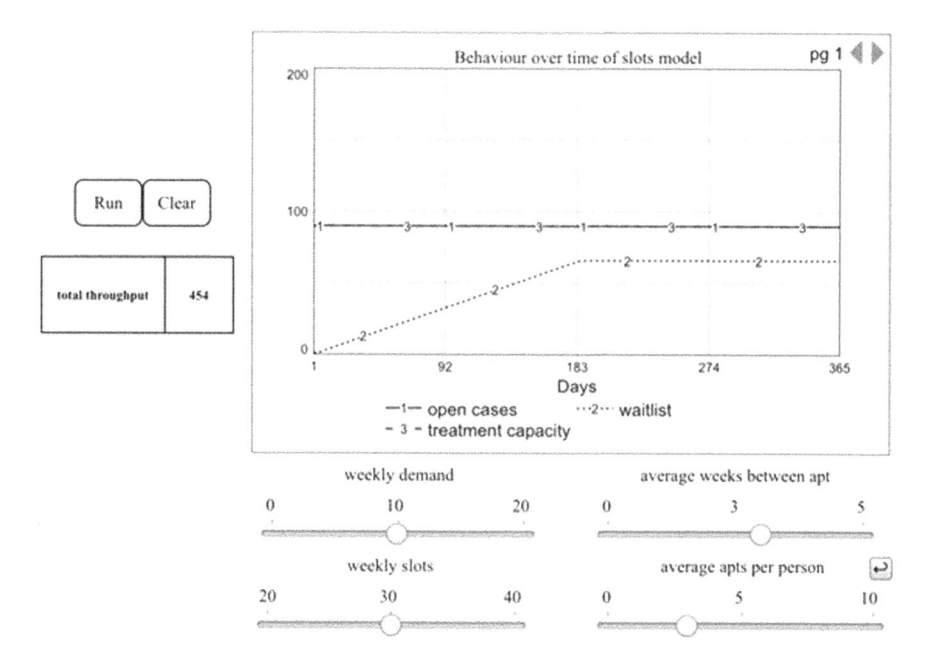

Fig. 2.12 Experiments to reduce the average number of the appointments per person

terms, we are increasing the capacity of the stock but also increasing the length of stay, meaning that exactly the same number can flow in or out.

Figure 2.12 shows that reducing the average appointments per person has a dramatic effect on stabilising waiting. This is because the capacity remains the same but the length of stay reduces, meaning that people can flow in (and out) at a higher rate. But there may well be unintended consequences of doing so on treatment efficacy. In times of urgent need for inpatient care, reducing or suspending outpatient appointments for less urgent surgical and long-term medical conditions is not uncommon in many hospitals.

Screening, Brief Assessment (Triage)

A specific case of a slot-based capacity is where a brief, one-off assessment is needed, perhaps to do an initial screening of the suitability of a referral. In this case, the capacity is simply 'the maximum number that can be processed per time unit (probably day)'. When simulating this, unlike the examples given above, note that the service intervention (assessment) 'takes place' within a flow rather than a stock. Chapter 4 goes into some detail about the difference between interventions, including whether they are best described as happening within a stock (called treatment) or a flow (called assessing or diagnosing, for example).

2.10 A Word on Variation and Costs

It will be appreciated from the discussion so far that system dynamic models tend to be formulated primality in terms of averages values for major parameters such as length of hospital stay. This does not mean that variations around these averages cannot be built into models, which clearly happen in practice, both on a day to day basis and seasonally, say due to demand surge of illness in winter. In fact, variation is built into many of the models described later in the book. However, such inclusion, whilst bringing an additional element of reality, can sometimes results in some modelling clarity being lost.

It will also be appreciated that no mentioned has been made so far of costs within models. Some sorts of modelling such as spreadsheets are often totally financially based. The contrast here is that the models are focused primarily on operational activities. The justification is that illuminating pathways is the way to externalising and sharing mental models and that it is within pathways that the best intervention and leverage points are located. Models can and do include costs, often as performance measures, as will be shown in the later Chapters of the book.

2.11 Concluding Remarks

This Chapter has given an overview of some common modelling structures for treatment and capacity embedded in most project models throughout this book. The importance of these structures will become clearer in subsequent chapters. It has (hopefully) demonstrated the challenge and rewards of thinking through time.

In more complex models the structures become less clear and are often buried in supplementary elements associated with input and outputs, data conversions and the addition of dashboards and other interfaces aimed at allowing users to manipulate models as microworlds. This is why it is important to surface the constructs here both in their own right and to demonstrate that the more complex models are also driven by similar dynamic elements which makes them different from most other approaches to modelling available.

2.11 Concluding Remarks

Appendix: The Answer to the Exercise in Fig. 2.2

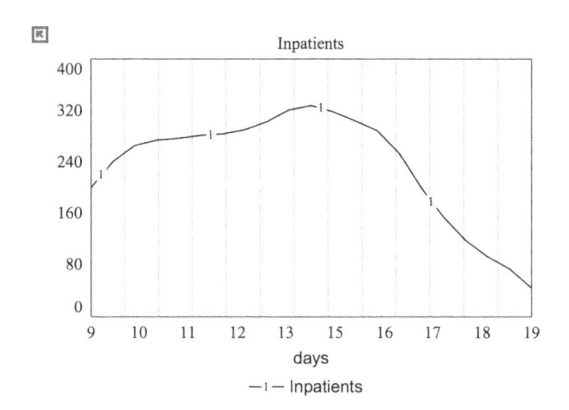

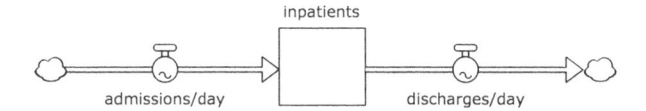

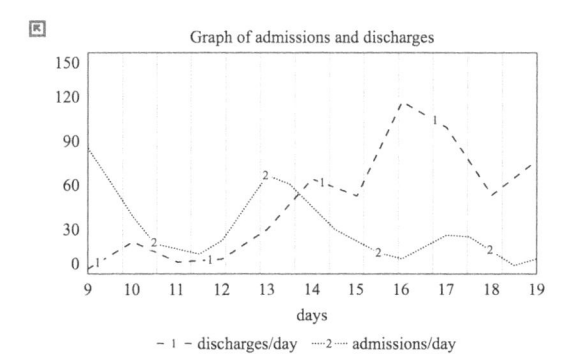

[Graph: Inpatients over days 9–19, y-axis 0 to 400]

[Stock-and-flow diagram: admissions/day → inpatients → discharges/day]

[Graph of admissions and discharges over days 9–19, y-axis 0 to 150; legend: –1– discharges/day, ···2··· admissions/day]

The graph above shows people being admitted to and being discharged from hospital per day over the a 10 day period. Please answer the following questions:
1. During which day did most people get admitted?
2. During which day did most people get discharged?
3. During which day were there most people in the hospital?
4. During which day were there fewest people in the hospital?

Answers:

1. Day 9 The number of admissions per day is shown by the dotted line (2), which peaks at week 9
2. Day 16 The number of discharges per day is shown by the dashed line (1), which peaks at week 16

3. Day 14 During the first 14 days the number of admissions is greater than the number of discharges and after that time the number of discharges is greater than the number of admissions. So, most people are in the hospital at day 14.
4. Day 19 This is perhaps the trickiest of the questions. We know from answer 3 that the number of people in the hospital goes up until day14 and down until day 19. But we do not know by how much. To find out, it is necessary to estimate whether more people are admitted before day 14 than are discharged after day 14. That is whether the area between the two curves up to day 14 is greater or less than the area between the two after that time. Observation will show that it is greater. More people leave after day 14 than are admitted before day 14. So, the fewest people are in the hospital after 19 day.

Answers 3 and 4 are made much clearer by studying the graph of inpatients at the top of the answer, which is the result of the net flow of admissions and discharges.

References

Sterman, J. (2002). All models are wrong: Reflections on becoming a systems scientist Jay wright Forrester prize lecture. *System Dynamics Review, 18,* 501–531.
Wolstenholme, E. F. (1996). A patient flow perspective of UK health services. *System Dynamics Review, 15*(3), 253–273.

Chapter 3
Performance Measurement—The Fallacy of Waiting Time Targets

Chapter Summary
This chapter uses the simple two-stock hospital model introduced in Chap. 2 to explore the concept of treatment waiting time targets in common use to measure the performance of health treatment services. The results suggest that the setting of such targets is purely arbitrary and perhaps more of a political aspiration than a concrete aim since achieving them is out of the practical control of hospital management. In fact, the only way to attain them would be by having the ability to continuously change service capacities over impossible ranges to track changes in referrals or by continuously adjusting lengths of stay.

3.1 The Relationship Between Capacity and Waiting Times

A question we are often asked by a potential client is 'what capacity do we need in order to achieve a given waiting time?' This is typically a number of weeks for elective procedures and a number of hours for unscheduled emergency care.

Such questions arise because governments (differently across the UK) set 'target waiting times', meaning 'the longest acceptable wait between being referred for, and starting, treatment' for a given procedure. Performance measures of this kind are used extensively in most organisations with the aim of providing benchmarks, holding staff to account and improving productivity. However, it is questionable whether they are effective in achieving these goals.

The requirement to meet a target inevitably generates unintended consequences often centred on perverse behaviour by those working within the system. For example, by redefining stages in a process. Examples in health and social care would be:

- ambulances delivering emergency patients might queue in a car park because the waiting time clock only starts ticking when the patient enters the hospital door and time spent in a hospital car park or slow lane is not an official 'delay'.
- starting treatment and moving the wait to 'within' the treatment.
- redeploying staff to where the current bottleneck is and creating bottlenecks elsewhere.

Ultimately when targets are not met the well-known system archetype of 'drifting goals' takes place with targets being reduced to what the system can feasibly achieve (Senge 1990, Wolstenholme 2003).

While such observations may be correct, we have a different take on waiting times. Using a simple simulation of the two-stage hospital model introduced in Chap. 2, we explore the 'physics' of the system to generate this useful insight:

– *Although there undoubtedly is a relationship between 'capacity' and 'waiting time', the **nature** of that relationship is not as generally imagined by policy-makers, commissioners and even those working within the system—THE IDEA THAT ANY GIVEN CAPACITY WILL GENERATE A SPECIFIC WAITING TIME IS FLAWED.*

In fact, the existence of a (false) belief that for every capacity (input) there must be a particular waiting time (output), leads to its own perverse outcomes. A policy-maker holding this mental model may well pass on that misperception to those charged with commissioning services, who will hold providers to account for failing to achieve something that is actually impossible. Experts in 'improvement science' may be deployed to work with providers in order to help them to achieve this impossibility.

This way of thinking might be compounded by the current emphasis on an 'outcome-focus' where the commissioning process emphasises the outcomes to be delivered by the provider rather than the inputs. This has some logic. In commissioning public services, we want to involve those who actually use services, and deliver the outcome they want (e.g. recovery). But that should not absolve commissioners from paying attention to the actual processes involved in getting there; otherwise how would they know that a service specification is feasible and sustainable?

Our simple insight is this. Either there is enough capacity or there isn't. With enough capacity, there is no need for a waiting time.[1] Without enough capacity, waiting times will rise relentlessly, never levelling off.

---

[1] Apart from the absolute minimum time it takes to process a referral and arrange commencement of treatment, which may be several weeks.

3.2 The Two-Stock Hospital Model

To explore the dynamic relationship between capacity and waiting times, we will explore a very simple model of referrals to a waiting list, admissions from the waiting list to inpatients, and discharges based on an average length of stay. This model shown in Fig. 3.1 was introduced in Chap. 2.

The flow relationships of this model are described in Chap. 2 and summarised here:

Admissions = minimum (spare beds, waiting)
Spare beds = beds – inpatients + discharges
Discharges = inpatients/los d (length of stay in days)
Wait time w (waiting time in weeks) = waiting/admissions (divided by 7 to convert days to weeks).

This model runs for five years in days. The graph plots what has happened to waiting times (dotted line) during the run, alongside an 18-week target. The numbers on the diagram show the values of all of the variables in the model at a particular point on the timeline. The numbers in boxes refer to inputs that a user can change (not shown, user can also set the 'initial number' in the waiting stock). In this run, the key inputs are:

- 20 referrals per day
- 130 beds (capacity)
- Length of stay of 7 days

In these runs:

- we set the 'initial number' in the waiting stock to 1,400 (i.e. there is a waiting list at the start), and we vary ONLY the number of beds.
- we set the inpatients to automatically equal the beds (by filling every spare bed, if enough people are waiting) so the hospital is working at capacity

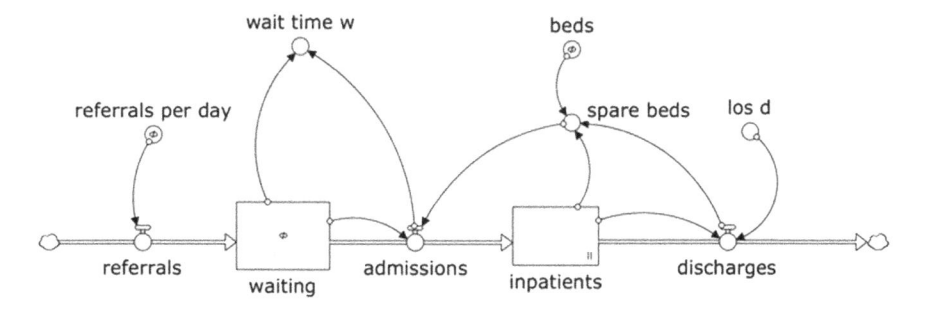

Fig. 3.1 The two-stock hospital model

The key question we are exploring is:
How many beds should we have to produce a waiting time of 18 weeks
When the model starts, the waiting time is already at 9 weeks.

Run 1 (Fig. 3.2)—**bed capacity set to 130**

In this run, the waiting time steadily increases from 9 weeks. It does not find any kind of equilibrium value. The number waiting at the end of the five years is 3,896.

Reviewing the numbers at the end of five years, note that the key numbers are the **flows**:

- 20 referrals per day
- 19 admissions per day
- 19 discharges per day

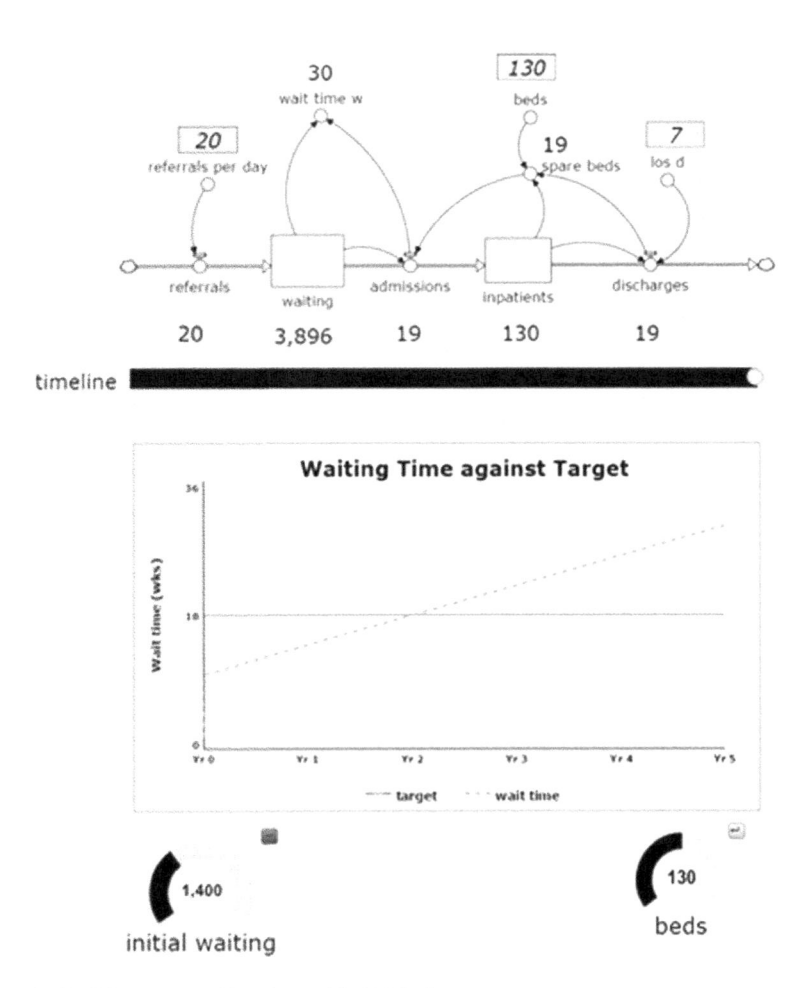

Fig. 3.2 Model output: waiting time with 130 beds

3.2 The Two-Stock Hospital Model

Clearly, if referrals are always greater than admissions, the number waiting will be rising by that amount every day.

A key metric, therefore, is to compare the 'referrals' flow with the 'discharges' flow.

Run 2 (Fig. 3.3)—bed capacity set to 145

(paused at year 3 of 5)

In this run, the waiting time steadily reduces from 9 weeks. We have paused the model after three years, at which point the waiting time is 3 weeks.

At this point, there are:

- 20 referrals per day
- 21 admissions per day
- 21 discharges per day

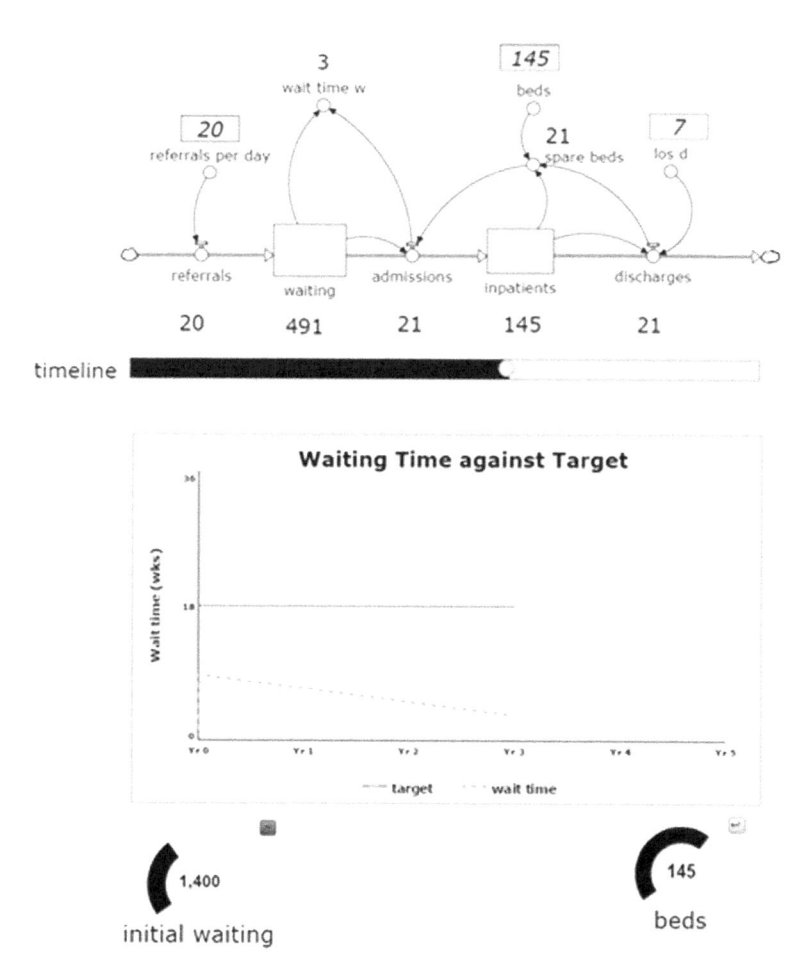

Fig. 3.3 Model output: waiting time with 145 beds

50   3 Performance Measurement—The Fallacy of Waiting Time Targets

Clearly, if referrals are always fewer than admissions, the number waiting will be falling by that amount every day.

Run 2 (Fig. 3.4)—**bed capacity set to 145**

(paused at end of 5-year run)

This is the same run, but the focus is on what happens towards the end of the model run.

The waiting time had been steadily reducing (because admissions/discharges were always greater than referrals). It is clear from the graph that towards the end of the simulation, the waiting stock has completely cleared.

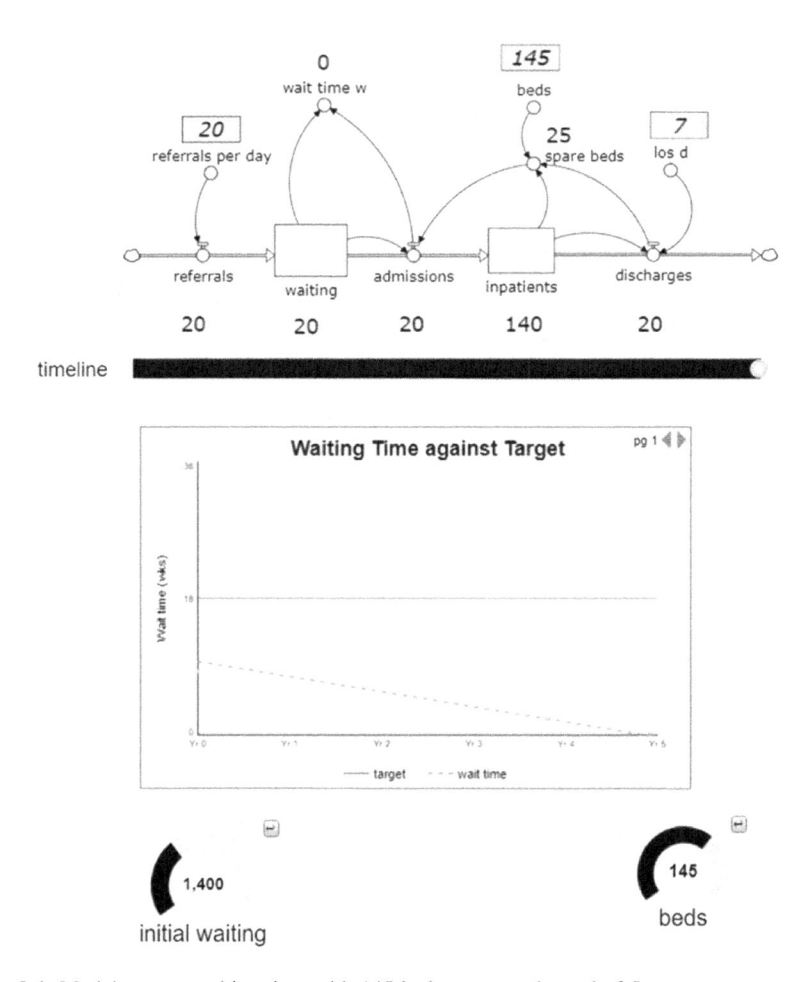

Fig. 3.4 Model output: waiting time with 145 beds pause at the end of 5 years

3.2 The Two-Stock Hospital Model

From this point onwards, there is effectively no waiting time (when measured in weeks—technically, there is always at least one day's referrals in the waiting stock at any time) and the model is operating in equilibrium.

There are:

- 20 referrals per day
- 20 admissions per day
- 20 discharges per day

Note also that the 'inpatient stock' settles at 140 which is equal to 'admissions per day * length of stay'.

Run 3 (Fig. 3.5) Discontinuities and Tipping Points

In this run, we exaggerate the effect shown in Run 2 by increasing bed capacity to 150, leading to a sharper reduction in waiting times.

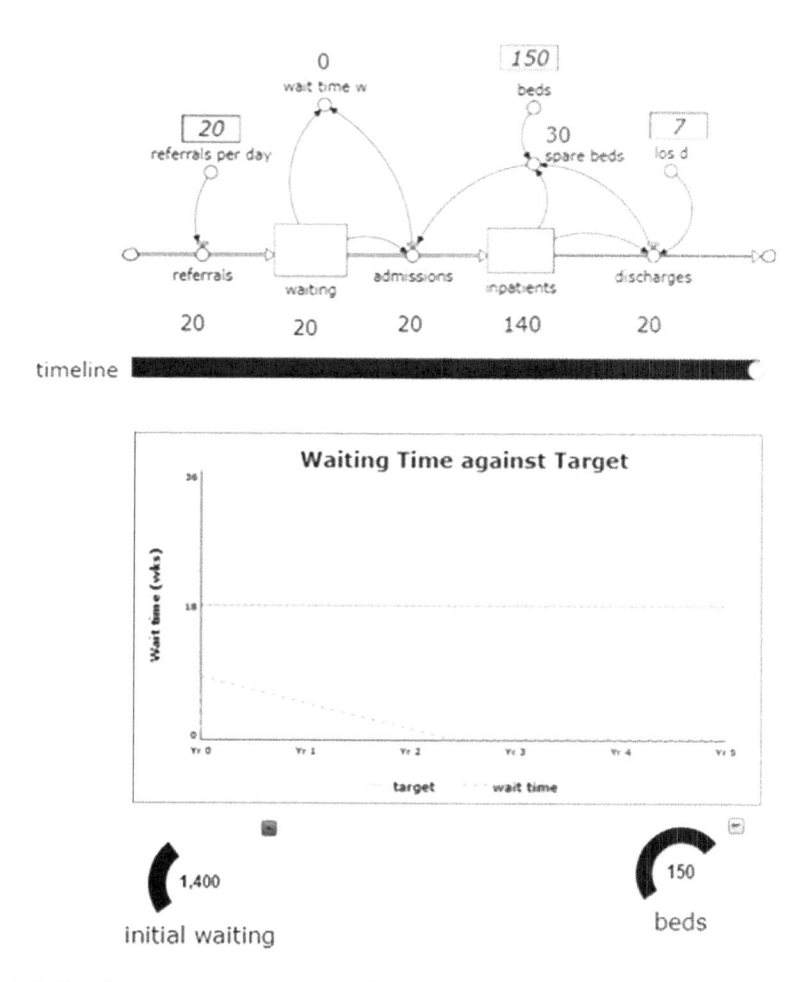

Fig. 3.5 Model output: waiting time with 150 beds

This clearly shows that just about 2½ years into the run, the waiting list is cleared, and waiting times reach 0. Although the model is simple and looks linear, because it contains stocks its behaviour might demonstrate discontinuities or tipping points.

In this case, the waiting time has been steadily decreasing, but when it approaches 0, its lower limit, it flattens out.

Run 4 (Fig. 3.6)—**bed capacity set to 140**

It should be obvious by now that if we have enough capacity to admit 20 people per day (in line with referrals) the number entering and leaving the waiting stock will remain level, and waiting times will also remain level, throughout the model run.

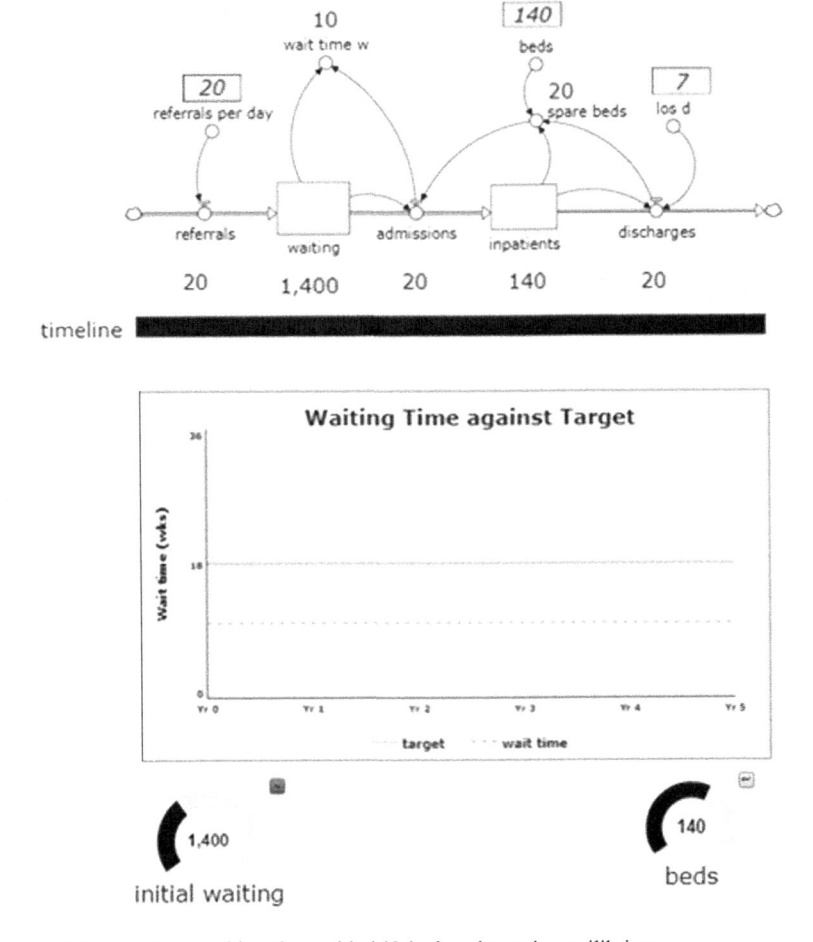

Fig. 3.6 Model output: waiting time with 140 beds—dynamic equilibrium

3.2 The Two-Stock Hospital Model

It so happens that the waiting time throughout this model run remains level at 10 weeks, but why 10? The reason is that this derives from the 'initial number waiting' (1,400). Because the number waiting does not change in this run (referrals = admissions throughout), and admissions are 20 per day, dividing the stock by the outflow gives 70 days (10 weeks).

What we have shown in these examples is that (other things being equal) there definitely is a relationship between **capacity** and **waiting times** but it is not 'linear'. There is not a 'waiting time' that corresponds to a particular 'capacity'. The relationship is actually better understood to be between 'capacity' and the 'gradient of the waiting time', Fig. 3.7.

In the real world, rather than the model, the 'physics' of the stock/flow relationships may be obscured by the 'noise' of another variable, perhaps rising over time, referral rate, or, more likely, as a result of the various coping strategies adopted by those working within the system. If waiting lists are rising, perhaps patients will be discharged earlier (with consequences for other parts of the system), so there will be pressure to reduce length of stay. If waiting lists are falling, perhaps we can ease off in various ways, by keeping some beds empty (it is not considered good practice to run a service at capacity), or by holding onto patients for a little longer (length of stay rises), or even by allowing patients from other, over-stretched, parts of the hospital to 'board' in these wards. The combined impact may well be to maintain waiting times at the desired level for a prolonged period.

3.3 Other Implications

Another implication of our model is this:

If there is enough capacity to maintain waiting times at 18 weeks for a prolonged period, it should also be possible to maintain them at a lower level (given a short-term injection of capacity).

Not only that, it seems hardly likely that the discharge rate per day from a service (which, for a service running at capacity is equal to beds/length of stay) would be

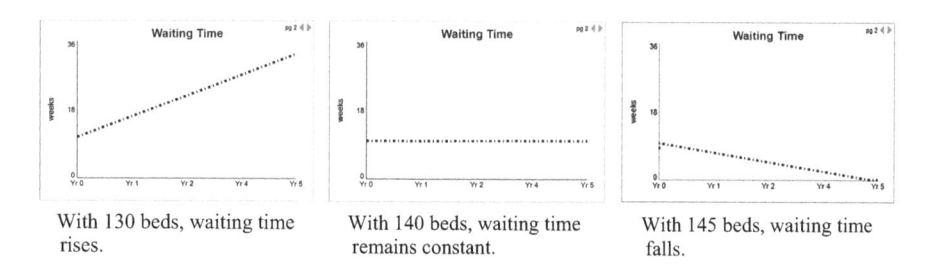

With 130 beds, waiting time rises.	With 140 beds, waiting time remains constant.	With 145 beds, waiting time falls.

Fig. 3.7 The relationship between capacity and the waiting time GRADIENT

exactly equal to its daily referral rate (the conditions under which waiting times stay level). It is much more likely to be the case that:

- There is more capacity than the minimum required
- There is less capacity than the minimum required

The question then is, 'why create the impression that maintaining waiting times at a particular level (12 weeks, 18 weeks, whatever) is a desirable outcome?'

3.4 The Arbitrariness of Waiting Times

Another way of spotting that the level of any particular stock in a model is not under control is to distinguish between time dependent stocks and buffer stocks, as defined in Chap. 2.

A *time-dependent* stock is one where a resource passes through the stock over an average period of time and the outflow is a function of the level of the stock. A *buffer* stock is one where the inflows and the outflows do not directly relate to the size of the stock which can only be changed indirectly through other parts of the chain in which it resides.[2] The buffer simply acts as a means of delaying and dampening a fluctuating inflow into a smoother outflow, or vice versa.

In other words, the content of a time-dependent stock is controlled by an inflow or outflow whereas the content of a buffer stock has no such direct control.

It should be noted that in the model diagram we have shown in the various Figures above, that *inpatients* is a *time-dependent* stock the duration of which is the length of stay, whereas *waiting* is a *buffer* stock, the purpose of which is to protect a fixed hospital capacity from fluctuating referrals.

Recognising 'waiting' as a buffer stock implies that the numbers waiting are not directly controlled and hence the number of people waiting and the waiting time at any point is quite arbitrarily determined by the difference between referrals and admissions.

---

[2]We do show a connection between 'waiting' and admissions but this is just to imply a restriction on admissions so the waiting stock cannot go negative, rather than to generally control the level of the stock. Many buffer stocks are part of more complicated capacity-constrained stock/ flow chains, and their behaviour would require a more detailed explanation than we offer here.

3.5 The Infeasibility of Implementing a Relationship Between Capacity and Waiting

In order to underline our assertions, we now present some simulated evidence of what would be needed to accept that there is a viable relationship between waiting times and beds.

It is possible to construct a management control mechanism which allows the waiting time to be kept to a target, but this is only at the expense of continually adjusting the number of beds, perhaps by opening and closing wards, so that admissions can track referrals.

This mechanism is analogous to 'just-in-time' manufacturing, where order backlogs and raw materials inventories are kept to a minimum to reduce order lead time and costs—but requiring a flexible manufacturing rate to respond quickly to incoming orders.

The required changes in beds and hence staffing levels to keep waiting times to a target will be determined in the following simulation to demonstrate how totally impractical such an arrangement would be.

Figure 3.8 shows a feedback mechanism capable of adjusting bed capacity to keep the waiting time exactly at 18 weeks applied to the two-stock hospital model. The structure of this is shown along the top of Fig. 3.8. (Note that in order to adjust the number of beds and to allow for a time delay in doing this, 'beds' is formulated as a stock variable.)

The target waiting time (18 weeks) is multiplied by the referrals to give number of people needed to be waiting to achieve the waiting target. This is then compared with actual number of people waiting. The difference is the number of beds needed to be added to cope with any excess of people waiting or the number needed to be withdrawn if there is a shortfall of people waiting. (Obviously, we could have also left the beds and staff in place and accepted a large and costly underutilisation of

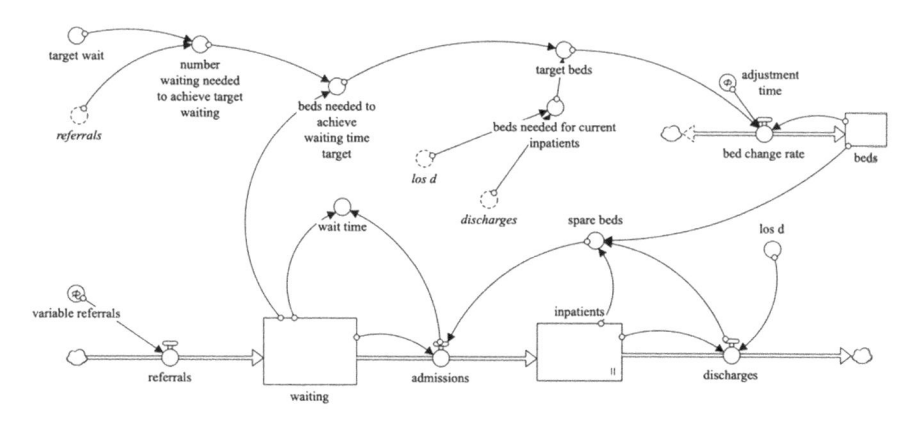

Fig. 3.8 The two-stock hospital model with a control mechanism to adjust bed capacity in line with referrals

capacity). These beds are added to the number of beds needed to cope with current inpatients to give the target beds. The actual number of beds is then adjusted by any difference between the target and actual beds.

Figure 3.9 shows the results from an experiment with the model. It is assumed that beds are fixed at the equilibrium number of 140 initially and then an upward and fluctuating change in the number of referrals is imposed, rising from 20 per day to 28 per day. The top graphs shows how the admissions track the referrals and how the actual beds track the target beds. The bottom graph shows how the wait time tracks the target. It is assumed that each change in bed numbers requires an average of 30 days.

In order to keep the actual waiting time within a week of the target the number of beds required ranges from130 to 182.

A second way to construct a management control mechanism which allows the waiting time to be kept to a target is to change the length of stay in line with deviations between the target and actual waiting time. There are a few ways in which this can be achieved and Fig. 3.10 shows one of these. Here variation in the ratio of waiting time to target waiting time is used to increase or decrease the length of stay (again formulated as a stock variable) between feasible upper and lower bounds. In policy terms, this would represent clinicians trying to maximise discharges when waiting times are under pressure and adopting a more relaxed approach when waiting times are well within target.

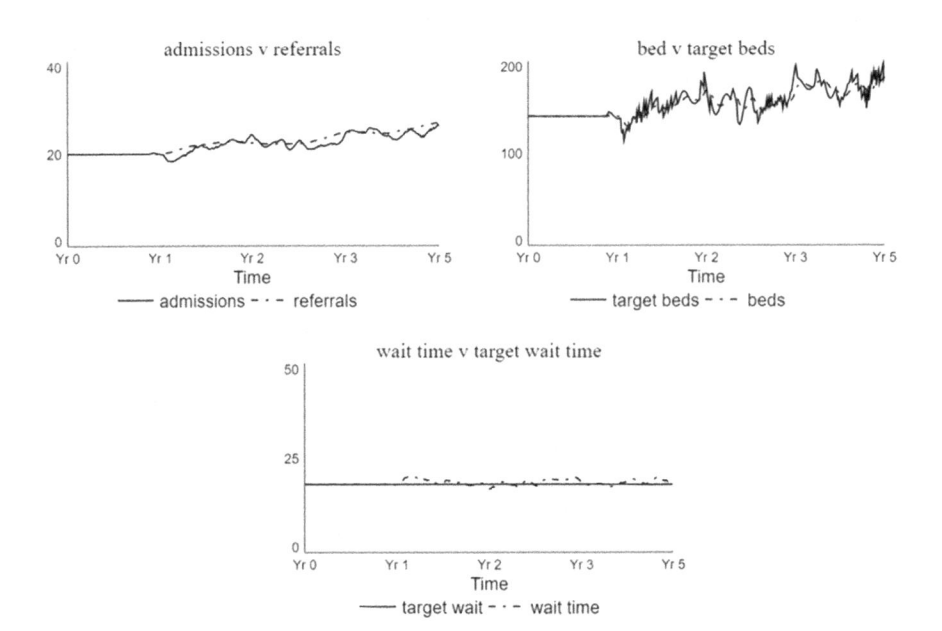

Fig. 3.9 Output from the model with a control mechanism to adjust bed capacity in line with referrals

3.5 The Infeasibility of Implementing ...

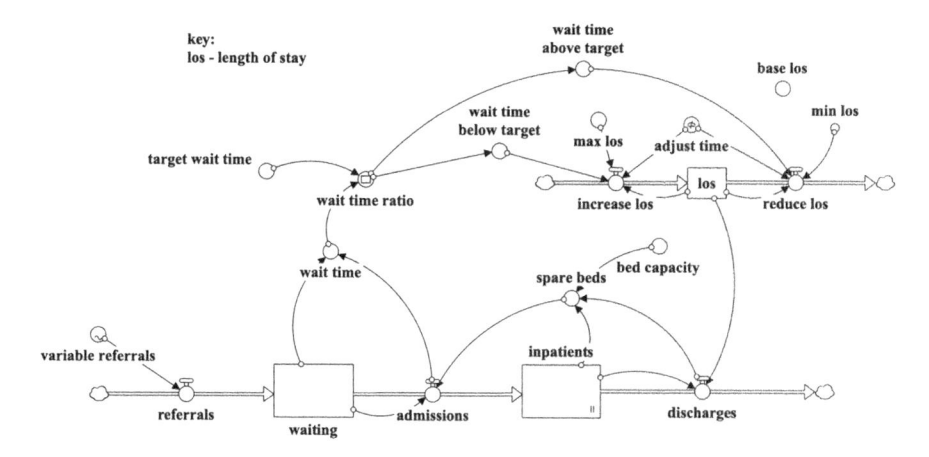

Fig. 3.10 The two-stock hospital model with a control mechanism to adjust length of stay in line with waiting time variations

Figure 3.11 shows the results. The model is run under the same scenario as before (a fluctuating and rising referral rate) and it will be seen that waiting time is kept precisely to the target. However, this time the control is at the expense of progressively decreasing the length of stay.

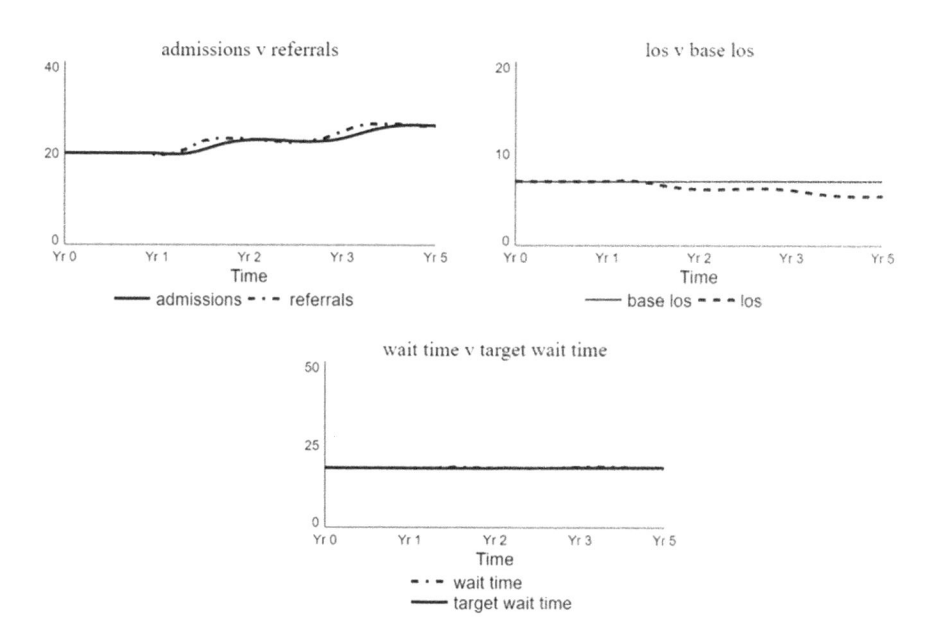

Fig. 3.11 Output from the model with a control mechanism to adjust length of stay in line with waiting time variations

Length of stay is in general following a decreasing trend over time with the increased use of day-surgery and a desire to minimise exposure to the hospital environment for vulnerable patients. However, it is a contentious issue which can be detrimental to patient safety and lead to readmissions (which we have, unrealistically, not included in this model). Although primarily a clinical *parameter*, based on patient need and condition, it has the potential of being a strategy *variable* as demonstrated here. Its use in this context is discussed at length in Chap. 10 as one of a number of strategies by which hospitals cope in time of high demand.

3.6 Conclusions

This chapter has explored the often-asked question 'how many hospital beds are needed to produce a patient waiting time of 18 weeks'? Although there undoubtedly is a relationship between 'capacity' and 'waiting time', the nature of that relationship is not as generally imagined by policy-makers, commissioners and even those working within the system.

Our conclusion is that the idea that any given capacity will generate a specific waiting time is flawed and that patient waiting times are not within the control of hospital management. Indeed, to have waiting time within control would require a totally impractical ability continually to change bed and associated staff numbers or lengths of stay.

From a system dynamics point of view, the chapter demonstrates that a very simple model linking relating 7 major hospital variables; bed occupancy, bed capacity, referrals, admissions, discharges, length of stay and people waiting, can produce powerful conclusions.

References

Senge, P. M. (1990). *The Fifth Discipline: The Art and Practice of the Learning Organization.* New York: Doubleday/Currency.
Wolstenholme, E. F. (2003). Towards the definition and use of a core set of archetypal structures in system dynamics. *System Dynamics Review, 19*(1), 7–26.

Chapter 4
The Shape of Illness and the Impact of Interventions

Chapter Summary

This Chapter uses the language of stocks and flows to represent some generic templates used in modelling the demand and supply of health and social care services. On the demand side, we look at the dynamics of population ageing and health conditions. On the supply side, we show different ways of modelling intervention services and present the beginnings of a taxonomy of these. Understanding how people flow through population ageing chains and health condition chains is important in designing treatment capacity and at which stages it is best to apply this capacity. The simple templates described here will be deployed in a number of the models described in Parts II and III of the book.

4.1 Introduction

So far, the discussions of the dynamics of treatment pathways have assumed that referrals to those pathways have been made from outside the boundaries of the models. One of the thinking processes in dynamic modelling is always to bear in mind whether it is useful to expand the model boundaries and much of the work in this book has involved combining treatment/service pathway models with models of the dynamics of population ageing and health conditions.

Forrester wrote of how, in engaging with a client and a new problem, the modeller's discussion is 'filtered through one's catalogue of feedback structures into which the behavioural symptoms and the discussion of structure and policy might fit' (cited in Sterman 2018, p. 23). In the course of our modelling work in health and social care, we have accumulated a catalogue of model structures. In Chap. 2, we outlined a classification of 'service capacity types'. In this chapter we describe some common 'condition types' along with an account of how the purpose and impact of the service might be understood in stock and flow terms.

The impact of a service intervention depends on the nature of the condition it is designed to treat or manage. Here, we outline some commonly found structures.

On the demand side:

- Ageing
- Acute, episodic illness
- Degenerative long-term conditions and states
- Chronic but not degenerative, but with possibility of improvement, if not cure
- Chronic with acute episodes
- Lifelong conditions/states.

On the supply side, interventions include the following but we will focus on the last four categories:

- Assessment, referral, diagnosis
- Cure-type
- Care-type, including slowing down progression of a condition
- Management of a condition
- Prevention and screening.

4.2 Population Dynamics (Ageing Chain)

Figure 4.1 shows the simplest possible representation of population dynamics using stocks and flows. People are born, live, and die, and this can be captured in a simple model driven by a birth date and death rate.

To recap, stocks are cumulations (or bathtubs) of resources (here, people) and are visible when time is frozen as in a picture. Flow variables such as births and deaths feed and drain stocks and are time-dependent with units of people per time-step. Flow variables act as taps or control valves on the pipe and change in two distinct ways. They either operate in response to natural laws or to human actions. The distinction between stocks and flows characterises the language of system dynamics.

It is extremely unlikely that we would deploy the Fig. 4.1 structure in a serious, healthcare model. The structure is too high-level/over-simplified to be of much use in modelling health care. We normally aim to build population chains into models at a level of detail commensurate with what is required to inform a discussion of the

Fig. 4.1 The dynamics of population

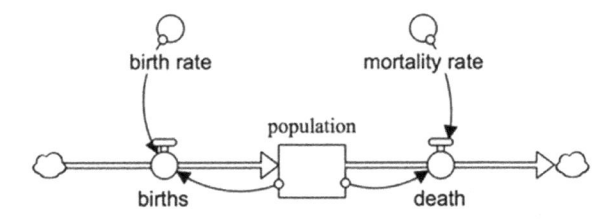

relative impacts, including impacts on other parts of a 'whole system' (which might affect people with other conditions or care-needs), and associated costs. Although we rarely need to represent stocks in terms of single-year steps; some disaggregation is necessary. Figure 4.2 shows a minimal level of disaggregation of the population into children, young people, adults and older people.

But perhaps a more likely possibility would be a model focusing on a particular segment of the population such as children, or older people. When modelling the older population, disaggregation into five- or ten-year age bands is normally enough. There are in fact many approaches to modelling age-detailed demographic analysis capable of dissecting populations down into many different categories.

One characteristic of a chronological ageing chain[1] is that all people 'age' at exactly the same rate. Without exception it takes everyone exactly 60 years to reach the age of 60. Therefore, when representing chronological ageing, it is better to use a special type of stock which does this ('conveyor' or 'box-car' stock). The expression *outflow = stock/average duration* as used to model hospital discharges in Chap. 2 will not do. Later in this chapter, we will encounter 'long term conditions' as a type of ageing chain where people do not degenerate at exactly the same rate.

4.3 Health Condition Dynamics (What Shape Is the Condition?)

Many system dynamics models in healthcare are of specific conditions, or classes of condition. It is possible to think, in stock and flow terms, of conditions taking one of a number of generic 'shapes', depending on whether the condition is short-term and acute (episodic), long-term, or lifelong. Long-term conditions may be degenerative, or, sometimes, with the possibility of improvement, if not cure.

Acute, Episodic Conditions

The simplest condition is an acute illness, with an onset (incidence), a duration (leading to a stock of people having the condition) and recovery (or death). Figure 4.3 shows a typical representation of an acute illness. People become ill, and either recover or die, but do not remain ill for ever.

A rather more sophisticated representation of something similar, known as an SIR (susceptible, infected, recovered) model is shown in Fig. 4.4, commonly used in modelling the life cycle of epidemics.

---

[1] In System Dynamics, the term 'ageing chain' denotes a broad category of stock/flow structures and the concept may be applied to stocks of materials, not just people.

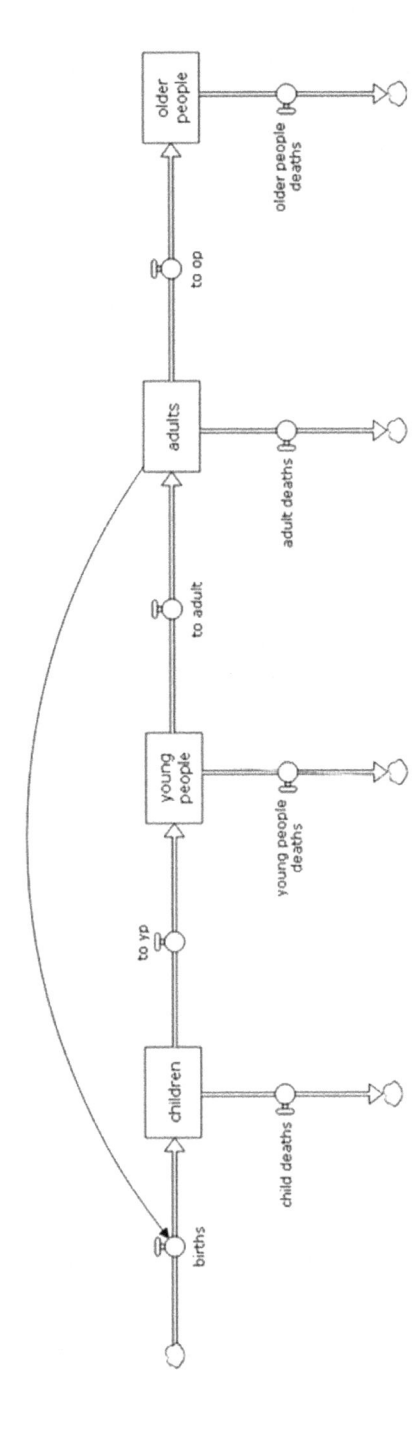

Fig. 4.2 The dynamics of population ageing

4.3 Health Condition Dynamics (What Shape Is the Condition?)

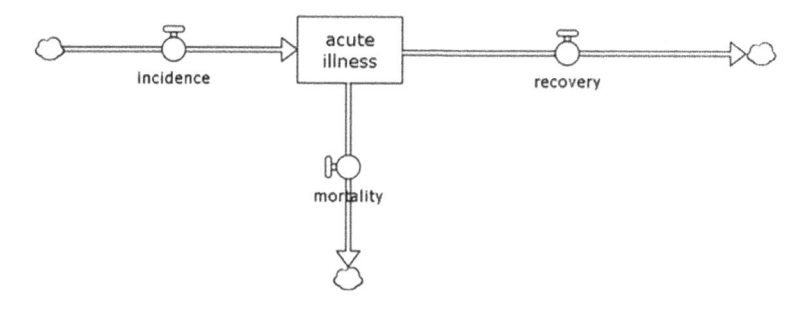

Fig. 4.3 Acute condition and treatment

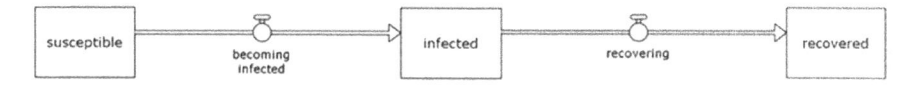

Fig. 4.4 SIR (susceptible, infected, recovered) model

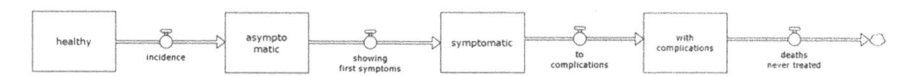

Fig. 4.5 The dynamics of degenerative health conditions

SIR models are used to model both treatment and also prevention of spread of an infection.

Long Term Conditions (Degenerative)

Figure 4.5 shows a common construction for a stock and flow chain for a condition that is first asymptomatic (people do not know they are ill), then symptomatic, then has complications.

There are numerous examples of system dynamics models of degenerative conditions such as diabetes or dementia.

A key characteristic of a degenerative condition is that the flow is always in one direction, towards deterioration.

Figure 4.6 shows a typical representation of a 'management and treatment of long term conditions' model in system dynamics (stock and flow) terms. Although a condition is not reversible,[2] many conditions can be managed differently, their symptoms relieved, and progression sometimes slowed down. The challenge in

---

[2]Or is believed not to be reversible; as medical science progresses, conditions once considered irreversible may turn out to be treatable.

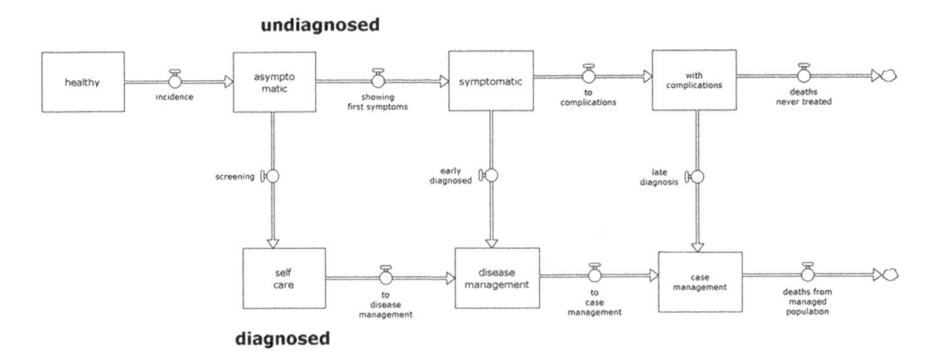

Fig. 4.6 Diagnosis and management of degenerative conditions

such a model is to show the logistics and potential benefits of early identification and treatment. Asymptomatic states may be detected by means of screening, and early diagnosis is preferable to late diagnosis, by which time a condition may be in the 'with complications' state.

The kind of template shown in Fig. 4.6 owes much to the work of Jack Homer and Gary Hirsch in the USA.

This approach to modelling, particularly the high level of aggregation, can therefore be used to simulate the likely effectiveness of strategies based on risk stratification approaches such as the 'Kaiser Permanente Pyramid' (see Chap. 14).

Long Term Conditions (Not Degenerative, Improvement May Be Possible)

For some chronic conditions, some improvement is possible, and people can therefore move both in the direction of degeneration or recovery. In fact, the whole of the purpose of healthcare can be defined as finding treatments to impact deterioration in health conditions.

In our experience, this kind of 'illness shape' is more typically found in mental health conditions or with broader problems, such as in models of alcohol consumption or 'general wellbeing'. In other words, people move up and down a chain whose main states represent 'states of being'. In this book, probably the best example is the Alcohol Systems Model in Chap. 12.

Figure 4.7 shows a simplified version of this kind of model, where the main stocks represent 'levels of alcohol consumption' and people move between low, medium and high consumption in both directions.

As Fig. 4.7 shows, measures might be taken to reduce the probability of people moving up (consumption increasing) the chain, and interventions can be offered that increase the probability of people moving down (consumption reducing) the chain. The main 'policy' shown here is the implementation of a minimum unit-price

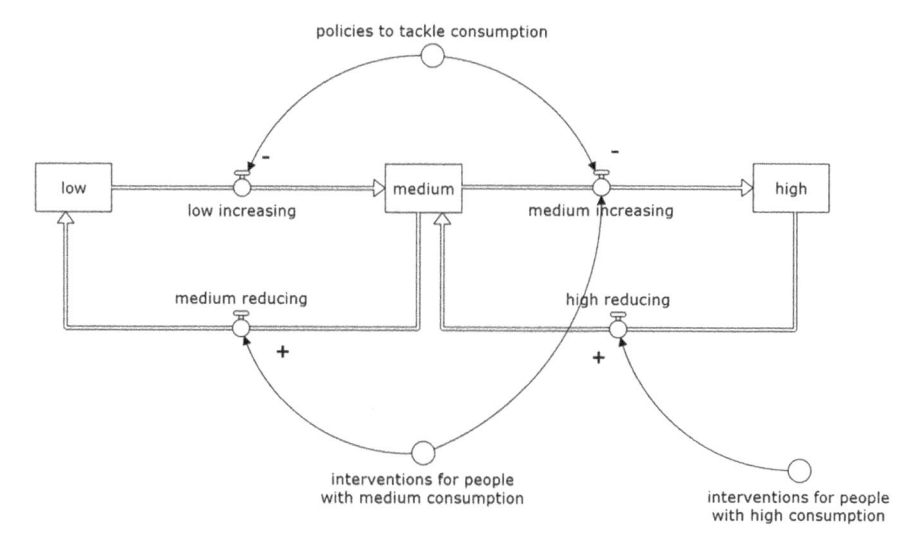

4.3 Health Condition Dynamics (What Shape Is the Condition?) 65

Fig. 4.7 The dynamics of reversible health conditions

for alcohol (something recently implemented in Scotland, but not in the rest of the UK). This single policy might reduce the probability of people moving from low to medium, or from medium to high.

In addition, specific 'interventions' (such as 'brief advice in hospital' or 'opportunistic brief advice in primary care') can have multiple impacts. People in the medium group might be more likely to reduce their consumption, or have a reduced probability of increasing consumption. People in the high group cannot move any further up this chain (although movement WITHIN the aggregated stock is possible, but not simulated), but may be supported to reduce their consumption.

The Alcohol Systems Model is fully explained in Chap. 12.

Chronic Illness with Acute Episodes

Figure 4.8 shows a simplified representation of people suffering from psychosis, a form of 'severe mental illness'. The main characteristic of this structure is its cyclical, rather than degenerative, nature. In mental health, often the main challenge is to maintain and support people whose conditions are chronic in such a way that avoids the possibility of the onset of another crisis, which might lead to hospital admission, including also an increased risk of suicide or self-harm.

The structure also draws attention to the needs of people in the early stage of illness. in some versions, the 'acute no history' stage might include people in their first two or three years of illness (the concept of 'early intervention' as a treatment opportunity, when it is believed that a better recovery might be possible and the modelling/capacity planning challenge is to allocate sufficient resources to this group in the hope that their condition will not progress to a chronic condition).

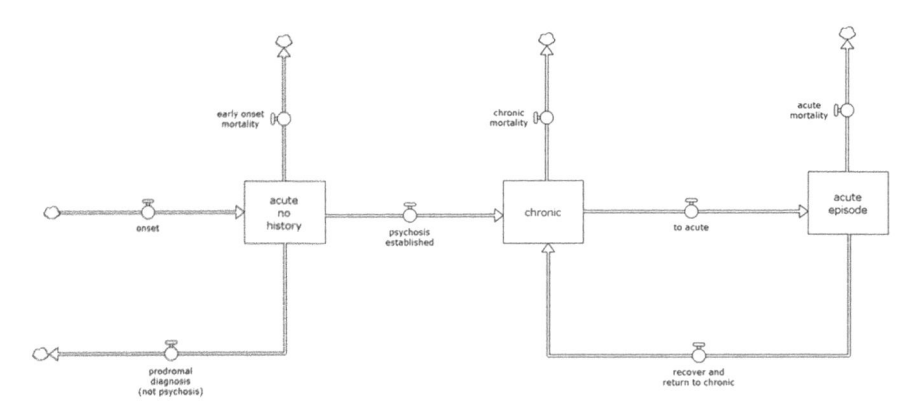

Fig. 4.8 Chronic with acute episodes (e.g. psychosis)

We have developed a range of such stock/flow structures in various projects. Some go into much more detail about the different levels of severity the chronic state might reach, and most differentiate between people whose care is being managed (including, increasingly, self-management[3]) and those who drop out of the treatment system, not least because some people with severe mental ill health lead a transient life on the edge of society, with no permanent address and a high risk of homelessness, which militates against them being able to maintain regular contact with the kind of community services that most appropriately meet their needs.

Typically, our models of the severe mental illness treatment system represent complex treatment pathways as people move between short and long-term hospital stays, into supported housing arrangements, to moving into more mainstream accommodation with 'floating support'. On reflection, whilst we understand that making sense of a complex treatment pathway is often the main driver that generates client-demand for a model, often the model we would like to have built would have been based around understanding the 'structure of the condition' rather than the more service capacity-driven type.

Lifelong Conditions—Physical and Learning Disabilities

The main characteristic of a 'disability', compared with an illness, is that it is normally a lifelong condition, which might exist from birth, or result from an accident or other trigger-factor, such as a physical illness, in later life. It is interesting to reflect that we have rarely been commissioned to develop any models in this field, and the small number that we have undertaken, for example Miller and McKelvie (2016), have been in the learning disability field.

---

[3] A key theme of the 'recovery' movement, along with ideas that services should be co-produced.

4.3 Health Condition Dynamics (What Shape Is the Condition?)

The 'condition progression' part of such a model will most likely be a straightforward chronological ageing chain, similar to that shown in Fig. 4.2. The size of the affected population should be reasonably predictable, given the lifelong duration of a disability. But the service pathway might also be complex, drawing on the 'chronic versus episodic' insights explained earlier and the likelihood of multi-morbidity because people with certain disabilities may be more likely to experience other forms of ill-health. The modelling process is likely to reflect the principles of service user involvement and indeed, the use of participatory group model building could be a particularly good match with current practice in coproduction, self-directed support, and service redesign.

4.4 Combining Population Ageing Dynamics and Health Condition Dynamics

In modelling practice, we often need to combine both ageing and condition dynamics and Fig. 4.9 shows a matrix approach to achieving this. Using the same states of the previous figures, a 4 × 3 matrix is constructed with age running horizontally and health condition running vertically.

Note that the hypothetical condition described in Fig. 4.9 is NOT degenerative (as we discussed earlier) because condition progression is shown as a two way process where remission is possible. To show this, the diagram uses bi-flows, which are an alternative to the uni-flows deployed so far. Our preferred modelling style is to use bi-flows sparingly; even where it is possible to move between stocks in opposite directions, we would normally draw two flows, representing the reality that they are describing two different processes (such as 'becoming ill' and 'recovering').

Dynamic equilibrium in this type of representation is one where progression of the condition and remission work as a net effect. Indeed, this type of dynamic model, by having the ability to recognise this balance, can often demonstrate that the impact of treatment might be less than imagined because some people would have recovered anyway, and at all times, those who recover may be replaced by people becoming unwell. We go into much more detail about this in Part III, which looks at 'dynamic impact of treatment'.

Of course, the matrix demand-structure of Fig. 4.9 is only useful when it forms part of a model of a treatment or care management system. We saw in Fig. 4.6 a slightly different matrix, where the horizontal dynamics represented stages in a condition, and the vertical represented 'diagnosed' and 'undiagnosed'. If we were to explore the dynamics of treatment using the Fig. 4.9 demand structure, which already deploys two dimensions (age and condition-state), on paper, at least, we have run out of dimensions, and this is challenging, given the visual nature of system dynamics. Questions also arise about the level of disaggregation and whether this is an 'appropriate' use of system dynamics. Chap. 14 details an example of a model with this level of disaggregation that provided dynamic insights which a client had not gained by any other means.

We require three dimensions now (age, condition-state, treatment-status), and system dynamics software provides multiple ways of representing these (such as

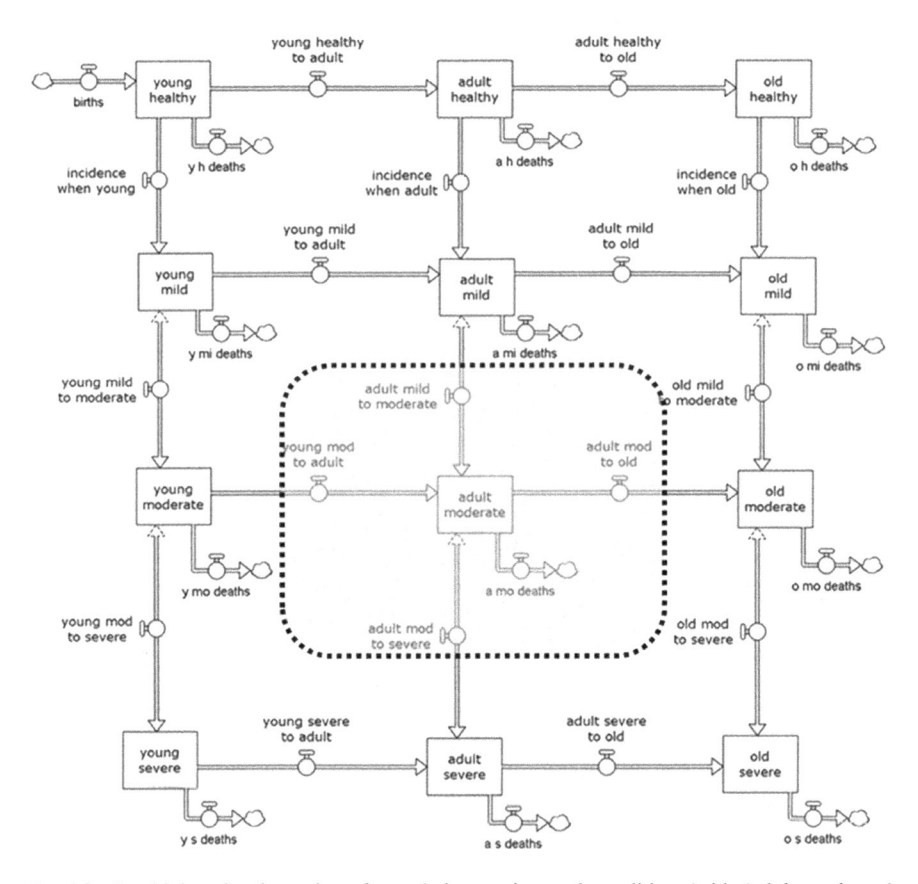

68   4 The Shape of Illness and the Impact of Interventions

Fig. 4.9 Combining the dynamics of population ageing and condition (with 'adult moderate' stock highlighted)

co-flows, arrays, and modules[4]). In this example, we use a co-flow structure (which we would position somewhere away from the matrix diagram, but most likely would embed within a module) to 'drill down' inside one stock in Fig. 4.9, the 'adult moderate' stock, which we highlighted in the diagram. The term co-flow should be more obvious after the following discussion.

Figure 4.10 shows how any of the 12 stocks in Fig. 4.9 could be disaggregated by treatment status, here modelled as a three stock structure (untreated, waiting for treatment, being treated) but other possibilities, for example some kind of long-term 'care management' service exist (as we will discuss in the next section on the purpose and nature of treatment). 'Ad mod' is used as a prefix to these states because all are part of the adult moderate stock.

---

[4]This reflects the options available in Stella, the software we use mostly; other possibilities include more 'object-oriented' software, such as Ventity.

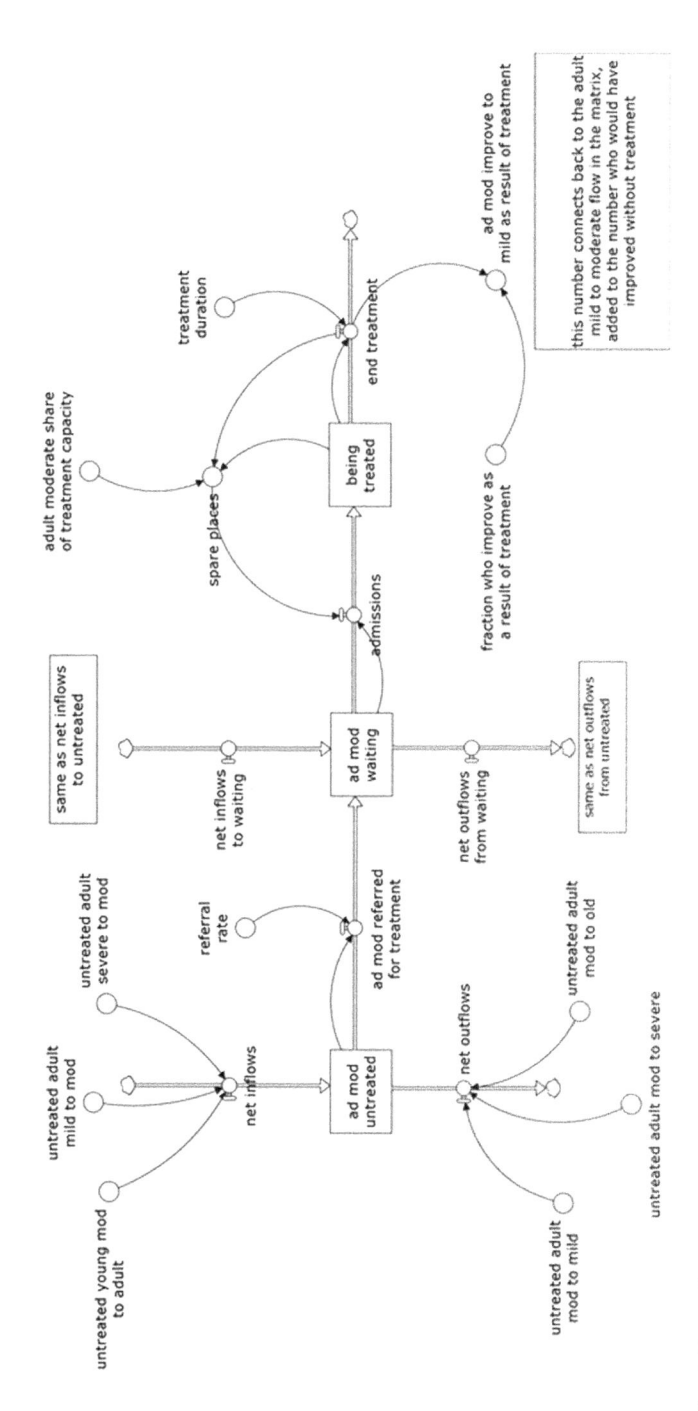

4.4 Combining Population Ageing Dynamics and Health Condition Dynamics 69

Fig. 4.10 Adding a treatment-status dimension to one stock in the matrix: the diagram disaggregates what is happening 'inside' the adult moderate stock

The 'net inflows' and 'net outflows' to the 'untreated' stock show in some detail how this structure is connected to the other stocks in the matrix. People arrive in the 'adult moderate untreated' state from the three flows that connect into 'adult moderate' in Fig. 4.9 (from young moderate, adult mild and adult severe). And people may leave the stock in three ways (to old moderate, to adult mild, to adult severe).

The stock of people 'untreated' might be referred for treatment, for which we require a 'referral rate'. Assuming that treatment is capacity constrained, new referrals go into a 'waiting' stock. It is necessary to repeat the 'net inflows' and 'net outflows' structure to the 'waiting' stock. This may seem pedantic, but if this kind of model were to be tested in extreme conditions (such as, 'how does the model run if there is no treatment capacity?') if the only exit from the 'waiting stock' was to treatment, and if no treatment capacity existed,[5] there would be a build-up of people inside the waiting stock, where their status could never change (no remission or deterioration and, crucially, no deaths).

These 'net inflows' and 'net outflows' structures introduce an underlying 'churn' which gives a model like this its key dynamics, as we outline in Chap. 14.

Finally, in Fig. 4.10, people progress to treatment, based on a capacity allocation calculation (depending on the condition, there might be separate treatment capacities based on either/both age or severity of condition; where people in different condition-states share the same treatment capacity we need to determine the rules under which spare capacity is allocated). On ending treatment, a fraction of people improve (moderate become mild, for example), and this number (adult moderate improve to mild as a result of treatment) is added to the flow from adult moderate to adult mild in the main diagram (Fig. 4.9).

Similar co-flow structures would operate for all of the stocks in Fig. 4.9. Obviously, this is a detailed and painstaking process, whose results/benefits are explained in Chap. 14.

4.5 Models that Are Not Condition-Based

We noted in the Introduction that many health and social care models do <u>not</u> include a representation of the nature of a specific condition because many services are designed to treat or manage people with multiple conditions. For example, models to support capacity planning in general hospitals may draw on exogenous variables such as 'referrals per day' (perhaps stratified by age, or by unscheduled/elective), reflecting the reality that, in a general hospital, patients with a wide variety of conditions share the same treatment resource (often, hospital beds); indeed, meeting that mix of needs with the same resource is probably what makes managing healthcare systems, especially hospitals, but also wider hospital and social care integration issues, one of the most complex management tasks known to humankind. The problem is that that very mix of patients provides managers and clinicians with the possibility of coping with daily demand pressures by moving

---

[5]Leaving aside the question why there might be a referral rate if there is no treatment capacity.

people into the 'wrong' kind of bed, leading to complex patterns of delays and blockages, where problems appear far from their underlying cause. We deal with that in some detail in Chap. 8 (Integrated Care).

Similarly, in social care, the core service of 'care at home' is provided for people with a wide variety of problems. The majority are frail, older people who are likely to need the service until such time as they can no longer manage to live at home. However, others use the service for a short term, as part of a rehabilitation or reablement process, perhaps following surgery or illness.

4.6 The Purpose, Nature and Intended Impact of Interventions

In modelling health and social care our main purpose is to explore the likely impact of an intervention of the type classified in the introduction to this Chapter and some interventions have already been noted in the descriptions of conditions.

Most models will therefore contain elements of:

- The nature of the condition (acute, chronic, degenerative or not, state of being)
- The cost, based on capacity and duration, of the treatment
- The impact of the treatment on the 'whole system' including unintended consequences
- A comparison of the impact of intervening against what would have happened.

Just as particular conditions have a 'shape' (acute, long-term, state of living), so too do interventions. Some interventions are brief, perhaps a single consultation, or a small number of tests, resulting in a decision to refer for treatment or service. The treatment might be longer-term, perhaps involving a stay in hospital of several days, or it might consist of a complete change in one's living-status, such as a permanent move into a residential or nursing home or, less radical, receiving lifelong support to enable one to continue to live at home.

Many models will include at least one type of condition, and more than one mode of treatment. The health and social care systems contain multiple examples of services (primary care physicians, unscheduled/emergency hospital beds, the home care system) that are used, differently in intensity and duration, by different needs-groups. It is this mixing of 'people with different types of need', combined with the flexibility, to some extent, for managers of the system to move resources around depending on immediate utilisation and demand, that makes the health and social care system much more complex than most industrial processes or supply chains.

Importantly, interventions can, of course, also be capacity constrained and as indicated in Chap. 2 capacity constraints can be applied to both flows AND stocks. In some cases, for example hospital beds or a social worker's caseload, we think in terms of a 'capacity constrained stock' where there is a limit to the number of people who can be in the stock, which limits the flow into the stock. In other cases, such as assessment or diagnosis, we tend to think in terms of a 'capacity constrained flow' where it makes more sense to think about 'the maximum number of people who can flow through this part of the system in one time period' (for example appointments per week). Therefore, the 'nature' of some interventions is that they happen inside a flow, and others happen inside a stock.

Basic Assessment and Treatment

In the next sequence, we want to explain where in the model diagram an 'intervention' takes place and how we express its effectiveness or impact, in stock and flow terms. This is probably best explained step-by-step (Figs. 4.11 and 4.12).

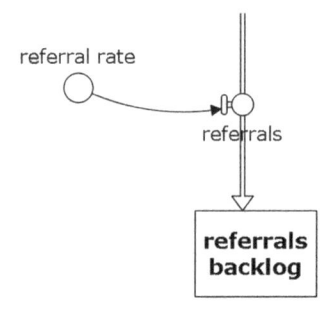

Fig. 4.11 Simple referrals

To start at the beginning, people enter a treatment system by being referred, which is best thought of as an inflow. The system might have a finite capacity to deal with referrals, therefore we represent them going into a stock, referrals backlog, of referrals that are not yet processed.

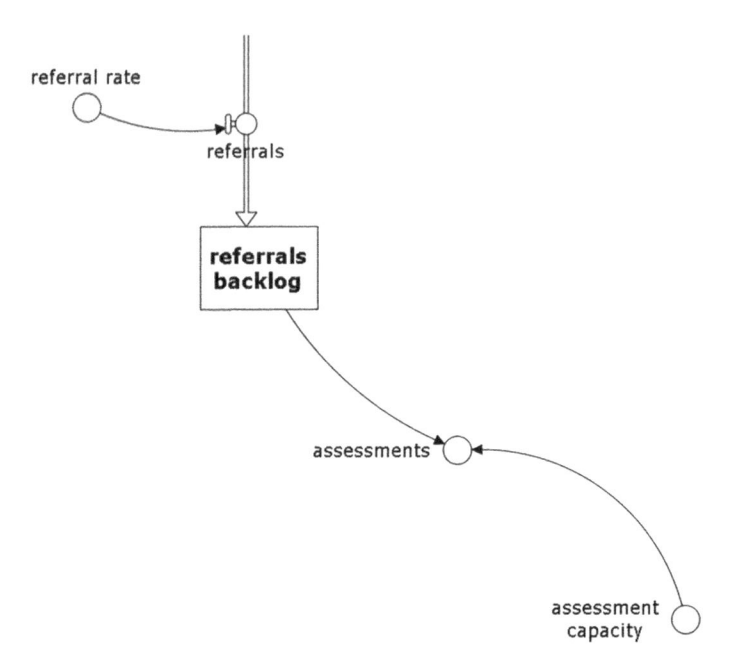

Fig. 4.12 Assessment

4.6 The Purpose, Nature and Intended Impact of Interventions

The intervention that is required now is a simple assessment. In this case, assessment is a one-off event; a practitioner reviews the referral and decides to accept, or not accept for treatment. Assessment capacity would be formulated as 'max number who can be assessed per time step (e.g. day)' and assessments would be the minimum of the assessment backlog or the assessment capacity. The intervention is simulated as 'happening' inside a simple variable (assessments). The next thing is to consider impact. The impact of an assessment is to make a decision whether or not to accept a referral for treatment (Fig. 4.13).

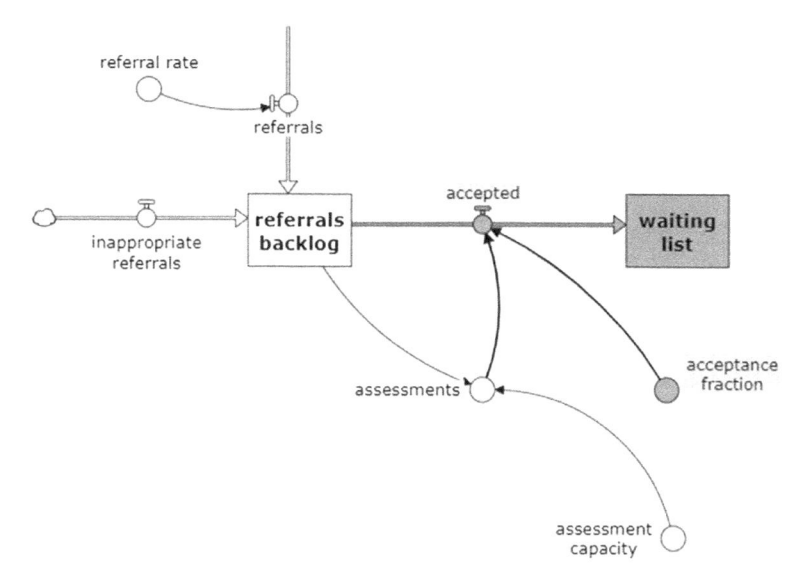

Fig. 4.13 Assessments accepted to waiting list

This impact is captured in the variable 'acceptance fraction' which means the fraction of assessments that are accepted for treatment. The number accepted are a flow of people onto a waiting list (assuming that the service has limited capacity) (Fig. 4.13).

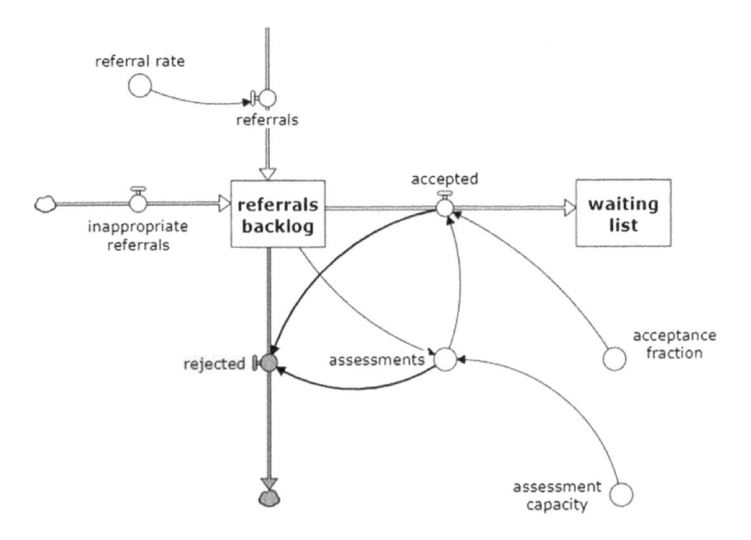

74　　　4 The Shape of Illness and the Impact of Interventions

Fig. 4.14 Assessments rejected (no further action)

The assessments that are not accepted (assessments minus accepted), also flow out of the backlog through the 'rejected' flow (Fig. 4.14).

To summarise the nature and impact of the intervention called assessment, it takes place inside a simple variable, and its impact is to drive two flows, accepted and rejected. Perhaps the key point is that there is no stock of 'people being assessed'. (Of course, this is not a rule. Some types of assessment take place over an extended period of time and involve multiple consultations and tests. In such cases, there would be a stock.)

The next intervention is treatment. In this example, treatment takes a period of time and is capacity-constrained in that there is a limit (such as beds, or a professional's caseload) to the 'number of people who can be in treatment at any point in time'. Therefore, we formulate treatment as a stock (Fig. 4.15).

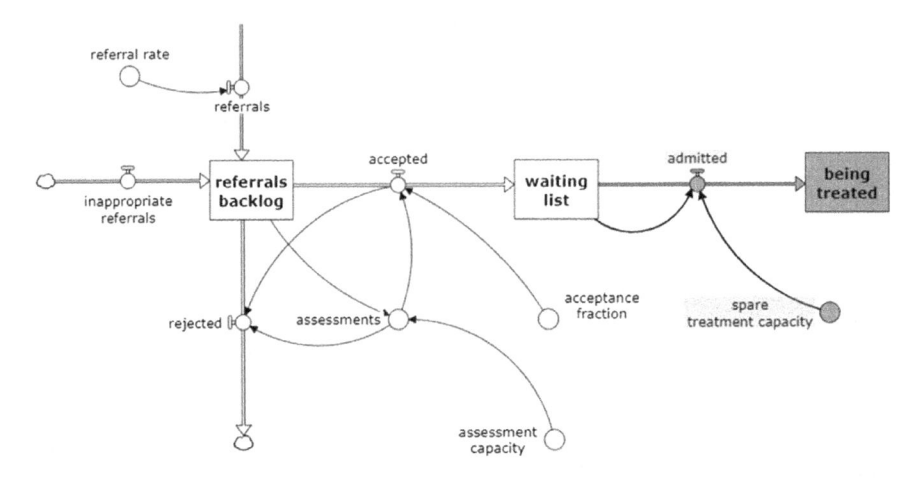

Fig. 4.15 Admissions

4.6 The Purpose, Nature and Intended Impact of Interventions

People are admitted to being treated, based on whether there is spare treatment capacity (as explained in Chap. 2) (Fig. 4.15).

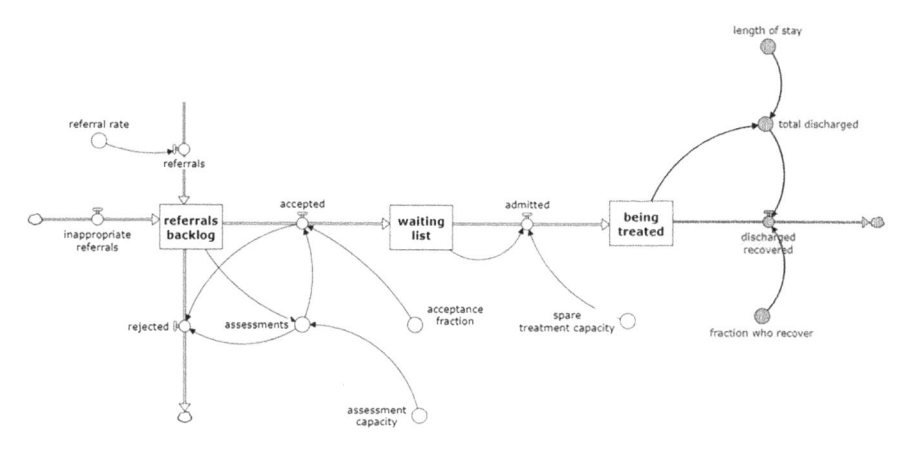

Fig. 4.16 Discharged and recovered

The treatment stock outflows are driven by an average length of stay calculation. In this case, we want to cover the impact of treatment, and so will differentiate between people who recover and those who do not. We therefore derive the total outflow number first (total discharged is stock divided by length of stay), and then represent the impact as being the fraction who recover. This gives our discharged recovered outflow (Fig. 4.16).

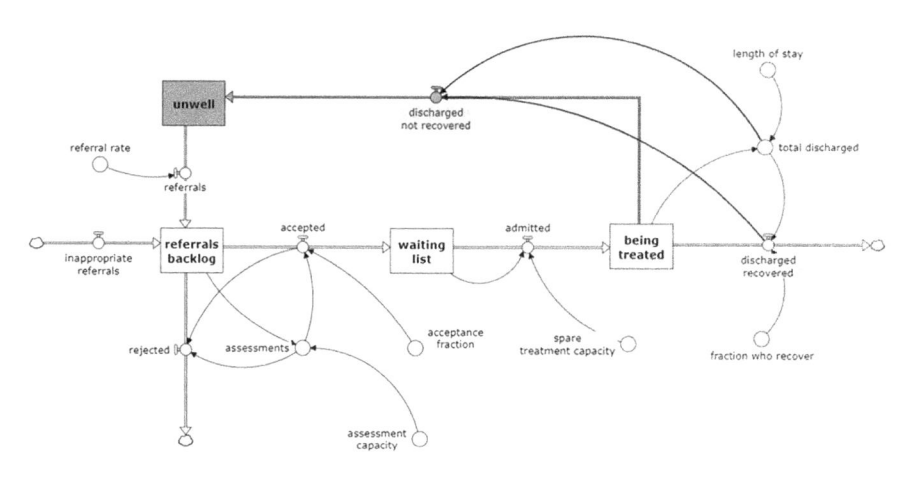

Fig. 4.17 Discharged but not recovered

76   4 The Shape of Illness and the Impact of Interventions

The discharged not recovered outflow (Fig. 4.17) is simply the total discharged minus the discharged recovered. Here, we make it explicit that they are discharged to a stock of 'unwell' people, who were the source of the original referrals.

The important points to note are that the intervention called 'treatment' takes place inside a stock, rather than inside a flow. And its impact is to produce a flow of people who are recovered, with a by-product of people who are not recovered (but have ended treatment).

Now we can complete the spare treatment capacity calculation (below) (Fig. 4.18).

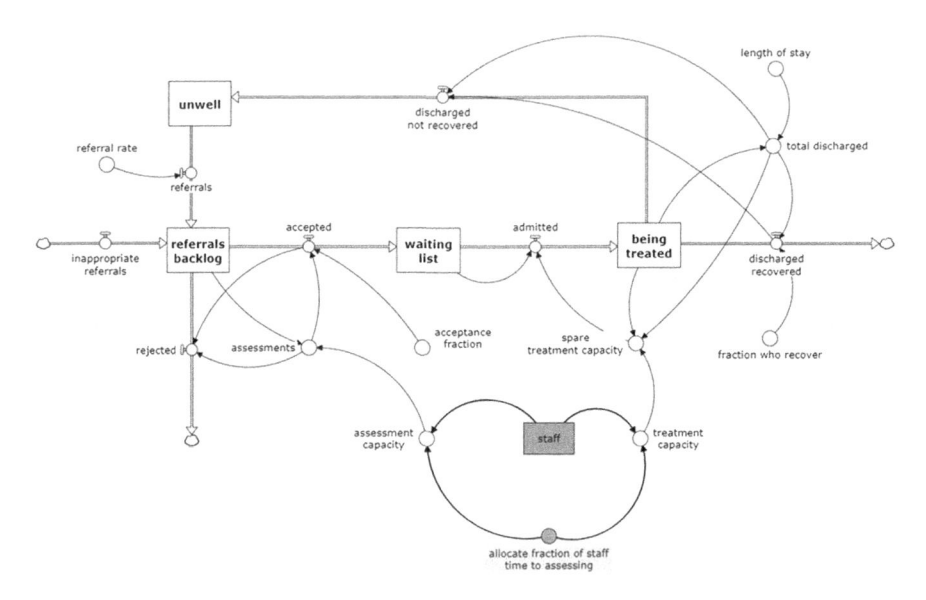

Fig. 4.18 Staff capacity allocated to treatment and, spare treatment capacity calculation

Finally (in this sequence) note that the same resource, such as staff, can provide different types of intervention. The structure at the bottom of the diagram shows that staff time can be allocated between assessment and treatment. Staff might spend most of their time treating people on their (capacity constrained) caseload, and the rest of their time undertaking assessments. How that time is allocated (here represented as a simple fraction) might help us understand the trade-offs between having a referrals backlog or a waiting list.

And, as we explain at various points in this book,

spare treatment capacity = capacity − stock + total outflows.

Care Interventions

The purpose of the treatment intervention in the previous section was to move people OUT OF a state of ill-health. We can call that a 'cure' intervention.

By contrast, 'care'[6] interventions, such as care at home, are designed to slow down deterioration of people in a dependency state. If effective, their impact has two impacts. The obvious impact is to meet the immediate need for support. A secondary consequence is to slow down the process by which people become more dependent. Rather than MOVE PEOPLE OUT of a state of ill-health, the intervention purpose is to KEEP PEOPLE LONGER in a particular level of dependency. These interventions are best understood using the kind of stock-flow structure shown in Fig. 4.19.

Figure 4.19 represents the process where in the latter years of life people generally move in the direction of increased dependence (with the possibility of mortality from an acute condition or accident at any stage). The three stocks mean:

- Independent: capable of living at home without assistance
- Dependent: living at home but needing help such as is provided by a 'care at home' service
- Very dependent: no longer capable of living at home/need some form of 24 h care (nursing home type).

The focus in this diagram is on the middle stock, and the impact of the 'care at home' service as a specific intervention. Note that the actual flow into the home care service is not shown in this simplification; the use of the service is simply determined by the capacity of the service.

Two impacts are shown:

- 'impact of care service on deterioration' means that, compared with people who do not receive care, people receiving care spend more time managing to live at home before moving on to the 'very dependent' state (where they will need institutional care). For example, they are more likely to be eating a balanced diet, and less likely to experience adverse events such as falling. This means that the outflow 'no longer coping' slows down, meaning that the dependent stock is relatively bigger than it would have been had no one received care
- 'impact of care service on mortality' means that people receiving care are less likely to die (their mortality rate reduces) so, as service use increases, the fraction of deaths reduces, making the 'dependent' stock relatively bigger than it would have been had no one received care.

Another way of putting it is that a successful 'cure' intervention means that prevalence of a condition reduces because people recover faster; a successful 'care' intervention actually increases prevalence (prolongs life). The corollary is that one of the consequences of providing home care is that it increases the population of

---

[6]A Symmetric associate, Angèle Pieters, coined the phrase 'care or cure' in a slightly different context (Dutch Perinatal Care), see Pieters (2013).

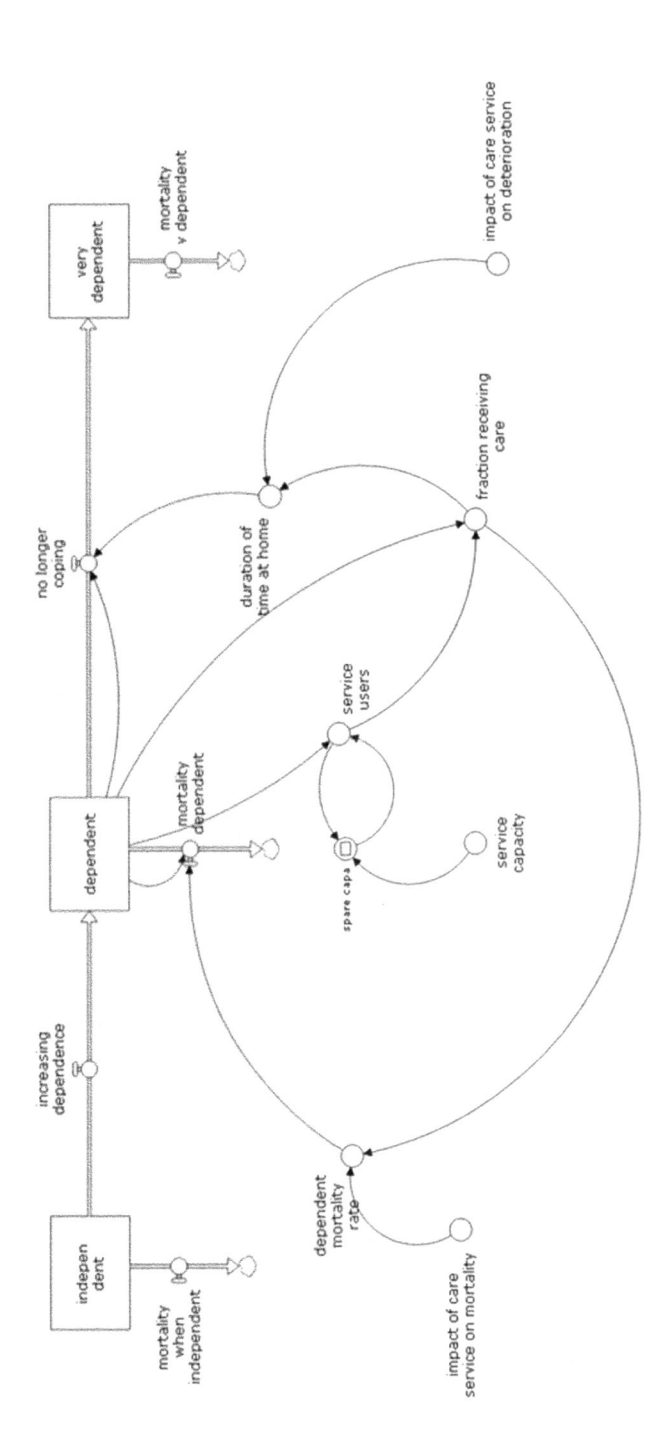

78   4 The Shape of Illness and the Impact of Interventions

Fig. 4.19 Care at home, as more care is provided the number of people in the 'dependent' state increases and more care is required [Causal connections and loops relating to the independent and very dependent states are not shown]

people who need home care, and therefore yet more home care capacity is needed. This is a comparatively rare example of a reinforcing feedback loop in health and social care service dynamics. Feedback Dynamics is the subject of Chap. 5.

This reinforcing feedback loop can sometimes baffle clients who, because of public policy imperatives to save money, may often think in terms of 'invest to save' (if we do more of this, we will do less of that). In these instances, the reality might be characterised as 'invest to invest more'. We have often found that, by modelling a possible increase in capacity, clients often discover that the dramatic saving they were expecting is confounded by some other aspect of the 'whole system'. Of course, what we are describing here is an increase in the length and quality of life of old, frail people, a cause for celebration, but perhaps not a guaranteed way of saving money. However, as we discuss in Chaps. 7 and 8, when home care services are considered as part of the whole system of health and social care, it remains most likely that increasing expenditure on home care is likely to produce significant reductions in spend on hospitals.

A variation of this phenomenon is where a condition is degenerative, and it is not possible to slow down the degeneration, one might imagine that it would be impossible to prolong the average life-expectancy (which would lead to an increase in prevalence, because it equals incidence times average life expectancy post-onset). For example, we understand that currently, for people with Alzheimer-type dementia, no treatment exists that would delay the process of brain-degeneration. Therefore, it should not be possible to prolong the length of time spent at each disease stage (generally characterised as mild, moderate, severe). However, with long-term conditions there are two processes at play; degeneration to the next stage AND mortality (for other, perhaps related, reasons) at this stage. For someone with moderate dementia, it is possible that treatment and management of the condition will improve some other aspect of a person's living conditions. With appropriate care, they may be less likely to encounter adverse events such as falls, or the effects of eating out-of-date or inadequately cooked food. As a result, even although the brain degeneration continues apace, at the earlier stages fewer people die from adverse events with the result that the 'average life expectancy' of people with the condition may increase.

Management of a Condition

Whereas the 'care' intervention discussed above was primarily about looking after, or taking care of, someone, the purpose of other interventions is to enable someone to manage a health condition. Impacts would include improving their quality of life, while also making it less likely that they will suffer adverse events whose consequences might include the need for acute medical care, including hospital admission. This phenomenon has been well-described by Hirsch and Homer (2016).

Typically, this structure is used in relation to a condition with several stages, but for simplicity's sake, Fig. 4.20 shows a condition with only one, 'chronic', state.

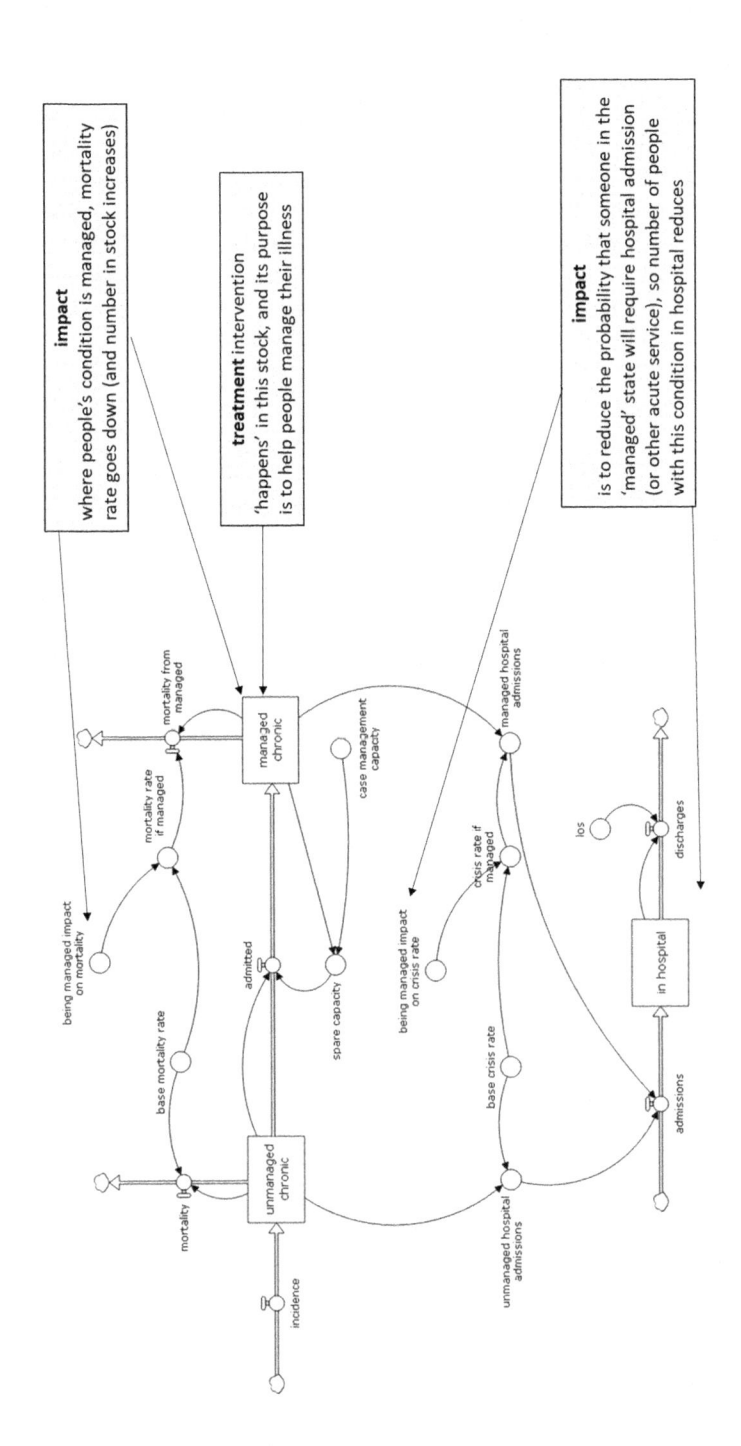

Fig. 4.20 Intervention with purpose of managing a condition and reducing the demand for other services

4.6 The Purpose, Nature and Intended Impact of Interventions 81

The 'main stock—flow chain' is at the top of the diagram. People acquire a chronic illness, from which there is no recovery, only long-term degeneration. Mortality is driven by a base mortality rate. An intervention in the form of some kind of 'condition management' is introduced. Those referred move into a 'managed chronic' state (if the service has capacity). In this example the treatment takes place INSIDE the 'managed chronic' stock, and lasts until the end of life. The intervention has two main impacts. It reduces the mortality rate (people with the condition live longer if it is managed, increasing the number of people with the condition). And it reduces the probability of an acute hospital admission, so, at any time, there will be fewer people with this condition in hospital.

Prevention

The concept of prevention can be modelled in various ways, depending on its nature, therefore it is hard to produce a generic template of 'prevention'. Figure 4.21 provides a simple example of the impact of a health promotion measure to encourage people to adopt an active lifestyle.

The example shows a condition whose incidence (flow from general population into the prevalence stock) can be reduced if some of the population adopt a more active lifestyle. Therefore, the intervention, in this case some kind of 'health promotion' activity (which will most likely be an exogenous variable) has as its immediate impact that more people adopt an active lifestyle. The impact of having an active lifestyle is a lower probability of becoming unwell.

In general terms, therefore, 'prevention' takes place at population level and its intended impact is to reduce the incidence flow, thereby reducing the prevalence. Of course, it is also possible that adoption of an active lifestyle will have an impact on the recovery rate (flow), but this is probably not an example of pure 'prevention'.

Screening

For serious conditions that are asymptomatic, screening is the best approach to identify those in need of treatment. Screening involves inviting the 'at risk' population to take a simple test, or undergo a simple procedure. Leaving aside the important considerations about the whole concept of 'risk' (the false positive and false negative problem, for example), Fig. 4.22 provides a simplified view of how screening works, in stock and flow terms.

The stocks represent a population in relation to a condition. The condition is first asymptomatic, therefore initial incidence is not noticed. The condition then progresses to a symptomatic stage. If screening is offered to the whole population 'at risk', this will include people in the at-risk group (typically on grounds of age and gender), along with people who have the condition but are as yet undiagnosed. Not

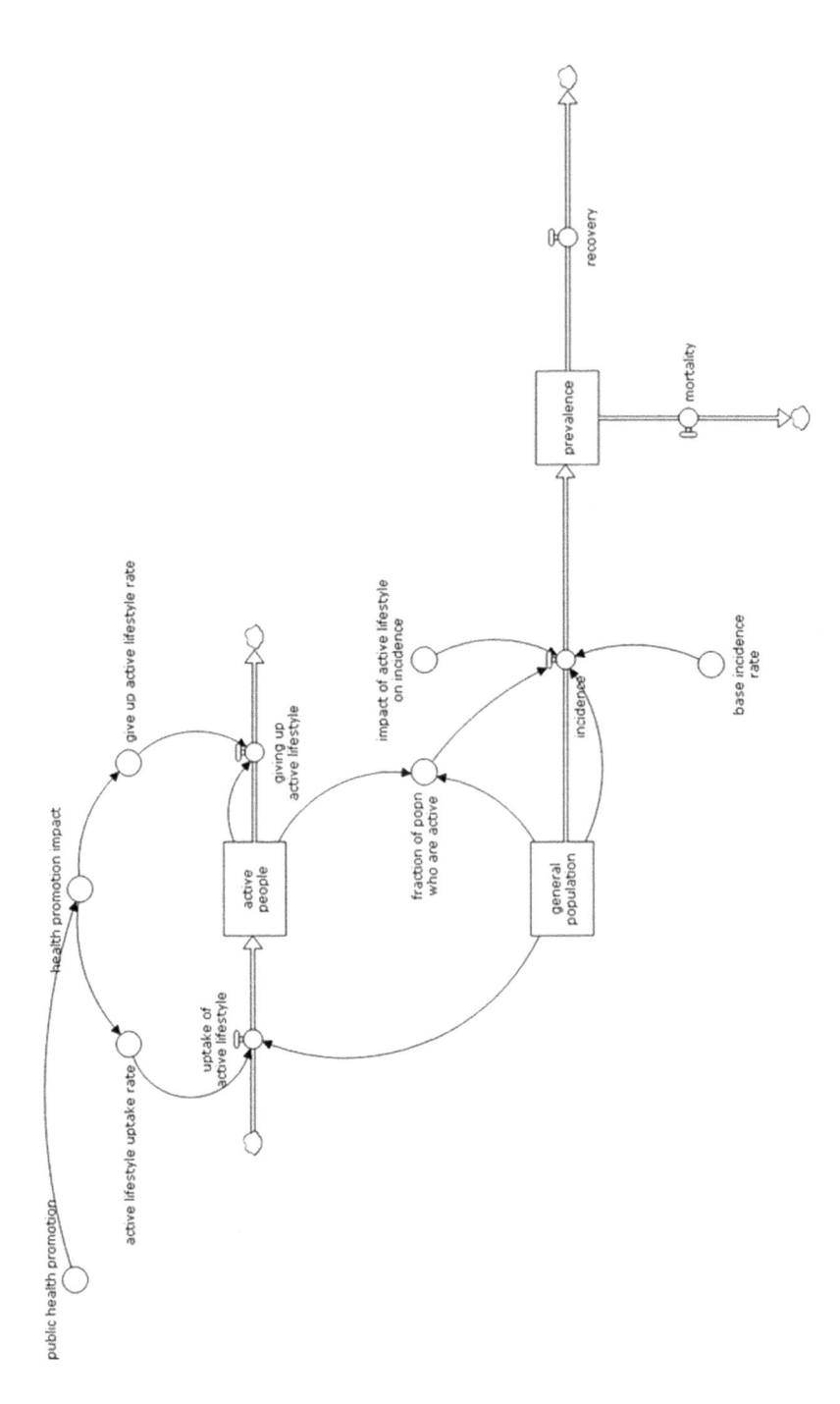

Fig. 4.21 A very simplified view of prevention

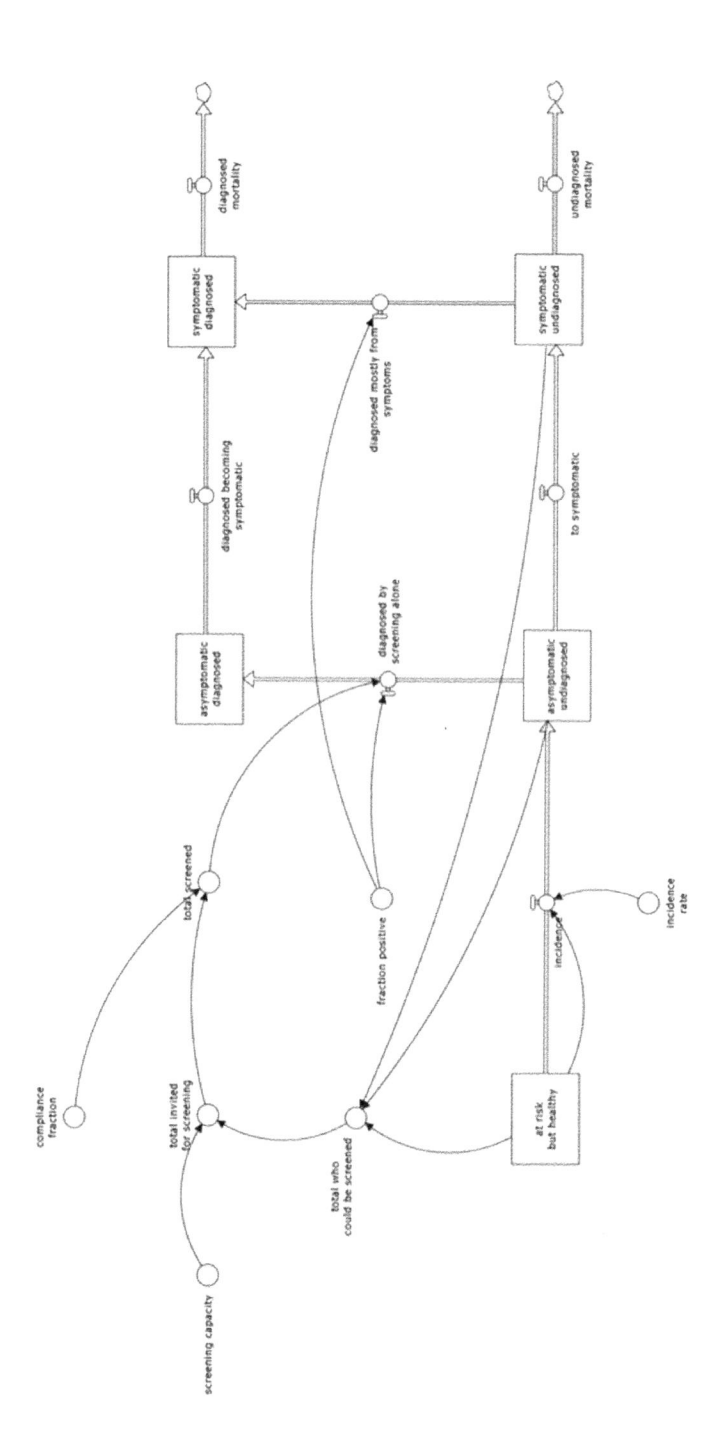

4.6 The Purpose, Nature and Intended Impact of Interventions

Fig. 4.22 Simplified view of screening

shown in the diagram, only a small fraction of this population will be called for screening in any time-step of the model (perhaps people are screened every five years). Not everyone called for screening will attend (compliance fraction), and a fraction of those screened will be diagnosed.

In terms of this discussion, whether the intervention is modelled as being stock or flow-like, and how impact is modelled:

- The intervention itself will show on the model as a variable (total screened in this time step) that drives a flow (diagnosed) rather than a stock; of course, modelling the intervention capacity in detail would require the use of stocks, most likely a stock of staff
- The impact of the intervention is therefore to move people out of the undiagnosed state and into the diagnosed state.

4.7 Towards a Taxonomy?

In modelling the health and social care system it is important that we accurately represent the nature and impact of interventions (treatments). Sometimes that means representing interventions as taking place within a flow; more often interventions happen within a stock. Specific interventions might have multiple impacts. Cure-type interventions have the desired impact of reducing the number of people who are unwell by speeding up recovery. Care or management-type interventions may typically reduce the possibility that service users will experience adverse events, such as mortality or hospital admission. A less-often noticed impact is that these interventions may actually also increase the prevalence of a condition (or dependency-state), which is something to celebrate. This phenomenon might, at the same time, confound the expectations of those who expect that the impact of any new intervention ought to be that it saves money.

The following table of intervention-types is not intended to be comprehensive, but gives a flavour of the range of types of intervention that it is possible to model, whether they are best conceptualised as stocks or flows (often this depends on whether the average duration of the service is longer than the time-step in the model).

Intervention	Stock or flow—like	Intended impact
Brief assessment e.g. determining a person's eligibility to receive a service	Most likely represented as a flow (maximum number who can be assessed per time-step)	To drive a flow of people into a 'treatment' stock (which might well mean joining a backlog stock first)
Diagnosis identifying the nature of an illness or condition	Depending on how long it takes in relation to the model time-step, or the purpose of	To flow people from the 'undiagnosed' to the 'diagnosed' stock

(continued)

4.7 Towards a Taxonomy?

(continued)

Intervention	Stock or flow—like	Intended impact
	the model, could be represented either as a flow or a stock	(and possibly also onto a waiting list for treatment)
Simple treatment treatment of an acute condition	Most usually, stock, if the model is of the treatment system In a large-scale public health model, treatments of acute conditions would most likely be flows or simple output variables	In practical terms, in the model, to drive the 'discharged from treatment' flow Which should also mean flowing people from the 'unwell' to 'recovered' state
Care service a service that looks after people in the long-term, such as 'care at home' or 'care in a nursing home'	Stock Almost always, because the service describes someone's 'state of living' and not just an episode	To look after people, by RETAINING them inside the 'using care' stock for as long as possible To increase the 'quality of life' of people with an identified condition. To reduce the probability of a person suffering an adverse event that would lead to hospital admission or death
Care management service A service that enables people to manage to live with a long-term condition. It might consist of helping people to 'self-manage', or it might comprise a more active form of treatment	Stock	To flow people from the 'unwell, not managed (or not known)' state to the 'unwell but managed' state To slow down the rate of degeneration (reducing the flow out of this stage of the condition, and increasing the stock of people at this stage) To make it less likely that a person will suffer complications or an adverse event that might result in hospital admission or death
Intermediate Care Various services that sit between different parts of the health and/or social care system	Stock Probably with multiple stock-flow chains	Here, we are using 'intermediate care' as a generic term to describe a wide range of services that may be provided either in institutional, hospital-like, settings, or as a form of enhanced home care The intended impacts include: • Providing an alternative to hospital admission,

(continued)

(continued)

Intervention	Stock or flow—like	Intended impact
		therefore reducing the in-flow to hospital • Supporting people to leave hospital at an earlier stage, therefore reducing the length of stay in hospital for some • Improving the possibility of rehabilitation, reducing the number of people who flow into long-term care services (known as reablement)
A single service that treats people who have a wide range of conditions, or have differing needs, for example: • general hospital	Stock Perhaps better as multiple stocks, representing the range of types of condition treated or stages of treatment	Most likely represented by several, parallel, stock/flow chains, having variable admission-rates and lengths of stay Intended impacts could include any of the treatment interventions covered earlier
A single service that treats people who have a wide range of conditions, or have differing needs, for example: • care at home	Stock Perhaps better as multiple stocks, representing the range of types of care-need	Several parallel stock/flow chains representing, for example: • younger disabled people who will need lifelong support • people whose need is temporary, and are in a process of rehabilitation/recuperation following hospital treatment • older, frail people who will need the service in the long-term until their needs change (most likely a transfer to nursing home, or death)
prevention	A range of possibilities. The actual intervention could be some kind of public information campaign, or population-level policies such as banning smoking in public places or imposing a minimum price for alcohol, designed to reinforce a particular kind of behaviour	The intended impact is that the general population should behave in a particular way The result of that change in behaviour is that the inflow of **incidence of a condition** goes down, leading, in time, to fewer people with the condition

(continued)

(continued)

Intervention	Stock or flow—like	Intended impact
		But such a reduction may take some time to show, given the nature of long term conditions
screening	Flow In a model, the number being screened is a flow	The intended impact of screening is to create a new flow (asymptomatic, and some symptomatic, people being diagnosed as a result of screening) This, of course, leads to an increased stock of people 'needing treatment'

4.8 Conclusions

This Chapter has presented a classification of some generic templates used in modelling the utilisation (demand and supply) of health and social care services. On the demand side, we have described the dynamics of population ageing and health conditions. On the supply side, we have shown different ways of modelling and classifying services, focusing on their purpose and impact/effectiveness. Understanding how people flow through population ageing chains and health condition chains is important in designing treatment capacity and at which stages it is best to apply this capacity.

The simple templates described here will be deployed in a number of the models described in Parts II and III of the book.

References

Hirsch, G., & Homer, J. (2016). System dynamics applications to health care in the united states. In R. Meyers (Ed.), *Encyclopaedia of complexity and system science*. Springer: Berlin, Germany. ISBN 978-0-387-75888-6.

Miller, R., & McKelvie, D. (2016). *Commissioning for complexity: exploring the role of system dynamics in social care*. London: NIHR.

Pieters, A. J. H. M. (2013). *Care and cure: Compete or collaborate? Improving inter-organizational designs in healthcare. A case study in Dutch perinatal care*, Tilburg: Center, Center for Economic Research.

Sterman, J. (2018). System dynamics at sixty. *System Dynamics Review, 34*(1–2), 5–47.

Chapter 5
Feedback Dynamics

Chapter Summary
The chapter introduces feedback structures and their importance both in the world at large and in systems thinking and system dynamics modelling. It introduces reinforcing and balancing feedback loops and their classic behaviours over time and how to recognise them within stock-flow models. The language of causal loop maps is also introduced as an alternative means of describing feedback loops. Causal loop maps are useful as a means of simplifying feedback structures and summarising model behaviour. They can also be used as a starting point for the conceptualisation of news models. The chapter finishes with a look at how reinforcing and balancing feedback loops can combine to create system archetypes. These are combinations of feedback loops which give rise to specific behaviours. In particular they capture how well-intended feedback actions can result in unintended consequences and how to pre-empt and counter these. This section is a particularly relevant background to the use of archetypes in Chap. 10, 'Towards a Dynamic Theory of how Hospitals Cope in periods of High Demand'.

5.1 Feedback

Up to this point dynamic models have been described in the language of stocks and flows, but an important characteristic of such models is that they subsume information feedback loops. These loops play an important role in determining how models behave over time and have an important role in helping to explain and understand behaviours.

The work on problem and solution archetypes described in this chapter was first published in Wolstenholme (2003) and extracts published here are with the permission of Wiley Publishing.

Feedback is everywhere in the world around and within us and a feedback loop is created wherever information about the level of a stock is measured and then used to as a basis for an action to change flows, which then feed or deplete that stock.

In nature, there exists a web of interconnected feedback loops working in combination with one another that create cycles over time, which hold nature in a state of dynamic balance. For example, water, atmosphere, ocean, carbon, nitrogen and rock cycles. The driving forces of these feedback loops are the fundamental forces of nature or their derivatives in the form of temperature and pressure differences.

Inside living organisms, literally thousands of feedback loops combine to create the rhythms of our lives and to balance the functioning of our brains, organs, hormones and temperature. These loops and their driving forces are hard wired into our brains and, until they go wrong, we are not even conscious of their existence. For example, feedback acts to quickly protect us in the event of emergency by such mechanisms as blood coagulation and subsequently to reduce coagulation to prevent clots. The internal balance created by feedback within organisms is often referred to as homeostasis—the capacity to sustain internal stillness (Cannon 1926; 1929).

Also, important, particularly to our everyday lives, is that feedback operates both between living organisms and between living organisms and their environment. For, example reading body language and the hand-eye coordination that enables us to eat and drink.

In both nature and organisms, rhythms are vital to well-being and changes or breakdown in feedback processes can be catastrophic for both nature, society, organisations and people. In fact, ill-health could be defined as a breakdown in our internal feedback mechanisms.

Health and Social Care professionals are experts in the feedback of the body and mind but are perhaps less aware of how application the same feedback could be used to hold organisations in balance and improve the productivity of the application of their knowledge.

5.2 Reinforcing and Balancing Feedback Loops

Feedback loops consist of variables that are causally related (rather than statistically related through correlation) and there are only two types of feedback loop. These are reinforcing (or positive) feedback loops and balancing (or negative) feedback loops and each is characterised by their behaviour over time.

Reinforcing feedback loops are *growth* or *decline* loops, where each element in the loop reinforces the behaviour of other elements under the influence of feedback multipliers. In reinforcing loops change causes more change, resulting in exponential growth (virtuous spirals) or decline (vicious spirals) which, alarmingly, can double in magnitude in each time period. Such spirals are so called because they

5.2 Reinforcing and Balancing Feedback Loops

can be very difficult to break out of and start so innocuously that we are often trapped in them before we realise.

Population growth, addiction and compound interest on savings are good everyday examples of reinforcing growth. In fact, reinforcing feedback is increasingly the common parlance by which to describe climate change. For example, where initial warming is reinforced by reducing the quantity of ice reflecting heat into space and by melting permafrost to liberate more potent greenhouse gases, such as methane.

Balancing feedback loops on the other hand are *control* loops and their behaviour over time is *target seeking*. Here change in one part of a system feeds back to causes less of the same change—in other word to control behaviour over time towards the target. We encounter this type of loop in many contexts in everyday life, in a variety of control and regulatory settings.

For example, automatic control is used extensively in engineering and has its own branch of study devoted to it. Control engineering is used to design automated controls for a multitude of applications from robots, heating and cooling systems to missiles to space probes. Control of such systems is achieved using mechanical, electronic and algorithmic servomechanisms, which convert instructions to actions and increasingly have in-built learning.

When we interact with our environment we ourselves become part of a feedback loop. We are part of a balancing feedback loop whenever we drive a car or eat. In each case we take information from the environment to steer the car or to directing our hands to our mouth—or both at the same time!

Balancing feedback is used extensively in organisations, both to ascertain customer reactions to performance and as the basis of performance management. The setting of targets and the monitoring of performance against these is common practice in many industries. Health professionals in government health settings in particular are probably more aware than many others of the use of targets as management control tools for a whole range of service wait times.

Feedback loops are often hidden in system structures and tools are needed to extract them and make them visible. There are two ways of revealing feedback loops. One is to mark them on a stock-flow maps and the other is to draw an explicit map of them known as a causal loop map. Both have their pros and cons.

5.3 Revealing Feedback Loops on a Stock-Flow Map

Figure 5.1 shows an example of a stock-flow representation of a single—reinforcing feedback loop, describing the way an infected population increases as more people are exposed to the infection. The behaviour of this single loop is exponential growth and the feedback multiplier is the 'exposure to infection'.

We define the loop in Fig. 5.1 as a reinforcing loop by examining the *polarity* of each of its individual causal links.

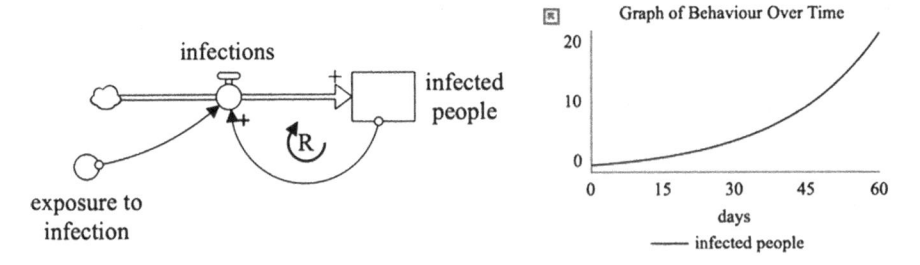

Fig. 5.1 A single reinforcing feedback loop and its behaviour over time

If an *increase in the tail variable* of a link produces an *increase in the head variable* of the link (above what it would have been) and vice versa, then the polarity of the link created is said to be a positive and marked with a '+' (or an 's' for *same* direction in some literature).

So, in the example, infections add to infected people and more infected people leads to more infections. In a reinforcing feedback loop the net effect of all of the link polarities is positive and the resulting behaviour over time is that of self-reinforcing growth. Such a loop is designated by a letter R.

Figure 5.2 shows an example of a stock-flow representation of a single balancing loop describing, the recruitment of nurses to achieve a target number in service.

We define the loop in Fig. 5.2 as a balancing feedback loop by again examining the polarity of each of its individual links.

This loop has one positive link and one negative link. If an *increase in the tail variable* of a link produces a *decrease in the head variable* (below where it would have been) and vice versa, then the link created is said to be a negative link and marked with a '-' (or 'o' for *opposite* direction in some literature). The negative link is between 'nurses' and 'nursing gap'. Nursing gap is defined here as ('target nurses'-'nurses') so, more nurses lead to a smaller gap and fewer nurses lead to a larger gap. As nursing numbers increase the gap closes and causes a gradual

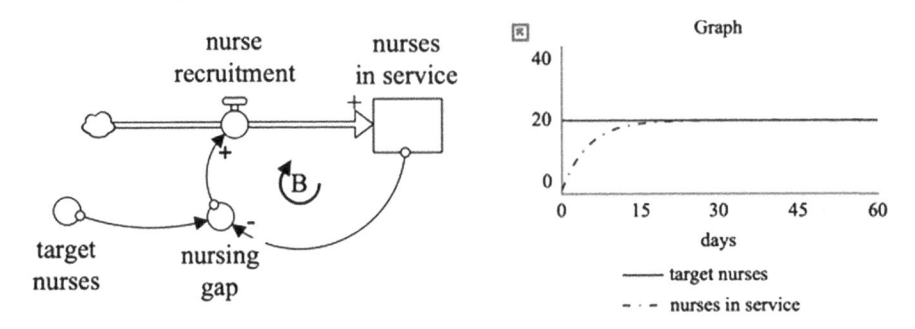

Fig. 5.2 A single balancing feedback loop and its behaviour over time

5.3 Revealing Feedback Loops on a Stock-Flow Map 93

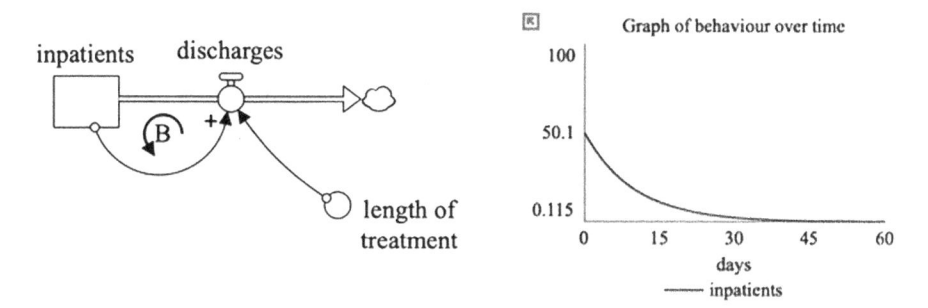

Fig. 5.3 A single balancing feedback loop depleting a stock

reduction over time in the rate of nurse recruitment. Fewer and fewer are recruited as the number of nurses approaches the target.

In a balancing feedback loop the *net* effect of all the link polarities is negative and hence the behaviour over time is target-seeking. Such a loop is designated by a letter B. By having one negative link, the net effect of the loop polarity in Fig. 5.2 loop is negative.

In general, any feedback loop can contain numerous *'positive'* and *'negative'* links and a more general rule for loop polarity is that a feedback loop is reinforcing if it contains an *even* number of *negative links*, since these cancel one another out, and *balancing* if it contains an *odd* number of *negative links*.

Drawing feedback loops on stock-flow maps works fine and clearly shows the *circular causality* of feedback loops for flows *which increase stocks*.

However, this method of exposing feedback does not work well where there are flows which *deplete stocks* as shown in Fig. 5.3. This is a balancing feedback loop, taken from Chap. 2, where a hospital discharge rate is defined as the inpatients/ average length of treatment and the target of the loop is zero. Over time without admissions the number of inpatient will decline to zero. However, the *circular causality* of the process is not readily apparent.

5.4 Causal Loop Maps

A second way of drawing feedback loops is by using causal loop maps and Fig. 5.4 shows the same balancing feedback loop as Fig. 5.3, displayed as a causal loop map. Here discharges are shown to have a negative influence on inpatients.

It should now be clear that a *circular balancing feedback loop* is present and has one negative link. It should be equally clear that this has been at the expense of hiding the stock outflow pipe and not distinguishing between the flow of people and the flow of information.

The simple difference between a stock-flow map and a causal loop map is that out-flows from stocks are shown not as flow pipes, but as a negative causal link

Fig. 5.4 A causal loop map of a single balancing feedback loop depleting a stock

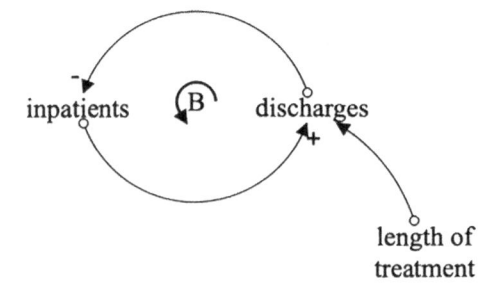

between the outflow variable and the stock. This causal link is not an information link which determines a policy, but a consequential influence.

In summary, showing feedback loops on stock-flow maps has the advantage of distinguishing stocks from flows and physical links from formation links. However, it is not easy to see the circular causality of loops which involve stocks depletions. On the other hand, showing feedback loops as causal loop maps clearly shows the circular causality of all loops, but loses the distinction between variable and link types.

To consolidate the thinking on feedback loops, Fig. 5.5 shows the feedback associated with the simple two stock treatment model of Chap. 2 as a causal loop map and Fig. 5.6 as a stock-flow map.

As explained in Chap. 2, an efficient hospital admissions policy is to both close the gap between hospital capacity and inpatients (this is the role of the balancing feedback loop B1) and to replace those discharged (this is the role of the reinforcing feedback loop R1). There is also a second balancing feedback loop B2 which controls the discharge rate according to the average length of treatment.

Of particular importance to the behaviour produced by both balancing and reinforcing feedback loops are delays (lags). There are always delays within

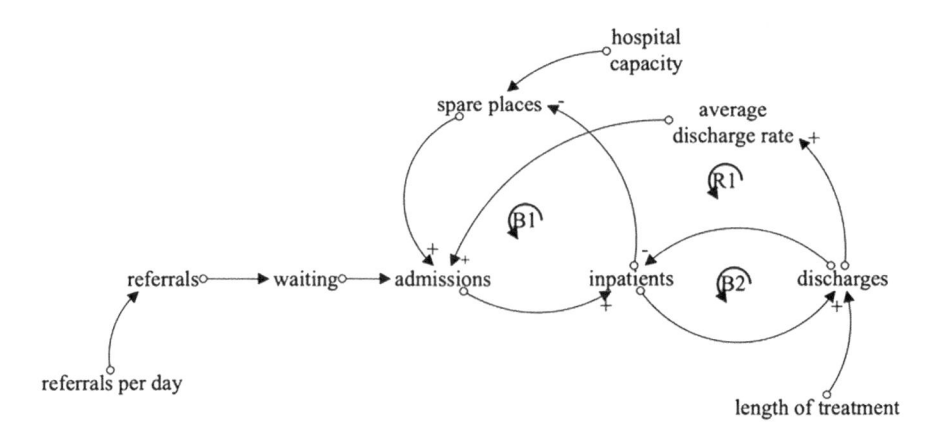

Fig. 5.5 The hospital model of Chap. 2 expressed both as a causal loop map

5.4 Causal Loop Maps

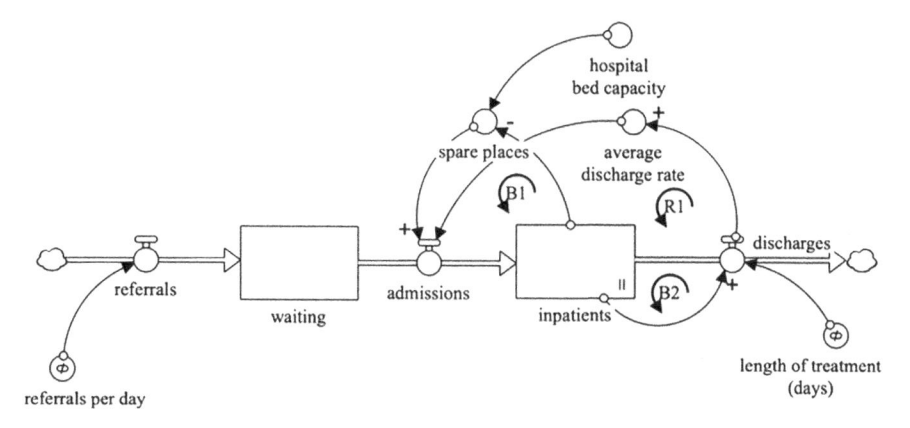

Fig. 5.6 The hospital model of Chap. 2 expressed as a stock-flow map

individual feedback loops, such as delays in observation or measurement of what is happening, delays in formulating action or delays in the process of carrying out the action in the loop. Delays can slow the growth rate of reinforcing feedback loops and cause overshoot and undershoot of a target and hence oscillations in balancing feedback loops. Delayed feedback loop behaviour over time is one of the main reasons why we often misinterpret what is really happening in systems when we take a point-in-time view.

5.5 Summary of the Rules for Drawing Feedback Loops

Feedback loops will be used in later chapters of the book and the following summary of the rules for drawing feedback loops will be reproduced in those chapters where appropriate.

Balancing (or negative) feedback loops are *target* seeking *control* loops and have just *one* or an *odd* number of *negative* links between variables.

Reinforcing (or positive) feedback loops are *growth* loops and have *all* or an *even* number of *negative* links between variables.

Positive links are when an *increase in a tail variable* of a link gives rise causally to an *increase in the head variable* (and vice versa).

Negative links are when an *increase in the tail variable* of a link gives rise causally to a *decrease in the head variable* (and vice versa).[1]

---

[1] It should be pointed out that generally in causal loop maps these rules work fine but in certain cases technically the vice versa rule for causal links does not strictly apply (Richardson 1986; Sterman 2000). Whilst increasing an inflow increases a stock, reducing an inflow does not reduce the stock but increases it less quickly. Here the '+' sign simply means that the inflow *adds* to the

5.6 Multiple Feedback Loops, Unintended Consequences and System Archetypes

Understanding single feedback loops and their behaviours over time is informative in itself.

However, feedback loops are rarely found in isolation. For example, there are mixed loops present in Fig. 5.6, which work to complement each other and we could add additional loops to Figs. 5.1 and 5.2 to treat infected people and to allow for nurses leaving, respectively.

Moreover, it is when reinforcing and balancing feedback loops work together to counter one another and produce unintended consequences that their behaviours over time really become counter intuitive and interesting.

An important use of causal loop maps is capture the essence of these multi-loop situations and to simplify the details of models by exposing their underlying feedback structure, which perhaps cuts across many different stock-flow pathways. They can also be useful as part of the model conceptualisation process. Perhaps most importantly, they also form the foundations of system archetypes as used extensively in Chaps. 7 and 10.

System archetypes (Senge 1990) are a formal way of categorising groups of feedback loops responsible for generic patterns of behaviour over time, such as oscillation and over-shoot-and-collapse.

Categorising multi loop situations is not as complicated as it might sound because we are helped in our thinking by the fact that there are only two types of feedback loop. Hence, there are only four basic combinations of two loops to consider and hence a core set of only four system archetypes (Wolstenholme 2003).

The generic form of these four archetypes is shown in Fig. 5.7.

The characteristics of an archetype are as follows:

1. First, it is composed of an *intended consequence (ic) loop* resulting from an *action* initiated in *one sector of an organisation* with an intended consequence for some outcome over time in mind (blue).
2. Second, it contains an *unintended consequence (uc) loop* resulting from a *re-action within another sector of the organisation or outside*, which creates an unintended consequence diminishing the outcome of the intended action over time (red).
3. Third there is a delay (//) before the unintended consequence manifests itself.
4. Forth, there is a boundary that often masks the unintended consequence from the view of those instigating the intended consequence. This boundary can be a real organisational boundary or a mental barrier to which we prefer to turn a blind eye.

---

stock. Similarly, whilst increasing an outflow reduces a stock, reducing an outflow does not increase the stock but reduces it less quickly. Here the '-' sign simply means that the outflow *subtracts* from the stock.

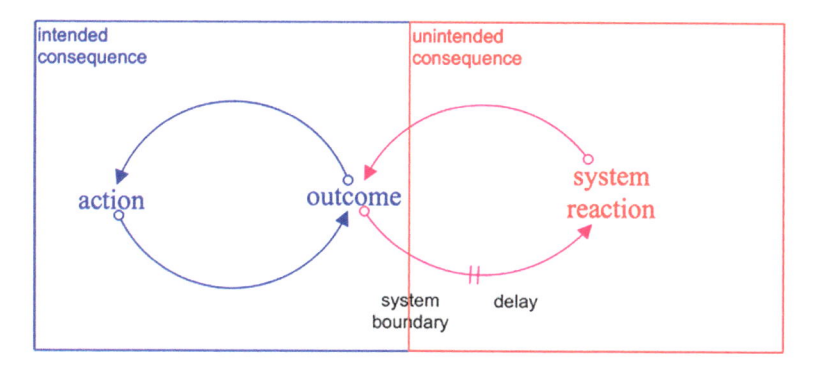

5.6 Multiple Feedback Loops, Unintended Consequences and System Archetypes 97

Fig. 5.7 The generic structure of a two-loop 'problem' archetype

5. Fifth, for most problem archetypes there is often hidden a potential solution archetype whereby a further action can be taken in parallel with the intended action to help unblock the unintended consequence and support the intended consequence.

5.7 Problem Archetypes

The combination of an intended and unintended consequence is referred to as a *'problem archetype'* the outcome of which over time is far from that intended by the people creating the *ic* loop.

It should be noted that reactions can come from the same system participants who instigate the original actions (perhaps due to impatience with the time taken for their original actions to have effect). However, it is more often the case that the response comes in the form of action from other sectors of the organisation or externally. These responses might also be natural or arise from the reactions of collaborators or competitors.

It can be argued that, whilst side effects are well established and understood in health care, where it is known that the treatment can sometimes be worse than the disease, side effects are less well understood in management and many other social systems. Because such systems are dynamic, self-organising and adaptive, every action will be countered by a reaction and hence no one strategy will ever dominate.

5.8 Solution Archetypes

The idea of a two-loop system archetype with problem behaviour leads to the idea of a *solution archetype* to minimise any side effects of the intended action. The generic form of a solution archetype is shown in Fig. 5.8.

The key to identifying solution archetypes lies in understanding both the magnitude of the delay and the nature of the organisational boundary present. In particular, solutions require that people instigating a new action should attempt to resist being too reactive, allow for the delay and remove or make more transparent the organisational boundary masking the side effect. Effort can then be directed at introducing a 'solution link' to create a new feedback loop. The purpose of this loop is to counter or unblock the *uc* loop in parallel with activating the *ic* loop. The result could be that the intended action might be much more robust and capable of achieving its purpose.

5.9 The Four Problem/Solution Archetypes

Intended actions can be condensed down to one of two kinds.

These are actions which attempt to improve *success* or *achievement* in an organisation by initiating *reinforcing feedback* effects and those which attempt to *control* an organisation by introducing *balancing feedback* effects. Reactions can also be condensed to one of the same two kinds.

Hence, four possible two-loop archetypes can be defined to represent these basic action-outcome-response situations. These are named here:

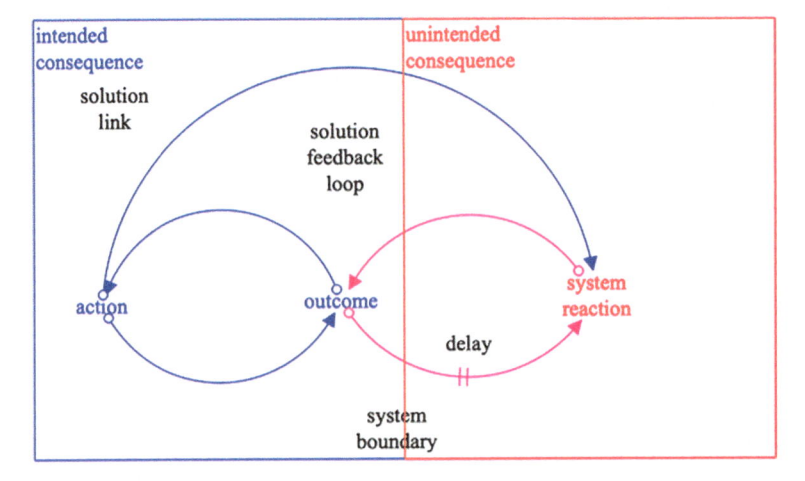

Fig. 5.8 The generic structure of the two-loop 'solution' archetype

- *Underachievement*, where intended achievement fails to be realised,
- *Out of Control,* where intended control fails to be realised,
- *Relative achievement*, where achievement is only gained at the expense of another,
- *Relative control,* where control is only gained at the expense of others.

Attention here will be focused on the first two of these archetypes, since these are used later in the book and are much more common in health and social care than the last two. All are discussed in detail elsewhere (Wolstenholme 2003).

5.10 Underachievement Archetype

(composition: ic loop is a reinforcing loop, uc loop is a balancing loop)

Figure 5.9 shows the problem form of this archetype.

This archetype consists of a reinforcing ic loop intended to achieve a successful outcome from an initiative, but the reaction from another sector of the system is the creation of a balancing uc loop which causes a delayed underachievement of the outcome over time. This archetype is a more general description of the *'Limits to Success'* or *'Limits to Growth'* archetypes described elsewhere in the literature (Senge 1990).

Figure 5.10 shows the solution form of this archetype. It is suggested that the solution to an underachievement archetype lies in introducing a solution link to reduce the system reaction which, by introducing two negative causal links, creates a further *reinforcing* loop to counter the system reaction and complement the intended action.

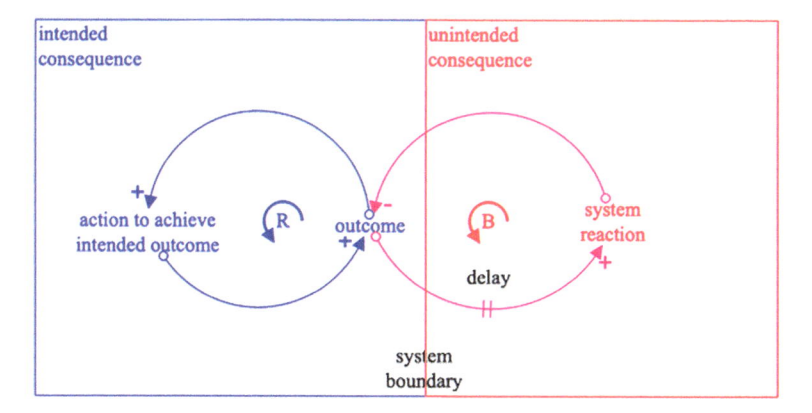

Fig. 5.9 The 'problem' structure of the 'under achievement' archetype

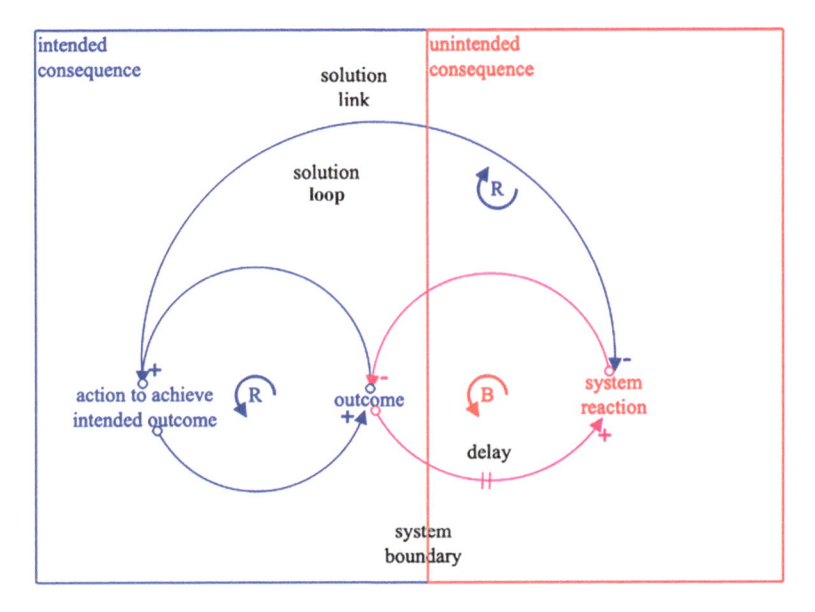

Fig. 5.10 The 'solution' structure of the 'under achievement' archetype

5.11 An Example of the Underachievement Archetype in Health and Social Care

An example from health and social care of a problem underachievement archetype is shown in Fig. 5.11.

Here, investment in health initiatives are intended to increase health interventions and encourage further investment (the reinforcing loop R on the left), but increased interventions can lead to delayed hospital discharges (the balancing loop

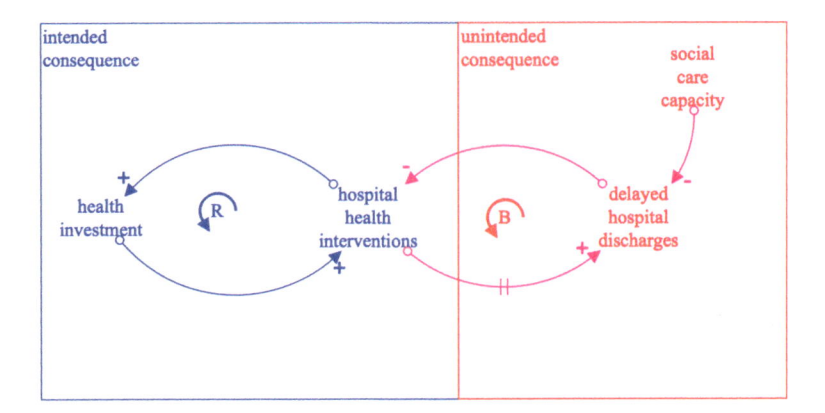

Fig. 5.11 An example of an underachievement 'problem' archetype in health and social care

5.11 An Example of the Underachievement Archetype in Health and Social Care   101

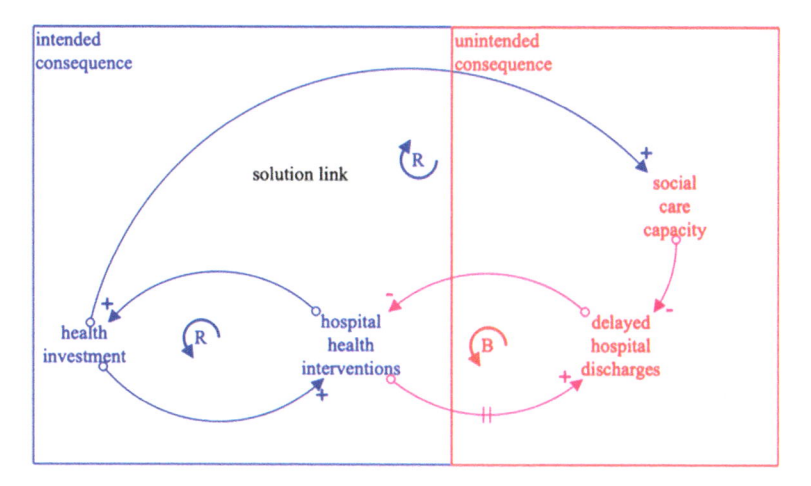

Fig. 5.12 An example of an underachievement 'solution' archetype in Health and Social Care

B on the right), due to problems with social care capacity, which actually reduces the success achieved.

The potential solution suggested by archetypal thinking (Fig. 5.12) is to invest in unblocking the constraint in social care in parallel with investing in the health interventions. This is to create another reinforcing feedback loop which supports the intended one.

This is a succinct archetypal dress rehearsal of a matter which will be discussed in detail in Chaps. 7 and 10.

5.12 Out-of-Control Archetype

(composition: ic is a balancing loop, uc loop is a reinforcing loop)

Figure 5.13 shows the problem form of this archetype. This consists of a balancing ic loop intended to control the magnitude of a problem but the reaction from another sector of the system is a reinforcing loop, resulting in a possible worsening of the problem, which gets more and more out of control. It is useful to note in this archetype that it is usually the control action itself, rather than the outcome that provokes the system reaction.

Figure 5.14 shows the solution form of this archetype. It is suggested that the solution to an out-of-control archetype lies introducing a solution link which forms a further *balancing* loop to mitigate against the system reaction and to complement the intended control.

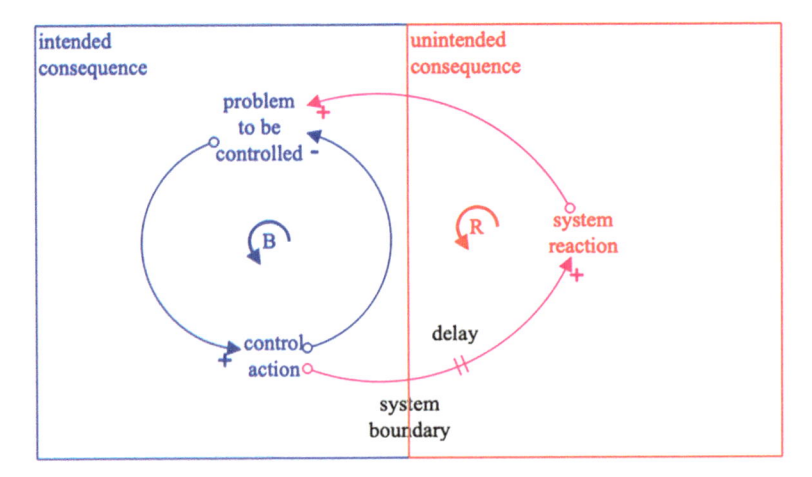

Fig. 5.13 The 'problem' structure of the 'out of control' two-loop archetype

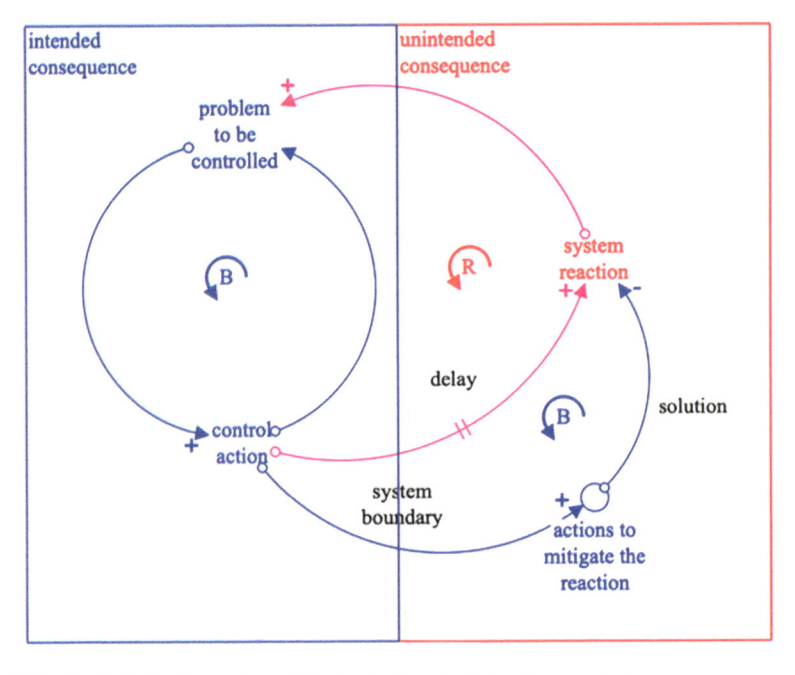

Fig. 5.14 The 'solution' structure of the 'out of control' two-loop archetype

5.13 Examples of the Out-of-Control Archetype in Health and Social Care

An example of an out-of-control archetype from health and social care is shown in Fig. 5.15. Here, employing more social workers is deemed to be a way of coping with increases in reported cases of child abuse (the balancing loop on the left), but more social workers lead to more discovery of abuse (the reinforcing loop B on the right) which requires more and more social workers.

A potential solution (Fig. 5.16) could be, in parallel with deploying more social workers to existing cases, to devote more social worker time to reducing the underlying occurrence of child abuse. This in turn reduces the discovery and reporting of child abuse. This is an example of balancing prevention and treatment which is a very common theme in health and social care.

A further example of an out of control archetype is shown in Fig. 5.17. Here home care capacity is installed to reduce the number of older people at home who are not coping. The unintended consequences are that degeneration is reduced and longevity increased, both of which actually add to the numbers needing help and hence drive the need for more home care capacity. Unintended consequences are often seen as vicious cycles and hence undesirable, but here the effect is actually virtuous and very desirable and should perhaps be referred to an unforeseen bonus. The success of health interventions by definition are intended to improve life but in general they are not often perceived as success stories which lead to the need for more of the same. Of course, the ultimate limitation here is the funding of capacity.

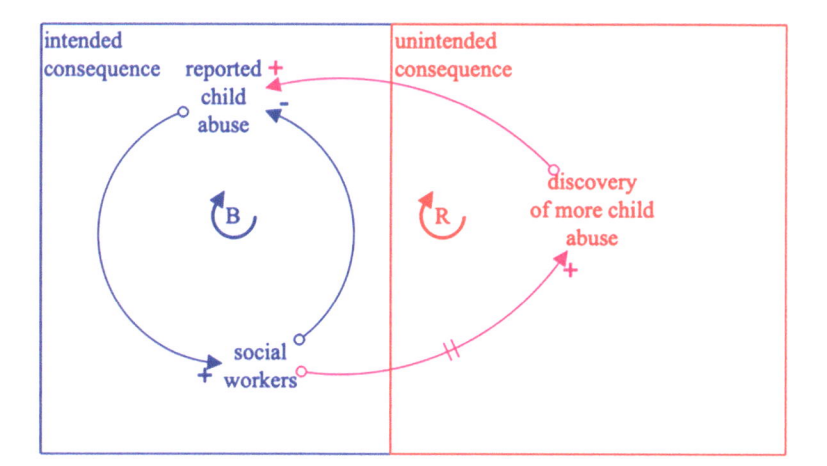

Fig. 5.15 An example of an 'out of control' 'problem' archetype in health and social care

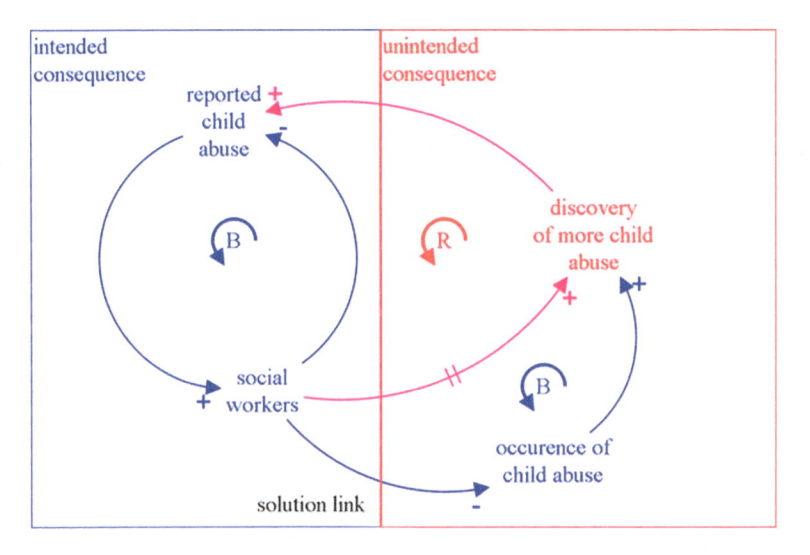

Fig. 5.16 An example of an 'out of control' 'solution' archetype in health and social care

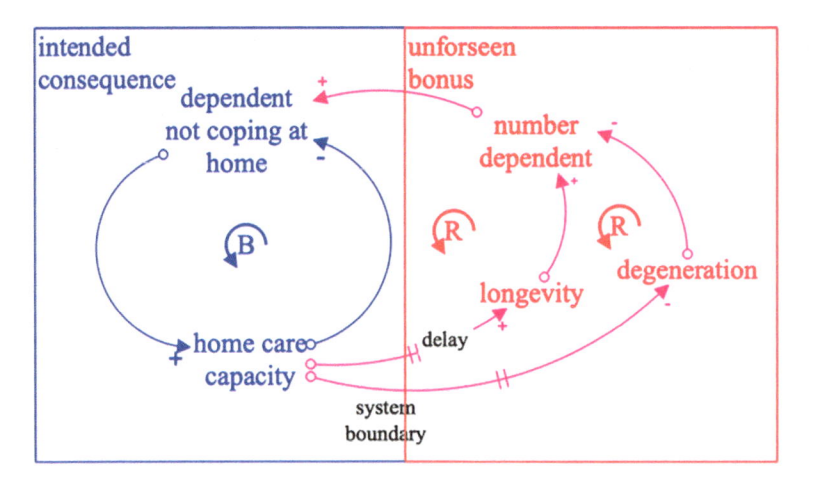

Fig. 5.17 The unforeseen bonus of helping to keep older people at home

5.14 Conclusions

This chapter has introduced feedback as an important, inherent component of the world around us and of systems thinking and system dynamics models and has classified feedback into two types—reinforcing and balancing. It has also covered the ways in which to make reinforcing and balancing feedback loops visible on stock-flow maps and by using causal loop maps. It has emphasised how understanding of feedback and delays across system boundaries can help interpret and explain the behaviour of systems over time.

The idea of using two-loop archetypes where reinforcing and balancing feedback loops work together to counter one another and produce unintended consequences has been examined. Such archetypes can help with thinking about how to pre-empt unintended consequence at the time of taking well-intended actions. This sort of temporal thinking is not easy to do as decisions gain their own momentum and are difficult to challenge. It is only too easy to be prisoners of our own structures and events and to feel that the system pushes back against our best initiatives to make balanced change.

It could be argued that not fully considering unintended consequences over time results in so many of today's problems being the result of yesterday's imperfect solutions. It is only too easy to take short term solutions to make problems go away, rather than finding sustainable answers. And fixing does not make a problem go away. A major issue inhibiting our thinking over time is that cause and effect are not closely related in either time or space and that the best levers for problem interventions are well removed from the symptoms of the problem—and often on someone else's patch. As a result, identifying the most appropriate levers for change in any given situation can often be very counter intuitive.

An important message is that often you can have your cake and eat it. Investing ahead of time beyond the minimum necessary to initiate the intended action can avoid later side effects that cost more than the cure.

Two loop system archetypes are used in Chap. 7 to explain the unintended side effects of more obvious policies to tackle delayed hospital discharges and extensively in Chap. 10 to explain how hospitals cope with excessive demand and the unintended consequences of some of these actions for cost, efficacy and staff in health and social care.

References

Cannon, W. B. (1926). Physiological regulation of normal states: some tentative postulates concerning biological homeostatics. In A. Pettit (Ed.), *A Charles Riches amis, ses collègues, ses élèves (in French)*. Paris: Les Éditions Médicales.

Senge, P. M. (1990). *The fifth discipline: The art and practice of the learning organization*. New York: Doubleday/Currency.

Sterman, J. D. (2000). *Business dynamics, system thinking and modelling for a Complex World*. Boston: Irwin Mcgraw-Hill.

Richardson, G.P. (1986/1976) Problems with causal loop diagrams. *System Dynamics Review, 2*(2) (summer), 158–170.

Wolstenholme, E. F. (2003). Towards the definition and use of a core set of archetypal structures in system dynamics. *System Dynamics Review, 19*(1), 7–26.

Chapter 6
Applying System Dynamics

Chapter Summary

This chapter describes the steps in building system dynamics models in health and social care. It covers the process of group model building by which system dynamics models are constructed and validated with management/clinical teams and positions the approach of the authors. It also references alternative modelling and simulation methods and their software and alternative approaches to health and social care analysis and improvement.

6.1 An Overview of the Process of Building and Validating System Dynamics Models

Ideally, system dynamics models are built in response to a dynamic concern, that is a trend over time which is considered problematic. This dynamic trend is referred to as a reference mode which is used to guide the model development (Fig. 6.1).

An important first step is the assembly of an expert group, most of whom should have some responsibility for the concern. This expert group is then facilitated to build a stock-flow map of the health and social care pathways through which people flow, relevant to the concern, perhaps aided by causal mapping. The pathways defined constitute the shared mental models of the team about how the pathways work and, importantly, the model and its assumptions are owned by the team.

The model is then populated with appropriate data and relationships between variables. Data may need to be estimated and parameter estimation forms an important part of the subject (Sterman 2018). In this book extensive use is made of big data and triangulating parameter estimates from diverse sources. Data definitions used in the health sector are usually based on those needed for performance management purposes and to enable comparisons between organisations.

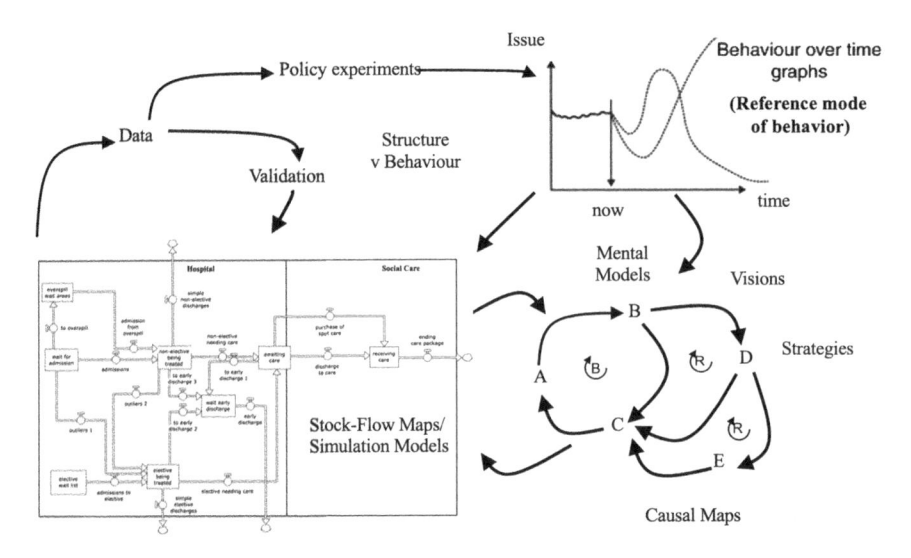

Fig. 6.1 The iterative cycle of building a system dynamics model

Performance indices are rarely developed from a stock-flow perspective. In our view, stock-flow thinking about data provides information that supports a whole system view and would make for a better decision-support system than conventional performance data. The performance dominated view of data also means that clients seldom have a coherent set of time-series data for model reference modes.

Model validation is an integral part of the model development process and many formal approaches have been developed. These include sensitivity analysis, extreme behaviour testing, dimensional analysis, rigorous fitting of model output to historic data and partial model calibration. It is beyond the scope or intent of this book to explore these in detail and they are well documented elsewhere (Forrester and Senge 1980; Graham 1980; Sterman 2000; Yucel and Barlas 2006; Homer 2012; Lane 2015). Increasingly, model testing techniques such as optimised curve fitting are built into system dynamics software.

In this book model validation is largely carried out relative to the needs of the expert groups owning the issues of concern. Ultimately, the modelling team must have confidence that the model is capable of reproducing a reference mode of behaviour consistent with their data or mental models and many of the early iterations of model building centre on building client confidence both in their own mental models and the emerging simulation model. In general, our approach and that of our clients has been to construct models based on sound quantitative relationships and to leave contentious, qualitative relationships for retrospective discussion and possible later inclusion.

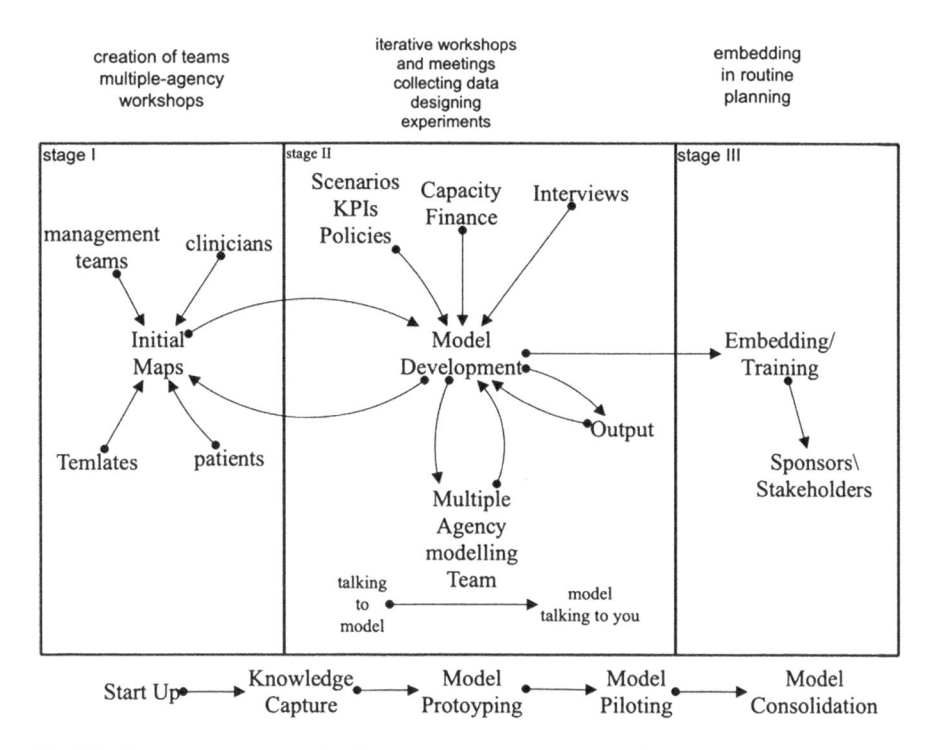

6.1 An Overview of the Process of Building and Validating ... 109

Fig. 6.2 The iterative stages of building a system dynamics model

Once validated a model can be used to test alternative pathway designs and policies under different scenarios and performance measures in a laboratory setting without disturbance to the real pathways. Experimentation with the models is helped by constructing accessible interfaces through which users can perform experiments by moving controls such as slider bars and observing multiple numeric and graphical outputs.

There is no ideal duration for a model building project. The key principle is that the purpose of a model is always to improve ability to think about a complex issue and the iterative stages of the dialogue between the model and an expert group is captured in Fig. 6.2.

An important point is that at which there is a switch between 'talking to the model' and 'the model talking to you'.

6.2 The Author's Approach to Group Model Building and Modelling as Learning

System dynamics practitioners have devoted a great deal of attention to methodology, and the idea of "group model building" provides a practical way forward (Vennix 1996, 1999; Lane 1992; Lane et al. 2003).

Some authors go into some detail about the roles that are needed to achieve successful facilitation of group model building, including the facilitator/knowledge elicitor, modeller/reflector, process coach, recorder, and gatekeeper, while noting that experienced group modellers can normally get along with just two facilitators (Richardson and Andersen 2010).

The account given here reflects the experience of the authors of using system dynamics mainly within consulting engagements, where a typical client would be a service commissioner or government agency/department. The key requirement is always to secure client engagement in an iterative learning process.

A typical group model building project in health and social care requires:

- An "expert group" containing people who have an operational understanding of the range of services/interventions, as well as familiarity with the nature of the population and issue of concern (whether that is ageing, deprivation, mental health);
- At least one member, or access to someone, who is familiar with the range of data sources/information systems in which data might reside; but it is important to emphasise that the process of model-building does not begin and/or end with data. The model will probably draw on both data from academic research, as well as secondary analysis of local datasets;
- Facilitators who, between them, have both some understanding of the domain and, obviously, knowledge and skills in model-building.

There should be scope for a series of iterations; around five is a minimum but it is difficult to be too prescriptive. Not least, the building of a model can trigger awareness that a larger enquiry is necessary; as the work progresses the model boundaries can be extended. Nevertheless, a group must resist the temptation to model "everything" in great detail. The best models focus on a specific problem and work out from it.

A typical sequence of meetings will include:

- An introductory session, where participants are given some background knowledge about the modelling approach, the "problem" issue is introduced and described, and some initial stock-flow and causal maps are generated; this is similar to process mapping but generally at a more aggregated, higher-level view of each process;
- A second session where perhaps an embryonic model based on the maps generated at the first meeting is presented. Moving quickly to simulation can accelerate learning, even if the actual model at this stage lacks detail; after this meeting the modeller will go away and aim to build something that begins to resemble "the" model;

6.2 The Author's Approach to Group Model Building ... 111

- A third session where the model is presented; this will likely lead to a discussion that covers:
  - The need for some amendments to the model structure;
  - Evidence that the group is beginning to learn something new about the issue;
  - A discussion about data and data sources;
  - Identification of a range of scenarios that might be tested;
- At least two more sessions, in between which further work is carried out by the modeller and different group members, including a search for data/evidence.

Normally, a group will not manage to meet any more frequently than monthly (based on experience of how much time senior managers and frontline staff can afford to devote to, and meet about, any issue). Probably, half-day sessions are enough. Any less, and not enough material is covered, but spending a whole day on model-building, requiring detailed work and attention can be draining. Achieving a consistent group attendance makes a difference because this avoids the need to engage in lengthy re-explanations of previous material in order to bring newcomers up-to-speed. Against that, if a group becomes too exclusive there can be a risk of groupthink, where the group adopts a particular interpretation that becomes the peceived wisdom.

Modelling as an iterative learning cycle is often referred to as 'modelling as learning', a phrase originating from 'planning as learning' (de Gues 1988) and developed by others (for example, Lane 1992) where it is possible to reconsider and revisit anything from one meeting to the next. However, as the project progresses the focus of attention shifts:

- Initially, focus is on model structure and gaining an understanding of the problem/issue;
- As the structure is consolidated, so a more detailed conversation about data and evidence is more possible;
- Estimation of data parameters tends to come towards the middle of the process (unless, a project has been triggered by some problematic observations in "the data"); the kinds of data sought will include:
  - Population data about levels of need and, more difficult, the dynamics of need—so not just "how many people need something" but what is the flow rate at which people enter into this state and exit from it. Flow variables are perhaps the most important but least monitored data items. There is also often a problem in health and social care of databases not linking to one another across boundaries. For example, health might classify hospital discharge data in a completely different way to social care records of admissions to care packages;
  - Service capacity and throughput data;

- Data about interventions and their impact;
- Financial data, mainly the costs of services and interventions;

- As the model moves from being a mere diagram to a functioning simulation, the focus moves on to an exploration of possible scenarios;
- The issue of "how the model is to be used" beyond the immediate project will become more prominent; the shelf-life of some models may simply be for the duration of the project, other models might be intended for continued use by a client, or even distributed.

'Service Design' and Group Model Building

One very welcome development in recent years has been the incredible growth in interest in 'service design' to support the reimagining of public services, in the UK, but also internationally. Service design takes the concept of design as taught in art schools and applies it to the improvement of public services, with user-engagement, empowerment, or 'co-production' as central themes. This is probably most evident in services for people with mental health problems or disabilities, where service users increasingly give voice to what they know they need, rather than accept the service that has traditionally been provided.

Typically, this approach deploys highly participative workshops or engagement-events, with an emphasis on skilled facilitation, and a structured approach to drawing diagrams and flow-charts of service processes as imagined by participants. The similarities with the best approaches of SD practitioners to 'group model building' are obvious, because stock-flow and causal-loop thinking are compatible visual tools for helping people to think differently. Some, such as at Peter Hovmand's Social Systems Design Lab,[1] or Sarah Wylie's contribution to the Northern Ireland government's Innovation Lab, have already engaged productively with the service design community. What system dynamics offers the service design process is a quantitative element to what is mostly undertaken as a qualitative approach. We hope to return to this subject.

6.3 Other Modelling Approaches

Dynamic modelling can be implemented using a wide range of methods (Sterman 2018) and there are numerous modelling methods available for simulating patient flows.

---

[1] At Washington University in St. Louis.

The most obvious candidates of these are spreadsheet models and discrete event simulators.

Spreadsheets are well used across the whole spectrum of business analysis and reasonably well understood tools. However, they are used predominantly for financial rather than operational calculations. They can incorporate accumulations, perform simulations and incorporate information feedback but, unlike system dynamics software, are not easy to configure for these purposes.

Spreadsheets are also far from transparent and less than ideal for supporting thinking about behaviour over time. For example, a typical SD model might run for five years with a time step of days, a total of 1826 steps. Given a DT (delta time) of 0.25, meaning that the model recalculates every variable four times per day, that makes 7,305 time increments per model run. In a spreadsheet, that would mean recalculating each variable down 7,305 rows, or across 7,305 columns, cumbersome to say the least. This contrasts strongly with system dynamics models which start with a visual representation of the system in the form of a diagram which makes the connections/inter-connections between variables explicit and transparent, and generates behaviour from a set of built–in rules about what makes flows happen in each time period.

However, spreadsheets are familiar tools and can complement system dynamics modelling, both for data input and as a means of exporting model outputs in a format that people can access without investing in system dynamics software. The dementia, alcohol, predictive risk and well-being models described in later chapters all make extensive use of spreadsheets for input and output of results.

Discrete event simulation does exactly what the name implies (Brailsford 2013; Viana et al. 2014). It is concerned with the statistical modelling of individual entities, rather than aggregated flows and, as an extension of the Operational Research technique of queueing theory, separates flows into queues and activities. It is a very visual and transparent approach and uses its own range of dedicated software tools (for example, Simul8).

Agent-based simulation is a hybrid method which combines both discrete and continuous methods and also has dedicated software (Luke et al. 2005; Borshchev et al. 2005; XJ Technologies 2007). Here populations are represented as collections of agents each linked with their own attributes and parameters.

There are numerous initiatives to try to contrast and consolidate some of the approaches (Viana et al. 2014; Brailsford et al. 2014; Brailsford 2014; Luke and Stamatakis 2012; Sadsad et al. 2014; Marshall et al. 2015a, b; Roberts 2015).

6.4 Other Approaches to Health and Social Care Analysis

There are numerous inter-related approaches to health and social care analysis varying from whole disciplines to specific toolsets. System dynamics is distinct from, but complements, many of these approaches.

One of the most prominent disciplines is that of health economics, which as its name suggests is the application of economic thinking to the analysis of health care (Sloan and Hsieh 2017; Wonderling et al. 2005). Health economics subsumes many toolsets, mostly statistical but increasingly including simulation, mainly in the form of discrete event simulation. Also prominent are Decision Theory and Markov techniques used primarily within the pharmaceutical industry, particularly for randomised control trials of new drugs.

A particularly apposite link exists between system dynamics and health economics in the area of cost benefit analysis (CBA). Cost benefit analysis in health and social care is used in a wide range of situations to choose between alternative policies for improvement by:

- deriving detailed costs and benefits of new treatments and procedures on a per capita basis, then multiplying these up by very broad estimates of the numbers of people expected to benefit, to derive the total financial case for decisions.
- predicting the outcome of each alternative in terms of costs and benefits *after* a relevant time period. These *external* estimates are then converted into a common financial currency and discounted to provide a set of comparative net present values using spread sheet models.

What dynamic modelling can add to this type of analysis is:

- To provide a much more thorough investigation of the people who will benefit over time, where they will flow from and flow to.
- To *generate* the costs and benefits at each time point as a result of *internal feedback* connections and examine the impact of a change in policy as it *evolves over time* under that policy.
- To provide the transitional impact as well as the final.

Such extensions to conventional thinking help to convert static cost benefits analyses into what we call *dynamic impact analysis*. This complementarity is demonstrated clearly in the work described in Part III of the book.

Another approach gaining prominence in health and social care is Lean Thinking (Liker 2004). Lean thinking focusses on stock, waste, error and cost reduction, together with efficiencies and improvements. In order to do this lean thinking now subsumes many independent techniques arising from total quality management and operational research. These include; process and value mapping, statistical techniques and problem-solving methods, all usually wrapped in a cyclic method of process improvement and training. The emphasis is on easily assimilated concepts applicable to individual processes, which can be rolled out across individual organisations for immediate gains in very tangible performance measures. The plan-do-study-act (PDSA) cycle of lean thinking used in implementing stepped care for depression in Chap. 9 is a good example of the two methods working together.

6.5 The Authors' Positioning of System Dynamics for Health and Social Care Modelling

The authors have experience of a wide range of analytical methods and have always thought that what has been missing the most is a *strategic* modelling approach and system dynamics lends itself to this role.

It is felt important when analysing complex, dynamics concerns to bring to bear an array of methods, but to apply these in a specific order from the strategic to the operational.

Without a long-term strategic direction, operational tools can often miss important foci of change. Or improve one organisation or sector of a supply chain or patient pathway, but possibly to the detriment of others. There is also a danger that problems simply get moved around in a time-consuming set of activities, which are themselves inefficient and create an initiative overload that detracts from core business. The converse is perhaps also true. Without detailed implementation assistance the potential outcomes of strategic studies, which often demonstrate the location rather than the type of effective interventions, might not be fulfilled.

To realise the best of both strategic and operational methods, it is suggested that system dynamics simulation should be applied first to identify effective global intervention points since they are often well removed from observable problem symptoms.

6.6 Big Data

It has been demonstrated that system dynamics has important implications for the design of information systems (Wolstenholme et al. 1993) and it was highlighted in Chap. 2 that system dynamics can assist with checking for the consistency of data. The triangulation of missing data is also very much to the fore in the dementia work in Chap. 13. However, understanding flow has particular implications for current trends in Big Data and Chap. 14 highlights this with reference to risk assessment tools in health.

The idea behind Big Data is that with enough information we can make better informed decisions. In the health system, real-time databases have the potential to describe health or dependency states of everyone in a population. For example, researchers in the UK have developed 'predictive risk models' (Lewis et al. 2011) to identify those people most at risk of readmission to hospital. In contrast to Big Data approaches, whose algorithms identify patterns but not causes, system dynamics draws attention to the need to understand flow. The same distribution of people into stocks over time can result from different underlying churn (flow). The same intervention introduced to two populations with identical stock over time values, but different underlying flow rates, will have significantly different impacts, including on cost. To understand the dynamics of interventions we must understand flow. To understand flow, we often require the kind of data that has not hitherto been routinely collected or, if collected, analysed with flow in mind.

One way of expressing this is that Big Data approaches might be capable of making reasonably accurate predictions of what might happen next, based on a large amount of real-time data about the present state of the system. But because it does not have an explicit representation of the causal relationships within the system, it would be much harder to simulate 'what might happen if we were to change a parameter/model input?' This, of course, may change in the future as big data subsumes more developments from artificial intelligence, machine learning, algorithmic approaches and neural networks.

6.7 System Dynamics Software

A number of commercially available software packages have been developed by the system dynamics community. The choice of software will be determined by a range of circumstances and each offers a range of options for making models available to people who want to use them, including access over the internet, without needing to know how to build a model.

It is not possible to provide an exhaustive list of software options, but the field is still limited to a relatively few providers. The picture is always changing and the interested reader should put "system dynamics software" into a search engine and explore. Alternatively, the System Dynamics Society website (www.systemdynamics.org/) has links to the main software vendors.

Important current simulation environments include:

- Vensim (Ventana Systems, www.vensim.com),
- STELLA and iThink (isee Systems, www.iseesystems.com),
- PowerSim (www.powersim.com),
- AnyLogic www.anylogic.com)
- Sysdea (www.strategydynamics.com)

References

Brailsford, S. C. (2013) Discrete-event simulation is alive and kicking. *Journal of Simulation*. https://doi.org/10.1057/jos.2013.13.

Brailsford, S. C. (2014). Theoretical comparison of discrete-event simulation and system dynamics. In S. C. Brailsford, L. Churilov, & B. Dangerfield (Eds.), *Discrete-event simulation and system dynamics for management decision making* (pp. 105–124). (Wiley Series in Operations Research & Management Science). United Kingdom of Great Britain and Northern Ireland, GB: John Wiley & Sons.

Brailsford, S. C., Churilov, L. & Dangerfield, B. (Eds.) (2014). Discrete-event simulation and system dynamics for management decision making. (Wiley Series in Operations Research & Management Science). United Kingdom of Great Britain and Northern Ireland, GB: John Wiley & Sons.

References

Borshchev, A., Osgood, N., McDonald, G., Paich, M., Rahmandad, H., Heffernan, M., et al. (2005). Agent based modelling: Why bother? In International conference on system dynamics 2005.

De Gues, A. (1988, March). *Planning as learning, managing uncertainty, Harvard business review*.

Forrester, J. W., & Senge, P. M. (1980). Tests for building confidence in system dynamics model. *System dynamics, TIMS studies in the management science* (Vol. 14, pp. 209–228). North Holland: New York.

Graham, A. L. (1980). Estimating lengths and orders of delays in system dynamics models. In Randers (Ed.) *Elements of the system dynamics method*. Cambridge, MA: MIT Press. Reprinted by Pegasus Communications: Waltham, MA.

Homer, J. (2012). *Models that matter: Selected writings on system dynamics*. New York: Grapeseed Press.

Lane, D. C. (1992). Modelling as learning: A consultancy methodology for enhancing learning in management teams. *European Journal of Operational Research, 59*(1), 64–84.

Lane, D. C. (2015). Validity is a matter of confidence—but not just in system dynamics. *Systems Research and Behavioural Science, 32*(4), 450–458.

Lane, D. C., Monefeldt, C., & Husemann, E. (2003) Client involvement in simulation model building: Hints and insights from a case study in a London hospital. *Health Care Management Science, 6*, 105–116.

Lewis, G., Curry, N., Bardsley, M. (2011). *Choosing a predictive risk model*. London: Nuffield Trust.

Liker, J. K. (2004). *The Toyota way*. New York: McGraw-Hill.

Luke, S., Cioffi-Revilla, C., Panait, L., Sullivan, K., & Balan, G. (2005). MASON: A multiagent simulation environment. *Simulation, 81*, 517–527.

Luke, D. A. I., Stamatakis, K. A. (2012, April). Systems science methods in public health: Dynamics, networks, and agents. *Annual Review of Public Health, 33*, 357–376. https://doi.org/10.1146/annurev-publhealth-031210-101222. Epub 2012 Jan 3.

Marshall, D. A., Burgos-Liz, L., IJzerman, M. J., Osgood, N. D., Padula, W. V., Higashi, M. K., et al. (2015a). Applying dynamic simulation modelling methods in health care delivery research—The SIMULATE checklist: Report of the ISPOR simulation modelling emerging good practices task force. *Value in Health, 18*(1), 5–16).

Marshall, D. A., Burgos-Liz, L., IJzerman, M. J.,Crown, W., Padula, W. V., Wong, P. K., et al. (2015b). The ISPOR emerging good practices task force, selecting a dynamic simulation modelling method for health care delivery research—part 2: Report of the ISPOR dynamic simulation modelling emerging good practices task force. *Value in Health, 18*(2), 147–160.

Richardson, G., & Andersen, D. (2010). Systems thinking, mapping and modelling in group decision and negotiation. In D. M. Kilgour & C. Eden (Eds.), *Advances in group decision and negotiation: Handbook of group decision and negotiation* (Vol. 4, pp. 313–324).

Roberts, M. S. (2015). *Dynamic simulation in health care comes of age. Value in Health, 18*(2), 143–144.

Sadsad, R., McDonnell, G., Viana, J., Desai, S. M., Harper, P., & Brailsford, S. (2014). Hybrid modelling case studies. In S. Brailsford, L. Churilov & B. Dangerfield (Eds.), *Discrete-event simulation and system dynamics for management decision making*. Chichester, UK: John Wiley & Sons Ltd. https://doi.org/10.1002/9781118762745.ch14.

Simul8, www.simul8.com.

Sloan, S. A., & Hsieh, C. R. (2017). *Health economics*. Cambridge: MIT Press.

Sterman, J. D. (2000). *Business dynamics: Systems thinking and modelling for a complex world*. New York: Irwin/McGraw-Hill.

Sterman, J. D. (2018) *System dynamics at 60: The path forward, system dynamics review* (Vol. 34), Numbers 1–2, January-June, 2018.

Viana, J. Brailsford, S. C., Harindra, V., & Harper, P.R. (2014, August 16). Combining discrete-event simulation and system dynamics in a healthcare setting: A composite model for Chlamydia infection. *European Journal of Operational Research, 237*(1), 196–206.

Vennix, J. (1999). Group model building: Tackling messy problems. *System Dynamics Review, 15* (379), 401.

Vennix, J. A. M. (1996). *Group model building: Facilitating team learning using system dynamics.* Chichester: Wiley.

Viana, J., Brailsford, S. C. Harindra, V., & Harper, P.R. (2014). Combining discrete-event simulation and system dynamics in a healthcare setting: A composite model for Chlamydia infection. *European Journal of Operational Research.* https://doi.org/10.1016/j.ejor.2014.02.052.

Gruen, Wonderling D. R., & Black, N. (2005). *Introduction to health economics.* Maidenhead, Berkshire: Open University Press.

XJ Technologies, Software Program "AnyLogic", ver. 6, St. Petersburg, Russia, 2007.

Yucel, G., & Barlas, Y. (2015). Pattern recognition for model testing, calibration and behaviour analysis. In H. Rahmanda, R. Oliva, & N. Osgood (Eds.), *Analytic methods for dynamic modellers* (pp. 173–206). Cambridge, MA: MIT Press.

Wolstenholme, E. F., Henderson, S., & Gauine, A. (1993). *The evaluation of management information systems: A dynamic and holistic approach.* Wiley: Chichester.

Part II
Projects for Dynamically Balancing Health and Social Care Capacities

Chapters 7–10

Overview of Part II

Part II presents four chapters describing examples of projects used in practice with management and clinical teams to help understanding on the complex issue in government-funded health economies of balancing health and social care capacities over time. The common theme of these chapters centres on boundary issues. This is the complexity caused by the flow of patients through long pathways which cross boundaries between very different and often autonomous agencies.

We start in Chap. 7 by presenting two examples of our models to shed light on the persistent and costly problem of delayed hospital discharges (delayed transfers of care). This is the situation where patients who are clinically ready to leave hospital are unable to do so due to waiting for post-hospital health and social care services. The work dispels some obvious solutions to the problem and points to the need to balance social care spending with health care spending to sustain good patient flow.

This is followed in Chap. 8 by a comprehensive model of flows into and out of social care from both the community and hospital and capturing elements of integrated care between health and social care. The works show that there are small changes which can make a difference but that ultimately, it is difficult to avoid the underlying problem of lack of social care capacity.

Chapter 9 also deals with balancing capacities, but this time across mental health services for depression. Our example model here was used to improve access to depression services by introducing stepped care between primary and specialist services.

Chapter 10 builds on the delayed hospital discharge work to develop a systems hypothesis of how hospitals handle excessive demand by employing numerous coping strategies at many points along patient pathways. System archetypes are used to describe the coping strategies and their unintended consequences. It is suggested that insufficient social care capacity is again a major determinant of all coping strategies, and that coping strategies could lead to more risks and costs to patients and staff than balancing health and social care capacities in the first place. Also important is recognising the symptoms of coping early and taking steps to return to working within best practice capacities.

The models in Part II can be thought of as focussing on *where* to intervene in patient pathways to effect best leverage on patient flows. This is in contrast to Part III of the book where the emphasis is more on models to test *how* the impact over time of alternative preconceived ideas will improve patient flows and costs.

Chapter 7
Hospital Delayed Transfer of Care (Delayed Discharges)

Chapter Overview

This Chapter describes the persistent issue in health care delivery of delayed hospital discharges, its proposed solutions and the contribution of system dynamics modelling to clarify the problem and provide insights. Two models are described which are typical of the many studies carried out by the authors on this subject.

The first is a simple variation on the hospital model introduced in Chap. 2 with an extension of the patient pathway beyond hospital discharge and into Adult Social Care. This model captures the basic characteristics resulting from a single patient pathway passing through different organisations and having inevitable boundary issues.

The second model was one built soon after the delayed discharge issue came onto the legislative agenda in England. It was developed in a project carried out jointly for the NHS Confederation as the representative of the NHS and the Local Government Association (LGA) as the representative of Social Care. It represents a typical health community in England and comprises medical and surgical hospital beds, three components of post hospital care and 'intermediate care' initiatives.

Numerous conclusions are drawn but the most important is the importance of keeping adult social care spending in line with hospital spending. That is to prevent Social Care being a bottleneck and to balance patient throughput across the whole patient pathway.

7.1 The Issue

Delayed transfer of care is a long-standing issue in the UK which can be traced back to the closure of convalescent homes but occurs to differing degrees in many other countries. In fact, wherever hospital discharge is government funded and constrained by multiple agencies providing services required by those being discharged. In systems terms, it is a problem of a single patient pathway passing through different organisations and having inevitable boundary issues.

The issue centres on patients occupying hospital beds although they have been declared as "medically fit" for discharge. This situation can happen in such cases as mental health patients waiting for housing but is most prevalent in the case of older people in hospital waiting for places in adult social care and continuing health care. It is basically an artefact of a caring society where care places are subsidised to try to ensure everyone is looked after post-discharge.

Although small compared with the total number of hospital patients, delayed discharges constitute significant loss of hospital capacity for crucial elective procedures, significant risk of infection associated with longer hospital stays and increased cost.

In the UK, the main organisations involved in delayed discharges are health and adult social care—health being funded by central government and social care funded (and delivered in part) by Local Government Authorities (except in Northern Ireland). Social care also consists of many different services broadly classifies as nursing homes (private and local authority controlled) which provide nursing care, care homes which provide social care, domiciliary care (which means care at home) and NHS continuing care, which embraces services such as district nurses.

The scale of the problem is significant. In 2016/17 there were 2.3 million delayed transfer days in England, an average of around 6,200 per day and 25% higher than the previous year. Approximately half of these transfers was attributable to waiting for further health services and half to waiting for social care.

Estimates of the cost of delayed transfers to NHS providers vary but all are significant sums of money. The National Audit Office in its 2016 report found the total annual cost to the NHS was £820 m (National Audit Office 2016). Delays attributable to social care have been estimated as £173 million in 2017 (Bate 2017) and £289 m in 2018 (Age UK).

Additionally, local government social care is reported to be on the brink of crisis with budgets having shrunk by £7 bn since 2010. It is estimated there will be a £2.5 billion funding gap by 2019/20, which is considerably more than can be met by the current government offer of £2bn over the next 3 years from 2017. Further, a government target for delayed discharges of 3.5% of hospital bed days by September 2017 has not been met. It is suggested that, unless additional funding is found, more people will be denied access to care and pressures will increase for service users, their families and carers. The situation is not helped by the low esteem in which social care staff have been traditionally held. Staff turnover was recently reported as being 28% (Kings Fund/Nuffield Trust 2017).

Proposed Solutions

Delayed hospital discharges were made part of the legislative agenda with the Delayed Discharge Act of 2003 and this was replaced by the Care Act 2014. The underlying principles embedded in these acts ranged from fining local authorities for delayed hospital discharges, to improving joint working between health and social care. The latter has taken the form of combining health and social care budgets (NHS Wales and Scotland and small parts of England now operate in this way), to the recently proposed establishment of a "Better Care Fund" (NHS England 2016). This is a pooled budget between Local Authorities and the NHS to better integrate health and social care services. A further proposed solution has been to move medically fit patients to separate pathways for discharge assessment. In order to emphasise their commitment to better integration in 2017 the UK government recently renamed the post of the England Secretary of State for Health to the Secretary of State for Health and Social Care.

However, Health and Local Government Social Care are vastly different organisations with their own budgets, power, culture and information systems and there remains distrust between the two. In addition to Social Care, Local Government is responsible for local services of all kinds, including budgets for education and waste disposal and in times of austerity has to prioritise its own spending. These other sectors of Local Government are also in crisis, with Education in particular suffering significant cuts to teacher numbers.

There are also significant differences in the order of magnitude of the stock and flow parameters of the two agencies. Hospitals are characterised by high throughput and short stays (days). Many parts of social care, such as care and nursing homes, on the other hand, are characterised by having low throughput and long stays (weeks/months) which can sometimes lead to differences in their pace of change.

Despite growing awareness by many of the role of social services in improving hospital patient flow, there is still some evidence of denial and the issue remains an intractable problem.

The Contribution of System Dynamics to the Issue

This chapter describes how system dynamics simulation of the whole system pathways through hospital and out into social care and NHS continuing care has been used to clarify the problem and provide insights both nationally and regionally. Two models are chosen for presented which are typical of the many modelling projects carried out on this subject by the authors beginning in 1999 (Wolstenholme 1999).

But before describing the example models it is important to put the work in context and to clarify what it does and does not do. Ultimately the work is related to the remits set.

There are a multitude of constraints which lead to delayed discharges. These vary from the number of beds and care packages available in different wards and establishments to capacities associated with assessments, equipment availability, funding, disputes, family choice and rehabilitation. All these could be modelled in detail but, as discussed briefly in Chap. 1, there is always a choice in modelling between being sufficient aggregate to help simplify complex situations, whilst being sufficiently detailed to be meaningful. In practice, finding the right perspective for a model generally requires starting at a reasonably high level of abstraction followed by some expansion and contraction.

The first model described is an extension of the simple hospital model introduced in Chap. 2. It represents almost the minimum detail necessary to capture the interconnections of health and social care and results from simplifying a number of more complex models without losing their integrity. Such controlled simplification is an integral part of good modelling practice and result in good training models.

The second is a more complex model built to capture the interplay of the many different types of pathway encountered in hospitals and social care. For example, the emergency, surgical, medical and intermediate sectors of hospitals and the nursing home, care homes and domiciliary pathways of social care. This model is referred to as the 2004 national model, first used in a project carried out soon after the delayed discharge issue came onto the legislative agenda. This was carried out jointly for the NHS Confederation (as the representative of the NHS) and the Local Government Association (LGA) as a representative of Social Care. At the time of this modelling the government's solution centred on a proposal to fine local authorities for delayed hospital discharges and the purpose of the project was to help the LGA explore the consequences of this proposal. The remit was for consultants working with the representatives of the two organisations to create a system dynamics model of the 'whole patient pathway' extending upstream and downstream from the stock of people delayed in hospital, to identify and test alternative interventions.

In both cases the objective was to demonstrate the effects of constraints in general, rather than any one in particular. Moreover, it was to demonstrate the unintended consequences of intuitive solutions and to identify what might be win-win rather than lose-lose policies between the agencies.

7.2 A Two-Capacity Patient Pathway Model

Figure 7.1 shows a map of a simple two capacity patient pathway model which builds on the models introduced in Chap. 2. The model consists of 4 stocks, 'wait for hospital' and 'being treated' as before in Chap. 2, plus 'awaiting care' and 'receiving care' in adult social care. The social care sector of the model is described by care packages but actually is representative of all types of post hospital services.

7.2 A Two-Capacity Patient Pathway Model

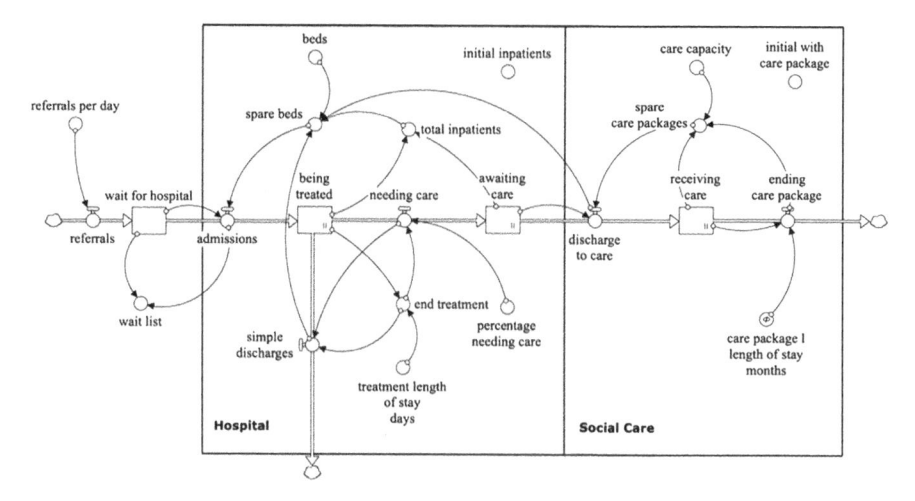

Fig. 7.1 Two capacity patient pathway model

In Fig. 7.1, organisational sectors are superimposed on the pathway to clearly show the boundaries between hospital and adult social care and hence to demark which pathway variables are under the influence/control of which organisation.

The map in Fig. 7.1 recognises that most people will be simple discharges to home, but that a small percentage of people will need post treatment care packages and will move to the stock 'awaiting care'. The people in this stock are those who have finished treatment, but whose discharge is dependent on the availability of care packages in adult social care. The total number of people in hospital is now the sum of two stocks (being treated and awaiting social care) and the length of stay in hospital is the sum of the treatment time and the time total awaiting care. Also, the 'wait for hospital' stock has been moved outside the hospital boundary, although some wait will actually be within the hospital.

In this representation, the hospital discharge rate is now shown to be outside the hospital boundary indicating that it is largely under the control of adult social care. So, the emphasis here is on delayed discharges due to social care. This sector has a stock of 'receiving care' and its own discharge rate and care capacity. It should be clear from Fig. 7.1 that the structure of the patient pathway in the social care sector is exactly the same as is described for the hospital sector. To recap, admissions to either sector are only possible if there are spare places, calculated as the gap between the capacity of each sector and the patients in the sector, plus the discharges from the sector.

This two-capacity pathway representation of Fig. 7.1 forms the core of many of our later models and is powerful map in its own right, capable, when simulated, of demonstrating some interesting insights.

Data

The data for the model, which is typical of many situations found in practice, is as follows:

beds = 520
care capacity = 1600
care package length of stay = 12 months
initial inpatients = 520
initial with care package = 1500
needing care = 5%
referrals = 100 per day
treatment length of care = 5 days
cost of a hospital bed = £400 per day
cost of an adult social care package = £40 per day
simulation time horizon = 6 months (914 days).

Performance measures for the model are as follows:

Waiting for hospital
Beds
Inpatients
Awaiting care
Care capacity
Cumulative total costs
Cumulative discharges to care

Design of Experiments—Dynamic Equilibrium

The concept of dynamic equilibrium was introduced in Chap. 2 and it is good experimental design practice to set a model up in equilibrium and then introduce shocks and solutions to see how the behaviour over time is affected. This procedure ensures that there is nothing happening in the model until change is introduced and the procedure is a cornerstone of model validation.

Unlike static equilibrium, where an object is at rest, dynamic equilibrium is a balanced state of a stock which appears static, but where there is movement through it. Dynamic equilibria exist in many forms through nature and managed systems and by definition it is created when the rates of inflow to a stock are equal to the rates of outflow.

In nature clouds are excellent examples of dynamic equilibrium. Clouds are created by moving currents of air activated by pressure and temperature differences. In particular, orographic clouds are formed when winds encounter an obstacle like a mountain and are forced upwards to pass over it. When air rises it expands causing it to cool and droplets of water condense to form the cloud. As the air falls beyond

Fig. 7.2 Orographic clouds in dynamic equilibrium

the mountain these droplets evaporate. Individual droplets may only have a life of 10 min, but if the rate of condensation equals the rate of evaporation the cloud appears to exist apparently motionless over mountain tops for hours when it is actually in an airstream flowing at 70 mph or more. See Fig. 7.2.

We could describe (and model) the phenomena in terms of stocks and flows, where the condensation rate and the evaporation rate respectively feed and drain the stock of water in the cloud which remains effectively constant. In dynamic equilibrium, the rates that feed and drain stocks are always equal but not static.

It is often said particularly in economics and social science that equilibrium is an impossible and ideal state. However, dynamic equilibria often occur in all managed systems when rates of demand and supply are equal.

Simulation Results

The base experiment is to run the model in equilibrium over the whole period of 12 months, to calculate the base cumulative costs and cumulative discharges to care resulting from no interventions. These are £247 million and 408,000 people respectively and are reproduced at the top of all subsequent figures for comparison with a number of intervention experiments.

Intervention experiments involve running the model of Fig. 7.1 in equilibrium until time 220 (days) (with just a little spare capacity), when the rate of referral is increased, causing the wait list to rise and then trying alternative interventions to counter this rise at time 240.

The first experiment is to increase hospital beds and the results are shown in Fig. 7.3. There are 3 graphs shown. The first is the number of people waiting for hospital, the second the hospital capacity, inpatients and numbers of people awaiting care and the third the adult social care capacity and the people receiving social care.

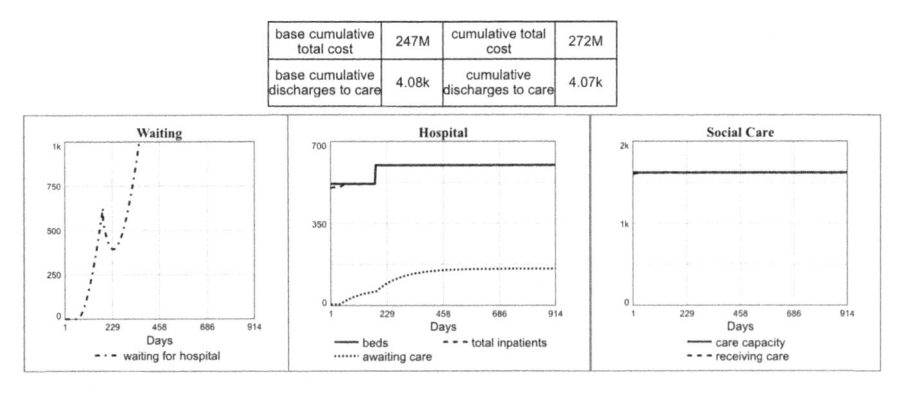

Fig. 7.3 The effect of increasing hospital capacity on costs, throughput and waiting

At time 240 the hospital capacity is raised from 520 to 600 beds. This has a dramatic effect in reducing the numbers waiting for hospital, but the effect is very short-lived. As soon as the new beds are full the waiting rises sharply again. The cost of these beds is significant but, despite their implementation, the cumulative discharges to adult social care is little different to that without these beds.

These results contrast strongly with the second experiment of increasing adult social care capacity. Figure 7.4 shows a similar simulation, but this time with adult social care capacity increased from 1500 to 1850 at time 240. As will be seen, this policy change causes waiting lists to rapidly decline to zero and there is actually a little spare capacity in hospital.

Further, the cumulative discharges to care are much higher and the costs not much above the base experiment.

In a patient pathway where there are 2 capacity constraints in series, it would appear that relieving the first (upstream) one can only result in temporary respite,

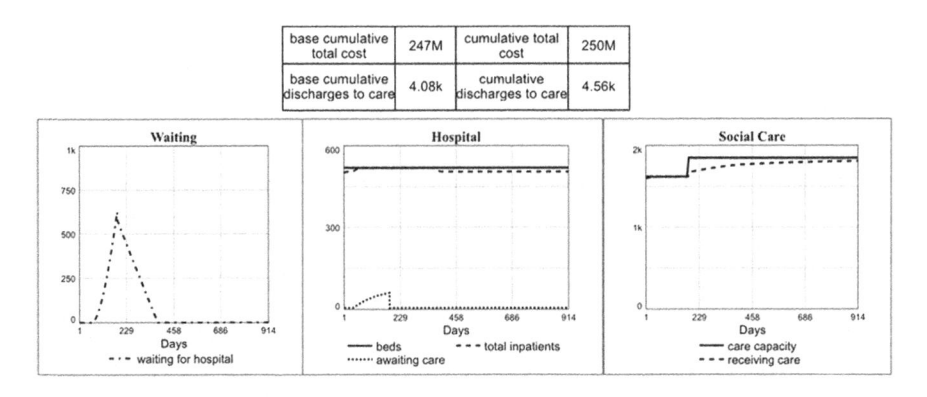

Fig. 7.4 The effect of increasing social care capacity on costs, throughput and waiting

7.2 A Two-Capacity Patient Pathway Model

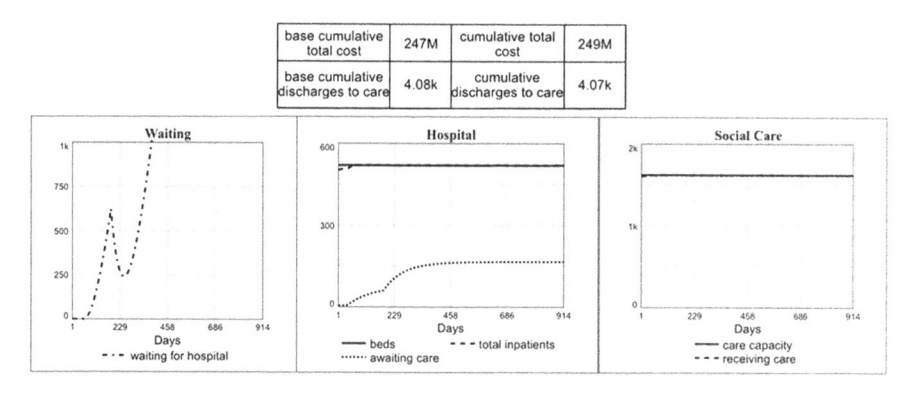

Fig. 7.5 The effect of reducing hospital treatment time on costs, throughput and waiting

whereas relieving the second (downstream) one can provide sustainable throughput increases and cost reductions.

This leads to the thinking that, as in many supply chains, it might be a beneficial win-win solution if the trapped organisation in the chain (in this case the hospital) invested in the organisation trapping them (in this case social care).

Figure 7.5 shows an additional experiment and results from reducing the length of hospital treatment and a similar pattern emerges to Fig. 7.3. Reducing hospital treatment time has only a transient effect on waiting.

The lack of impact of reductions in hospital treatment times here is interesting. Unlike the simple two-stock model in Chap. 2, where it was possible to increase throughput by reducing hospital treatment times, this is no longer possible in the case where there are two capacity constraints.

The perhaps worrying element of this statement is that it indicates that hospital productivity innovations can be negated by social care capacity constraints. To fully realise the effect of reductions in hospital treatment times it is necessary to increase social care capacity at the same time.

Figure 7.6 shows an experiment to demonstrate this. Here, at time 240, hospital length of treatment is reduced to 4 days and social care capacity is increased to 1850. Rather than realising the benefits in terms of increased throughput, hospital capacity is reduced in this experiment to realise the benefits in terms of cost reductions. It will be seen that this gives similar throughput to Fig. 7.4, but at significantly reduced costs.

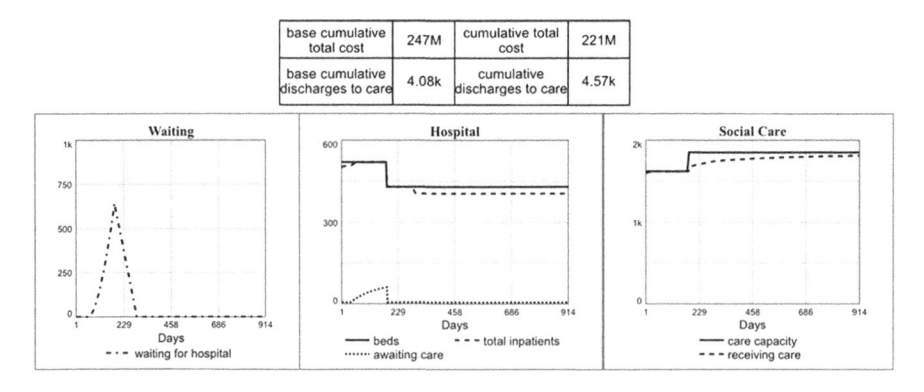

Fig. 7.6 The effect of reducing hospital treatment times in parallel with increasing social care capacity and reducing hospital beds

7.3 The 2004 National Model of Delayed Hospital Discharge[1]

Figure 7.7 shows a simplified overview of this model which represents a typical health community in England and comprised medical and surgical hospital beds, three components of post hospital care and 'intermediate care'. Post-operative intermediate care was included as an intermediate sector where patients with complex assessment needs might be moved to free up acute beds. Some pre-operative intermediate care was also included as a means of diverting some patients from hospital altogether.

Again, all sectors in the hospital were capacity constrained and the shorthand term "beds" used to mean essentially the total number of hospital places of a particular kind and subsuming staff and theatre constraints and set at the acute hospital's intended level of occupancy (90% of the number of beds available).

Patients with relatively straightforward conditions and few onward care needs were assigned relative short average lengths of treatment whilst those with more serious conditions having very specific onward care needs were moved into the state of awaiting discharge to meet those needs.

The model also included a number of assumptions:

1. Medical and surgical emergencies would always be admitted.
2. If surgical elective beds were not available, patients for these would stay on the elective wait list.
3. Coping strategies could be brought into play in times of need. For example, if medical beds were under pressure some patients could be treated in surgical beds; these are referred to as outliers or boarders. These people will be referred

---

[1] A description of this model first appeared in Wolstenholme et al. (2008) and is reproduced with the permission of Springer-Verlag.

7.3 The 2004 National Model of Delayed Hospital Discharge

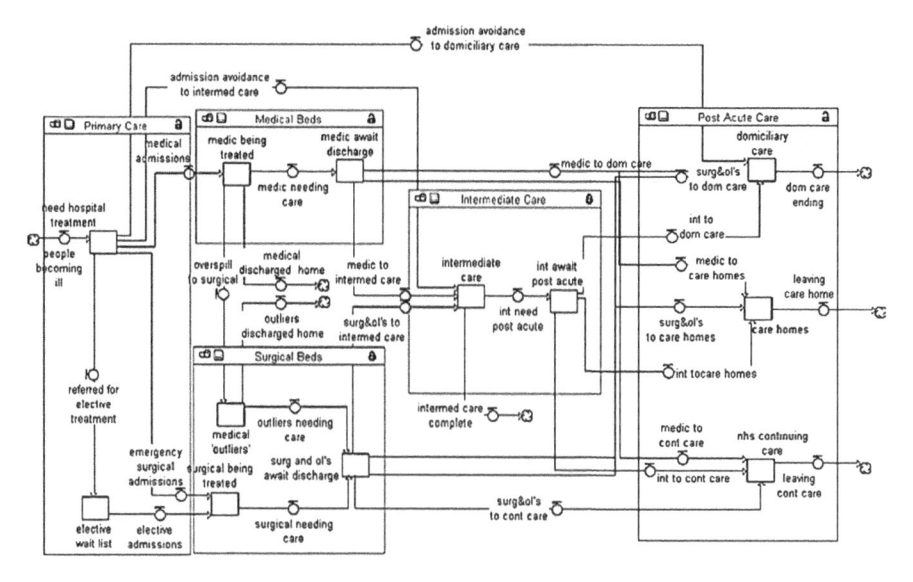

Fig. 7.7 A simplified representation of the 2004 delayed discharge model

to throughout the book as boarders. This strategy would deal with the immediate problem of emergency patients needing to be admitted but would result in the cancellation of elective operations.
4. Patients with onward care needs would be held in "await discharge" stocks until care packages became available for them.

Data and Experiments

The data used for the model was that of a typical health community and involved demand, capacities, average lengths of treatment and percentages of patients typically using each pathway.

The model was set up to simulate a typical health economy over a 3-year period in days when driven by a variable demand (including three winter "peaks"). The capacity constrained sectors of the model were given barely sufficient capacity to cope with winter peaks. This situation was designed to created shocks against which to test alternative policies for performance improvement. Major performance measures in use in the various agencies were incorporated. These included:

1. cumulative episodes of elective surgery
2. elective wait list size and wait time
3. numbers of patients in hospital having completed treatment and assessment, but not yet discharged (delayed discharges).
4. number of 'boarders'

Numerous polices were tested using the model with the three major experiments as follows:

1. Adding additional acute hospital bed capacity. This was seen at the time as the classic response used over many years by governments throughout the world to solve any patient pathways problem and was a favourite 'solution' at the time of the study.
2. Adding additional social care capacity, both nursing and residential home beds and more domiciliary care packages.
3. Diverting more people away from hospital admission by use of pre-hospital intermediate capacity and also expansion of treatment in primary care surgeries.

Example Results from the Delayed Hospital Discharge Model

The following figures show some typical outputs for the delayed hospital discharge model. Figure 7.8 captures the way capacity utilisation was displayed (actual beds occupied v total bed capacity available for both medical and surgical sectors of the hospital) and shows the occurrence of 'boarders' (transfers of patients from medical to surgical beds) whenever medical capacity was reached.

The next two Figures show comparative graphs for 3 policy experiments of the model.

Figure 7.9 shows delayed hospital discharges and Fig. 7.10 cumulative elective procedures in hospital.

In each case the base experiment result is line 1. Line 2 shows the effect of increasing hospital capacity by 10% and line 3 shows the effect of increasing Social Care capacity by 10%.

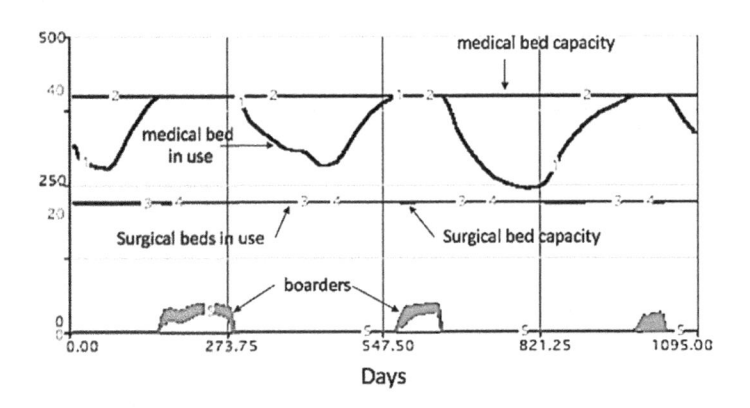

Fig. 7.8 Boarders plus medical and surgical bed 'Capacity' and 'In Use'

7.3 The 2004 National Model of Delayed Hospital Discharge

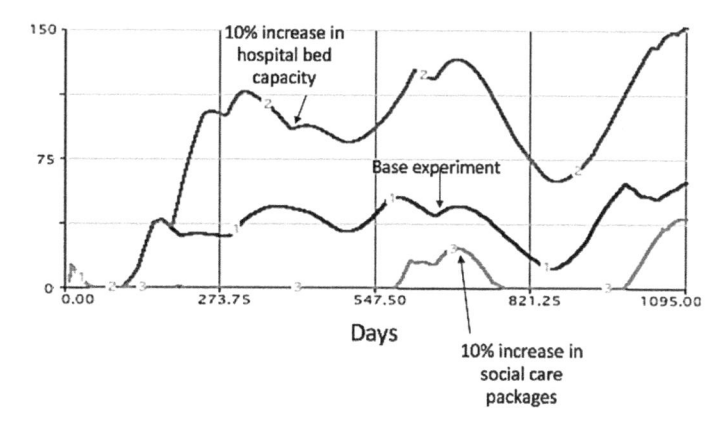

Fig. 7.9 Delayed hospital discharges for three policy experiments with the model

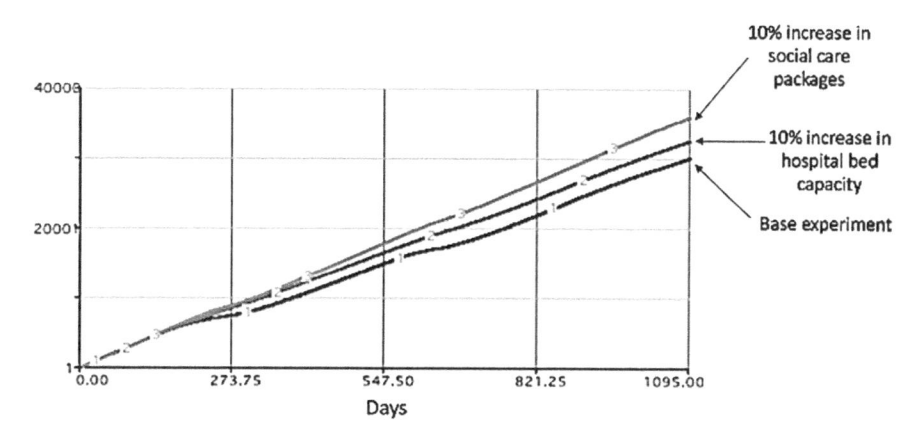

Fig. 7.10 Cumulative elective operations for 3 policy experiments of the model

The interesting feature of this example output is that the cheaper option of increasing social care capacity gives a lower level of delayed discharges and a higher level of elective operations, whereas the more expensive option of increasing acute hospital beds benefits the hospital a little but makes delayed discharges worse.

The key to this counter intuitive effect is that increasing social care capacity results in higher hospital discharges which in turn reduces the need for the 'boarders' coping policy in the hospital, hence freeing up surgical capacity for elective operations.

7.4 Conclusions from the 2004 Delayed Hospital Discharge Model

The main learning for the modelling team was that common-sense solutions can be misleading.

The obvious unilateral solution by health of adding more hospital capacity can exacerbate the delayed discharge situation as also demonstrated in the results for the two-capacity pathway model in Fig. 7.1. More hospital admissions will be made in the short term, but no additional discharges will be possible. Hence, the new capacity will simply fill up and the medical backlog will increase again.

This effect can be described as an 'out of control' system archetype introduced in Chap. 5, where a well-intended control action is undermined by an unintended consequence which has the opposite effect to that intended.

The characteristics of this archetype are shown in Fig. 7.11. The intended control action is a balancing feedback loop (B) on the left. Here a control action is taken as a problem increases and the purpose is to reduce the problem. The unintended consequence is a reinforcing feedback loop (R) on the right which represents a system reaction to the control. This latter loop makes the problem worse but only manifests itself well after the intended control action and is often hidden by some real or imagined boundary. In other words, the unintended consequence may be known when the control is introduced, but the need for control is so urgent that short-termism rules and the later unintended consequences which undermine the control are often ignored.[2]

Figure 7.12 shows how this archetype plays out for the introduction of more beds to solve delayed discharges from hospital.

Delayed hospital discharges cause an increase in waiting time for hospital admissions. The policy of increasing hospital beds is intended to allow more admissions and reduce waiting. This is shown by the balancing loop. However, increased admissions leads to more inpatients and after a delay to more delayed discharges (assuming the mix of patients stays the same) and increases waiting again. This is shown by the reinforcing loop.

Similar archetype thinking can also be used to demonstrate the unintended consequences of fining Social Care for delayed discharges as captured in Fig. 7.13.

---

[2]Summary of the rules for drawing feedback loops:

1. Balancing (B) (or negative) feedback loops are target seeking control loops and have just one or an odd number of negative links between variables.
2. Reinforcing (R) (or positive) feedback loops are growth loops and have all or an even number of negative links between variables.
3. Positive links are when an increase in a tail variable of a link gives rise causally to an increase in the head variable (and vice versa).
4. Negative links are when an increase in the tail variable of a link gives rise causally to a decrease in the head variable (and vice versa).

7.4 Conclusions from the 2004 Delayed Hospital Discharge Model

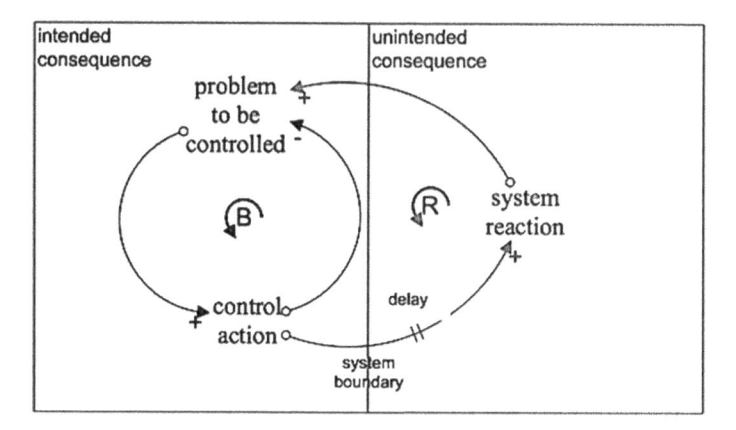

Fig. 7.11 The 'problem' structure of the 'out of control' two-loop archetype

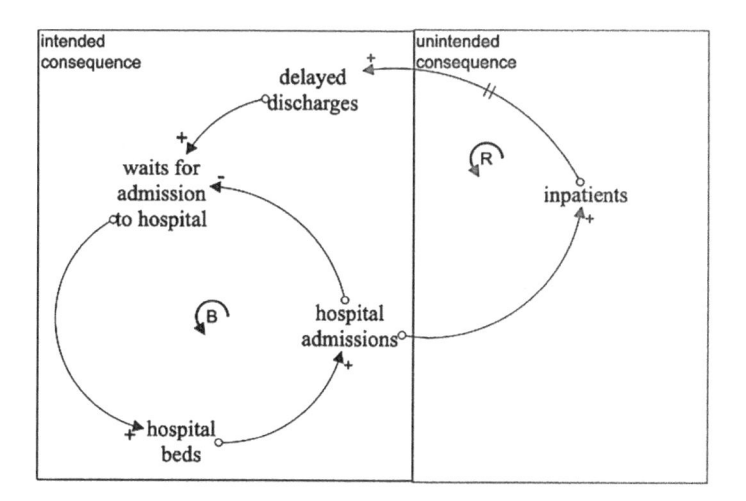

Fig. 7.12 Adding more hospital beds as an 'Out of Control' system archetype

Here, the introduction of a balancing feedback loop to control rising numbers of delayed discharges by fines is overtaken by a number of reinforcing feedback loops.

If introduced on a large scale the fines could both increase social care costs and hospital revenues. This solution would be at its worst if hospitals used the money levied from social services to finance additional capacity and if social care had to cut capacity. The effects of service cuts could also spill over into other areas of local government including housing and education.

Both these effects would have the opposite effect on delayed discharges to the intended.

It was concluded that there were some interventions that could help:

- As in the first model in this chapter, increasing social care capacity was demonstrated to provide a win-win solution to both health and social care. This

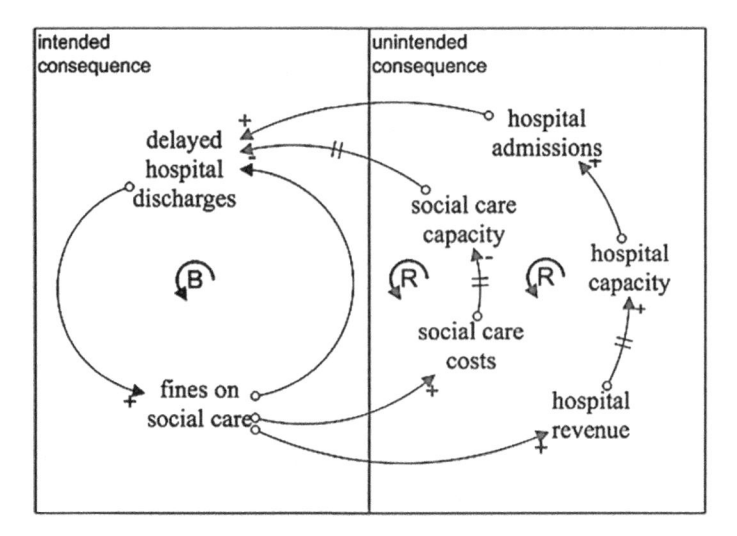

Fig. 7.13 Fining social care as an 'Out of Control' system archetype

solution improves all hospital and social care performance measures used here and allows hospital capacity to be better utilised and increased if necessary with no unintended consequences.
- Further, counter intuitively, increasing medical capacity in hospital was shown to be more effective than increasing surgical capacity for reducing elective wait times. Primarily, this effect is because the need for 'boarders' is avoided.
- Reducing assessment times and lengths of stay in all sectors would be beneficial to all performance measures.
- Increasing diversion from hospitals into pre-admission intermediate care was almost as beneficial as increasing social care capacity, but this assumes that those diverted do not also have on-going care needs.
- If fines are levied they need to be re-invested from a whole systems perspective. This means re-balancing resources across all the sectors (not just adding to hospital capacity).
- Improving the quality and compatibility of data system in health and social care is paramount to realising the benefits of all policies.

In systems terms an interesting generalisation of the findings was that increasing *stock* variables where demand is rising (such as adding capacity) is an expensive and unsustainable solution. Whereas increasing *flow* variables, by reducing delays and lengths of stay, is cheaper and more sustainable.

Impact of the National Delayed Hospital Discharge Model

This model was demonstrated at the Labour Party Conference of 2004 and generated considerable interest. It was instrumental in causing some re-thinking of the intended legislation. Social Care was provided with investment funding to address capacity issues, and the "fines" (re-titled "re-imbursement") were initially delayed for a year. Fines were subsequently used intermittently and eventually banned in the 2014 Act. Reference to the model was made in the House of Lords (see Insert 7.1).

Insert 7.1
"Moving the main amendment, Liberal Democrat health spokesperson Lord Clement-Jones asked the House to agree that the Bill failed to tackle the causes of delayed discharges and would create perverse incentives which would undermine joint working between local authorities and the NHS and distort priorities for care of elderly people by placing the requirement to meet discharge targets ahead of measures to avoid hospital admission….. *He referred to the whole systems approach being put forward by the Local Government Association, health service managers and social services directors involving joint local protocols and local action plans prepared in co-operation*"

Concluding Remarks

This Chapter has provided two examples of the contribution system dynamics modelling can provide to the issue of delayed hospital discharges.

Both clearly demonstrate that in a patient pathway which has two separate agencies with individual capacity constraints in series it is important to:

- free up both capacities together:
    - to increase total pathway throughput
    - fulfil the potential of the upstream agency
- not be tempted to make matters worse by increasing the capacity of the upstream agency alone or by penalising the downstream agency.

The 2004 national model, which allowed for some aspects of intermediate care demonstrated that freeing-up very expensive acute hospital beds is useful in that it reduces costs. The idea of multiple levels of step-down care for delayed discharges is taken further in the integrated care modelling in Chap. 8 which incorporates more sophisticated representations of how such services connect both in *parallel* and in *series*. However, these facilities do not get away from the overwhelming fact that patients are still trapped by Social Care capacity constraints and the need to balance capacities across the different stages of the patient pathway.

The overall conclusion from both models is the importance of keeping adult social care, spending in line with hospital spending. That is to prevent social care being a bottleneck, to take away the need for 'boarders' and to balance patient throughput across the whole patient pathway.

The use of boarders is a hidden strategy widely used in practice and built into the 2004 National Model. Although not seen like the major policies tested in the models, it is one of the key informal policies by which hospitals cope with delayed discharges. It is vital when modelling to surface and include such informal strategies as they are the key to understanding why a system behaves as it does. More generally, the use of boarders is one of the ways hospitals cope with high demand and will be explored further with other such coping policies in Chap. 10. Indeed, the conclusion here of keeping health and social care spending in balance to reduce delayed discharges works well to also reduce many more expensive coping measures used by hospitals to withstand periods of high demand and Chap. 10 and should be read in conjunction with this chapter.

A final point on this issue is to highlight that it is only a relatively small number of frail elderly patients, like Mrs Jones of Chap. 1, who contribute most to the delayed hospital discharge problem. Current hospital practice, and hence an assumption of our modelling, is that this cohort of frail elderly patients is mixed with all other patients in undergoing hospital treatment. This leads to the thought that if patients with a potential to cause delayed discharge could be identified at the time of admission to hospital it might be possible to:

1. Monitor their progress differently from other patients
2. Design a separate pathway to cater better for their needs
3. Start the social care discharge process at a much earlier stage of their hospital treatment.

This idea is taken further in the risk assessment work described in Chap. 14. Here a risk stratification tools and are used alongside a case management approach to interrogate a 'patient at risk of readmission' database to identify those at high risk of being admitted to hospital. The use of system dynamics in this project suggested that identification and impact could be increased if the 'churn' (flow) of patients through the data base was measured as well the number of patients (stock) in each stratum of risk.

References

Age UK Press release 9/7/2018.
Bate, A. (2017, June). *Delayed transfers of care in the NHS*. Briefing paper no 7415. House of Commons Library.
Kings Fund/Nuffield Trust. (2017). *The autumn budget: Joint statement on health and social care*. Nuffield Trust, Health Foundation, Kings Fund.
National Audit Office Annual Report. (2016).
NHS England. (2016). *Better care operating guide*. NHS England.

Wolstenholme, E. F. (1999). A patient flow perspective of UK health service. *System Dynamics Review, 15*(3), 253–273.
Wolstenholme, E. F., Monk, D., & McKelvie, D. (2008). Influencing and interpreting health and social care policy in the UK. In H. Qudrat-Ullah, M. J. Spector, & P. I. Davidsen (Eds.), *Complex decision making: Theory and practice* (pp. 155–185). US: Springer-Verlag.

Chapter 8
Integrated Care

Chapter Summary
Current thinking to improve hospital flows and provide benefits to people in both health and social care is to move towards integrating health and social care delivery by introducing a much wider range of linked services. This chapter describes a modelling approach to test out some aspects of integrated care. The model and its experiments are described which demonstrate the effects on flows and costs of 'balancing' care in this way. As before, it is shown that obvious solutions are not the best but that small changes in reducing flows from social care to hospitals can have a significant impact on the problem of delayed hospital discharges. Ultimately however, it is also suggested that whilst many of the ideas of integrated care are helpful there is no escaping the need to balance social care capacity with health capacity. Finally, a discussion of the challenge of modelling services which are connected in both series and in parallel is discussed in an appendix.

8.1 Integrated Care

'Integrated care' denotes ways of co-ordinating the delivery of diverse services to the same person, based on the belief that services should be centred on the person, not the provider (Ham 2018). Versions exist in most countries.[1] Within the UK, there are different variations in each of England, Scotland, Wales, and Northern Ireland. Although it is tempting to frame the discussion in terms of integration *between* health and social care, it is also important to integrate service delivery *within* each of health and social care. It may also be argued that in some respects health services are already TOO integrated. Large general hospitals

---
[1] See, for example, the International Foundation for Integrated Care.

integrate so many multiple specialties that managers and clinicians are often able to make their own pragmatic operational decisions. The use of 'boarding' to accommodate unscheduled hospital admissions in elective beds is an obvious example of the flexibility they have. However, as discussed at length in Chap. 10 such coping strategies can have serious unintended consequences for patient efficacy and costs.

In the UK, the nature of the integration challenge is largely political. What each part of the UK has in common is that healthcare is provided by the National Health Service, whose founding principle is that the cost is borne by the state out of general taxation, and treatment is free at the point of delivery.[2] Social care (care at home or in residential settings) is the responsibility of local government,[3] and many service users are charged.[4] Therefore, if health and social care were to be fully 'integrated' under the NHS principle of 'free at point of delivery', that would mean providing social care free of charge, leading to major cost increases. Successive governments have struggled to square this circle.[5] Moreover, as more powers are devolved to Scotland, Northern Ireland and Wales, any debate about how to fund social care becomes harder to frame or follow.

Nevertheless, there does seem to be a broad consensus in favour of integration (Ham 2018). In Scotland, parts of the NHS along with the social care system are now jointly run by statutory Health and Social Care Partnerships (legal entities), with greater powers to move funding between services. In England, the integration debate is framed in terms of Sustainability and Transformation Partnerships, which are evolving into becoming (non-statutory) Accountable Care Systems or Organisations (NHS Providers 2018) with similarities to USA models such as pioneered by Kaiser Permanente. In Wales, legislation underpins a partnership approach. Northern Ireland always had a more integrated approach, with social care provided by the same body that delivers health services; Health and Social Care Northern Ireland (HSC).

However, it is framed legally, the challenge in planning, designing and commissioning integrated services,[6] is to balance capacity (and flow) across a wide range of services. The pathways of integrated care are much more complicated (and somewhat more complex) than in the delayed discharge example shown in the previous chapter. We will illustrate this with a model that was developed in Scotland.

---

[2]With some exceptions, for example, charges exist for (a small fraction of) prescriptions, and dental services.

[3]Except in Northern Ireland.

[4]There are various 'means tests', and in some parts of the UK some services, or elements within services are free.

[5]It was a major issue in the 2017 General Election.

[6]Terms that will mean slightly different things in different places.

8.2 Modelling Integrated Care (the 'Balance of Care')

This more recent model of (just about) the 'whole system' of health and social care generates precisely the same insights as in the earlier ones, about the need to balance capacities across the different stages of a service-chain, but with more sophisticated representations of how services connect both in parallel and in series, to produce a wide range of behaviour. In particular, this model represents social care dependency states and flows into social care from the community as well as flows into and out of social care from health.

A high-level view of the model is shown in Fig. 8.1 showing how demographics and dependency states are linked to health treatments, community facilities and finance.

As Table 8.1 shows, the model captures, in much more detail than the delayed discharges models in the previous chapter, a key difference between health and social care services, that health services tend to be **episodic**, and that adult social care services tend to be **long-term**, representing life-stages, including 'end-of-life'

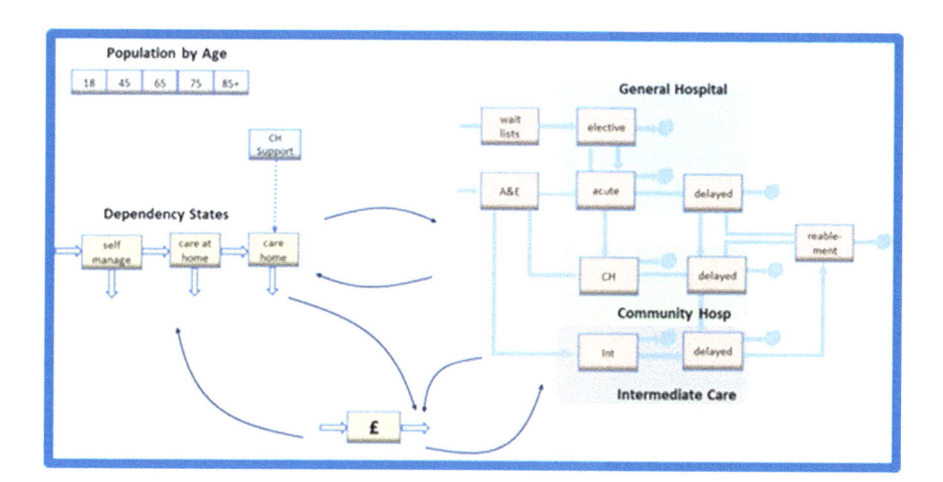

Fig. 8.1 High-level view of an integrated care model

Table 8.1 Comparing long-term and episodic services

Long term (dependency) services	Episodic hospital and intermediate services
• Thought of as 'social care' • Commissioned by local authorities • Focus on 'care' • States or stages of being	• Thought of as 'health care' • Commissioned by the NHS • Focus on 'cure' • Episodic
Success looks like • 'holding onto people' • prolonging length of stay • keeping people well	Success looks like • 'moving people on' • reducing length of stay • making people better

stages. To use Pieters' (2013) characterisation of 'care and cure', health services are more (but by no means entirely) about 'cure' and social care services about 'care'.

With 'cure' services, reducing length of stay without compromising treatment effectiveness is almost always a good thing; the less time spent in hospital the better. By contrast, **increased duration** of use of a 'care' service (such as care at home) may be a positive indicator because it represents the slowing down of a person's loss of independence. As a result of good care at home, a person will live at home for longer, because they are more likely to be eating good food in a safer environment, and less likely to be experiencing accidents, such as falls or food poisoning. Increased 'length of stay' in a care service is almost always a positive indicator, and, as such, a rare example in health and social care of a virtuous reinforcing feedback loop.

In order to represent the nested stock/flow structure of this type of model, full use is made of the modular capabilities of the Stella Architect software. Without modules, drawing such a complicated stock/flow diagram would be challenging. To communicate what is going on inside such a model also requires a carefully-designed model interface as shown in Fig. 8.2.

Figure 8.3 shows a high-level view of the 'health' part of this model.

By 'high-level' view, we mean that there is further detail, and behaviour, within each of the stocks shown.

The main pathways are, simply, an elective pathway which is almost self-contained. People are referred onto elective waiting lists, admitted when a bed is available, and discharged, based on a relatively short length of stay. This should

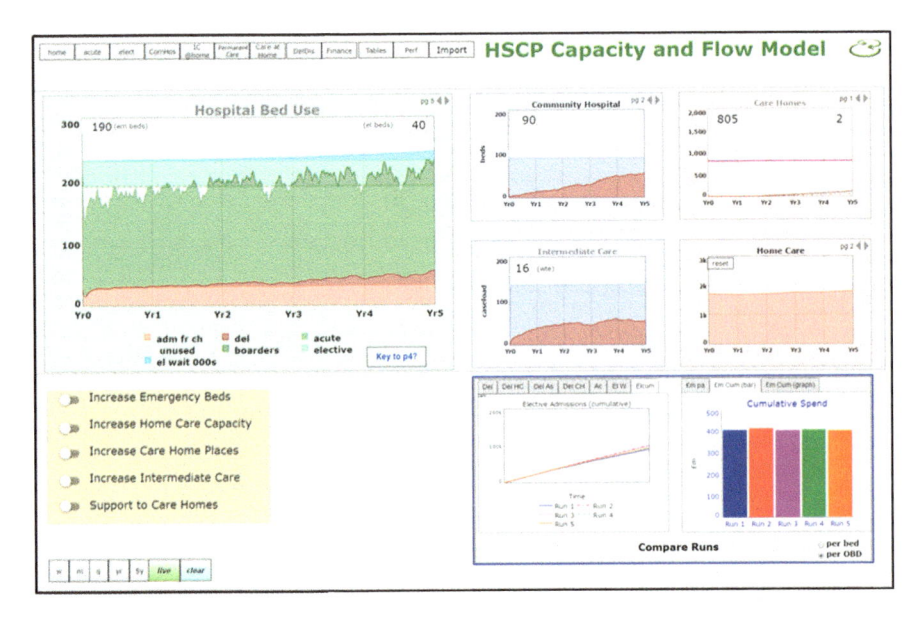

Fig. 8.2 Integrated care model interface

8.2 Modelling Integrated Care (the 'Balance of Care') 145

Fig. 8.3 High level representation of health services in the integrated care model

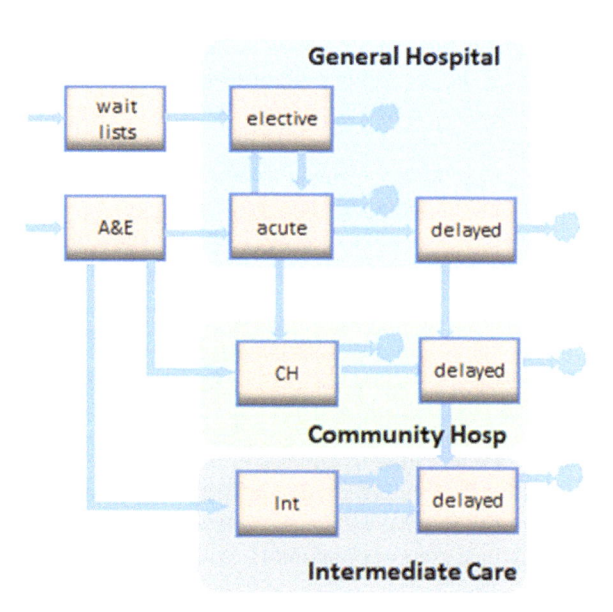

make it straightforward to calculate the required elective bed capacity, but the significant complication that arises is that acute (non-elective) patients may be transferred into elective beds at times when the hospital system is under pressure, especially in winter, resulting in the cancellation of elective procedures and larger waiting lists with longer waiting times.

The emergency pathway begins with arrival at Accident and Emergency (there are some other entry points depending on local circumstances, for example, patients referred by primary care). Here, patients are assessed, some are admitted, others, such as frail older people with less-acute conditions, may be admitted to 'community hospitals' (often with a long stay) or to 'intermediate care' (which takes multiple forms, sometimes bed-based, sometimes, as in this example, intensive home care).

Integrated Care, Delayed Discharge and the 'Balance of Care'

In all three settings (general hospital, community hospital, and intermediate care) it is possible for people to become 'delayed', because they need a form of social care. In this model, there are two main types of delay (waiting for a care package at home, waiting for a place in a care home).

People admitted to general hospital, go through various stages (represented in stock/flow structures not shown in the high-level diagram but similar in nature to those used in Chap. 7).

- Initially, they are in a stock of 'need acute', they are in an acute hospital because that is the appropriate place to be
- Then they move to a stock of 'no longer need acute/onward needs being assessed', representing people who could now manage in a less-intense setting (e.g. community hospital or intermediate care) but whose future needs (for care) are not yet assessed
- Finally, they move to a stock of 'delayed', meaning that their onward need (for home care, or a care home) is known, but there is not yet a place available ('delayed discharges').

Depending on the interplays of available capacity, therefore, as shown in Fig. 8.3 it is possible for people to transfer from general hospital to community hospital or intermediate care

- as an alternative to admission (for some)
- whilst their future needs are still being assessed
- when they have become a 'delayed discharge' (because it is better to wait in an intermediate or community setting than in an acute bed).

This type of system dynamics model with its multi-level pathways and linkages between health treatment dynamics and population/dependency/episodic dynamics can shed light on a broad range of problems associated with the treatment of older people.

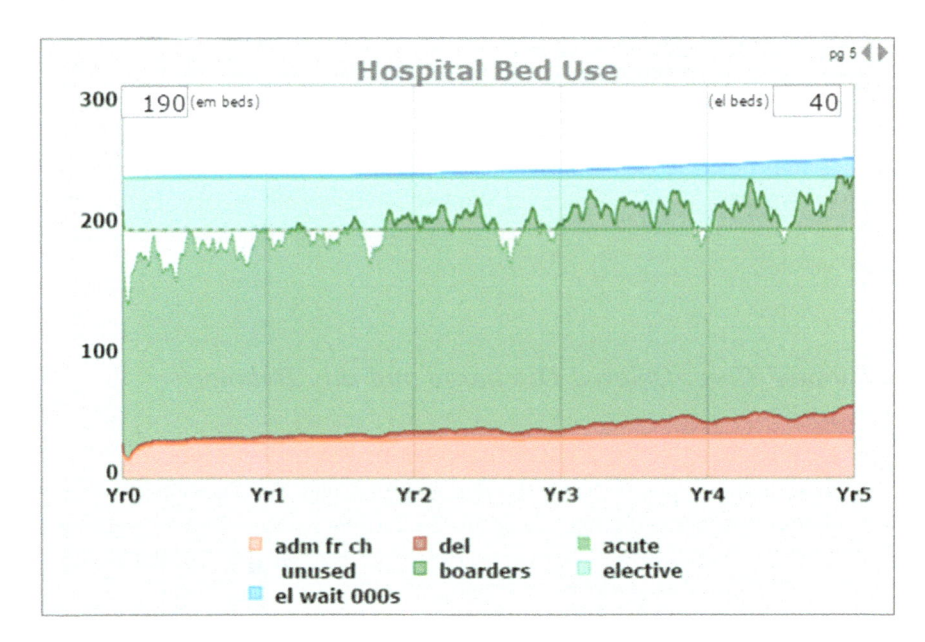

Fig. 8.4 Bed use in general hospital (integrated care model 'base run')

8.3 Running the Integrated Care Model

These dynamics can be shown in a series of experiments, the main outcomes of which can be demonstrated on a single graph.

Base Run

This one graph, although at first glance quite complicated, cleverly summarises a great deal of this model's behaviour by showing the impact of various interventions on the general hospital, with capacity divided between Emergency Beds (190) and Elective Beds (40).

The horizontal line crossing the graph at a value of 190 represents the total emergency (unscheduled) bed capacity. Elective bed capacity is shown above this line between a value of 190 and 230 (i.e. 40 beds). Unscheduled referrals vary from day to day (exogenous input). And referrals gradually increase over time in line with changes in the population (particularly, in this version, growth in the older population).

Occupancy of emergency beds is, from the bottom:

- people whose normal residence is a care home, many of whose admissions are believed to be preventable
- 'delayed discharges'—mostly people waiting for a 'care package' at home or for a care home place
- 'acute', hopefully the largest segment, people who currently need to be in an emergency bed (people appropriately admitted and not ready for discharge)

'unused' capacity, if applicable, is shown (most obviously in years 1 to 3, but thereafter, population growth renders that a rare occurrence)

Occupancy of elective beds is more straightforward:

- at peak times, 'acute' patients occupy elective beds (known as 'boarders'), a well-known coping mechanism in general hospitals
- elective patients (appropriately placed); because their need is not urgent, when boarders overspill into elective beds, fewer elective patients can be accommodated
- the graph could show empty elective beds, but there are none.

Finally, to get a picture of the impact of model scenarios on waiting lists, the elective waiting list (divided by 1,000 to fit the scale of the graph) is stacked on top.

In the example shown in Fig. 8.4, at the start of the five years, emergency patients do not overspill into elective beds, which are mostly fully-occupied by elective patients. As time passes, a combination of increased demand (growing older population) and increasing numbers of delayed discharges result in more

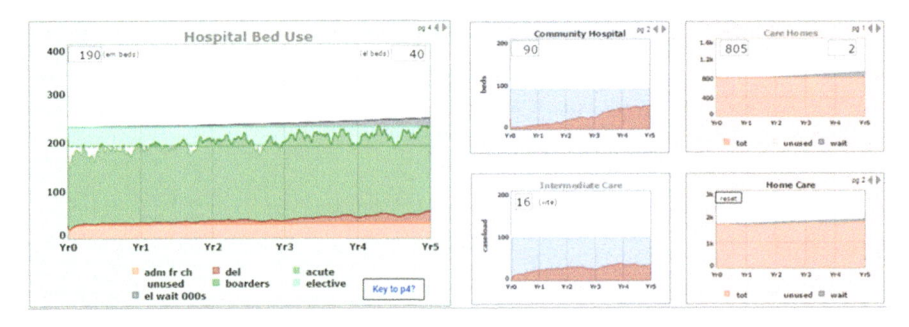

Fig. 8.5 Model dashboard (base run)

emergency 'boarders' in elective beds, and the elective waiting list rises relentlessly.

To get a more detailed picture of what is happening, the model dashboard also shows the occupancy/utilisation of the other key services (Fig. 8.5).

The dashboard layout shows hospital on left, and long-term services (people's 'state of living') on the right. In the middle are intermediate-type services (community hospital and intermediate care). In these graphs, the red-shaded area shows the occupancy of these services that is itself 'delayed discharges', of people awaiting either home care or care homes. The grey-shaded area above the red shows the waiting list for each of those services.

There are innumerable scenarios that could be explored.

Adding Emergency Bed Capacity (the '+Beds' Scenario)

This run simulates classic silo-thinking as used in Chap. 7. Noting that there is a problem with emergency patients spilling over into elective beds, what would happen if we increased emergency beds by 20? As expected, the number of emergency boarders reduces as the emergency system is better able to cope, but this is a costly option, because 20 extra beds have been commissioned, and no obvious savings made elsewhere in the system.

The impact is possibly best illustrated in Fig. 8.7 which compares these two graphs of 'admissions per day'. By increasing emergency capacity (graph on right), actual emergency admissions are exactly the same, and it is elective admissions that increase. These graphs also illustrate another of the challenges that is built into this model, which is a (realistic) increase in the older population, where emergency beds are mostly sufficient in the first year of the base run (note that elective admissions are largely flat). In the '+beds' scenario, it takes two years before this problem emerges; consequently, the wild oscillations in the elective admissions graph are less pronounced.

8.3 Running the Integrated Care Model

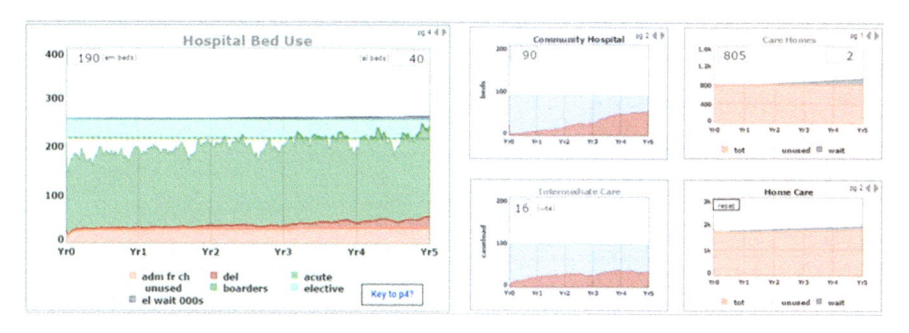

Fig. 8.6 Run '+beds'—emergency beds are increased by 20 throughout the run

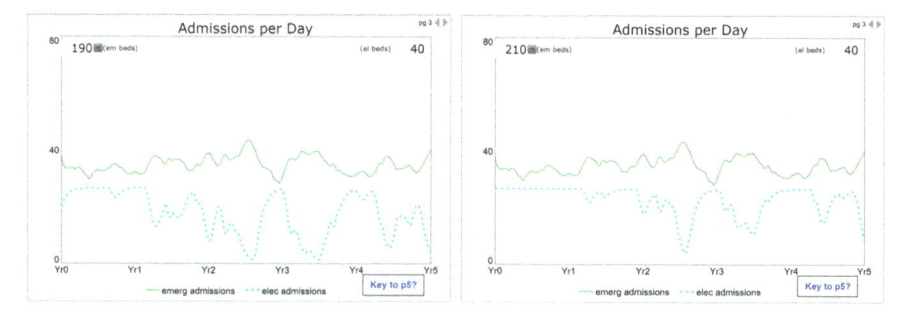

Fig. 8.7 Elective and emergency admissions comparing base run with '+beds'

As Fig. 8.13 and Table 8.2 (which summarise all of the model runs) show, the obvious downside to the '+beds' run is that it costs more, a cumulative increase of £7 m (increase from £401.7 m to £408.5 m spend over five years).

And as Fig. 8.6 makes very obvious, adding emergency capacity does nothing to help avoid 'delayed discharges' at any point in the system (Fig. 8.7).

Adding Home Care Capacity (the 'hc' Scenario)

In this run, home care capacity is increased gradually over the length of the model run, to take account of population change. As the main graph in Fig. 8.8 makes clear, this leads to a significant reduction in delayed discharges in hospital and in intermediate care (there are still delayed discharges in community hospitals, where people are more likely to be delayed because they need a care home place).

This results in lower emergency occupancy, fewer boarders in elective beds, and more elective admissions. This increase in elective activity is slightly less than in the '+beds' run, but, as Fig. 8.13 and Table 8.2 show, this increase in home care capacity results in an overall reduction in the five-year cost across the whole

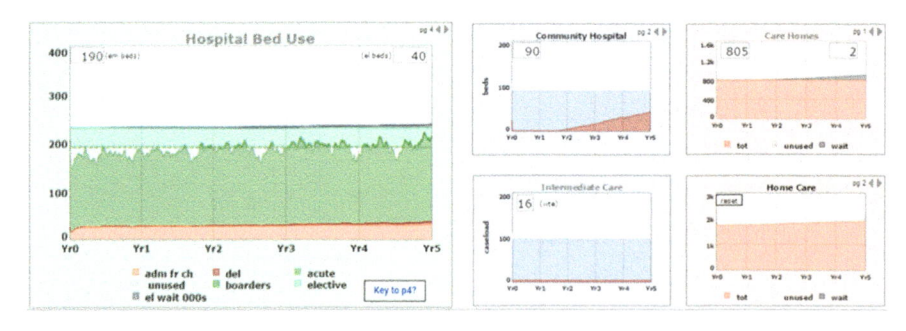

Fig. 8.8 Run 'hc'—home care capacity is increased gradually over time

system, and with about 10% more elective patients treated. Shifting the balance of care seems to work.

Adding Care Home Capacity (the 'ch' Scenario)

This run (Fig. 8.9) is similar to the 'hc' run, but with capacity added to care homes rather than to home care. In this case, there are reductions in delayed discharges in emergency beds and community hospitals, along with a welcome increase in elective admissions. Because there is less of a reduction in delayed discharges (compared with the 'hc' run), there is a slight increase in overall costs, compared with the 'hc' run.

Another possible scenario, not shown in this chapter, would be combining the 'hc' and the 'ch' runs, increasing capacity in both.

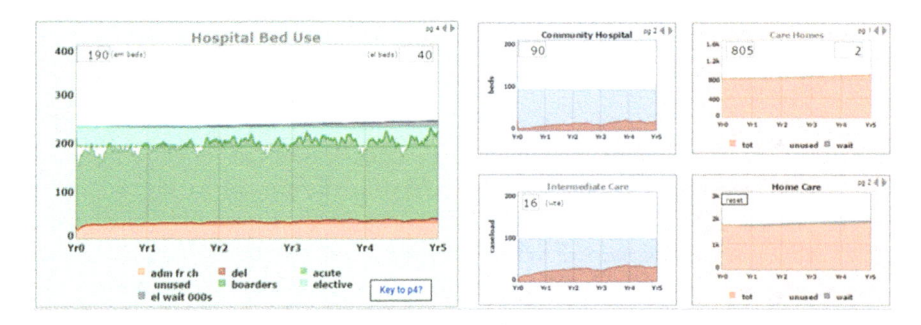

Fig. 8.9 Run 'ch' care home capacity is increased gradually over time

8.3 Running the Integrated Care Model   151

Adding Intermediate Care (the 'ic' Scenario)

The impact of intermediate care is more subtle because it sits between hospital and community-based services. The obvious benefits of intermediate care are that:

- some admissions can be avoided altogether
- some discharges can be made earlier
- some people whose discharge is delayed can, at least, move out of hospital
- for many people, it is a more appropriate setting than an acute hospital bed
- it is less expensive than acute hospital

However, capacity planning for intermediate care services is difficult, because its occupancy at any given time depends on what is happening in the connected services, especially downstream in social care. Ultimately, if there is insufficient home care capacity, there will be delayed discharges, and the impact of intermediate care might well be to provide a service for people whose discharge is delayed and who could be using home care. That is still a benefit, if we assume that people should move out of hospital at the earliest opportunity. But if intermediate care is regularly serving people who could be using a standard care package at home, it would be better to shift the balance of care more towards home care.

These issues are shown in Fig. 8.10 though perhaps hard to perceive on the Hospital Bed Use graph because the reduction in delayed discharges in hospital is small in relation to the graph scale. The increase in delayed discharges within intermediate care is more obvious. And, as Table 8.2 shows more clearly, in the extra intermediate care capacity scenario, elective admissions over five years increase from 87,429 (base) to 90,922 cumulative spend goes down from £401.7 m (base) to £399.4 m.

Adding Care Home Support (the 'chs' Scenario)

The 'care home support' (chs) scenario simulates the impact of a service whose purpose is to provide additional community nursing support to care homes. In many

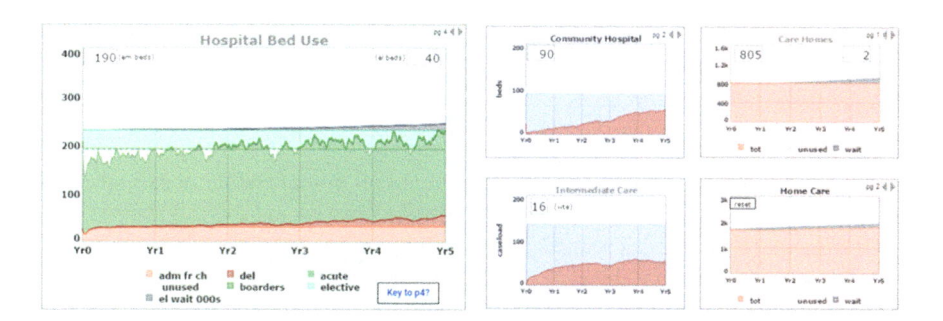

Fig. 8.10 Run 'ic'—intermediate care capacity is increased by 40 places

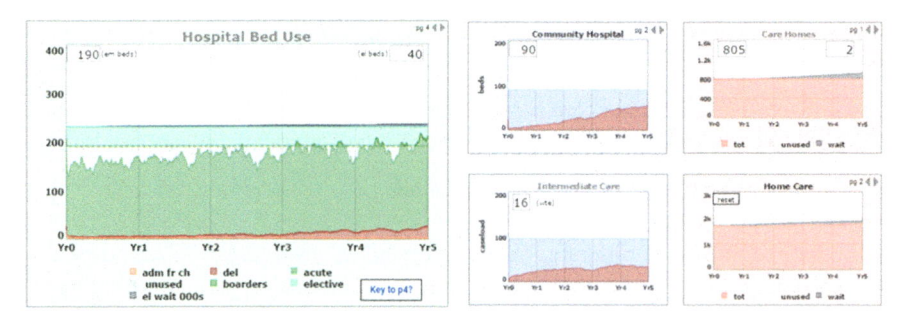

Fig. 8.11 Run 'chs'—care home support staff increased from 2 to 12

cases, it would be better if people who live in nursing homes are not admitted to hospital when their condition deteriorates or they become acutely ill, including when they are at their 'end of life'. There is a broad consensus that wherever possible people should not die in hospital, where it can be difficult for family members to visit/remain at the bedside. By providing nursing and medical back-up to care homes (there are various models of what such a service would look like) very many hospital admissions could be avoided altogether and, if admission does take place, the length of stay in hospital could be significantly reduced.

As is clear from the Hospital Bed Use graphs in the base case and all other scenarios, people who were admitted from a care home form a significant proportion of the acute inpatient population. Figure 8.11 shows what might happen if the number of nurses providing support to care homes were to increase from two to 12 (full-time equivalent).

This proves to be the scenario with the biggest impact by far (on increasing elective activity and reducing costs, but with no impact on delayed discharges).

The emergency inpatient population falls to a level that almost completely eliminates the need for people to be boarded in elective beds. As Table 8.2 shows, elective admissions over five years increase from 87,429 (base) to 99,878, and cumulative spend goes down from £401.7 m (base) to £388.7 m.

Adding All Capacity Increases (Except Emergency Hospital Beds)

Finally, Fig. 8.12 shows a scenario that combines all of the interventions in the runs described (except increasing emergency beds, for obvious reasons). Because this is a simulation of a complex system, it would be naïve and invalid simply to add together the net changes in expenditure, or in elective activity from each run, because of the way in which the impacts interact. A change in service A affects service B, and a change in service B affects service A. However, as one might

8.3 Running the Integrated Care Model

Fig. 8.12 Run 'multi'—where all of runs hc, ch, ic and chs (but not +beds) are deployed

expect, combining all of these interventions, effectively 'rebalancing' care across a range of interconnected settings, is more powerful, and affordable, than any intervention taken on its own. More home care and residential care means fewer delayed discharges, whilst more intermediate care means that many of the delays that do occur take place outside the hospital. And care home support reduces the emergency inpatient population further.

Note also that in the run shown above, there is still a problem of delayed discharges in intermediate care in years two and three (as shown on the intermediate care graph, and caused by the emergence of a waiting list for home care, the thin dark section on top of the home care graph) (Fig. 8.13).

A 'comparative graph' is a graph of ONLY ONE variable, plotted for a series of model runs. In this model, we track multiple indicators in this way, including different types of delayed discharges, acute occupancy, elective waiting lists, and various spending metrics, including, as shown, 'cumulative' spend, across the whole system, over five years. This latter graph, being a bar chart, does not show 'behaviour over time' but is useful because changes in spending might vary. In

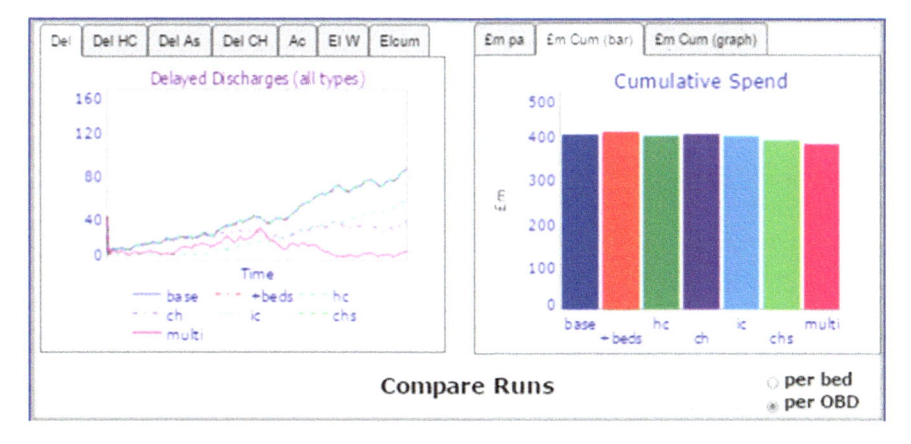

Fig. 8.13 Comparative graphs of all seven runs

Table 8.2 Total elective admissions and costs over 5 years for each scenario

	Elective admissions	Total cost (5 years)
Base run	87,429	£401.7 m
+beds	98,814	£408.5 m
Home care	97,811	£400.3 m
Care home	92,087	£403.5 m
Intermediate care	90,922	£399.4 m
Care home support	99,878	£388.7 m
Multi-intervention	100,474	£380.8 m

some runs, we spend more at the start then acquire savings over time. A good way to compare scenarios is therefore to track the cumulative spend over the whole period. Table 8.2 shows this alongside the cumulative elective admissions figure.

It is clear that the only scenario that costs more is, not surprisingly, to increase acute capacity (tackling the problem where it occurs, rather than tackling the underlying causes).

Of course, one should not track cost alone. A good example is that, increasing home care does not generate a great saving, but, **for roughly the same overall cost**, the system actually delivers 98,000 elective procedures rather than the baseline of 87,000 (on another graph, not shown).

8.4 Conclusions

This chapter has presented a comprehensive model of the interconnections between health and social care and the effects of both health and social care changes on a variety of performance measures, in particular overall costs and delayed hospital discharges. In terms of delayed hospital discharges it contributes to the debate on the merits of moving patients away from acute to less expensive settings, including 'at home' for discharge assessment. It has also demonstrated that small changes in the right place can make significant differences.

However, whilst these actions can significantly reduce costs, they can have an element of out-of-sight equalling out-of-mind and distracting from the issue that no matter where it happens any discharge still runs up against any lack of capacity in adult social care.

System dynamics helps to ensure that physical constraints of this type are always kept in mind and cannot be avoided. It applies what in engineering is referred to as 'mass balance', where models adhere to checks that inputs to a system equals outputs plus accumulations, so material ('people'!) can be neither created or destroyed within a model.

So, the bottom line is that this type of integrated care model still leads to the conclusions from the other models in Chaps. 7 and 10 that hospital delayed discharges must address the imbalances between hospital and social care investment.

8.4 Conclusions

Finally, this chapter has demonstrated how simulation helps thinking about impact, outputs, outcomes and performance measures in a very complex system and raises questions about what are the best ways of capturing the best summary data and presenting them on a dashboard. It also raises the challenge of how to deal with multiple two-way flows which are discussed in the Appendix.

Appendix: The Challenge of Modelling Integrated Care—Transparency, Allocation and Alternative Pathways

Transparency

When encountering public services, it can be tempting to make the analogy with a supply chain, where products make a journey from factory, to warehouse, to distributor, to retailer, to customer and as shown in earlier Chapters this can be helpful in health and social care. However, sometimes in human systems things are less straightforward and the health and social care system is arguably much more complex than any industrial process.

Unlike production, where materials mostly flow in one direction,[7] in health and social care people flow in multiple directions, miss out some stages and perhaps repeat others. The same service capacity might be used for different purposes; for example in Fig. 8.14, an 'intermediate care' service which has a single capacity, might be used BOTH 'upstream', as an alternative to hospital admission, AND 'downstream' to facilitate hospital discharge of people who have recovered somewhat, no longer need to be in hospital, but are not quite ready to go home. In the same system, some people might be waiting in hospital to be discharged to an intermediate care setting at the same time as other people in an intermediate care setting now need hospital admission, perhaps because their condition has deteriorated. Alternatively, people might be admitted to hospital having been users of a home care package, losing that package on or shortly after admission, then, several weeks later, cannot be discharged from hospital until another, identical or more intensive, home care package can be procured. Such eventualities are not only possible, but common.

Therefore, at any point in time, people are waiting to be transferred between services, when capacity allows, in various combinations:

- (waiting in A and needing B)
- (waiting in A and needing C)
- (waiting in A and needing D)

---

[7]With the possible exception of faults resulting in 'rework'.

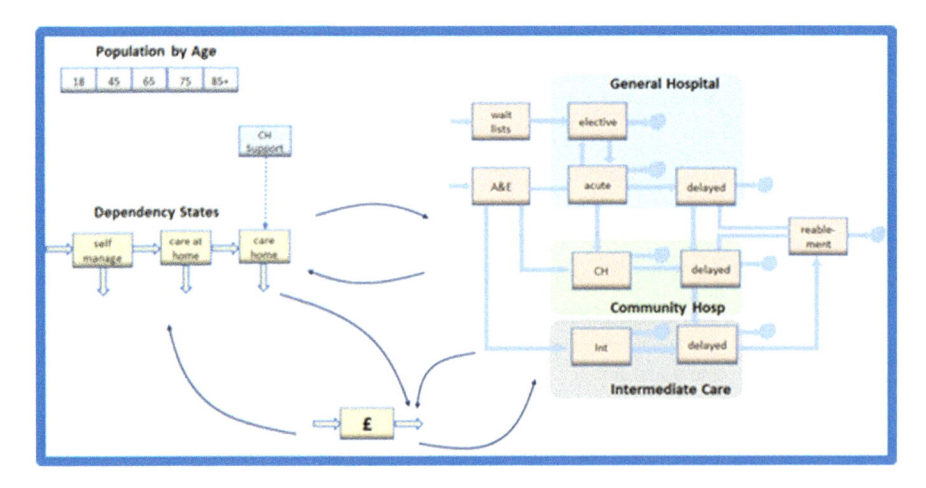

Fig. 8.14 (same as Fig. 8.1) High level view of integrated care model

- (waiting in B and needing A)
- (waiting in B and needing C)
- Etc. (but some pairings are not possible or likely).

This degree of disaggregation creates a challenge to the transparency of a stock/flow diagram. Depending on the software used, the model can be constructed with each service being represented as a single stock. These stocks are further disaggregated elsewhere on the model screen, using a co-flow structure and, in the case of Stella Architect software, using its modular capabilities.[8]

The disaggregated representation of each service will look something like the diagram in Fig. 8.15.

Each service might have people currently waiting for a place, of whom some are not currently using a service, and others are using other services. To make this diagram clearer, we have drawn 'sector frames' round the people who are 'waiting for A' and those who are using 'Service A'. Note that, in the diagram, those waiting but currently using other services are shown as 'ghosted' stocks (dotted lines), copied from elsewhere on the model. The stock called 'using service A' represents the number of people currently using service A and are appropriately placed. Service A is also being used by people who need, variously, services B, C, and E. And, in this example, nobody ever goes from A to D. The total number of people using service A is therefore the sum of the four stocks.

Note that another way of representing this degree of disaggregation more simply, would be to 'array' (or subscript) the 'waiting in' stocks.

---

[8]There is an interesting debate to be had about the benefits/drawbacks of using sub-model, or modular structures—ideally, we want to achieve the best possible means of conveying the essence of a system without concealing important structure.

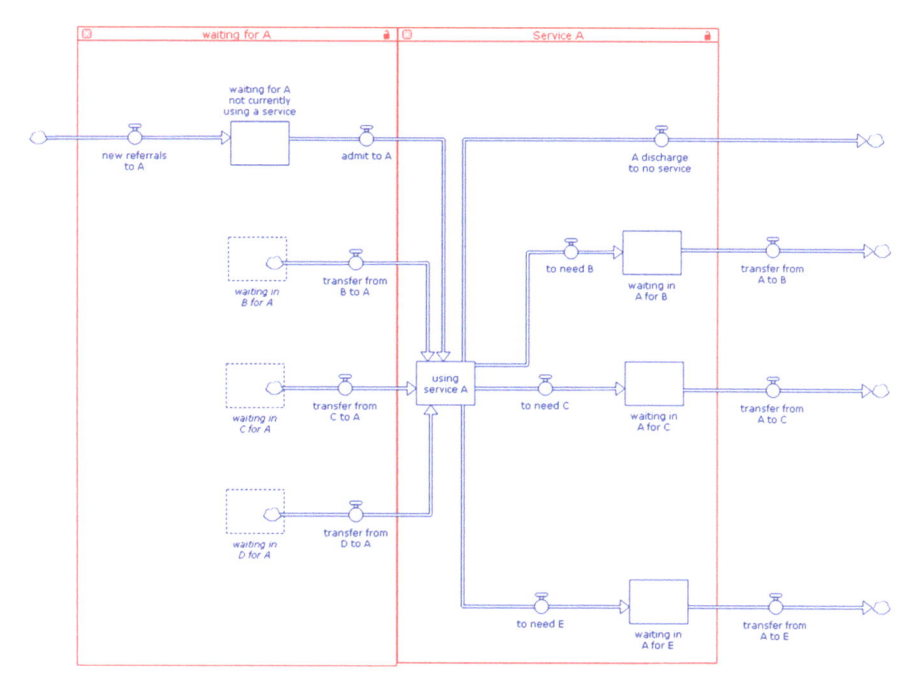

Appendix: The Challenge of Modelling Integrated Care … 157

Fig. 8.15 Disaggregated view of one service—note that the stocks drawn with dotted lines are copies of stocks that appear elsewhere in the model diagram

Allocation of People Waiting to Capacity Restricted Services

The key question that arises, for each service, is 'what is the policy for allocating spare places across the various waiting stocks?' Various possibilities apply, all of which can be modelled. For example:

- Spare places might simply be allocated in proportion to the number of people in each waiting stock
- Places might be allocated based on a very strict order of priority: we allocate spare places first to people waiting here, then to people waiting there, then there, and so on; one problem with this approach is that if the whole system is under pressure, some people 'waiting here, needing a place there' might never be allocated a place, in which case, the modeller must also bear in mind 'what happens to people who wait for a very long time?' because their state of health/ or need for care is likely to change
- Places could be allocated according to some kind of weighting system (we admit relatively more people from here but always some from there), which gets round the problem of some people never moving
- A variation might be to base that weighting on some kind of 'floating goal' derived from some other dynamic in the model, such as 'the length of time for

which people have been waiting to move from x to A'; for example, people waiting in B should wait no more than twice as long as people in C.

Obviously, the modeller should create an allocation policy that most closely matches the actual policies that are deployed (Sterman 2000, Chap. 15), assuming that these are known and can be codified. It is perfectly possible that what actually happens is the result of various informal decision-making heuristics that are brought to light by the modelling process itself and are poorly understood by key people across the whole system.

Alternative Pathways

A further important consideration with this kind of model is the question of 'what happens to people who wait for a long time in any one state?' Depending on where they are in the system, their condition might improve or deteriorate.

Where people are improving/recovering, it is common for people in hospital on reaching the status of 'no longer needing to be in hospital but needing something else' to 'step down' to some kind of intermediate care setting, the purpose of which might either be to provide care whilst a permanent home care package is organised, and/or to provide additional rehabilitation. In these cases, if intermediate care is NOT provided, they will remain in hospital for the duration of their recovery, then be discharged to a home care package when it is ready. Going back to Fig. 8.15, people waiting to transfer from A to B might actually transfer from A to C if B is not available in time (detail not shown in the diagram).

The opposite effect might happen in the case where the existing level of support for someone waiting is less than is needed (or completely absent). People waiting at home for a home care package to be arranged might be admitted to hospital. People on an elective waiting list might be admitted to hospital as an emergency.

To summarise, it is quite common in these structures to have at least two outflows from a waiting stock, the outflow to the service that is desired, and the outflow to the destination that will result if the desired service is not provided in time.

References

Ham, C. (2018). *Making sense of integrated care systems, integrated care partnerships and accountable care organisations in the NHS in England.*
NHS Providers. (2018). STPs and *accountable care background briefing.*
Pieters, A. J. H. M. (2013). Care and cure: Compete or collaborate? Improving inter-organizational designs in healthcare. In *A case study in Dutch perinatal care*. Tilburg: CentER, Center for Economic Research.
Sterman, J. (2000). *Business dynamics: Systems thinking and modelling for a complex world.*

Chapter 9
Implementation of a Stepped Care Approach to Depression Services

Chapter Summary
This chapter describes a novel approach to communicate and accelerate implementation of a stepped care approach to depression services in one region of England. The work was carried out in 2004 when guidelines for stepped care were first issued. It involved the development of a simulation model, combining the new guidelines with economic and resource allocation factors. This model was used to demonstrate to local health communities how rebalancing care resources across the whole patient pathway over time could result in significantly more patients being more appropriately treated, without any additional funding. A series of collaborative workshop was organised around the model. By providing an 'ideal' case for services, the model helped each member of the collaborative to operate a change management process. Each member could compare their own reality against the ideal as portrayed by the model, and identify gaps in commissioning, service provision and workforce together with incremental changes to move closer to the ideal service configuration.

9.1 Introduction

Like many other conditions the demand for mental health services is growing worldwide, both with population growth and the stress of modern life whilst supply of mental health services suffers from a lack of professionals. Mental health education and awareness is often lacking and there is a social stigma attached to the condition. Perhaps the biggest long-term problem has been issues with access to mental health services.

Traditionally, people presenting with a variety of mental health conditions have found themselves with either short episodes of general services or a long wait for specialist services. An almost all or nothing approach to service delivery.

In England the issue was addressed in 2004 for depression and anxiety with the publication of the National Institute for Health and Care Excellence (NICE 2004a, b) guidelines for 'stepped care'. This guidance described a range of easily accessed intermediate services between primary and specialist care applicable though primary care, community services and NHS Mental Health Trusts. The guidance was subsequently revised further in 2006.

The cornerstone of these services was the use of psychological techniques, in particular cognitive behavioural therapy. This technique received a further boost in 2006 with the role out by NHS England of a major programme for Improving Access to Psychological Therapies (IAPT), involving the recruitment of significant numbers of therapists. A model of this role out is described in Chap. 11.

In 2014 NHS England attempted to redress the problem further (Achieving Better Access to Mental Health Services by 2020, Department of Health, 2014) by accepting that for decades the health and care system in England had been stacked against mental health services and stacked against the people who use them by an imbalanced approach to health investment between physical and mental health.

The chapter reports on a study carried out at a regional level in England in the early stages of implementation of stepped care for depression in 2004. Here modelling was used not so much to assist with where to intervene but to add missing links in a programme of defined interventions to support the implementation of the NICE guidelines for depression in particular situations. The guidelines provided details of the services to be delivered but left it to regions to assess who would need them in the local population, the likely flows of people into and out of them and the staff capacity planning in each service. Apart from the health care communities in the region involved, this type of study was later implemented in 10 other mental health communities across England.

9.2 The NICE Guidelines for Depression and Implementation Issues

The NICE guidelines for a stepped care approach to depression services, specify clinically-proven, best-practice pathways to care via a series of steps, which recognise patient choice and preference. These steps involve: active monitoring (originally named watchful waiting), followed by primary care led guided self-help and other brief therapies, which only then lead to psychological interventions such a cognitive behavioural therapies (CBT) or medication and perhaps eventually to case management and longer-term specialist treatment. The main aim of a stepped care approach to depression is to simplify the patient pathways, provide access to more patients and to improve patient well-being and cost reduction. This is achieved by directing patient referrals, where appropriate, to low cost community-based treatments before high cost institutional or specialist services.

However, at the time of the study the guidelines had not been supported by robust implementation strategies and the uptake was left to local arrangements. Consequently, the concept of a stepped care approach to depression services was at very different stages of implementation across England and Wales.

Service providers (GPs and primary care mental health workers) were concerned that implementing the guidelines would take a lot of effort and cost. Commissioners were struggling with decisions of how to reallocate finite resources across a stepped system of care, where a large proportion of the available resources (people and money) were locked up in specialist services. The key challenge they raised was how they could make a case for the specialist part of the system to look at possible disinvestments and up-streaming of resources. Apart from communication and engagement of all parts of the patient pathway, commissioners were also concerned with more detailed matters such as the transition to stepped care, maintaining levels of care whilst adjusting current patient pathways at the same time creating new ones.

9.3 Using a System Dynamics Modelling Approach to Avoid Unintended Consequences in the Implementation of Stepped Care for Depression Services

In order to address some of the implementation issues the NICE guidelines had been extended locally by the Region concerned though its Care Services Improvement Partnership (CSIP). In the words of this organisation, the initiative was to translate the NICE guidelines locally in an attempt to change individual and organisational behaviour in respect of clinical interventions and commissioning of appropriate and cost-effective services for people with depression. The aim of the modelling project was to support the implementation and dissemination of its guidelines and to attempt to avoid some of the potential unintended consequences. The model effort was guided by both the localised guideline documentation and the help of an expert group of Mental Health clinicians, researchers and commissioners and was focused at pre-empting any resource allocation issues of stepped care and addressing them in parallel with implementing the reform.

The decision to utilise a modelling approach to support the implementation of a stepped care approach to depression, rested on three elements:

1. Documents are static and contain numerous hidden and often un-testable assumptions.
2. Whilst guidelines often represent best practice from a clinical perspective, they are often very light on the 'hard' economic factors (number of patients, finances,

workforce) that commissioners require to support the types of decisions they make.
3. Commissioning decisions are highly complex.

The specific objectives of the modelling were:

- To improve definition of patient pathways and support meaningful whole system/pathway redesign.
- To address detailed economic and resource allocation issues, particularly how to redistribute funding from specialist services across intermediate services and how to deal with accrued backlogs of demand.
- To facilitate the sharing and communication of the benefits of a stepped care approach to those responsible for delivery.
- To increase commissioners' active use of strategic scenario planning.

9.4 Description of the Model

Figure 9.1 illustrates the high-level structure of the stepped-care simulation model.

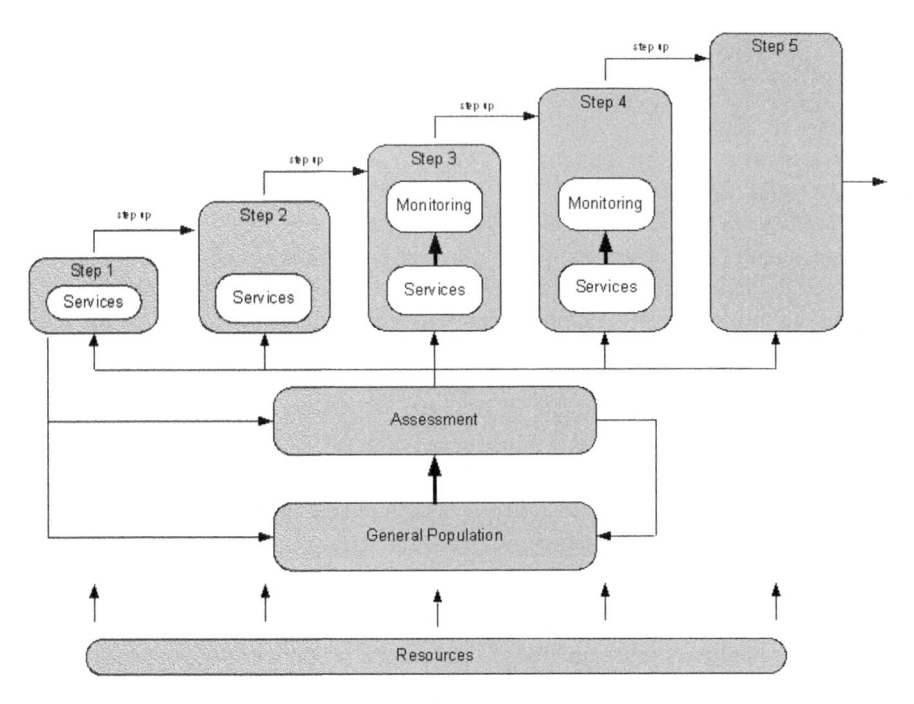

Fig. 9.1 High level map of the depression guidelines model

9.4 Description of the Model

Figure 9.1 shows that there is a general population of people in any mental health system. This could be nationally or locally. Some suffer from depression and come in contact with primary services. At this point they receive an assessment for depression. Based on this assessment of need, people flow to one of five service steps. Steps 1–3 are predominantly primary care delivered whilst steps 4–5 are secondary/tertiary acute services. Within each of these steps, services are delivered and if people improve then they flow back to the general population or for a re-assessment. If, however, a course of treatment within any particular step does not improve the patient's condition they either receive another package of care within that step or they step up to the next step. Decisions at these points are based on evidence and clinical judgement.

In addition to the patient pathway/flow elements described above the model incorporated the resource elements which are critical to commissioners. These resources included people and money.

Key elements that form the basis of the model included:

- A stepped care approach focusing on steps 1–4
- A chronic disease or long-term conditions orientation
- A population health perspective looking at the health of an entire population
- Care pathway and patient flow thinking.

In addition, three overarching criteria were used to focus the modelling. Any scenario run through the model was initially assessed against these criteria.

- System effectiveness as measured by the number of people the system can treat under different scenario conditions.
- Access (the length of time that patients wait for services).
- Cost effectiveness (the interaction of the two elements above to create the most advantageous outputs).

Any model has at its core a number of assumptions. The value of this modelling approach is that these assumptions can be modified and new scenarios tested, either by users themselves or live in workshops. Some of the key model assumptions included:

- The average percentages of people assessed as requiring different service steps
- The rates at which people relapse after recovering
- The average percentages of people that remit, require additional services within the same step or step up
- The length of the time delays in establishing a new service step or decommissioning others.

9.5 What the Model Enabled

The model was used to undertake detailed scenario analysis with commissioning groups who could adjust the data and policies of the model to suit their interests. To demonstrate this some example uses of the model are described, which provide general insights.

The basic run of the model was configured to represent the existing mental health services in England, operating as a two-step system as existed during the 1980s and 1990s. This is achieved simply by switching off steps 2 and 3 in the dash board of the model shown in Fig. 9.2. The important items to note are the graphs and the report measures for total waiting time and total people treated over the experimental runs.

The graph in Fig. 9.2 shows the average number of people waiting for step 4 under the traditional system. It can be seen that there is a significant wait for step 4 services as observed in current practice and that this wait simply gets longer over the 10 years covered by the model. Steps 2 and 3 are switched off during the experiment depicted so the resource allocation dial in Fig. 9.2 is inactive and the average waits shown in the graph for steps 2 and 3 are zero.

Figure 9.3 shows the model configured to represent the fully-implemented guidelines for stepped services (all 4 steps switched on).

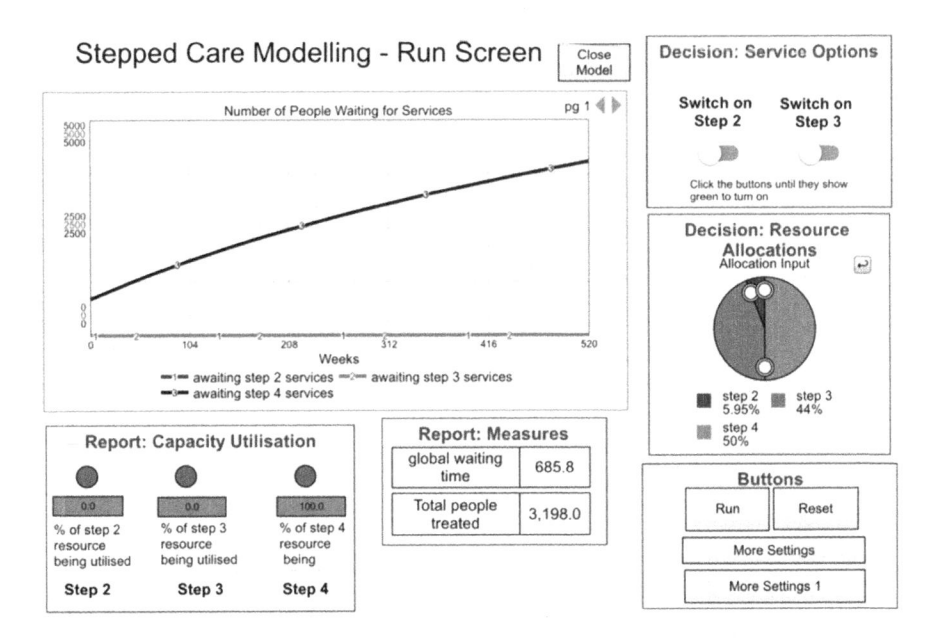

Fig. 9.2 The base experiment with the two-stage model showing large total waits across all services

9.5 What the Model Enabled

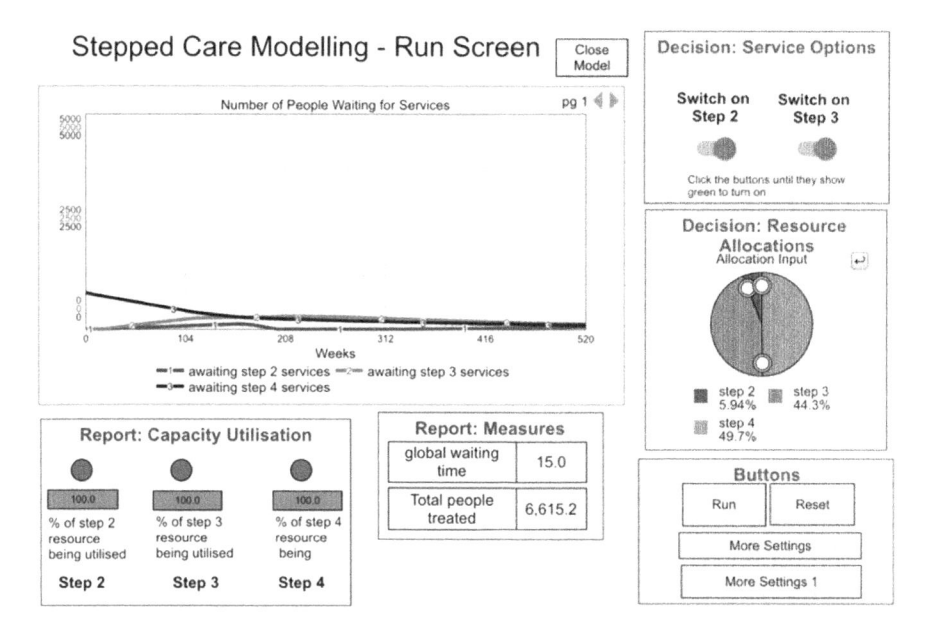

Fig. 9.3 Output from the three-stage model showing reduced total waits across all services

The graphs here capture a significant and dramatic reduction in the average total numbers of people waiting and a doubling of the people treated (see the figures under report measures on the dash board).

The model was configured so that users could allocate the percentage of a fixed pot of available finance across the steps at yearly intervals during the model run, using the resource allocation dial. Consequently, the exact results achieved depend on user-judgement. The particular result captured shows the best allocation achieved over time and demonstrates the ideal big gains feasible. This level of improvement is achieved because steps 2 and 3 provide a more appropriate, cost effective mix of services for people with less severe forms of depression.

Figure 9.4 shows the history of the resource allocation decisions across each step for the results of Fig. 9.3. The graph here shows how step 4 resources are reduced progressively as step 2 and 3 resources are built up. Experiments showed that it was necessary to initially still allocate significant money to step 4 to draw down the large backlog of outstanding cases. Then to progressively reduce this and increase the allocations to steps 2 and 3.

Figure 9.5 shows a comparative graph of the total numbers of patients treated between the two configurations of the system and it can be seen that a stepped approach gives significant benefits for this performance measure.

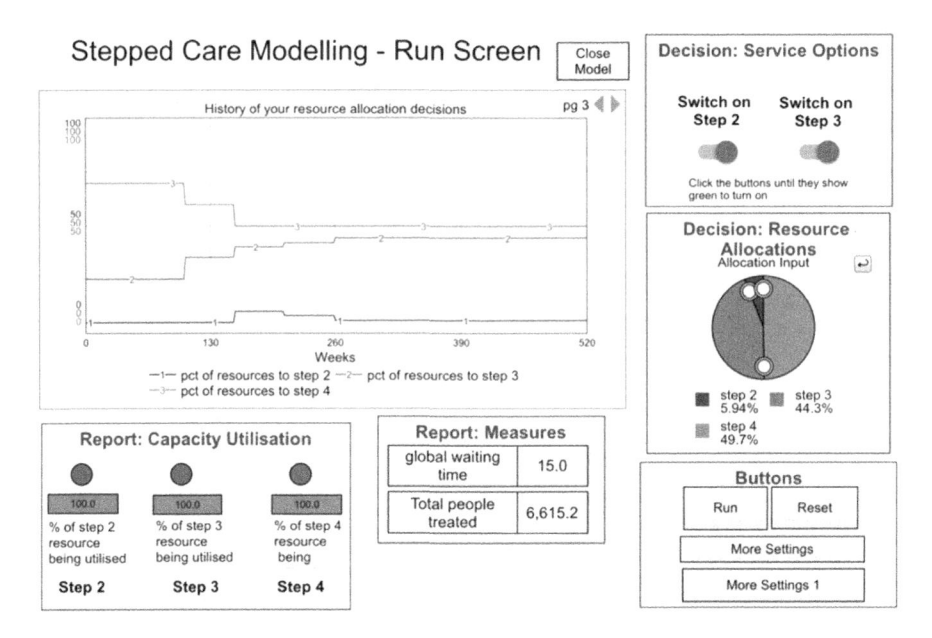

Fig. 9.4 Output from the three-stage model showing reduced total waits across tall services

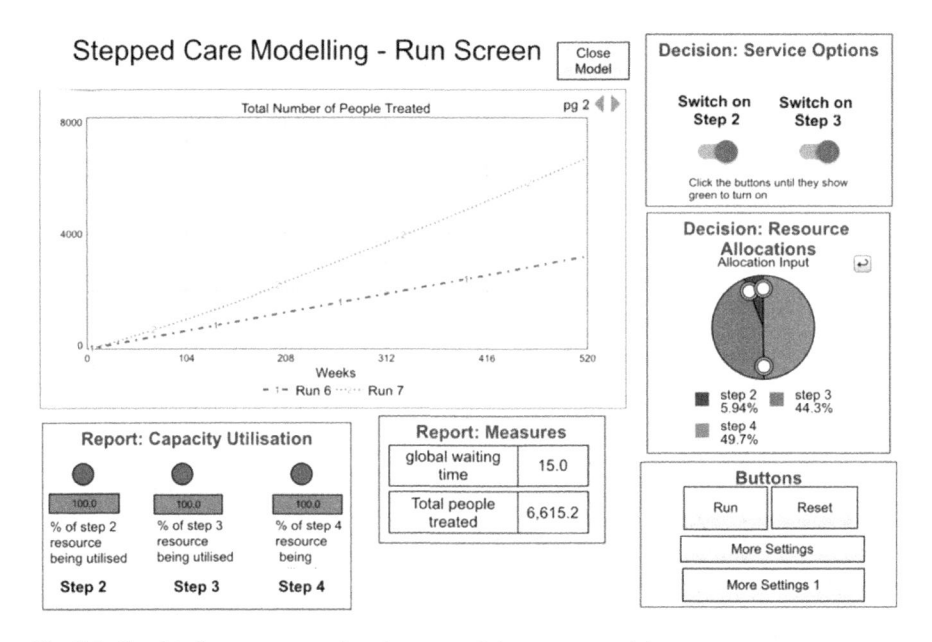

Fig. 9.5 Graphical output comparing the one and three-stage models

9.6 Using the Model to Support Implementation of the Guidelines—Running a Series of Model-Supported Collaborative Workshops

In order to assist the region with their implementation of the new guidelines for depression, a series of 10 collaborative workshops were held involving 10 mental health communities and Fig. 9.6 outlines the process used.

At each meeting representatives of each community were asked to describe their current stage of implementing the guidelines using maps of their own services based on pathways, boundaries, data, issues, and constraints. In particular, to articulate the 'coping strategies' used to match supply of services with demand. This constituted the 'what is' component in Fig. 9.6.

The model, as a unifying element of the new guidelines and the economics of resource reallocation provided a virtual representation of ideal stepped care system for depression services to which local health communities might aspire. This constituted the 'what might be' component of Fig. 9.6 and community members undertook their own experiments with the model using their own local data and assumptions. For example, about overall budgets and staff numbers, costs and treatment lengths at each step. The challenge was for groups of participants to find the allocation which gave the least total wait time and to set this as an ideal target to be achieved in practice. Of particular importance was the lesson to be learned from how to deal with the accrued waitlist for specialist services. Whether to leave sufficient funds with specialist services to clear this or whether to reallocate the waitlist over other services.

The aim at each meeting was for each community to communicate and share with other communities and to identify gaps in commissioning practice, service provision

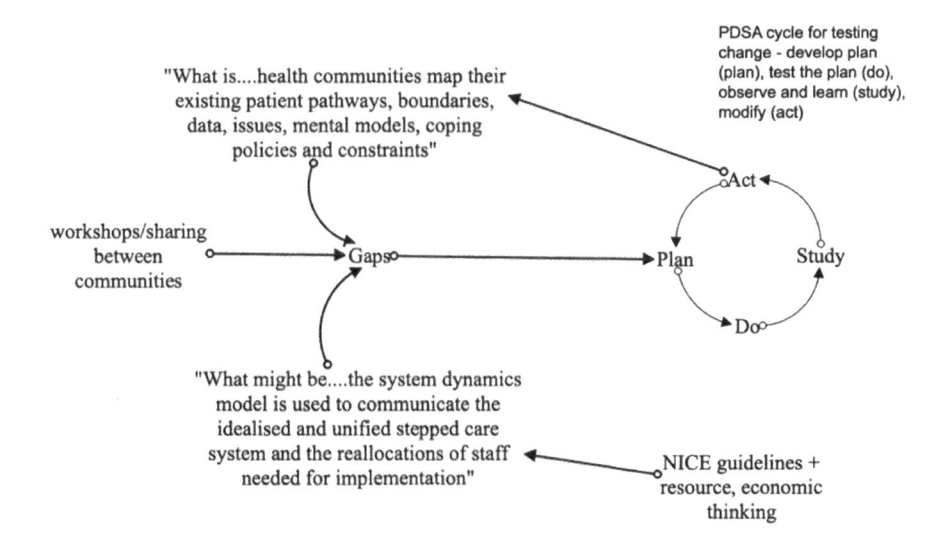

Fig. 9.6 An overview of the model-supported collaborative process

and workforce which could be incrementally closed. Between meetings the communities were asked to undertake initiatives to close these gaps, using process improvement techniques based on PDSA (plan-act-study-do) improvement cycles.

9.7 Factors Emerging from the Collaborative Process

At the start of the workshop process many communities were still essentially operating a two-step system for depression services which had largely evolved, rather than been designed.

Figure 9.7 shows a generic map capturing some of the major issues being described. Although essentially a simple two-step in nature, many treatment pathways were provided at each step by a complex mix of providers with multiple assessment points. Excessive wait times existed for specialist services and the system was characterised by a high level of risk aversion. Essentially, people seem to either receive no treatment or extensive and expensive treatment after a long wait. It was also common for patients to get caught between these states.

In contrast the ideal stepped care system shown in Fig. 9.8 seems to offer a designed, gradated 4/5 step system with much simpler patient pathways and service

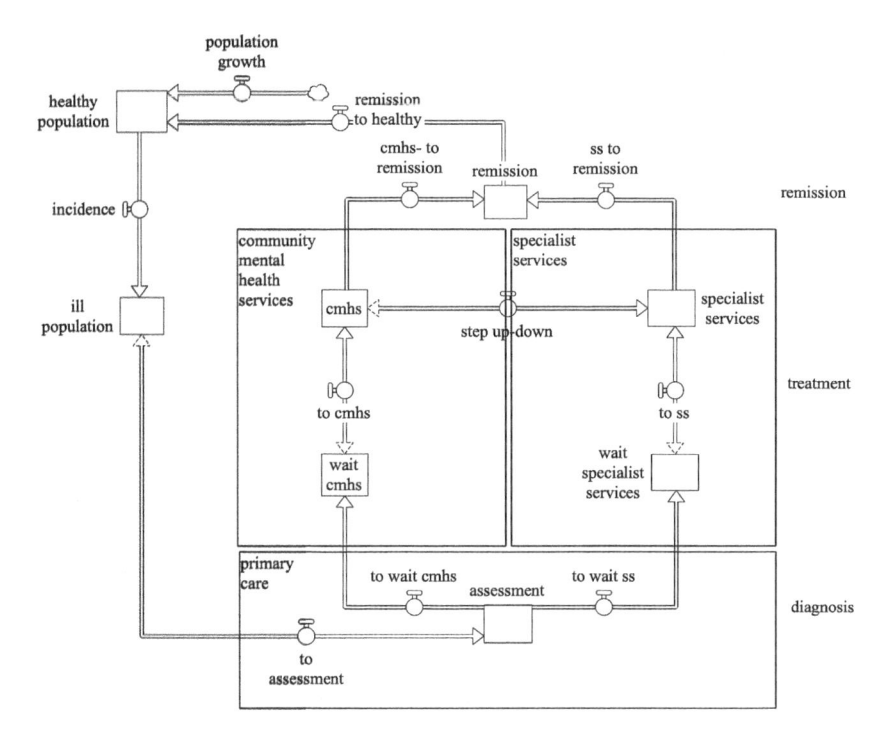

Fig. 9.7 Generic map capturing some of the issues of existing mental health practice

9.7 Factors Emerging from the Collaborative Process

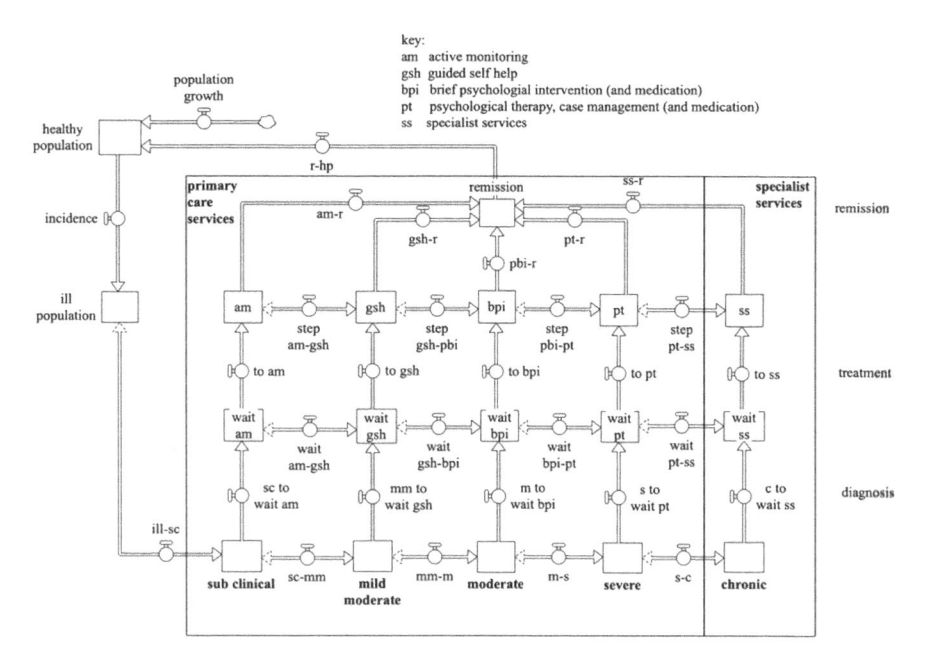

Fig. 9.8 The structure of stepped care services for depression

provider boundaries. This system would seem to suggest the need for communities to rationalise and balance their approach to risk management and to accept a trade-off between treating a few people very well after long waits or providing some treatment quickly to many people.

Feedback from participants suggested that the collaborative process was significantly accelerating implementation of stepped care. The average post collaborative waiting time across communities and across all steps was reported to be significantly less than achieved before the stepped care approach.

The preferred method of implementing stepped care seemed to be to create Primary Care Mental Health teams for services in steps 1–3, but largely staffed and managed by Specialist Mental Health Trusts. This arrangement created the necessary staffing resources at each step without enormous reallocations of money and people shifts and provided flexibility.

9.8 Conclusions

The work here using a system dynamics model of stepped care and a model-supported collaborative process to assist the implementation of a stepped care approach to depression demonstrated considerable benefits. The importance of providing very visual and animated communication of the ideal stepped care system acted as a catalyst to implementation.

References

National Institute for Health and Care Excellence. (2004a, December). *Depression: Management of depression in primary and secondary care—NICE guidance. National clinical practice guideline number 23.*

National Institute for Mental Health England, Regional. (2004b, December). *Enhanced Services Specification for depression under the new GP contract—A commissioning guidebook.*

Chapter 10
Towards a Dynamic Theory of How Hospitals Cope in Times of High Demand

Chapter Summary
This chapter builds on the research on delayed hospital discharge modelling work described in Chap. 7. It proposes a general, dynamic, hypothesis that the 'normal' mode of operation for many hospitals today is often well beyond their safe design capacity. This can be very risky for patients as well as expensive. A range of informal strategies which hospitals adopt to help cope with high demand are set out, together with their unintended consequences. These strategies and their unintended consequences are described in terms of the feedback loops and system archetypes introduced in Chap. 5. It is postulated that the unintended consequences for patients, staff and productivity result in an underachievement of the planned number and quality of hospital interventions. Moreover, the costs of using such coping strategies for lengthy periods could be much greater than the investment needed to avoid their use in the first place.

10.1 Introduction

Hospitals have to cope with whatever arrives at their door irrespective of their capacity and more and more find themselves overrun by demand pressures. Congestion has been readily apparent in recent years, particularly in winter, but the situation is long standing. For many years hospitals have appeared to cope and have seemed to be matching supply with demand but the reality is that this is due to them employing a variety of well-intended but costly survival strategies to attempt to meet performance targets and limit patient bottlenecks.

These practices mask some underlying problems and have severe unintended consequences for patients and costs and can lead to hospitals becoming trapped in a fire-fighting mode. The phenomenon of fire-fighting, where scare resources are allocated to solve unanticipated problems or 'fires', has been reported in a number of fields, such as market growth (Forrester 1968), new product development (Repenning 2001; Repenning et al. 2001), process improvement (Repenning and Sterman 2001) and quality (Oliva 2001; Oliva and Sterman 2001; Sterman et al. 1997). Some go as far as suggesting that the civil service, local government and the health service in the UK is operated consistently on a model of crisis management, which costs much more than it would to the tackle the cause of the problems (Dudman 2019).

It could be argued that a considerable portion of hospital budgets are spent on coping strategies at the expense of real improvements. When additional funding is forthcoming it is immediately absorbed by the cumulated deficits, rather than being available for development and whole systems improvement (Gainsbury 2017).

The first version of the dynamic hypothesis for how hospitals cope was first published in 2005 (Wolstenholme et al. 2005)[1] and is proving very real today. This a major expansion and rewrite of that paper using an improved method of representing systems archetypes in the Stella Architect software.

The hypothesis emerged from a wide range of hospital modelling studies associated with delayed hospital discharge modelling. Chapter 7 focused on the use of 'outliers' or 'boarders' as a coping strategy. In this book we shall adopt the use of the term boarders. This is the transfer of medical patients to surgical wards needed to free up medical beds. However, the subsequent work uncovered a much wider range of coping strategies along the patient pathway, which will be explored here.

It should be stressed that, unlike other projects in this book, which are based on models whose assumptions and evidence were provided by the management and clinical teams which commissioned them, the hypothesis compiled here is purely the construct of the authors and not that of clients. Some of the coping strategies described and their unintended consequences are well supported by documented evidence and some less so. Neither is it claimed that any one hospital deploys all these tactics. What the chapter does is, perhaps for the first time, to piece the strategies together in a systemic framework which presents a formidable composite explanation of how hospitals find themselves in difficulties in balancing budgets and patient efficacy in periods of high demand.

It is also important to point out that the hypothesis is qualitative. We remain true to our assertion throughout the book that it always important to quantify and test hypotheses by simulation. However, such a project would not be possible by modellers alone and would require the assembly of an expert modelling team willing to commit to quantification and sensitivity testing of what are very sensitive issues.

---

[1]Extracts from the original paper are published with the permission of Wiley.

10.2 An Overview of Hospital Patient Pathways

Figure 10.1 shows a simplified 'whole system' map of the main patient pathways through hospitals, building on those introduced in Chap. 7, to investigate delayed hospital discharges. The map is based on stock and flow variables as described in Chap. 2.

There are numerous ways of breaking down hospital patient pathways (for example, into emergency, medical, surgical and intermediate care) and social care pathways (for example, into residential care, nursing home care and domiciliary care).

Here, pathways are split into unscheduled and scheduled (elective) patients and all social care pathways are grouped together. Such a division provides a good way to capture the coping strategies under discussion and each hospital pathway subsumes an element of medical and surgical patients and intermediate pathways where patients can be stepped down into less intensive, faster and cheaper routes.

The map captures the fact that in normal circumstances most patients admitted to hospital are discharged after a relatively short length of stay, but, if continuing health and social care packages are not readily available, a small group of patients needing ongoing health and social care can become trapped in hospital despite being 'medically fit' to be discharged. The state of awaiting care in Fig. 10.1 represents these 'delayed discharges' or 'delayed transfers of care'.

In Fig. 10.1, blue pathways are those which patients normally follow along with hopefully speedy and good outcomes. The pathways shown in red are those resulting from well-intended clinical and management strategies to cope with demand pressures.

These coping strategies will be reviewed in the next section and their unintended consequences subsequently described.

10.3 The Coping Strategies

Figure 10.1 identifies patient flows associated with five informal Coping Strategies;

1. **Transfer of medical patients to surgical beds (boarders):**
   (Movement of medical patients to surgical beds, marked as Coping Strategy 1 in Fig. 10.1.)
   This strategy is widely applied to transfer unscheduled patients to scheduled (elective beds), whenever unscheduled referrals exceed the scheduled bed capacity. People moved in this way are referred to as 'outliers' or 'boarders'. In recent years the use of boarders has become a more formal government strategy in the UK with hospitals being advised to close down all elective procedures and to use all beds for unscheduled emergencies during periods of intense winter pressure. People can be 'boarded' on admission, but more likely existing, recovering inpatients are boarded.

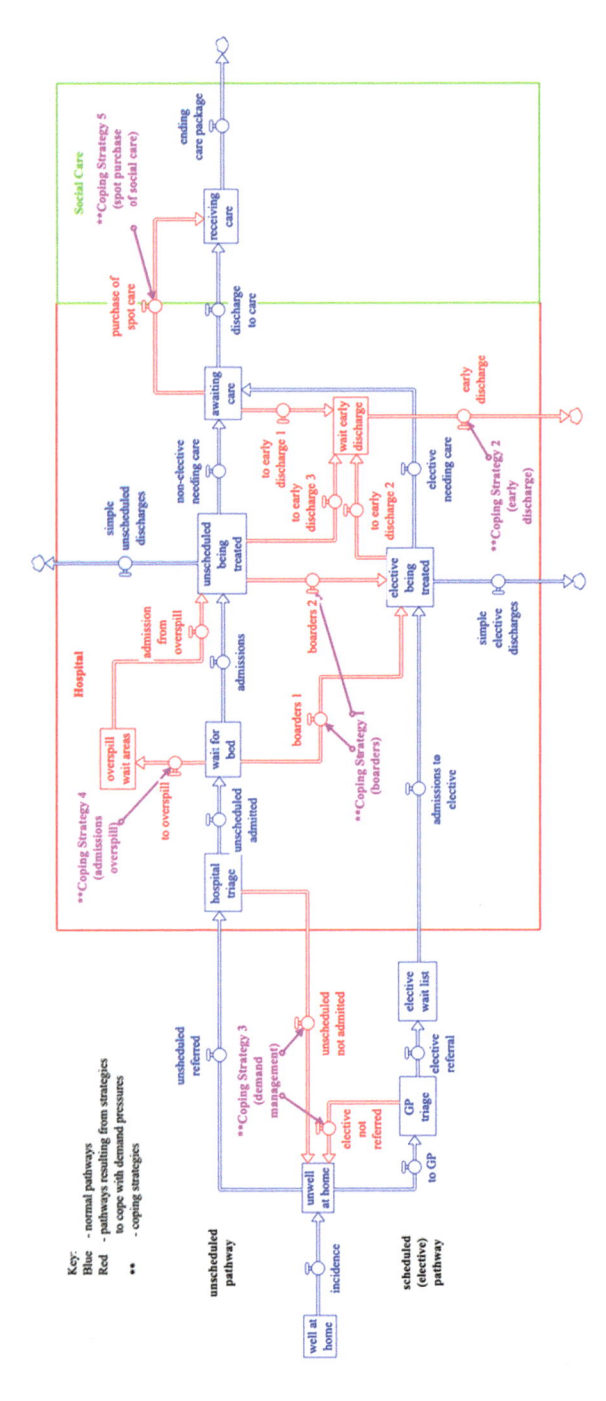

Fig. 10.1 An overview of normal hospital pathways and those used as a result of demand pressures

10.3 The Coping Strategies

2. **Early/premature hospital discharge**:
   (Premature discharge is marked as Coping Strategy 2 in Fig. 10.1.)
   Whilst delayed hospital discharges are well monitored, the other side of the hospital discharge coin—premature discharges—is perhaps less well understood. Over the past 17 years average lengths of stay in a NHS hospitals have fallen by more than 40% from 8.4 days to 4.9 days (Ewbank et al. 2017). Some of this reduction in length of stay results from an increased use of day-surgery and a desire to minimise exposure to the hospital environment for vulnerable patients. However, there is a growing concern that many patients may be discharged before being stabilised (Nguyen et al. 2017; Buie et al. 2006) leading to increased risk of mortality (Smith and Jackson 2017). Whilst length of treatment/recovery is generally assumed to be a clinical parameter, based on patient need and condition, it has the potential of being a strategy variable which could be reduced to increase patient throughput in times of high demand (Conversely, it could also sometimes be used to increase length of stay in periods of low demand). Length of stay has been described as a way of generating 'elastic' capacity and its use as a proxy for capacity has already been demonstrated by modelling in Chap. 2. Discharging patients based on available capacity rather than strict clinical need, has implications for patient recovery as well as the comparability of length of stay data.

3. **Hospital demand management**:
   (Hospital demand management is marked as Coping Strategy 3 in Fig. 10.1.)
   This book began in Chap. 1 with a discussion of the dilemma that exists between the needs of individual patients and the aggregate effect of patient demand on health and social care resources. General practitioners (GP's) in primary care are the main gatekeepers of the health care system and often face a dilemma between wishing to do their best for individual patients and their knowledge of the state of resources in downstream services when they decide on referrals to hospital. They will be only be too aware that when hospital are working at capacity raising referral thresholds is the only solution to relieve demand pressure. This, as a type of behavioural feedback, is very hard to quantify but difficult to dismiss as a real effect. In fact, it has emerged in recent press reports in the UK that there have been attempts to formalise the practice by commissioning groups offering GP's a share of the hospital savings resulting from deferrable cases during periods of winter pressure (Campbell 2018).

4. **Overspill wait areas**:
   (Overspill areas to accommodate emergency patients is marked as Coping Strategy 4 in Fig. 10.1.)
   In recent times demand on emergency facilities in hospitals as resulted in severe disruption due to lack of space for patients, with queues building up in corridors and in arriving ambulances. Some hospitals have gone as far as creating temporary admission wards to hold more people more comfortably.

5. **Spot purchase of social care beds by health and social care**:
   (Spot purchase to assist hospital discharge is marked as Coping Strategy 5 in Fig. 10.1)

When hospitals become overwhelmed by demand pressure and discharges to social care are taking too long, desperate strategies are required. At such times it is not uncommon for hospitals to both transfer patients for treatment to their competitors in the private sector and to buy beds in private sector care and nursing homes on the spot market to enable discharges (BBC 2018; Triggle 2016). Some are going as far as buying care homes (Smyth 2016). Such spot purchases of additional beds is also carried out by adult social care in the UK. Traditionally, adult social care has been commissioned by local authorities through block contract frameworks with care providers. However, with increasing and more complex needs of the elderly and an increasing turnover of providers, social care commissioning teams are more and more limiting the number of providers they work with and are increasingly turning to spot purchasing of services around framework agreements (Adam 2018).

The coping mechanisms described here are all well-intended strategies, aimed at keeping system performance within bounds and supply within capacity. The strategies represent ways of making it appear at the strategic level that the organisation is coping but mask the fact that organisations are working beyond their design capacity. A little over capacity is perhaps good for motivation and to ensure that scare resources are allocated to those who really need them, but operating organisations well in excess of capacity for prolonged periods and institutionalising the coping strategies can have serious repercussions.

These unintended consequences have implications for both patients and for the economics of health treatment delivery, each of which will be described in turn in terms of system archetypes (Senge 1990; Wolstenholme 2003, 2004) introduced in Chap. 5.

10.4 Unintended Consequences of the Coping Strategies for Patients

The coping strategies described in the previous section can be represented by *balancing* feedback loops aimed at trying to control various states along the patient pathways to informal targets.

The unintended consequences can be described by *reinforcing* feedback loops, which undermine the attempted control and which can sometimes feedback to make the original problem worse.

These loops could be superimposed on Fig. 10.1 in the manner described in Chap. 5. However, it is much clearer to show the intended and unintended consequences as a series of two-loop system archetypes in separate figures.

A *balancing* feedback loop aimed at control, coupled with a consequential *reinforcing* feedback loop which undermines the control is referred to as an 'out of control system archetype' and each of the following cases are of that type.

10.4 Unintended Consequences of the Coping Strategies for Patients

Fig. 10.2 The 'problem' structure of the 'out of control' two-loop archetype

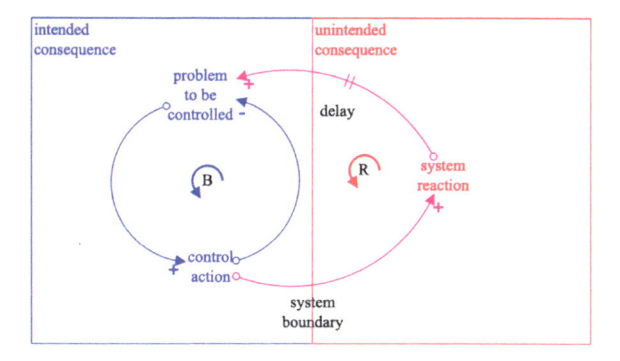

The generic characteristics of this archetype are shown in Fig. 10.2. The *balancing* feedback loop (B) coloured blue is established first and represents the intended control action. The *reinforcing* feedback loop (R) coloured red, which represents a system reaction to the control, only manifests itself after the intended control action. The delays on the links are shown by parallel lines (//) on Fig. 10.2. Further, the system reaction is often hidden by some real or imagined boundary. In other words, the unintended consequence may be known, but the need for control is so urgent that short-termism rules and the later unintended consequences which undermine the control are often ignored.[2]

10.5 The Coping Strategy Archetypes

Each of the coping strategies described are based on a reaction to the arrival at hospital of unscheduled patients expressed as 'waiting time for unscheduled patients'.

1. **Transfer of medical patients to surgical beds (boarders)**

Figure 10.3 demonstrates that the use of the boarders to reduce waiting times for unscheduled admissions has multiple unintended consequences. The main effect is that unscheduled patients occupying scheduled (elective) beds cause cancelled

---

[2]Summary of the rules for drawing feedback loops:
  1. Balancing (B) (or negative) feedback loops are target seeking control loops and have just one or an odd number of negative links between variables.
  2. Reinforcing (R) (or positive) feedback loops are growth loops and have all or an even number of negative links between variables.
  3. Positive links are when an increase in a tail variable of a link gives rise causally to an increase in the head variable (and vice versa).
  4. Negative links are when an increase in the tail variable of a link gives rise causally to a decrease in the head variable (and vice versa).

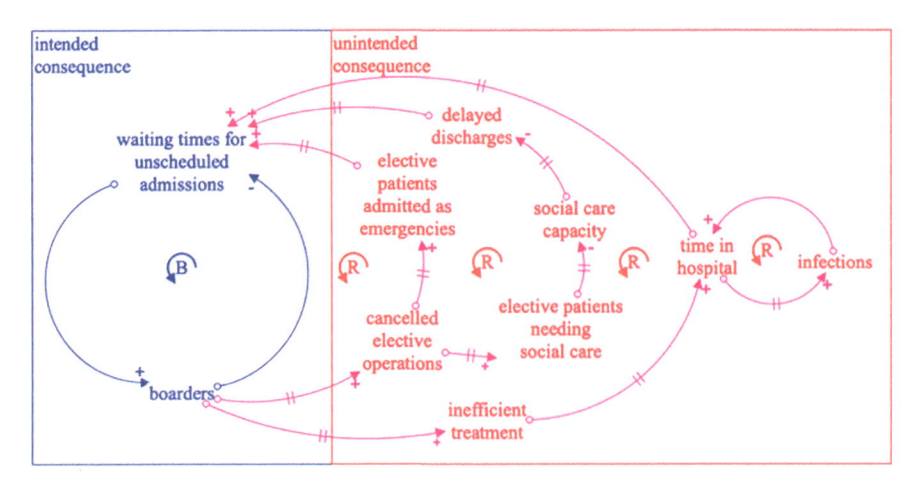

Fig. 10.3 A two-loop 'out of control' archetype for the 'boarders' strategy

elective procedures and long elective wait times. The elective waiting list becomes a key 'buffer stock' to enable unscheduled admissions.

Cancelled elective procedures not only result in enormous lost revenue to hospitals and underuse of elective teams, but increase the likelihood that some of those patients who are deferred will become future emergency admissions—adding directly to hospital demand. Others might need direct assistance from social care and take away social care capacity from those needing it to complete their discharge from hospital.

There is also a worrying efficacy issue associated with boarders in that it can result in numerous disruptive bed shifts for patients, discontinuities in treatment and inefficiencies for hospital consultants and other clinical staff, who often waste time and money locating their patients. Correlations have also been found between increased mortality rates and the practice of boarding (Portsmouth Hospitals 2018). On top of this there is often a strong association between time spent away from a patient's own ward and the number of emergency calls (Santamaria et al. 2014). The time in hospital for boarded patients can also be higher than for non-boarded (Stylianou et al. 2017) and hence the likelihood of infections is increased.

2. **Early/premature hospital discharge**

The most fundamental decision clinicians have to make is whether a patient is medically fit to leave hospital because mistakes here can compromise patient safety and lead to readmissions. Figure 10.4 suggests that premature discharge can be an effective option for hospitals to reduce their waiting time for unscheduled admissions in times of pressure but does have the potential to lead to later readmissions. It has been recorded that one million NHS patients are readmitted to hospital as emergency cases within 30 days of discharge at a cost of £2.4 billion per year (Healthwatch News Report 2017). In the US, research has shown that being

10.5 The Coping Strategy Archetypes

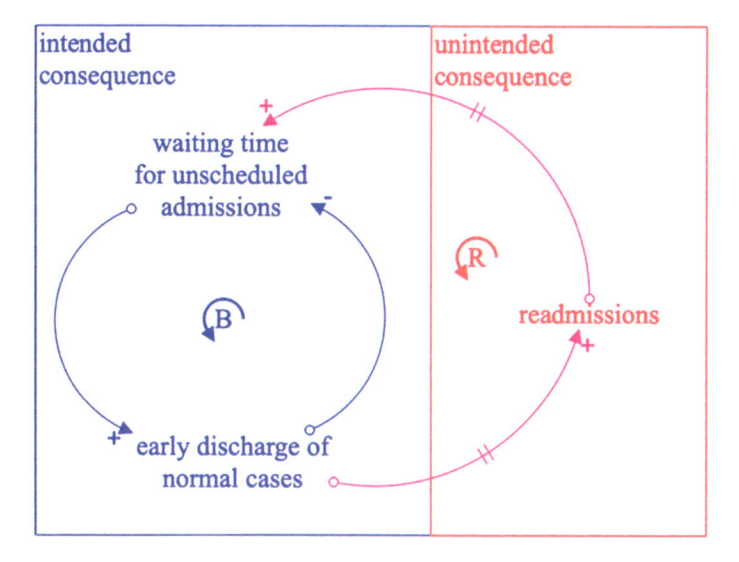

Fig. 10.4 A two-loop 'out of control' archetype for the early discharge strategy

discharged too early is a reality for nearly one in five patients (University of Texas Southwest Medical Center). Despite many discharge guidelines (NICE 2016) a recent report by the Health Service Ombudsman in the UK reveals many instances of poor hospital discharge (Oxtoby 2016).

3. **Hospital demand management**

Figure 10.5 shows that attempts to manage (reduce) inpatient referrals can reduce waiting times for unscheduled admissions, but such action pushes demand further back upstream and ultimately this has to be absorbed by stocks outside the health

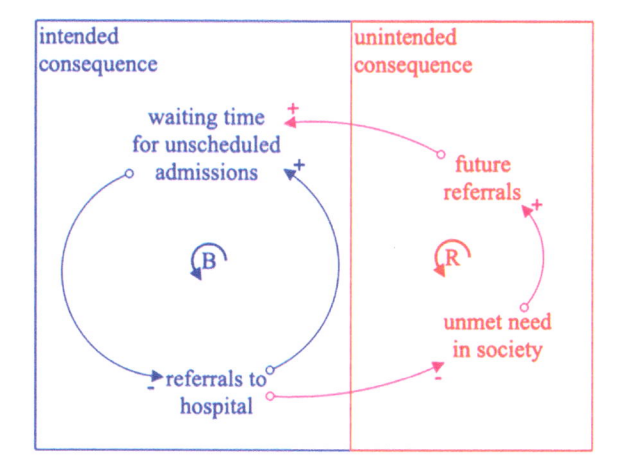

Fig. 10.5 A two-loop 'out of control' archetype for the hospital demand management strategy

and social care system. Demand can get pushed back on families, charities and communities to create a cumulative unmet need. Leaving families to cope with these additional responsibilities has implications for patient safety. In particular, it places a burden on women and their role in the wider economy. Unmet need eventually adds to demand on services when these begin to cope a little better.

4. Overspill waiting areas

In recent times demand on emergency facilities in hospitals has resulted in the impromptu creation of additional, informal, waiting areas often borrowing space from day clinics. Apart from further inefficiencies in treatment leading to longer length of stays, such moves mean the temporary closure of some services, particularly for those with long term conditions. Again, there is a strong likelihood of such patients needing to be admitted as emergencies or needing scarce social care assistance (Fig. 10.6).

5. Spot purchase of social care beds

Purchasing social service capacity on the spot market by hospitals can be very beneficial for drastically reducing the number of patients awaiting hospital discharge and hence unscheduled admission times. However, these beds are usually much more expensive than beds funded by social care. This is also true of special home care services purchased by social care outside block contracts. The higher costs inevitably mean that capacities in both health and social care are reduced OR cumulative deficits are increased which later absorb any funding increases (Fig. 10.7). These strategies can also result in more variable quality.

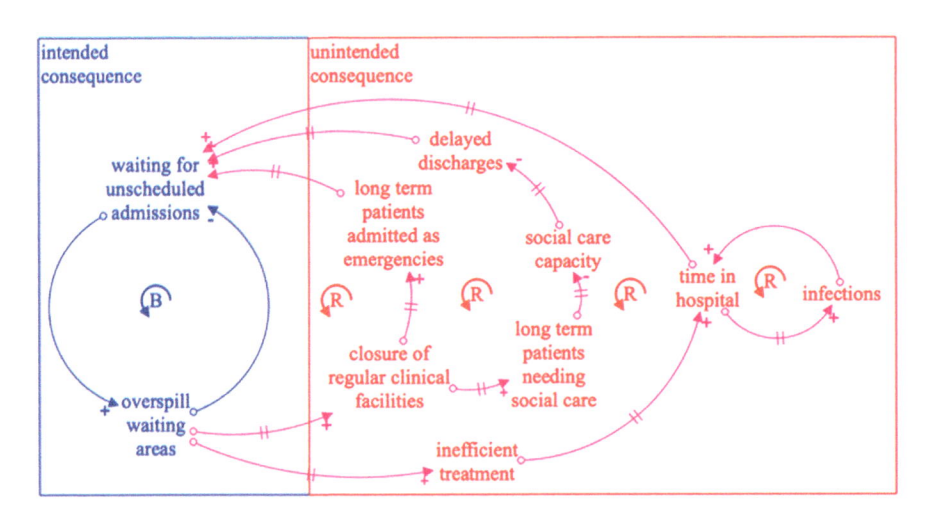

Fig. 10.6 A two-loop 'out of control' archetype for the 'impromptu wait areas' strategy

10.6 Unintended Consequences of the Coping Strategies … 181

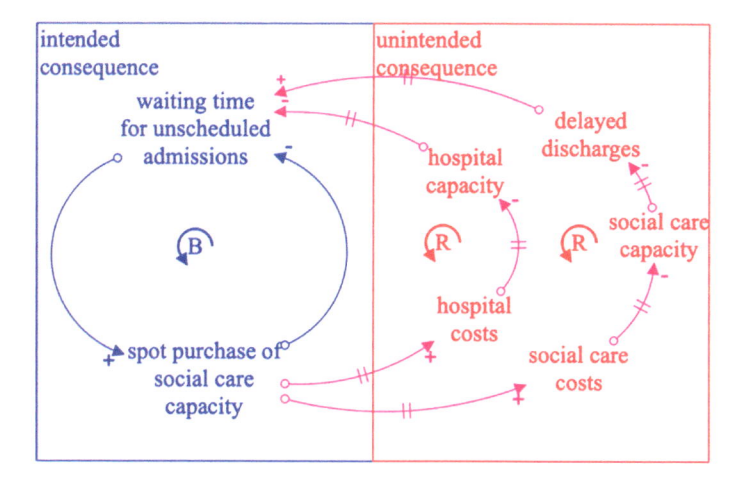

Fig. 10.7 A two loop 'out of control' archetype for the strategy of 'spot purchase' of social care by hospitals and by social care

10.6 Unintended Consequences of the Coping Strategies on the Performance of Hospitals

The problem with all the foregoing informal strategies is that they are potential 'fixes' to cope with working beyond the design capacity of hospitals and, so far, the main focus has been on the undesired consequences for patients and capacity costs. However, they additionally affect hospital performance through staff productivity, morale and turnover and by self-limiting the number of procedures and interventions achievable.

One way of looking at these aspects is through the lens of the other type of system archetype introduced in Chap. 5. This is the *underachievement archetype* whereby *reinforcing* actions to achieve intended outcomes are undermined by *balancing* system reactions often through resource constraints. Figure 10.8 shows the generic form of this archetype.

Figure 10.9 shows the intended consequences of health care investment as a reinforcing feedback loop. Here a rising older population ideally leads to increases in health investment, hospital capacity and service innovation, which in turn leads to more and smarter interventions. Successful use of such services in turn leads to longer life expectancy. Health care can then be a victim of its own success with longevity benefits, perhaps ironically, then leading to higher demand.

The reality, however, is that the aspirations of Fig. 10.9 are undermined by a set of unintended consequences resulting from underinvestment in social care. This results in a set of balancing feedback loops as shown in Fig. 10.10 involving delayed discharges, hospital congestion and the many coping strategies already described. All the coping strategies (boarders, early discharge, demand management, overspill and spot purchase) are all grouped together here. The costs of these

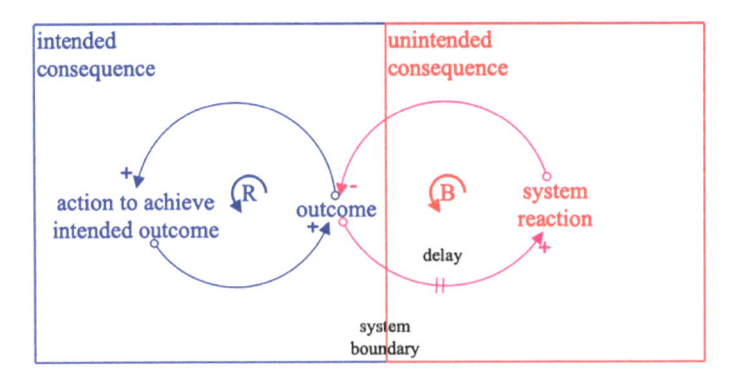

Fig. 10.8 The generic underachievement archetype

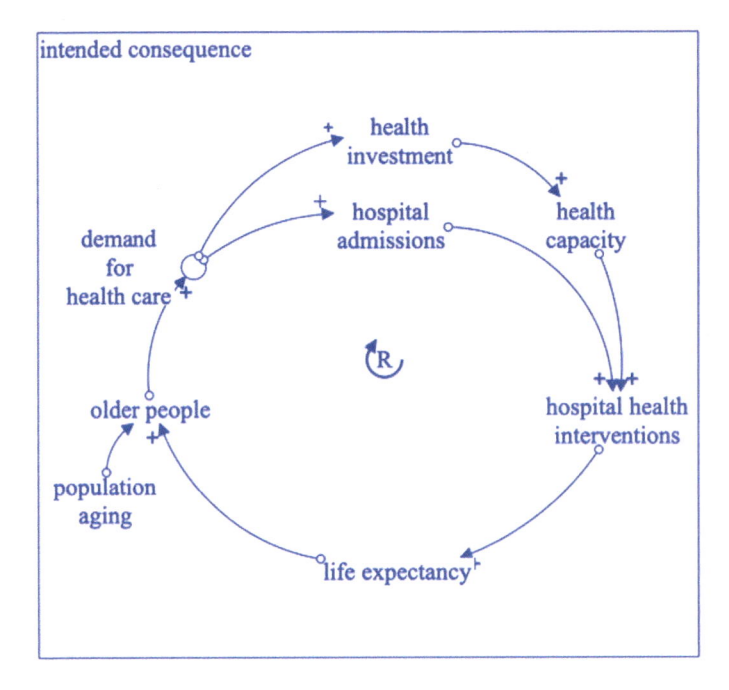

Fig. 10.9 The ideal intended consequences of health care investment

together with decreasing staff productivity and increasing staff turnover lead to limiting the number of interventions possible and affordable and an underachievement of the hospital's true capability. Under achievement has its own consequence since there is then a reason to justify a case against further increases in health spending.

This effect together with some of the unintended side effects of coping strategies —such as cancelled elective procedures, leading to elective patients being admitted

10.6 Unintended Consequences of the Coping Strategies ... 183

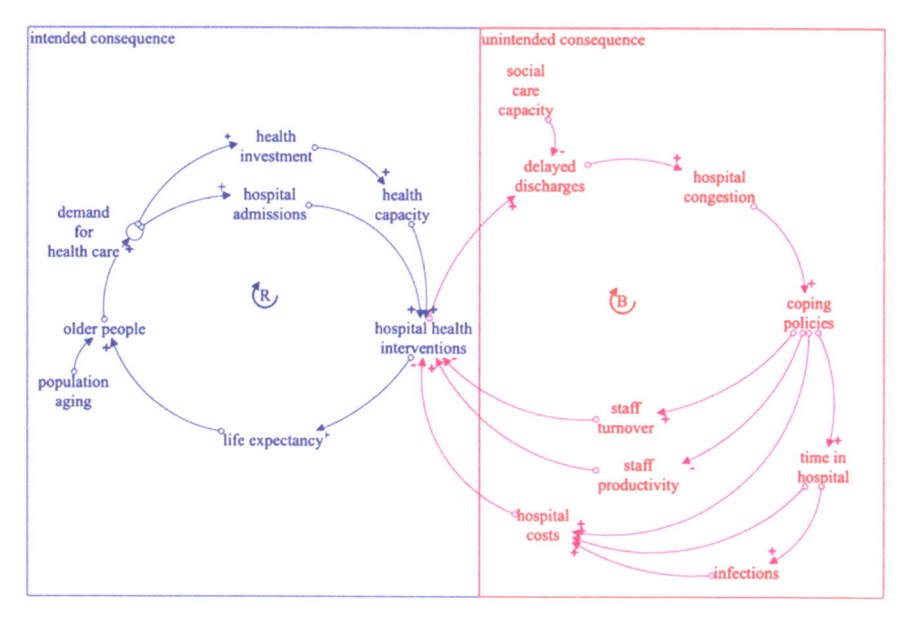

Fig. 10.10 The unintended consequences of underinvestment in Health

as emergencies, and early discharges leading to readmissions—reinforce demand even further. These are omitted from Fig. 10.10 for clarity.

10.7 Identifying Solutions

It was suggested in Chap. 5 that for any problem archetype there is often a solution which can be carried out in parallel with the intended action to pre-empt and counter unintended consequences. Figure 10.11 shows the generic form of the solution for an underachievement archetype where action is taken in parallel with the intended action to unblock the system reaction and consolidate the intended reinforcing loop.

Chapter 7 demonstrated quantitatively that increasing social care capacity was a win-win option for both health and social care by reducing delayed discharges and enabling increases in health procedures in hospitals. Here, it is suggested that it could do much more by also eliminating many other coping strategies as well.

Increasing Social Care investment in parallel with health investment is shown as a solution link to the archetype of Fig. 10.10 by the thick arrow in Fig. 10.12.

This link increases social care capacity in parallel with health capacity. Since increasing social care capacity reduces delayed discharges, the introduction of this link has the quite amazing effect of changing the unintended consequence loops from balancing to reinforcing, allowing them to work in partnership with the

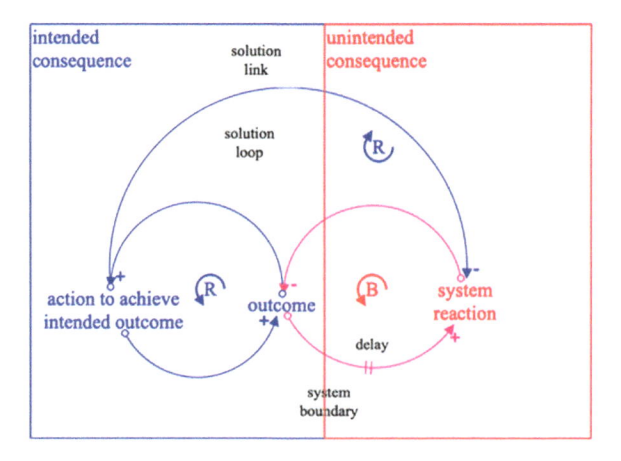

Fig. 10.11 The generic underachievement solution archetype

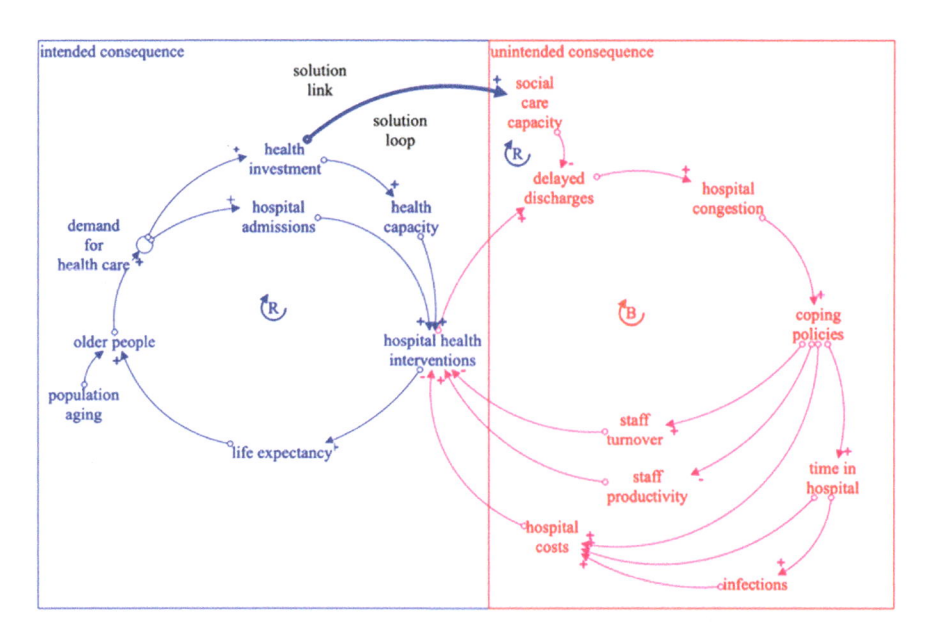

Fig. 10.12 Adding a solution link to the underachievement archetype

intended consequence loop. By reducing delayed discharges, it prevents the need for coping strategies at all, reduces time in hospital, increases staff morale, reduces costs and facilitates the funding of more interventions. Perhaps most importantly it actually frees up the intended consequence loop and allows the best use to be made of existing health investment.

Continued investment in health is clearly necessary to keep health services abreast of an ageing population. But irrespective of the level of health spending it is equally important to match this with similar spending in social care. Only in this way will the two agencies be kept in balance and the excessive costs of coping be avoided in the future. Indeed, the additional investment in social care needed to prevent coping strategies could actually be less than the cost of the coping strategies currently incurred by the NHS.

A further issue concerns understanding of the dynamics of the investment associated with the solution. Not only would spending be required for the future, but also a one-off sum to deal with the accrued backlog of cases from a long period of not coping. Not understanding this would result in it appearing that future balanced spending was not succeeding.

It would also be necessary to establish ways of guarding against a return to coping strategies. This might involve the definition of new performance measures to identify when they were being used. For example, in addition to recording delayed discharges it would be useful to monitor:

- the occurrence of boarders,
- early discharges
- spot purchase of health and social care services
- trends in hospital referrals
- clinic cancellations.

10.8 Concluding Remarks

This chapter has attempted to create a composite feedback hypothesis to explain discrepancies between the way health and social care organisations are described to work and their observed behaviour when they are faced with having to cope with demand well outside the design capacities.

The implication of the analysis is that coping strategies are necessary as being the only way for hospitals to remain functioning during times of high demand, but that they all, through their many and varied unintended consequences, conspire to increase costs and result in underachievement. The costs and under achievements associated with coping could be much more than the investment needed to avoid coping.

In the search for high leverage interventions, it is often said that the best levers in a system are often well removed from the location of the problem symptoms of that system. This is certainly true in the work discussed here in that the best levers for health have been shown to be in social care. But an interesting adjunct to this parable is that the best levers are often in the least powerful agency in the value or supply chain (Wolstenholme 2004) and it is often difficult for more powerful players to accept this. It might be difficult for hospitals to accept that it might be in their own interests to ensure or make investment in social care.

System thinking has been shown to be a very able toolset to both surface and explain informal structure and strategy and to expose the unintended consequences of such actions. It clearly emphasises the need to see health and adult social care as mutually dependent parts of the same system.

The key message is that much-needed systemic solutions and whole system thinking can never be successfully implemented until organisations are recognised as complex entities and are allowed to articulate and dismantle their worst coping strategies and return to working within best practice capacities. This is the ultimate new way of working.

References

Adam. (2018). Moving on from spot purchasing in domiciliary care commissioning. http://www.useadam.co.uk/news/moving-on-from-spot-purchasing-in-domiciliary-care-commissioning/.

BBC. (2018). Hospitals buying private nursing home beds for delayed discharge patients. BBC Documentary on Nottingham University Hospital March 2018.

Buie, V. C., Owings, M. F., DeFrances, C. J., & Golosinskiy, A. (2006). National hospital discharge survey: Summary. *Vital and Health Statistics*. Series 13, 2010 (168).

Campbell, D. (2018). GPs offered cash to refer fewer people to hospital. Health Policy Guardian Wed 28 February 2018.

Dudman, J. (2019). We've been wasting years trying to design Brexit, interview with Mara Airoldi, Director of UK Government Outcome Lab, Guardian 16th January 2019.

Ewbank, L., Thompson, J., & Mckenna, H. (2017). *NHS bed numbers: Past, present, future*. London: The Kings Fund.

Forrester, J. (1968). Market growth as influenced by capital investment. *Industrial Management Review, IX*(2).

Gainsbury, S. (2017). *The NHS deficit is here to stay Nuffield Trust*.

Healthwatch News Report (2017). NHS needs to do more to understand why people are returning to hospital after discharge.

NICE Guideline. (2016, December). Transition between inpatient hospital settings and community or care home settings for adults with social care needs. National Institute for Health and Care Excellence.

Nguyen, O. K., Makam, A. N., & Clark, C. (2017). Vital signs are still vital: Instability on discharge and the risk of post-discharge adverse outcomes. *Journal of General Internal Medicine, 32*, 42. https://doi.org/10.1007/s11606-016-3826-8.

Oliva, R. (2001). Tradeoffs in responses to work pressure in the service industry. *California Management Review, 43*(4), 26–43. Reprinted in (2002) *IEEE Engineering Management Review, 30*(1), 53–63.

Oliva, R., & Sterman, J. D. (2001). Cutting corners and working overtime: Quality erosion in the service industry. *Management Science, 47*(7), 894–914.

Oxtoby, K. (2016). Preventing unsafe discharge from hospital. *Nursing Times, 112*, 25, 14–15.

Portsmouth Hospitals NHS Trust. (2018). *Adult outlier policy, version 5*.

Repenning, P. N. (2001). Understanding fire fighting in new product development. *Journal of Product Innovation Management, 18*(5), 285–300.

Repenning, N., Goncalves, P., & Black, L. (2001). Past the tipping point: The persistence of fire fighting in product development. *California Management Review, 43*(4), 44–63.

Repenning, N., & Sterman, J. (2001). Nobody ever gets credit for fixing defects that didn't happen: Creating and sustaining process improvement. *California Management Review, 43*(4), 64–88.

Santamaria, J. D., Tobin, A. E., Anstey, M. H., Smith, R. J., & Reid, D. A. (2014). Do outlier inpatients experience more emergency calls in hospital? An observational cohort study. *Medical Journal of Australia, 200*(1), 45–48. https://doi.org/10.5694/mja12.11680.

References

Senge, P. M. (1990). *The fifth discipline: The art and practice of the learning organization.* New York: Doubleday/Currency.

Smith, K. O., & Jackson, S. (2017). *It's not all about reducing length of stay.* Carlike.

Smyth, C. (2016, October 15). NHS hospitals open own care homes to tackle beds crisis. *Times Newspaper.*

Sterman, J., Repenning, N., & Kofman, F. (1997). Unanticipated side effects of successful quality programs: Exploring a paradox of organizational improvement. *Management Science, 43*(4), 503–521.

Stylianou, N., Fackrell, R., & Vasilakis, C. (2017). Are medical outliers associated with worse patient outcomes? A retrospective study within a regional NHS hospital using routine data. *BMJ Open, 7,* e015676. https://doi.org/10.1136/bmjopen-2016-015676.

Triggle, N. (2016). *Care homes could solve NHS bed-blocking.* BBC Health.

Wolstenholme, E. F. (2003). Towards the definition and use of a core set of archetypal structures in system dynamics. *System Dynamics Review, 19*(1).

Wolstenholme, E. F. (2004). Using generic system archetypes to support thinking and learning. *System Dynamics Review, 20*(2), 341–356.

Wolstenholme, E. F., Arnold, S., Monk, D., Todd, D., & McKelvie, D. (2005). Coping but not coping in health and social care—masking the reality of running organisations well beyond safe design capacity. *Systems Dynamics Review, 23*(4), 371–389.

Part III
From Cost Benefit Analysis to Dynamic Impact Assessment as a Means of Understanding Complexity

Chapters 11–14

Overview of Part III

Cost-benefit analysis in health care and social care is used in a wide range of situations to choose between alternative policies for improvement by:
- deriving detailed costs and benefits of new treatments and procedures on a per capita basis and then multiplying these by broad estimates of the numbers of people expected to benefit.
- predicting the outcome of each alternative in terms of costs and benefits *after* a relevant time period.
- using spreadsheet models to provide a set of comparative net present values of the costs and benefits

What dynamic modelling can add to this type of analysis is:
- a focus on *flow* data.
- to provide a much more thorough investigation of the number of people who will benefit over time, where they will flow from and flow to.
- to *generate* the costs and benefits of policy changes as they *evolve over time* as a result of *internal feedback* connections. This characteristic is essentially what distinguishes system dynamics models from spreadsheet models as described in Chap. 6
- to provide the transitional as well as the final impact.

We refer to this use of system dynamics as dynamic impact analysis.

Figure 1 describes the generic idea of dynamic impact analysis:
- There is a dynamic population of concern represented as a stock/flow chain of a 'condition'—people in need for a particular reason, ageing, dementia, disability, health, substance misuse.

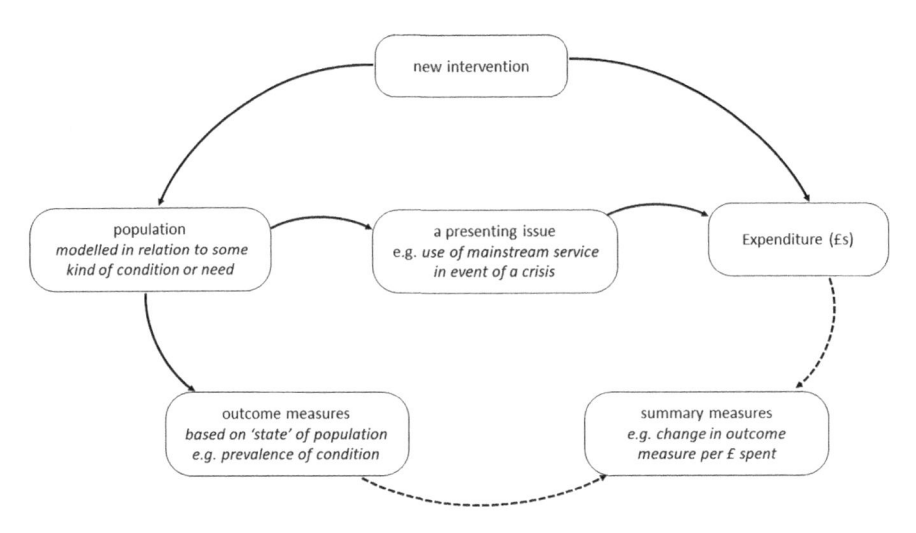

Fig. 1 Generic idea of dynamic impact analysis

- There is a presenting problem (either overuse of a mainstream service, which costs money, or perhaps underuse, because they have not been connected/referred).
- A new intervention is proposed; it also costs money.
- The new intervention has an impact on the population, so they move up or down the condition flow chain, and therefore use the mainstream service differently.
- It is possible to measure the 'quality of life' (qol) of a population, for example, by multiplying each stock/state by a qol index.
- It is possible to measure changes in quality of life in relation to changes in spending.

Part III presents four chapters describing examples of projects used in practice with management and clinical teams involving dynamic impact analysis. All reinforce the reasons to understand flows when designing capacities.

Chapter 11 describes the application of system dynamics to enhance traditional cost-benefit analysis in planning a significant expansion of therapy capacity for mental health treatment in the UK. Here, the cost-benefit analysis accurately determined the benefits per person but did not consider in detail the flows of recipients (where they came from and where they went to after treatment).

Chapter 12 reports on a model to assess the impact of three initiatives on different states of alcohol dependence and their effect on reducing alcohol-related admissions to hospital. This study emphasises the need to account for the movement of people both up and down the addiction chain when designing treatments.

Chapter 13 describes a project to explore the impact of diagnosis targets for dementia on diagnosis and treatment capacity. It suggests that the percentage of people it is possible to diagnose depends on the 'speed' of the flows of incidence, progression and mortality rather than just prevalence.

Chapter 14 explores why the impact of risk stratification tools designed to identify people at high risk of being admitted to hospital may fail to meet expectations. The study here suggests that for improved impact such tools should measure not only on stocks of people at risk but also the underlying flows (churn) in and out of these risk states.

Chapter 11
Dynamic Impact Analysis for Mental Health Reform

Chapter Summary

This Chapter describes the application of system dynamics to enhance traditional cost benefit analysis in planning a significant expansion of therapy capacity for mental health treatment in the UK. The aim of the initiative was to benefit the health of individuals, reduce costs to society and the exchequer and increase employment.

By focussing analysis on the dynamics of people flows over time, rather than static assumptions about the numbers benefiting, simulation is shown to assist understanding of the issue and its potential benefits. The numbers of patients expected to benefit is shown to depend on the treatment capacity, on the sources of people presenting, the number and type of treatment channels and their parameters, the success of treatment, the provision for patients moving between treatment channels, the dynamics of the labour market and employment opportunities.

The overall methodological conclusion is that dynamic factors are often left out of cost benefit analysis because they cause too much complexity for decision makers, whereas system dynamics allows these factors to be included without masking the clarity of the case. The paper suggests that cost benefit analysis and system dynamics are very complementary.

11.1 Introduction

This Chapter presents an example of the application of system dynamics modelling to support central government decision making on large scale investment in cognitive behavioural therapies (CBT) for treating mental health conditions.[1]

---

[1]This Chapter is based on a paper entitled Dynamic Cost Benefit Analysis for Mental Health Reform, first published in Kybernetics Vol.39 No. 9/10, 2010 pp 1645–1658 with the permission of the Department of Health, UK and the Improved Access to PsychologicalTherapies (IAPT) Programme. It is published here with the permission of Emerald Publishing.

It specifically focuses on the value that such modelling can add to cost benefit analysis.

A cost benefit analysis (CBA) is first described for planning the supply of new mental health treatments across England aimed at improving the quality of life, increasing the labour force and saving unemployment benefit payments (Observer 2006). This Improved Access to Psychological therapies (IAPT) programme centred on detailed calculation of the costs and benefits *per capita* after full implementation of plans and then converting these to gross benefits by making assumptions about the numbers of patients benefitting. The original cost benefit analysis was later broadened under the guidance of a wide Expert Reference Group, which examined and tested a range of assumptions in two trial sites. This later analysis will be referred to as the enhanced cost benefit analysis.

The development of a system dynamic analysis to both explore the original hypothesis and to assist the Expert Reference Group associated with the project is then explained. This subsumes the per capita coefficients of the conventional analysis into a patient flow perspective of treatment involving, treatment time, where patients originate from and where patients go after treatment. It also includes a therapist flow perspective involving their recruitment, training, case-loads and the provision of multiple service channels. In this way the modelling provides a platform for examining the transition of the plans to full implementation over time and the sensitivity of the analysis to many different assumptions about the demand and provision of services.

11.2 The Original Cost Benefit Hypothesis

In early 2006 plans were developed in England to assess the benefit of making cognitive behavioural therapy (CBT), as recommended by the National Institute for Health and Care Excellence (NICE 2004), widely available to treat depression and chronic anxiety. The plan suggested that investing £600 million in 10,000 therapists would enable the treatment/recovery of 800,000 people per year and create benefits to the UK exchequer and society of over £2 billion per year when fully established. The benefits would arise from extra output, reduced absenteeism, extra quality of life years, savings in medical costs associated with these conditions, increased tax payments and savings in invalidity benefits. It was known that there was an accrued backlog of around 1 million people on incapacity benefit (IB) due to mental illness and the CBA assumed that this level of investment and numbers treated might be expected to eliminate the backlog in 7 years.

Per capita benefit coefficients were derived based on well researched sources, averaged over 6 classes of mental health condition and taking account of spontaneous recovery rates. Cost coefficients were derived based on the costs of employing the number of therapists required to treat this number of people per year based on the number of people each therapist might treat. The overall net cost and benefit coefficients were then multiplied by estimates of the number of people

11.2 The Original Cost Benefit Hypothesis

whom it was thought might be possible to treat with CBT to give the annual return achievable in steady state, once the new treatment system was established.

The cost benefit analysis was thorough in its derivations of the *per capita* costs and benefits of the plan. However, three issues were identified for further analysis. First, the number of people expected to benefit. No detailed analysis was included of where the people would come from and how they would progress back to work after treatment. Second, no detailed account was taken of the treatment parameters —that is the length of treatment, success rate and drop our rate. Third, the analysis was only carried out in respect of the situation after full implementation of the plan in after 7 years. No account was taken of the transition to full implementation covering the build-up of treatment capacity by the recruitment and training of therapists.

11.3 The Enhanced Cost Benefit Analysis

In order to address the issues raised about the original CBA, a wide group of national experts and stakeholders were brought together in a Expert Reference Group and two trial sites set up to field test the approach. These groups were responsible for broadening the assumptions of the analysis.

In particular, these groups defined an alternative service configuration capable of treating 900,000 people per year. This required only 6800 therapists, 49 days treatment time and used a 50% success rate based on the field trial findings.

They also introduced the idea of having a mixed rather than single programme with two treatment channels using different types of therapists. The first channel would contain a high intensity programme for those with greater need and the second a low intensity programme for those with lesser needs.

A further element of the enhanced CBA was to try to assess how the programme would impact the labour market and other back to work initiatives.

11.4 The System Dynamics Model

The system dynamics model initially incorporated the derivation of the cost and benefit coefficients per person as in the cost benefit analysis. The idea of this was to demonstrate that the derivations were reproducible in a dynamic model and to allow changes in assumptions within these calculations. However, as the project developed the focus of the Expert Reference group centred more and more on assumptions about the numbers of people who might be treated, based on the flow of these people into and out of the proposed new service and the availability of therapy capacity. This trend resulted eventually in the *per capita* cost and benefit coefficients being fixed within the model to simplify the overall structure.

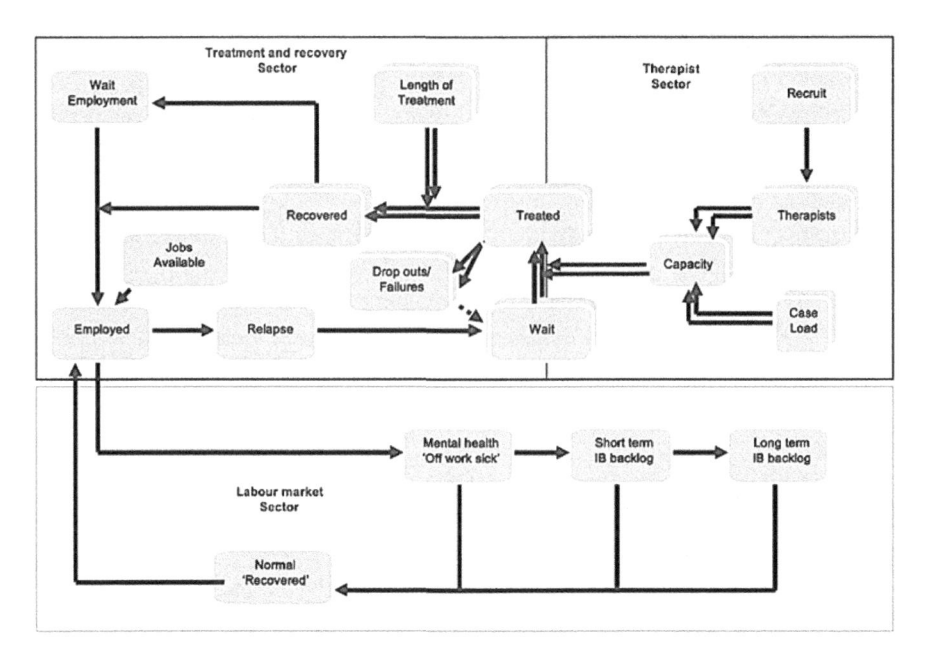

Fig. 11.1 Overview of the structure of the two-channel system dynamics model

Figure 11.1 Overview of the structure of the two-channel system dynamics model shows the system dynamics perspective for a two-channel system broken down into 3 sectors based on both the original and enhanced CBAs. These are the treatment and recovery sector—the dynamics of where people flow to, the labour market sector—the dynamics of where people flow from and the therapist sector— the dynamics of therapist capacity which acts as a constraint on treatment.

The treatment and recovery sector allows for assumptions about waiting for treatment, length of treatment, drop-out rates, recovery rates, employment rates (dependent on jobs available) and relapse rates.

The labour market sector allows for assumptions about the labour market and the flows of people into the new treatment system from those with mental health conditions in employment and from those out of work and claiming incapacity benefit (IB),[2] both short term and long term.

The therapist sector allows for assumptions about therapist recruitment, therapist leaving and case load.

Each of these sectors raised interconnected issues.

---

[2] A state benefit in the UK paid to people who are unable to work for a period of more than 28 consecutive weeks because of illness or disability. Now replaced by Employment and Support Allowance (ESA).

11.5 Issues Raised in the Treatment and Recovery Sector

The main issues raised were:

1. The distinction between treatment, recovery and employment. Although it was stated in the original CBA that there was a 30% failure rate associated with cognitive behavioural therapy, it was not clear whether it was being suggested that 2.5 million people would be treated to achieve 800,000 recovered OR 800,000 would be treated to achieve 270,000 recovered. The *benefits* expressed in the CBA were based on 800,000 people recovered and back in employment, but the feasibility of using 10000 therapists to treat 2.75 million people was questionable since the length of treatment achievable would be less than the minimum considered clinically feasible.
2. The original cost benefit analysis assumed that everybody treated had a job to return to, whereas the perspective here suggested that some people (varying with location) might not have a job to return to and that job availability and the stigma attached to mental health treatment would conspire against people in seeking a return to work.
3. The original CBA did not allow for any relapses after treatment.

The enhanced CBA did not allow for people failing the low intensity treatment and later 'stepping up' to receive the high intensity treatment.

11.6 Issues Raised in the Labour Market Sector

The main issues raised here were:

1. What would be the candidate population for the new treatment and how many people would be available for treatment? Although it was known that there was an accrued backlog of around 1 million people on incapacity benefit (IB) due to mental illness with inputs and outputs of around 260,000 per year, there was limited data available about the overall flow of people with mental health problems through the labour market. For example, the number of people off work due to mental illness. Figure 11.2 shows a more general structure of the labour market created by one of the trial sites from which the states of Fig. 11.1 were derived.
2. How did people recover from mental illness at present? The modelling led to thinking about and determining estimates for how long people were out of work due to mental illness and their rate of return. This led to an explicit statement that the main benefit of the new system would be, not only to increase the return to work of many more people than at present, but also to speed up their rate of return. The modelling also led to the thinking that there were really two states of people claiming invalidity benefit. A short-term cohort who recovered either without treatment from the current limited current NHS provision and a

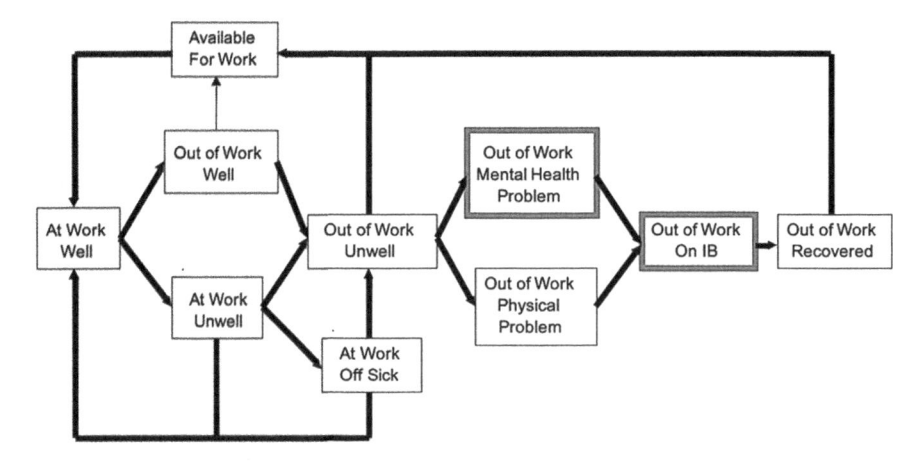

Fig. 11.2 A broader overview of the labour market

long-term cohort whose chances of returning to work diminished the longer they were in this state.
3. The link to other initiatives for assisting people to return to work from both physical and mental illness. It became clear that there were overlaps between the proposed use of CBT and numerous other central and local initiatives to help people back to work. Clearly any case for funding CBT needed to explain its how it complemented these other ideas.

11.7 Issues Raised in the Therapist's Sector

1. The number of therapists needed in steady state? With two service channels it was hypothesised that fewer therapists would be needed overall for a mixed programme than for a single programme.
2. The build-up of therapist capacity. The original CBA focused mainly on the steady state situation after full implementation of the new system but suggested that there would need to be a progressive increase in therapist recruitment and training from two sources over a seven-year period. The modelling added to this thinking by considering therapist turnover and by being able to test alternative training policies.
3. The number of therapists needed beyond seven years once the accrued backlog of people in the labour market had been drawn down and a new equilibrium had been established.

11.8 Model Experiments

The range of experiments carried out initially with the model fell into 2 groups and in each experiment the model was run for 7 years in days. The groups were:

1. Running the model to show the benefits when the programme was fully operational as a comparison with the original CBA for both single and for the mixed channel thinking, with and without step up from the low intensity to high intensity channels for some of those who failed to respond to the low intensity treatment. These runs assumed all therapists to be in place and a constant number of people per year presenting for treatment.
2. Running the model to show a phased build up to therapist capacity over 7 years for mixed treatments, again with and without step up and for a progressive drawdown of people from two states of the labour market ('off work with mental health conditions' and those people receiving 'short term invalidity benefit'). Assumptions were made here about the flow of people through the labour market. This data covered the length of time spent out of work due to mental illness and the current rates of return to work.

11.9 Results from Running Experiments to Show the Benefits of the 'Fully Operational' CBT Programme

A Single Programme

Figure 11.3 shows the number of therapists, number of people treated per annum, number of people recovered per annum, length of treatment in days and the overall net benefits per annum in £ billion to be expected from a fully operational single programme.

The first column on Fig. 11.3 is a direct validity comparison with the basic CBA and shows 10,000 therapists being used to treat 2.75 million people per year with a 30% success rate, giving net benefits of £2.27 billion. As indicated earlier, this situation was considered to be somewhat infeasible since a total treatment time of 44 days is too short given the number of sessions of treatment and the associated assimilation time needed for CBT.

The second column of Fig. 11.3 (alternative 1) shows the much more feasible interpretation of 10,000 therapists being used to treat 800,000 people per year with a 30% success rate. This result uses a minimum feasible figure for the average treatment rate of 77 days, but since only 270,000 people per year recover the net benefits per year are only 25% of those indicated by the original CBA.

A better return is indicated by column 3 in Fig. 11.3 which gives results for the alternative service design in the enhanced CBA capable of treating 900,000 people per year.

	Base run for comparison with the original CBA	Alternative 1	Alternative 2
Therapists	10,000	10,000	6,800
Numbers treated per annum	2,750,000	800,000	900,000
Numbers recovered per annum	800,000	270,000	450,000
Length of treatment in days	44	77	49
Net benefits per annum (£billion)	2.27 (infeasible)	0.56	0.8

Fig. 11.3 Model results for a single programme when established

11.10 A Mixed Programme

Figure 11.4 shows the results for a mixed programme when fully established for alternatives 1 and 2 from Fig. 11.1, for both 'no step up' and 'step up' between the programmes. These results assume a 50/50 spilt of people between the high intensity and low intensity programmes and a 50% failure rate from both the programmes.

Column 1 of Fig. 11.4 shows alternative 1 using a high intensity channel with 77 days treatment time and a low intensity channel with a 25 days treatment time. This configuration can treat 800,000 people per year and requires 4700 high intensity therapists and 1500 low intensity therapists. The net benefits per year of this configuration are double those from the single programme version of alternative 1 due to a higher assumed success rate and fewer therapists needed in total (6,200 compared with 10,000).

Column 2 of Fig. 11.4 again shows results for the mixed programme version of alternative 1, but this time assuming that people failing the low intensity treatment will step up to the high intensity channel. This effectively means treating 200,000 more people per year in the high intensity programme—1 million in total per year rather than 800,000. So this configuration means that 6400 high intensity therapists are needed in total not 4700. However, the net benefits per year are increased beyond the costs because more people receive treatment and recover.

Column 3 of Fig. 11.4 shows the results from alternative 2 using a high intensity channel with 49 days treatment time and a low intensity channel with a 25 days treatment time. This configuration can treat 900,000 people per year and requires

11.10 A Mixed Programme

	Alternative 1 no step up	Alternative 1 step up	Alternative 2 no step up	Alternative 2 step up
Therapists high intensity/low intensity (total)	4700/1500 (6200)	6400/1500 (7900)	3000/1500 (4500)	4500/1500 (6000)
Numbers treated per annum	800,000	1,000,000	900,000	1,125,000
Numbers recovered per annum	400,000	500,000	450,000	562,500
Length of treatment High intensity/ low intensity in days	77/25	77/25	49/25	49/25
Benefits per annum (£billions)	1.0	1.2	1.1	1.3

Fig. 11.4 Model results for a mixed programme when established

fewer therapists in total compared with alternative 1 (3000 high intensity and 1500 low intensity therapists), giving improved net benefits per year over both the single programme version of alternative 2 and the mixed programme version of alternative 1.

Column 4 of Fig. 11.4 shows the results assuming a step up of failures from the low intensity channel to the high intensity channel. This means treating 225,000 more people in the programme per year—1.125 m in total rather than 900000. So, this configuration means that 4500 high intensity therapists are needed rather than 3000. However, the net benefits are again increased because more people receive treatment and recover.

Overall, the mixed programme results would appear to give higher benefits than the single programmes and the use of 'step up' gives higher net benefits than 'no step up'.

11.11 Summary of First Insights from the System Dynamics Model

Although the system dynamics model was not really used as a dynamic model at this stage the stock-flow thinking of the model surfaced some interesting insights:

1. The differentiation between people treated and recovered. The clarification here indicated that the original net benefit claims of the CBA were unachievable since to attain 800,000 recovered people per year meant treating an infeasibly high number of people per year.

2. The mixed programme provides higher returns than the single programme and requires fewer therapists.
3. Step up. The consequences of allowing step up between channels would require 50% more high intensity therapists.

11.12 Results from Running Experiments to Show the Benefits of a Phased Build up to Full Operation of the CBT Programme Over 7 Years

This section of the work used the system dynamics model as a dynamic model. Figure 11.5 shows a similar output summary of results to Fig. 11.3. However, although the number of therapists is that achieved at the end of 7 years, the figures for the number of people treated per annum, the number of people recovered per annum and the overall net benefits per annum in £ billion are the *average* figures over 7 years.

	Alternative 1 no step up	Alternative 1 step up	Alternative 2 no step up	Alternative 2 step up
Therapists high intensity/low intensity (total)	4700/1500 (6200)	6400/1500 (7900)	3000/1500 (4500)	4500/1500 (6000)
Average numbers treated per annum	530,000	640,000	628,000	760,000
Average numbers recovered per annum	260,000	320,000	314,000	380,000
Length of treatment High intensity/ low intensity in days	77/25	77/25	49/25	49/25
Benefits per annum (£billions)	0.7	0.9	0.8	1.0
Change in stock of 'mental health off work sick' over 7 years	-50%	-50%	-58%	-58%
Change in stock of 'short term IB backlog' over 7 years	-15%	-33%	-15%	-33%
Change in stock of 'long term IB backlog' over 7 years	-36%	-36%	-42%	-42%

Fig. 11.5 Model results for a mixed programme phased in over 7 years and draw down of people from the labour market

11.12 Results from Running Experiments to Show the Benefits ...

These results are again presented with and without step up and, additionally, this time for a progressive drawdown of people from two states of the labour market ('off work with mental health conditions' and those people receiving 'short term invalidity benefit'). The final 3 rows show the percentage reduction in these stocks for each situation modelled.

Speculative assumptions were made here by the authors about the flow of people through the labour market to provide background assistance to the Expert Group. This data covered the length of time spent out of work due to mental illness and the current rates of return to work. It was assumed that the 'mental health off work' stock was 1.25 million people and had an inflow per year of 1 million people. Also, that the 'short term IB' stock was 0.8 million people and had an inflow of 260,000 people per year. The calculations for these draw down figures is a truly dynamic calculation since the draw down is in addition to the underlying normal throughputs of the stocks.

An important general point about the results of Fig. 11.5 is that the overall net benefits per year of the plan appear to be reduced relative to the fully operational situation, but this is due to the progressive build-up of capacity.

However, before discussing the Fig. 11.5 results in detail it is useful to relate some of the dynamic factors underpinning them. Figures 11.6 and 11.7 show example model results supporting the results summarised in Fig. 11.5. Figure 11.6 shows an example output of the progressive build-up of high and low therapy

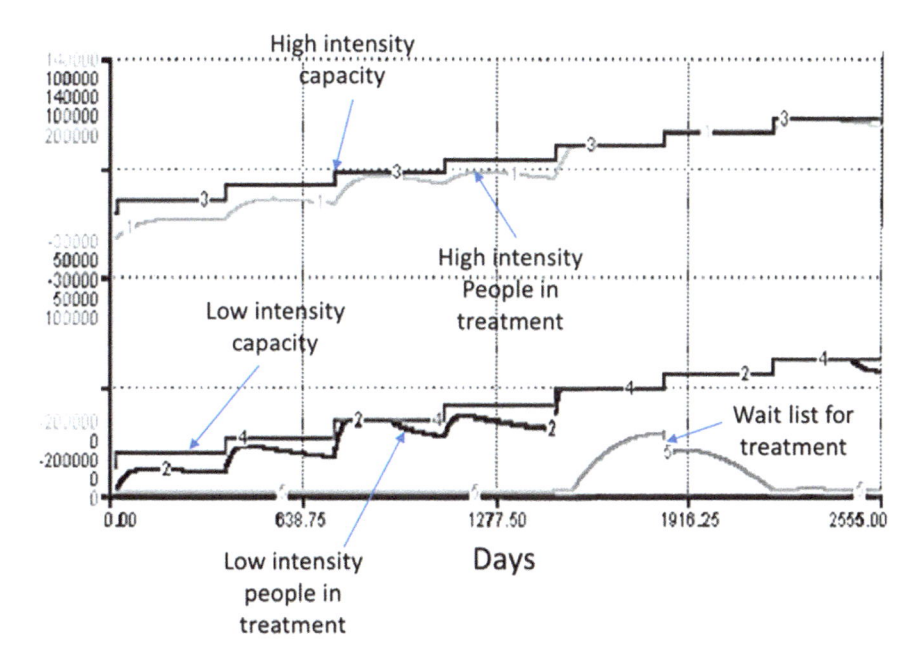

Fig. 11.6 Example model output showing the progressive build-up of high and low therapist capacity, people in treatment over 7 years and the waiting list for treatment

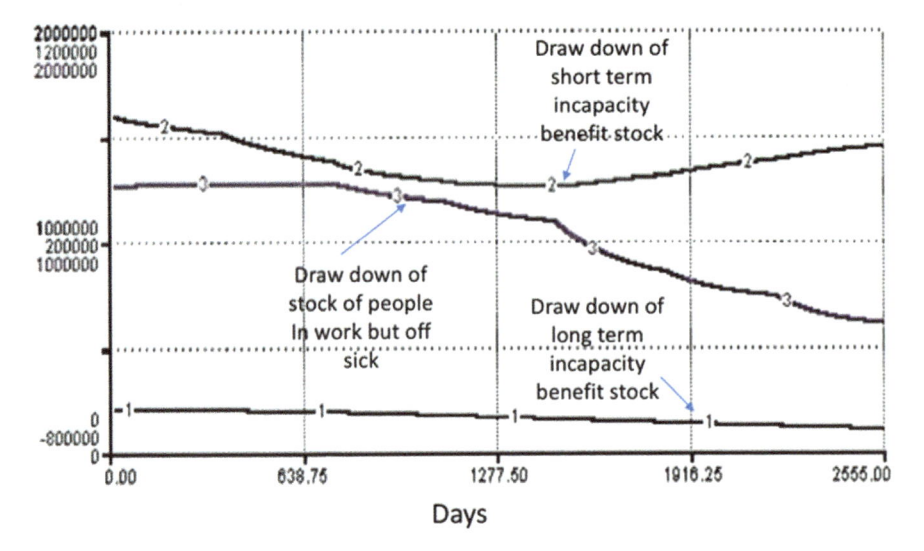

Fig. 11.7 Example model output showing the draw-down of labour market accrued backlogs over 7 years

capacity and people in treatment over 7 years. Figure 11.7 shows the corresponding draw down of the accrued labour market stocks over this period.

These graphs highlight two interesting counterintuitive factors.

The first is that the 'real' short term IB backlog is not just the one shown in Fig. 1, but the sum of this and those people failing to respond to CBT treatment. (Note that the people dropping out and failing to respond cannot be placed back in the short term IB stock because this would assume that they could be treated again). Consequently, and particularly in the case of no step up, as was the situation in Fig. 11.7, the real total short term IB backlog will not be drawn down as fast as linear, static thinking might predict. It will also start to rise in periods when therapy capacity is fully utilised as shown in Fig. 11.6.

The second factor is that although there is no direct draw down from the long term IB backlog, this stock will decline as an indirect consequence of the drawdown of the short term IB stock. Since this is upstream of the long-term stock, drawdown of it will reduce the flow into the long-term stock.

Returning to Fig. 11.5, column 1 shows the alternative 1 mixed model results with 'no step up'. The 'mental health off work sick' backlog is reduced by 50%, the short term IB backlog by 15% and by default the long term IB backlog is reduced by 30%.

Column 2 of Fig. 11.5 shows the same results as column 1, but with 'step up'. Here the impact on the 'short term IB' backlog is doubled, as more people are treated per year rather than placed back into the backlog (but obviously using more therapists).

Column 3 of Fig. 9.5 shows the alternative 2 mixed model results with 'no step up'. Here, the 'short term IB' backlog reductions are increased because this configuration allows more people to be treated than in the alternative 1 mixed model and introducing step up (column 4) permits even greater backlog reductions and more people to be treated per year (but again obviously using more therapists).

Although these results are not directly comparable with the CBA because two treatment channels and two backlogs are modelled and hence a greater total treatment rate used, it would seem that the impact of the plan on the labour market would take some time to show significant results. One reason for this is the treatment rate must not only be big enough to have an impact on the backlogs, but also on the underlying inflow rates into the backlogs. In health terms it must be large enough to cope with both prevalence and incidence. In system dynamics terms it must be large enough to cope with both stock correction and replacement as discussed in Chap. 2.

11.13 Summary of Further Insights from the System Dynamics Model

The simulation results from the system dynamics model created further insights about the overall plan in addition to those given earlier:

1. The annual net benefits of the plan would obviously build up progressively and on average over the 7 years be less than when the programme was fully established.
2. The results from the dynamic model give an indication of the time it would take to draw down the estimated accrues backlogs of people out of work in the labour market. Whilst very dependent on the assumptions about the normal build up and return to work from these stocks, the results show that significant impact could be made on the backlogs by the proposed programme. However, the impact is dependent on building sufficient therapy capacity to deal with people stepping up between treatment channels and on monitoring the true backlog, which includes those people failing treatment.
3. It would appear very important to run all other return to work initiatives alongside the new CBT programme.
4. Structurally the modelling suggested that the best strategy would be to reduce the expensive backlogs of claimants first and then to draw down people onto IAPT from as far 'upstream' as possible in the mental health/workforce chain.
5. Step up of from the low to high intensity programmes for those people failing the low intensity programme gives a bigger impact in reducing the accrued labour market backlogs of people off work sick and on short term IB benefits but requires more therapists.
6. The long term IB backlog would beneficially decline as an indirect consequence of the programme on drawdown of the short term IB stock.

7. Care should be taken to manage therapy capacity closely when the IB backlog was significantly reduced, to match long term capacity to the underlying flow into the backlog.

11.14 Sensitivity Results

All of the foregoing results assume that all people recovering as a result of the new programme would have no relapses and return to employment. The system dynamics model allowed the impact of these factors to be tested. Whilst such results were speculative they emphasised that monitoring relapses and new job creation would be key factors to support the aims of the programme.

11.15 Conclusions on the Content of the CBA

The use of system dynamics confirmed that the proposed IAPT programme had the potential to make an enormous financial net benefit to the UK economy in addition to the wellness benefits to individuals. These benefits are being brought out in practice. Taking in account the flows of people through treatment and the labour market allowed better understanding of assumptions and prompted actions to counter unintended consequences.

11.16 Conclusions on the Use of System Dynamics to Supplement CBA

It was shown possible to quickly develop a dynamic model to supplement the CBA which allows analysis and understanding to develop well beyond the CBA.

The characteristic of traditional CBA in health and social care is that enormous technical and clinical research effort is put into determining the per capita cost and benefit coefficients, but then these are often multiplied by single estimates of the underlying people flows.

System dynamics can include the derivations of static cost benefit coefficients, but its major contribution is to take up where the CBA leaves off and to apply the coefficients to an investigation of the underlying flow structure of the issue and to deal with transitional effects.

The overall methodological conclusion is that dynamic factors are often left out of cost benefit analysis because they cause too much complexity for decision makers, whereas system dynamics allows these factors to be included without masking the clarity of the case.

It is suggested that dynamic impact analysis as described here should be a prerequisite on all planning projects and starting with a CBA is an excellent way of showing the value of the system dynamics method.

References

Observer Leader. (2006). The Depression Report: A new deal for depression and anxiety disorders. *Centre for Economic Performance's Mental Health Study Group, the London School of Economics and Political Science*, June 2006.

The National Institute for Health and Care Excellence. (2004). Depression: Management of depression in primary and secondary care—NICE guidance. *National Health and Care Practice Guideline* Number 23, December 2004.

Chapter 12
Planning Investment in Alcohol Services

Chapter Summary

With costs escalating, the reduction of alcohol-related harm is seen as a priority in most health economies and this chapter describes a nationally developed model from 2009 to enable local NHS commissioners in England to work out which interventions are best at reducing alcohol-related harm for their populations. Using the model, commissioners can explore strategies that will reduce the need for alcohol-related inpatient admissions and reduce the overall cost of alcohol-related harm to the NHS. They can also demonstrate their effects to the Criminal Justice system and other partners engaged in reducing alcohol-related harm. The model uses four consumption groups (Abstainers; Lower Risk; Increasing Risk; Higher Risk) including 'binge' and 'dependent' drinkers in more than one group. Each group has a differing propensity for hospital admissions and a characteristic of the model is that it allows people to move both up and down the chain of groupings.

The project provides a dynamic impact analysis as interventions move people between groups hence changing their risk of admission to hospital. The model contains a set of policies parameterised by the Department of Health, but also allows for local settings. It shows the net impact on hospital admissions and cost from implementing three initiatives, Identification and Brief Advice, Alcohol Health Workers and Specialised Treatment. The model simulates the impact of developing each initiative, on its own or in combination with others. It also provides space for up to five additional service initiatives that can be user-defined by local commissioners. The project demonstrates that in all interventions costs will rise initially but break-even within 2–3 years and then continue to reduce on a recurring basis. The conclusion is that these changes are significant contenders for quality improvement projects locally and a potential major contributor to NHS efficiency gains.

The work relates to the search for consistent and cohesive policies by which central government can guide local actions. The approach of using dynamic models goes beyond action lists for guidance and allows localities to learn what will work for them.

12.1 Context and Client

The England Department of Health's Alcohol Improvement Programme (AIP) had a remit to promote a range of interventions designed to tackle alcohol-related harm caused by excessive alcohol consumption. Tackling excessive consumption is a worthwhile end in itself; additionally, the AIP wanted to test the economic case for such investment, whether savings made as a result of health improvement, particularly reductions in admissions to hospital and attendances at accident and emergency departments, might be greater than the cost of the new services.

Research into these interventions, mainly in the form of follow-up studies of those treated, suggested that savings were possible. Informed by this evidence, the AIP developed in-house a spreadsheet model, known as the "Ready Reckoner", as part of a suite of tools to be used by local service commissioners (normally at local health organisation level). Typical behaviour of this model showed a linear relationship between projected savings and investment in new services.

The remit for the project was to develop a system dynamics tool that was built on a less simplified set of processes and assumptions. It could be better adapted to fit local circumstances and requirements and could be operated over a longer time frame. The exercise used an expert-group model building approach. Once the model was developed and further tested, it was developed into a version designed for local use.

12.2 The Problem

Drug, alcohol and addiction problems have been studied in the past using system dynamics. The primary concerns of these models have included the supply chain, the issue of addiction, problems caused by anti-social behaviour resulting from intoxication, and even modelling the biology by which alcohol is absorbed into the blood stream (Moxnes and Jensen 2009).

The particular issue exercising this client was more mainstream, the wide range of damage done to the health of the general population through excessive consumption. Most, not all, of the interventions modelled here focus on reducing consumption, as a much wider concern than tackling dependent drinking (addiction) or episodic binge drinking. The Department of Health has sponsored considerable research into how this excessive consumption feeds its way into hospital admission. More than 40 types of hospital admission are found to be partly or wholly attributable to alcohol consumption.

The overall position is shown in Fig. 12.1 which displays the rise in "alcohol attributable" hospital admissions. This rise is attributed to increasing consumption combined with a rising adult population.

One way of tackling this problem is the provision of brief advice, combined with brief treatments (such as a series of four sessions with an adviser), to people believed to be drinking excessively. These services might be targeted on people

12.2 The Problem

Alcohol Attributable Admissions to Hospital (England)

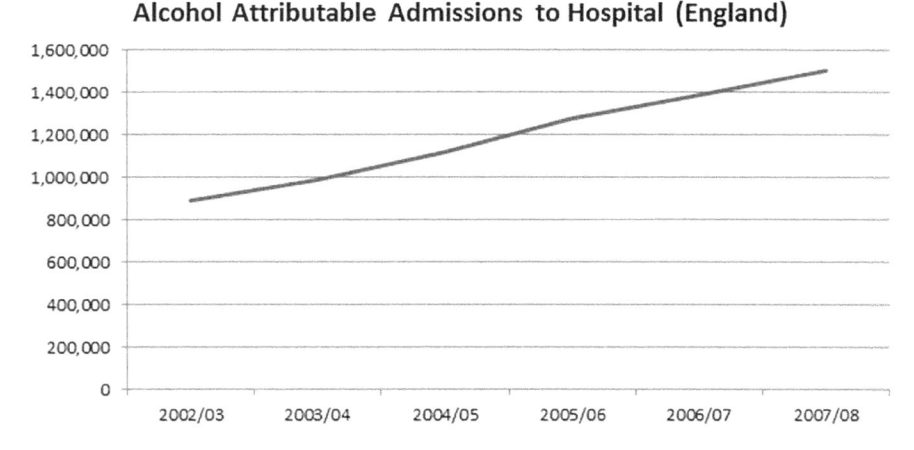

[Chart showing admissions rising from approximately 900,000 in 2002/03 to approximately 1,500,000 in 2007/08]

Fig. 12.1 Alcohol attributable admissions to hospital per annum

attending accident and emergency departments, people recently admitted to hospital, or through some basic screening of patients consulting general practitioners in primary care.

There is a very large body of research evidence supporting such opportunistic case finding for alcohol misuse and the delivery of simple advice including at least 56 controlled trials (Moyer et al. 2002). A recent Cochrane Collaboration review (Kaner et al. 2007) provides substantial evidence for the effectiveness of alcohol case identification and the delivery of brief advice. For every eight people who receive simple alcohol advice, one will reduce their drinking to within low-risk levels (Moyer et al. 2002). This compares favourably with smoking where only one in twenty will act on the advice given (Silagy and Stead 2003).

Evidence suggests that those drinking at increasing or higher risk who receive brief advice are twice as likely to moderate their drinking 6–12 months after brief advice when compared to drinkers receiving no brief advice (Wilk et al. 1997). Brief advice can reduce weekly drinking by between 13 and 34%, resulting in 2.9–8.7 fewer mean drinks per week with a significant effect on movement towards lower-risk alcohol use (Whitlock et al. 2004).

The dynamic hypothesis is that tackling consumption through these brief interventions will reduce alcohol consumption in the population, leading to health improvements that will show themselves in a reduction in alcohol-attributable hospital admissions, such that, in time, investment in new services is recovered from subsequent savings.

In the AIP's pre-existing spreadsheet tool, that causal chain is encapsulated in a simple statistical relationship between an input (brief interventions) and an output (reduction in hospital admissions). The effect is shown in the screenshot in Fig. 12.2 where some interventions (recruitment of alcohol health nurses) produce a linear reduction in hospital admissions. A key feature of this behaviour is that when

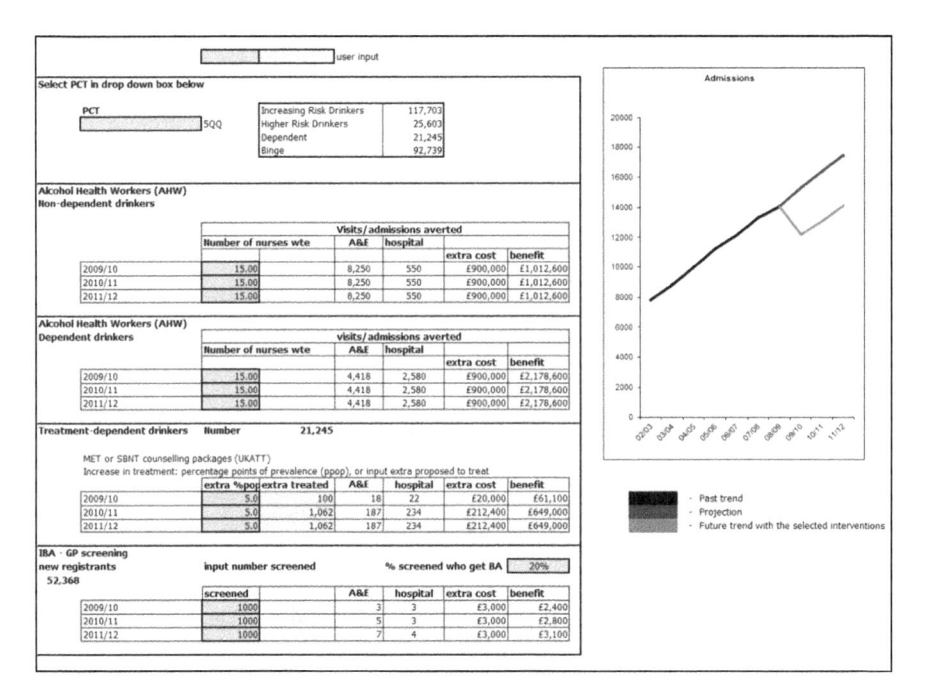

Fig. 12.2 Part of the spreadsheet "Ready Reckoner"

a constant change is introduced, there is an immediate stepped reduction (actual against trend) followed by a rise at the same gradient as the projection.

12.3 Method

The method adopted to build the model was group model building. The Department of Health assembled an expert group consisting of experts from the fields of public health, alcohol/substance abuse, health economics, academia, service commissioning, practice, policy development, operations research/data analysis and the "not for profit" sector. The group met at monthly intervals for eight months, facilitated by two consultants, both with a background of working in the health and care sectors combined with expertise in building system dynamics models. Although there were a few changes in membership, the group composition remained reasonably consistent; this contributed greatly to the success of the project.

After the model was completed (and no model is ever finished) a smaller, core group continued to meet, testing the model under a range of scenarios and, ultimately, refining some of its structure, assumptions and functionality.

During this phase, the model was converted into a "runtime" version, with detailed documentation and online help menus, and tested with a wide range of possible users of the model, mainly local service commissioners. The model interface was adapted in the light of their feedback.

12.4 Description of Model

The main stock-flow structure of the model is the adult population of a locality; in the development phase, a notional population of 250,000 was used (rising to just under 300,000 in 20 years). The four stocks represent the consumption groups (abstinent, lower risk, increasing risk and higher risk), defined according to average weekly consumption of alcohol in units. This classification is widely used by the Department of Health for policy planning purposes. Information for the groups is available from the General Lifestyle Survey,[1] an annual survey of a sample of households in Great Britain and is derived from questions about amounts of different drinks usually drunk on any one day during the last 12 months. The classification differs from international classifications of hazardous and harmful drinking based on the Alcohol Use Disorders Identification Test (AUDIT).

The benefit of using this classification is that much government planning data draws on it, but it does differ from international classifications of hazardous drinking.

Although the focus on consumption is foremost, the framework does contain within it other policy issues, such as dependence/addiction and binge drinking. A snapshot of how the adult population of England is distributed across these groups is shown in Fig. 12.3.

The main stock-flow chain (Fig. 12.4) represents people moving between these consumption groups. It bears some resemblance to system dynamics models of chronic health problems (Homer et al. 2004), with the crucial differences that:

- People can move up *and* down the chain; in most chronic conditions models, 0 only degeneration is possible
- Movement is not just to the adjacent stock; people can move between any stocks (for example movement from the "higher risk" group to "abstinent" would be a requirement for someone following a "12 steps" approach).

It is important to establish the main dynamics of this chain before applying the impact of additional interventions. These include:

- The model represents the entire adult (18 and over) population of a discrete area
- Therefore, at any point in time everyone is in one stock; the states are mutually exclusive and exhaustive

---

[1] Formerly known as General Household Survey, as in Fig. 11.3.

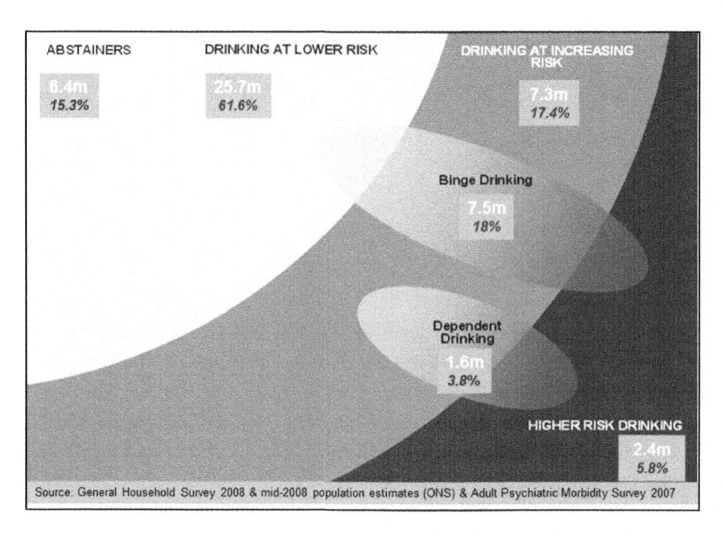

Fig. 12.3 Percentage in each consumption group, also showing how dependent and binge drinkers are distributed across consumption groups

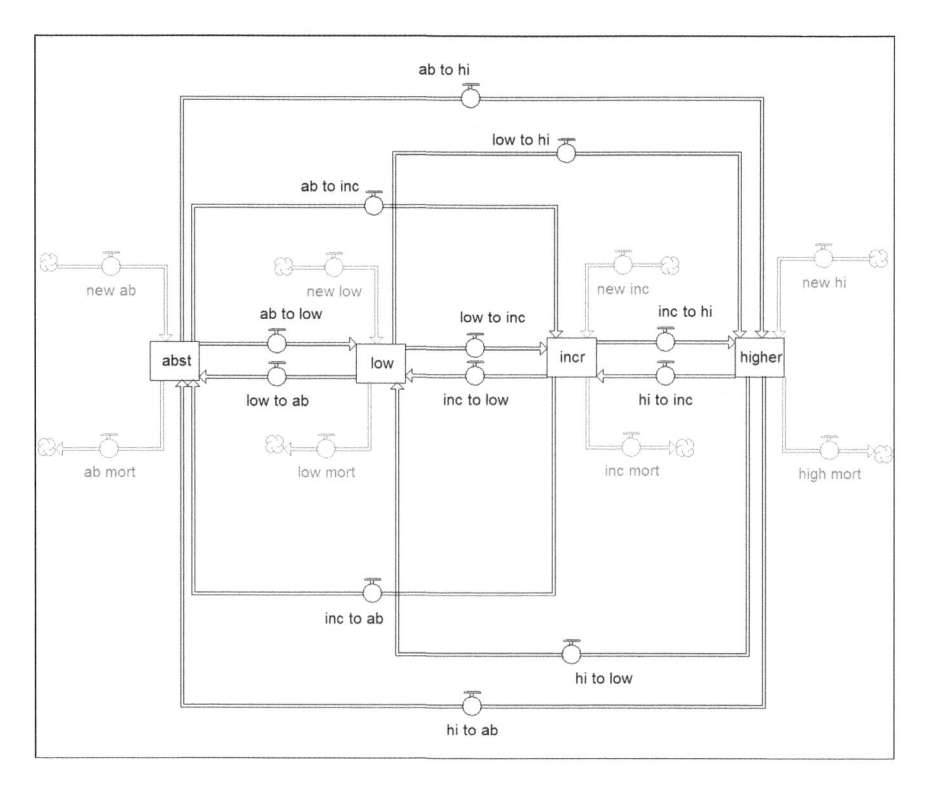

Fig. 12.4 Main stock flow chain for alcohol consumption

12.4 Description of Model

- The total population is given as an exogenous input, and for most areas is projected to increase over time
- The model runs for 20 years with a time step of days; it is now clear that months would have been a satisfactory time step but in the initial development period some stakeholders were interested in some detailed analysis of hospital episodes, whose lengths of stay are best measured in days (as with most models built in a consulting environment, this one contains more detail than is necessary, and time does not allow for subsequent refinement and simplification)
- National data are available to give the initial distribution between consumption groups
- Adjustments in population are based on different mortality rate inputs for each group, combined with a stock adjustment of "new" cases (mainly people reaching the age of 18)
- To make that adjustment, we need to know the distribution by consumption group of people at age 18 (people enter the model into any of the consumption groups)
- Further adjustments to population are made based on the effectiveness of treatment interventions (the population might therefore grow to a larger number than the exogenous input for scenarios showing particularly effective interventions because more people are in the lower consumption groups which have lower mortality)
- A key requirement is to estimate the "base" rate of movement between the stocks (see below).

Estimates of the historical distribution of the population between the four stocks are available at national level, and the Department of Health had made its own projections of the future distribution (not using system dynamics). There had been a steady rise in alcohol consumption in the 1990s which reached a plateau around 2004; this plateau was projected to continue.[2]

The client was able to undertake a secondary analysis of the General Household Survey data, comparing people's consumption in two successive years (this was not straightforward because the data set is of households rather than individuals). This estimated the annual rate of movement (in terms of the percentage of people who moved from each stock to each other stock in the course of a year) as shown in Fig. 12.5.

The model is designed to be operated by a variety of users, and it is possible to select from a range of starting years. Typically, the model has been run using 2005 as the starting point, but to produce a reference mode, the model was run from 2000. Without any additional dynamics resulting from the introduction of service interventions, the model's base-case behaviour is determined by:

---

[2] As things have turned out, there is some evidence of a reduction in consumption (perhaps as a consequence of the economic downturn).

From \ To	Abstinent	Lower Risk	Increasing Risk	Higher Risk
Abstinent		25	0	0
Lower Risk	5		8	0
Increasing Risk	1	21		11
Higher Risk	1	10	19	

Fig. 12.5 Percentage of people who have moved from each consumption group to each other group after one year

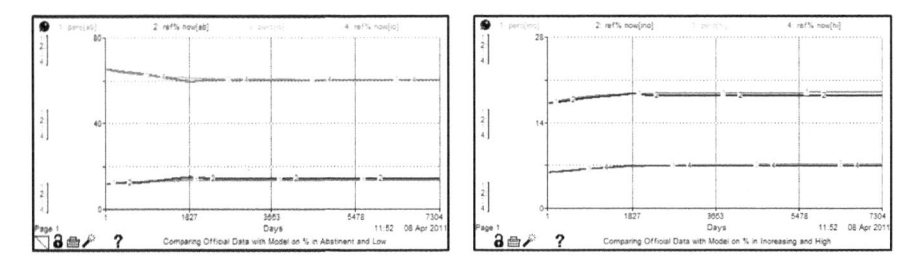

Fig. 12.6 Reference mode comparing base run of model output for percentage in each consumption group against reference data

- The flow rates set out in Fig. 12.5
- The initial percentage in each stock
- Assumptions about the distribution of people joining the model (drinking status on 18th birthday[3])
- Different mortality rates applied to each stock
- Population growth.

These inputs combined to produce a good match between the percentage distribution of people between drinking groups generated by the model and the (reference) historical plus projected data held by the Department of Health. Figure 12.6 compares the model outputs for the percentage in each stock in the base run against the reference data.

The total adult population is growing, as are alcohol attributable hospital admissions (see Fig. 12.7).

---

[3]Obviously, not based on behaviour on the day itself, the legal drinking age in England.

12.4 Description of Model

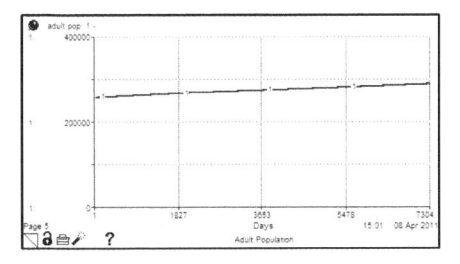

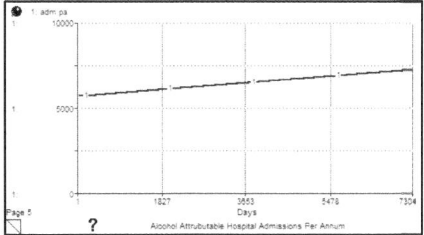

Fig. 12.7 Total adult population and alcohol attributable admissions in model base run

The two main output variables of concern are:

- Alcohol attributable hospital admissions
- Cost of services (including hospital and interventions, described below).

The purpose of the model, therefore, is to explore the extent to which spending money on specific interventions generates reductions in hospital admissions and therefore saves money. The causal mechanisms are that:

- Alcohol attributable hospital admissions vary by consumption group and are higher in the higher consumption groups
- Service interventions will increase the rate at which people move into lower consumption groups
- This takes place against a background of considerable churn between consumption groups in the base case
- With more people in the lower consumption groups, alcohol admissions will also reduce.

This is summarised in Fig. 12.8.

This diagram is neither a stock-flow map nor a causal loop diagram. In the Consumption part, people move between consumption groups. The distribution between groups determines the rate of hospital admissions, but there is also a delay here, because reductions in consumption are not immediately followed by improvements in health.

By commissioning interventions (services) it is possible to change the flow rates in the main model. After the time delay, this will show itself as a reduction in admissions.

(Note that although the diagram makes it look like services exclusively operate by speeding up the reducing consumption flows, and policies by slowing down the rate of increase, actually each will do a bit of both).

Hospital admissions are a mixture of acute (e.g. accident and injury) and chronic conditions (related to or exacerbated by alcohol consumption). It is possible to set a different time lag for each category of admission.[4] For example, following a reduction in consumption someone's propensity to have an accident is reduced

---

[4] Here, 44 types of admission have been collapsed into 10 categories in the model, using arrays.

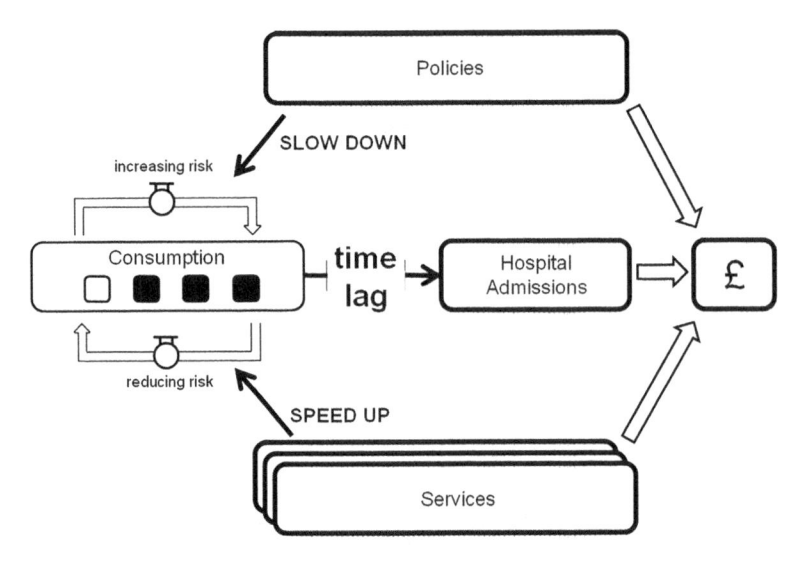

Fig. 12.8 Diagram showing assumptions behind causal relationships in the model

almost immediately, whereas chronic liver disease will continue (though some recovery is possible).

The financial implications are that both hospital admissions and services cost money. "Policies" may not cost a great deal or may cost the Department of Health nothing (being enforced by other means). Increased expenditure on services is incurred immediately, whereas any reductions in expenditure resulting from reductions in hospital admission will take time to show (because of the delay factor).

There are several service interventions modelled. They all have a similar structure:

- A demand function based on the main stock—flow chain or some other part of the model
- A capacity (the size of the investment, how much of the intervention to procure)
- An effect (the percentage of people receiving the intervention who reduce their consumption as a result) which feeds back into the main stock—flow chain
- A cost (based on the capacity utilisation)
- A setting determining how far into the model run the service should be switched on (typically the model is run for five years, then the intervention is introduced).

The characteristics of the main interventions are:

"Identification and brief advice" is provided in primary care. People visiting a general practitioner for any reason are asked some routine screening questions. Depending on the response to these questions, some supplementary advice about alcohol consumption is offered.

Brief interventions provided by "Alcohol Health Workers (AHWs) in hospital" (Owens 2005a, b and Owens and Morton 2007), in which people admitted to hospital, where there is reason to belief this might be alcohol-related, are offered brief counselling from a specialist (who might be a nurse). In this case, the maximum possible users of the service is governed by the alcohol-related hospital admissions figure that is itself generated by the model. Most model users to date have allocated a relatively modest capacity to this service, reflecting current reality that such a service tends to be targeted on dependent drinkers.

"Specialised services"—treatments for dependence, have tended to be less well explored in modelling sessions. They are the more traditional services geared towards tackling dependence/addiction, characterised by being typically more expensive and provided in smaller numbers. As the modelling work progressed, so the focus in the model was more on the "brief intervention" services which are tackling consumption.

12.5 Typical Model Behaviour

In the base case of the model, the overall population is rising, and the distribution of people between the consumption groups has plateaued as described above. The only expenditure being incurred is on hospital admissions, and also some specialised services.

The model dashboard (Fig. 12.9) enables a user to navigate to different service settings, and also to control which services are to be used in a particular model run through the use of switches.

The Service Settings consist of buttons enabling a user to navigate to a series of input screens for each type of service. As well as the three services identified above, the buttons headed Local A—E enable a user to describe up to five more locally-defined services (in terms of capacity, cost, effect on consumption). The "admissions and prevalence" settings do not have a switch because hospital services cannot be anything other than "on".

The Model Settings lead to:

- a series of population input screens that are mostly set-up once (to match the area being modelled) but not changed once scenarios are being run
- a series of output screens on which different graphs are displayed
- a "make base run" function (explained below).

1. **Base Run**

In the sequence of runs that follows, the start year is 2005 and the model runs for 20 years.

The base run of the model is normally a run with no additional services switched on.

At this point, we are most interested in the outputs for:

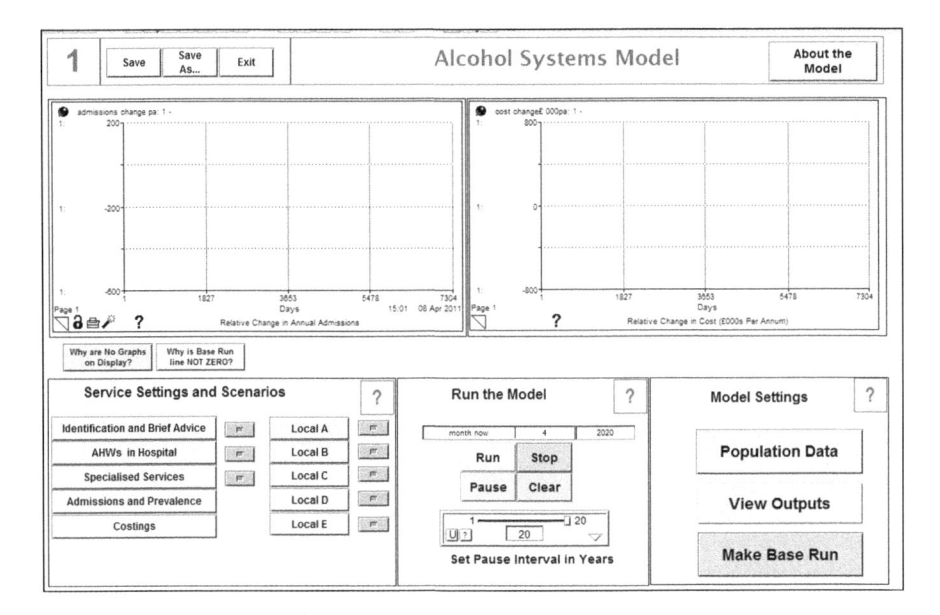

Fig. 12.9 The model dashboard

- number of hospital admissions per annum
- total cost per annum.

In the base case, both variables are rising (with similar gradients because hospital costs are the main costs) as shown in Fig. 12.10.

These graphs show the current run (admissions per annum or expenditure per annum in £000 s) mapped against variables called "base". Since this is the base run these lines are identical. Both admissions and costs are rising, mainly because of a rise in population (consumption having reached a plateau).

2. **Scenario Using Identification and Brief Advice in Primary Care (Fig. 12.11)**

In this scenario, a new intervention is switched on five years into the run. It consists of:

- 10% of primary care practices screening all "new registrations" where 8% of the population registers (normally following a change of address) with a practice per annum
- 5% of primary care practices screening every patient attending where 65% of the population visit a practice at least once per annum (people are screened only once in the year)
- Those identified as being in the two higher consumption groups are offered advice as a result of which 12.5% reduce their consumption enough to move into a lower group.

12.5 Typical Model Behaviour

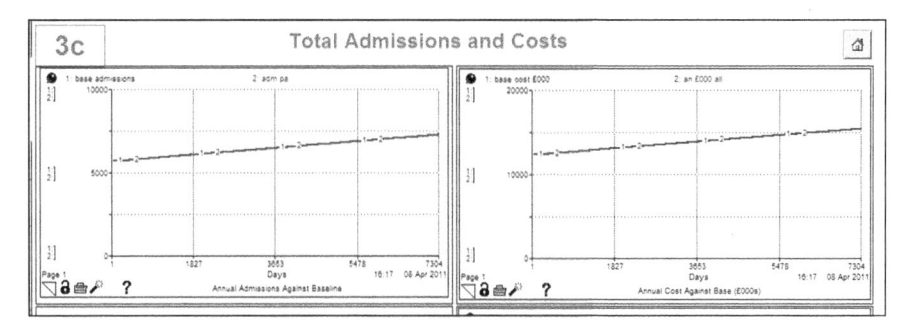

Fig. 12.10 Total admissions and costs outputs from base run

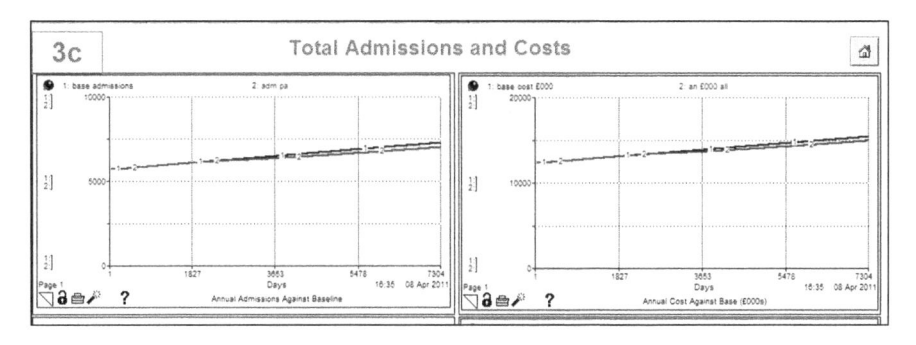

Fig. 12.11 Admissions and costs comparing scenario 2 against base

At this point, it becomes quite hard to discern much change. The intervention point is five years into the model (day 1827 on the graph), and after a considerable time, some reduction in admissions, then costs, begins to show.

Faced with these outputs, model users were finding it difficult to evaluate what the model was telling them. And in the model's earlier days these graphs were "comparative" graphs (plotting one variable over a series of runs) which tended to get quite cluttered.

What they really wanted was a graph of the gap between the current run and the base run, an output not readily generated in system dynamics software. By exporting several key variables (such as admissions and costs) to a spreadsheet, then importing these values into graphical variables called "base variable…" this problem was overcome, and new sets of variables plotting the difference between the current run and base were generated. These variables were ultimately selected to be the main variables displayed, as comparative graphs on the dashboard (Fig. 12.12).

Now, the base run is run 1, and the scenario is run 2. Obviously, in the base run, the difference between the variable and the base is 0. In the scenario, it becomes clearer that there is a reduction in admissions which is quite evident about two years

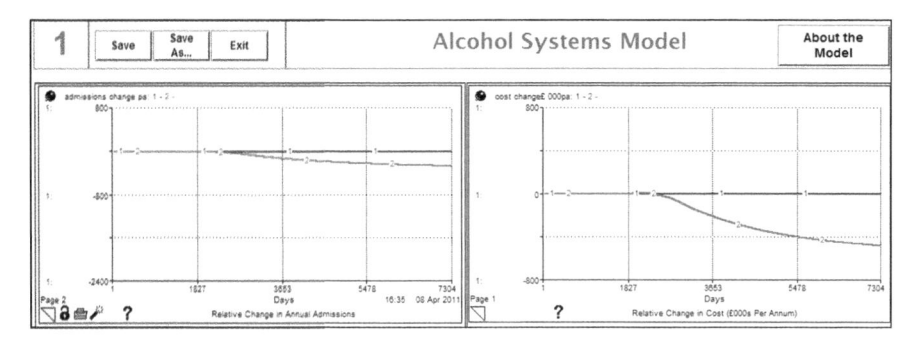

Fig. 12.12 Model dashboard showing "difference between this run and base run" graphs for admissions and costs (base and scenario 2)

after the introduction of the intervention, and that costs increase slightly (because when the intervention is first introduced there is a cost but no saving yet on admissions). These patterns become more obvious in the next scenario.

3. **Scenario: Introduce Alcohol Health Workers in Hospital (Fig. 12.13)**

In this scenario, four workers are employed to provide brief advice and interventions, typically a series of four appointments spread over 10 weeks, to people attending hospital (either accident and emergency/emergency room, or admitted) who are believed to have an alcohol attributable admission. As a result of the intervention, 60% of people seen reduce their consumption and move into lower consumption groups.

Most of the outputs produced by the model take this shape, an initial increase in expenditure (because a new service is introduced), followed by a subsequent reduction in expenditure as the reduction in admissions produces cost savings that are greater than the new service expenditure.

For the most part, service commissioners have been content to compare expenditure levels year on year and are content to consider the point at which the change in expenditure line crosses the X-axis as a "breakeven" point.

Strictly speaking, this is not the case, and some commissioners suggested that the breakeven point is the point at which cumulative change in cost is negative (so far, nobody has asked for a discounted cash-flow calculation).

The cumulative cost change graph (generated in the same way, by the export/import of base cumulative costs through a spreadsheet) for these model runs is harder to scale but shows the breakeven point for scenario 3 to be within the third year following the change (Fig. 12.14).

4. **Scenario: Combining Both Interventions (Fig. 12.15)**

Obviously, it is possible to switch on more than one service intervention. Run 4 represents the combined effect of using the services introduced in Runs 2 and 3.

12.5 Typical Model Behaviour

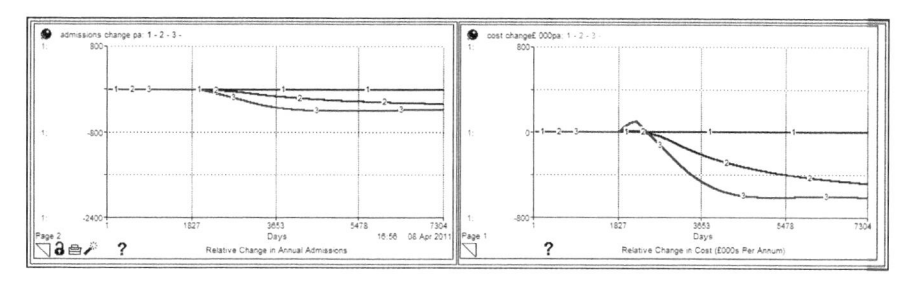

Fig. 12.13 Difference in admissions and costs for base, run 2 and run 3

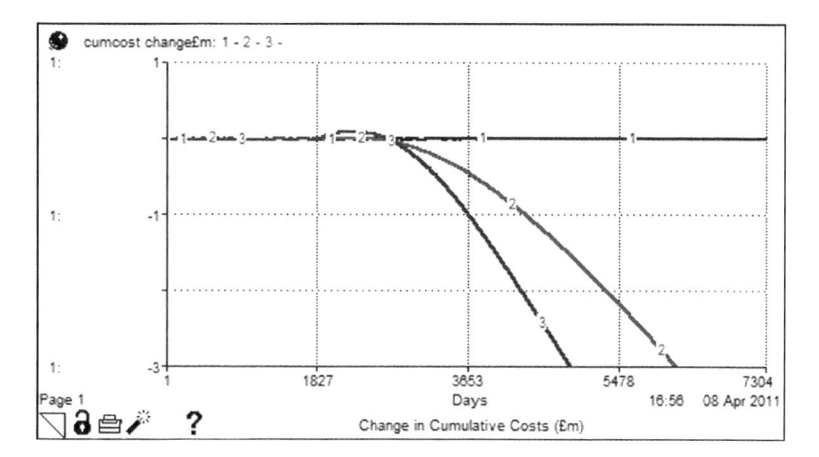

Fig. 12.14 Difference in cumulative cost compared with cumulative cost of base run for the same runs

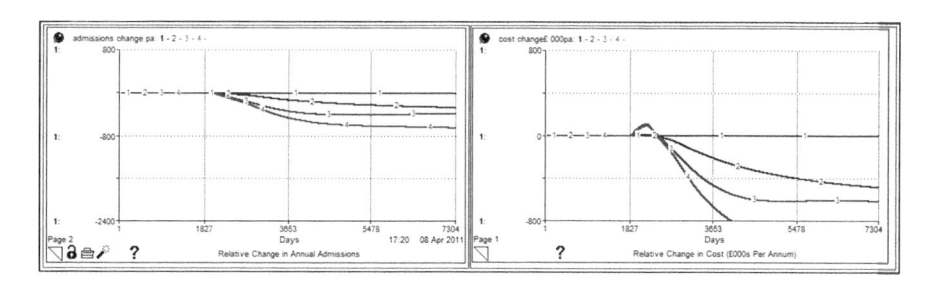

Fig. 12.15 Difference in admissions and cost graphs for all runs

12.6 Making Sense of the Findings

From the client's point of view, the model (disappointingly) showed less of a reduction in admissions (hence fewer savings) than the existing spreadsheet, which functioned essentially by extrapolating from a statistical relationship between service interventions and subsequent admission rates drawn from various studies. Because of this, the model was subjected to a prolonged period of testing and questioning, which established that the model faithfully represented the collective mental model of the client. The systems model could more readily represent the causal connections, delays and accumulations that had hitherto merely been captured within a statistical relationship, in particular:

- The basic assumption that alcohol-related ill health is caused by consumption—therefore those in the higher consumption groups will tend to experience more hospital admissions than those in the lower group
- That specific interventions will move people down the consumption chain
- Nevertheless, there is a time delay between change in consumption and improvement in some chronic conditions
- There is a cumulative effect because interventions move people into a different stock (thereafter, some will move back up, or continue down, the consumption chain).

There are other connections, for example, the *supply* of interventions located in hospital can be varied (e.g. by recruiting more staff) but *demand* (maximum number of alcohol attributable admissions) is a function of model behaviour (we might run out of people to treat). In the spreadsheet it is theoretically possible to go on recruiting staff, with a linear reduction in admissions, to the point where future admissions go negative because the number of admissions "saved" exceeds the actual number of admissions (an impossibility). In the systems model, the obvious "limit to growth" in the demand function means that beyond a certain amount, there is no point in expanding a service.

Ironically, because few will have tested the spreadsheet under these extreme conditions, the systems model tended to show that a much greater investment in hospital-based Alcohol Health Workers was indicated than any of the users who developed and piloted the model envisaged.

In the course of a long dialogue between the client and the modelling team seeking to explain the modest performance of the systems model, two further refinements were made:

- It would be possible that some people might reduce their consumption *within* a group but not enough to move into a lower stock
- When modelling the impact of interventions on people admitted to hospital with chronic conditions, using a treatment effect on the general population (only a fraction of whom have such a condition) dilutes the impact

12.6 Making Sense of the Findings

Further adjustments were made using co-flows, including a representation of prevalence and incidence of the chronic conditions modelled, which, as expected, improved the overall treatment effect in the systems model, but still showing fewer savings than were projected by the spreadsheet.

12.7 Wider Applications

Costs and Benefits

The model has been used to compare the impact of policy interventions on "costs". The model does not, as yet, make any attempt to quantify "benefits", although these benefits can be shown.

The most obvious benefit is that the general health of the population would improve if alcohol consumption goes down. In the last run of the model shown, combining brief interventions in hospital and in primary care, in addition to the main outputs shown (admissions and costs), it is worth looking at the distribution of the population by consumption group (Fig. 12.16).

The model does not at present quantify these population health improvements, such as in Quality Adjusted Life Years.

Another obvious benefit would look beyond the health sector. Such a reduction in consumption would also be shown in the criminal justice system, given a link between certain types of crime and alcohol consumption. There is interest in exploring this further but it is beyond the scope of the present enquiry.

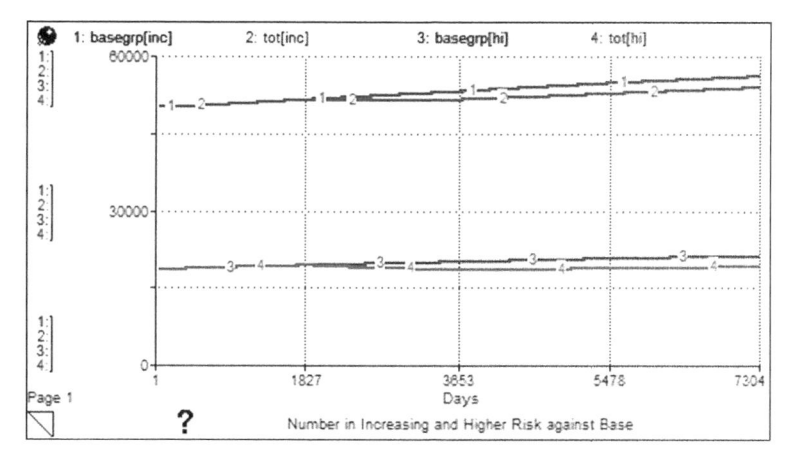

Fig. 12.16 Number in higher and increasing risk consumption groups compared against base run. In this model run, out of a final population of 297,000, the number in the increasing risk group has reduced from a base 56,500 to 54,300, and the number in the higher risk group from 21,200 to 19,100, a total reduction of over 4,000 from the two top consumption groups

Non-treatment Approaches to Tackling Alcohol Consumption

The model is currently limited to exploring the impact of specific treatment interventions on alcohol consumption. The model could also be expanded to include interventions not currently modelled, for example the impact of different pricing interventions on health and criminal justice outcomes.

The model does not offer a properly calibrated representation of the sensitivity of alcohol consumption to pricing, but it can be assumed that the intention of any minimum-pricing policy would be, in stock/flow terms, to reduce the rate at which people flow up the consumption chain and increase the rate at which people flow down the chain.

Introducing a very simple reduction to the flow rates, of "assume that the increase-in-consumption flows reduce by 10% and the reduction-in-consumption flows increase by 10%", after five years, produces a dramatic effect on hospital admissions and hence costs. Figures 12.17 and 12.18 show these outputs.

The most striking difference between these outputs and the outputs generated by the treatment intervention scenarios is that there is no rise in cost following the intervention point, because the policy would be introduced at no cost to the health system. There is no "investment" in services to be made.

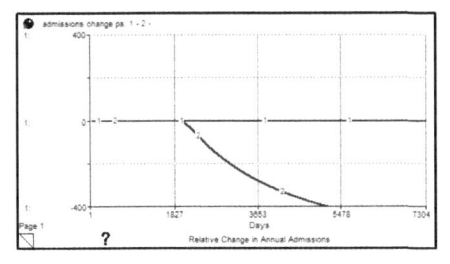

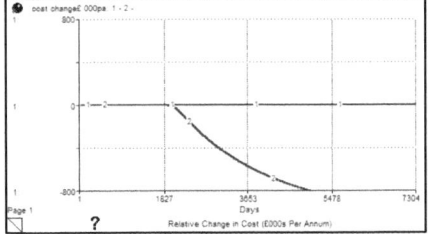

Fig. 12.17 Effect of "minimum pricing"

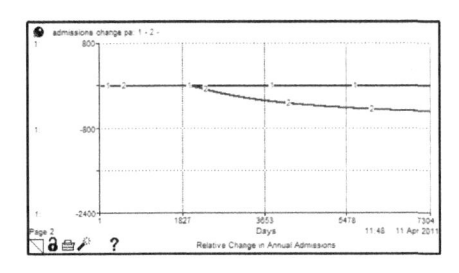

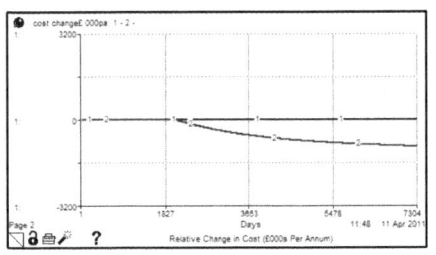

Fig. 12.18 The same graphs on a different scale

12.8 Making the Model Usable

The model has required an amount of secondary analysis by the client in order to estimate inputs for such variables as the "normal rate of movement between consumption groups". In addition, although a great deal of detailed analysis of alcohol attributable hospital admissions exists, largely based on the development of "alcohol attributable fractions" by which (all) admissions data are multiplied to report the number of alcohol attributable admissions by area, the model generated new data requirements, such as the need to have these admissions broken down by consumption group.

Although it would undoubtedly be possible to construct a simpler, higher-level model, showing only one category of admissions and only one treatment intervention (applied in varying degrees), to create a meaningful tool for service commissioners it is necessary to disaggregate admissions by type (by using an array function), and to separate out different types of intervention (partly because they each have different demand functions, such as people attending primary care, people admitted to hospital, people who are alcohol-dependent).

The model is also linked to various spreadsheets, both to create more comprehensive data reports and also to achieve the "create a base run" routine (involving exporting and importing a data set).

The model is now available to the NHS, and has been tested by a range of potential users. The runtime model interface has a range of features designed to make the model usable by service commissioners, including help menus, options to enter local data, the possibility of choosing from a variety of possible start years.

12.9 Conclusion

The model development has proceeded from an initial requirement for a tool to be used to communicate the benefits of a range of service interventions, so that local service commissioners might make more informed choices about future investment.

In the course of that development, which was supported by national experts in the field, questions arose about why the model projections differed somewhat from those that had been expected. This provoked a lengthy period of questioning of, learning from, and improvement of, the model.

The outcome is a tool that is capable of providing a more sophisticated analysis of the likely cost implications of new service investment, in a financial climate where increased investment in any area of public health may need to be justified by a business case showing overall savings. The model shows that any investment will be followed by a period in which more money is spent on services; in time the whole system of treatment might cost less, and it is possible to compute both the time at which expenditure will be less than baseline, and also when the initial investment might be recovered.

The system dynamics model arguably provides a more compelling picture of these phenomena than a spreadsheet approach that extrapolates from a particular statistical relationship, because it represents the subtleties of the impact of delays between changes in consumption and changes in health, as well as some limits to growth.

The model is capable of informing a wider debate, for example about the implications for the criminal justice system of these health interventions. There would be merit in extending the range of policy options modelled to include alcohol-pricing; a system dynamics approach would enhance that debate.

Finally, the model interface has been designed to make it usable by a wide range of (non-expert) users. The question of how much support such users will need and how it might be afforded given the current state of the public finances remains open, and the authors would hope to return to some of these themes of making complex models more accessible at a future date.

References

Homer, J., Hirsch, G., Minniti, M., & Pierson, M. (2004). Models for collaboration; how system dynamics helped a community organize cost-effective care for chronic illness. *System Dynamics Review, 3*, 20.

Kaner, E., Beyer, F., Dickinson, H., Pienaar, E., Campbell, F., Schlesinger, C., et al. (2007). Brief interventions for excessive drinkers in primary health care settings. *Cochrane Database of Systematic Reviews*, 2. Art No.: CD004148. https://doi.org/10.1002/14651858.cd004148.pub3.

Moxnes, E., & Jensen, L. (2009). Drunker than intended: Misperceptions and information treatments. *Drug Alcohol Dependence, 105*(1–2), 63–70.

Moyer, A., Finney, J., Swearingen, C., & Vergun, P. (2002). Brief Interventions for alcohol problems: A meta-analytic review of controlled investigations in treatment-seeking and non-treatment seeking populations. *Addiction, 97*, 279–292.

Owens, L. (2005a). *The burden of alcohol on the NHS*. Pharmacology & Therapeutics, The University of Liverpool. Doctor of Philosophy.

Owens, L. (2005b). How do NHS Hospitals in England deal with patients with alcohol-related problems? A questionnaire survey. *Alcohol & Alcoholism., 40*(5), 409–412.

Owens, L., & Morton, D. (2007). Effective nurse-led and patient-centred alcohol interventions. *Nursing in Practice* July/August, 50–55.

Silagy, C., & Stead, L. F. (2003). Physician advice for smoking cessation (Cochrane Review). In *The Cochrane Library*, Issue 4 (Chichester, Wiley).

Whitlock, E. P., Polen, M. R., Green, C. A., Orleans, T., & Klein, J. (2004). Behavioural counselling interventions in primary care to reduce risky/harmful alcohol use by adults: A summary of the evidence for the US Preventive Services Task Force. *Annals of Internal Medicine, 140*, 557–568.

Wilk, A. I., Jensen, N. M., & Havighurst, T. C. (1997). Meta-analysis of randomized control trials addressing brief interventions in heavy alcohol drinkers. *Journal of General Internal Medicine, 12*, 274–283.

# Chapter 13
The Impact of Diagnosis Targets for Long-Term Conditions: Dementia

Chapter Summary

This chapter uses a model derived from project work on dementia and developed by the authors to explore how much diagnosis capacity is needed in order to achieve a target percentage of 'people diagnosed' of people with dementia. The target is always expressed as a 'percentage of prevalence'. In England, the target is set at 67%.

The model and the thinking behind it are described. The results demonstrate that the same stocks (mild, moderate and severe prevalence) of people with dementia can arise from many different combinations of the flows (incidence, mortality and progression) into and out of each stage of prevalence. By comparing two sets of parameter combinations experiments show that the percentage it is possible to diagnose depends on the 'speed' of these (mostly unknown) flows (churn). The faster the churn the more diagnostic capacity is needed for people to be referred and go though the diagnosis process. When churn is higher the rate of new arrivals is higher and the number of deaths per annum is also greater. More people have dementia, but for a shorter period. Therefore, the same diagnostic capacity will have less impact on the population with the greater underlying churn.

As in many other projects in the book, the model highlights the need to know *flows* as well as *stocks* when designing dementia diagnosis (and treatment) capacity. As in Chap. 3, the work challenges again the arbitrary nature of performance targets. It is suggested that to achieve the current target might require unrealistic referral rates and have implications for the broader social care system.

Perhaps, more than any other, this chapter highlights the challenge and the rewards of thinking through time.

13.1 Introduction

System dynamics is perhaps at its most powerful when applied at whole population level and has frequently been deployed to model specific 'long term conditions'. Dementia is a good and topical example of a condition whose prevalence, diagnosis and management can be better understood through a system dynamics simulation.

Dementia is normally characterised as having three or four stages, known as mild, moderate and severe. In some descriptions, the mild stage is preceded by a stage known as 'mild cognitive impairment', which we do not cover in the model shown in this chapter. There are different types of dementia, the most commonly found being Alzheimer's Disease and Vascular Dementia, but all are characterised by being degenerative, life-limiting conditions. As discussed in Chap. 4, in system dynamics we can represent these stages of the condition as stocks and the movement of people between the stocks as flows, forming a 'condition' flow chain. We are then in a position to enhance understanding of the relationship between the stocks and flows, in particular, to distinguish the difference between the incidence of the condition (a flow) and the prevalence of the condition (the mild, medium and severe stocks). As we have pointed out numerous times throughout the book much more is known about 'stock' data than 'flow' data.

Health system planners and commissioners must use their data about and understanding of dementia to make decisions about how to invest in diagnostic and treatment capacity.

Therefore, a major question is: if prevalence, but not incidence, is known, is it possible to calculate how much diagnostic capacity to commission?

In the same way, if the underlying churn (people progressing through stages of ill-health) is not known, then anticipating the likely impact of diagnostic capacity on achievement of targets (typically, government has set a target for the percentage of people who should be diagnosed) is, we argue, impossible. One of the implications of this is that health bodies might be harshly judged for not meeting targets, even although those in charge of setting targets might, in fact, lack the capability of understanding the underlying dynamics of the condition,

- What we are trying to say here is that, once again (see Chap. 2 on waiting time targets), people who do not understand how things work often set infeasible or impossible targets by which they will judge whether things are working well or not.

It is frequently claimed, for example, that the main reason it would be impossible to achieve 100% of people with dementia being diagnosed is that 'not everyone would want to be diagnosed'. But this misses the point. That (not wanting a diagnosis) may be a factor, but the main phenomenon that confounds the achievement of diagnostic targets is churn. Every day, new incidence of dementia happens; people cross the threshold into mild dementia. And, every day, people with diagnosed dementia die, exiting the 'diagnosed' population. The reassuring news we can provide is that, faced with such uncertainty, system dynamics can provide realistic estimates of the extent to which it may be possible to diagnose dementia, so that more reasonable targets might be set, and health providers would be less unfairly judged.

13.2 Prevalence and Incidence—A Simple Model Structure

The model we describe in this chapter disaggregates the population of people with dementia into six stocks:

- three levels of severity (mild, moderate, severe)
- each with two states (undiagnosed, diagnosed).

But the simplest possible dynamic view of dementia is shown in Fig. 13.1. Onset (incidence) is based on a fraction of the general population per annum. The condition is degenerative, so (leaving aside migration) the only outflow is mortality. In this simple structure, we conceptualise the mortality rate as the mean duration of the condition.[1] (It is useful to note that this structure is basically the same as the first simple hospital model in Chap. 2.)

Elsewhere in this book (Chap. 2), we have outlined that for the type of structure in Fig. 13.1:

- Outflow is equal to stock/mean duration
- At equilibrium, inflow = outflow
- The stock is equal to the inflow * the duration
- The average time spent in a stock = stock/outflow.

In Chap. 2 we also pointed out that we can use the structure of Fig. 13.1 to expose inconsistencies in data and help to triangulate missing data. The case of incidence and prevalence encountered here is no exception.

Data Consistency

Anecdotally (for example, discussions with eminent experts), we find that these simple heuristics (stock = inflow * length of stay, length of stay = stock/outflow) are not commonly understood or applied to everyday events.

For understandable reasons (it is easier to measure prevalence), (Matthews et al. 2013) more is known about prevalence than incidence. Matthews et al. (2016) point out that although dramatic global increases in future numbers of people with

---

[1]Both amount to the same thing, a fraction of the stock departs every time unit (the model used in this chapter runs in months).

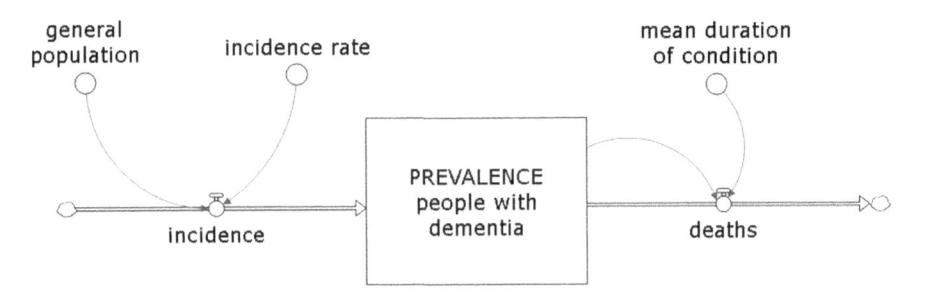

Fig. 13.1 Simple mental model of dementia

dementia have been predicted, no multicentre population-based study ... has reported dementia incidence. By comparing the results of two longitudinal studies, they report that over the past two decades, although the absolute numbers are increasing because of population growth the dementia incidence rate has dropped by 20%, driven by a reduction in men, because of factors such as improved cardio-vascular health. They estimate UK incidence to be 210,000 per annum.

This is slightly lower than the Alzheimers UK (2014, p. 67) estimate of a total incidence of around 225,000 per year in the UK, with a prevalence of 815,827 (all types of dementia). Although the report does not provide a figure for 'the average life expectancy post onset', it must be close to the prevalence divided by the incidence.

If we factor in that absolute incidence is rising, then this year's deaths will be of people whose incidence happened some time ago; in other words, the mortality figures will be equal to the onset after a time-lag, so perhaps we should assume that at the point in time where onset is 225,000, mortality might be around 200,000. From that, we calculate that mean life-expectancy post onset is just over four years (stock [815,827] divided by outflow [200,000]). Yet, experts tend to estimate a higher number for life-expectancy.

Interestingly, the Alzheimer Society of Ireland website states that 'on average, people with Alzheimers live eight to ten years from the time first symptoms emerge' and people with vascular dementia live for around five years after symptoms begin. Figures upwards of eight years appear in other sources, e.g. various USA sources.

We claim no expertise in measuring prevalence, incidence and mortality. Our contribution is to support domain experts by helping them to articulate their mental models. If different experts can hold the following views:

- The incidence of dementia is around 200,000 people per year
- The population with dementia is around 800,000 at any time
- The average life expectancy post-onset is around 8 years.

What we can affirm with some certainty is that this mental model cannot possibly be correct. The question becomes, in which of these figures do we have most confidence? If we were most confident in the prevalence and life-expectancy figures, we should conclude that the incidence must be closer to 100,000 per year. If we had most confidence in the incidence and prevalence estimates, the mean life expectancy must be closer to 4 years.

Clearly, there are complicating factors, such as the rise in population, or, over time, perhaps a change in the distribution of the population by age. If our objective was to replicate exactly the number of people in the population by age and sex, we would need to build a much more detailed model. But we can offer a more aggregate model that provides a means of estimating some of the main parameters (incidence, progression rates, mortality rates).

13.3 Developing the 'Condition Flow Chain' and Triangulating Missing Data

The big challenge comes with measuring/estimating incidence and transition rates between the stages of the condition. Where a condition has a gradual onset, and in its earliest stages may be managed by an individual along with their family and other carers without seeking help, the (incidence) date on which one passes from 'mild cognitive impairment'(a 'pre-dementia' state) to 'mild dementia' is not marked (whereas the onset of a stroke or heart attack is hard to miss). And people who do seek help, may be seeking help with some aspect of daily living rather than a formal memory assessment; people with dementia are known to various services, whether or not they have been formally diagnosed.

Assuming that the prevalence of dementia at each level of severity is reasonably well-measured, a system dynamics model can help us deduce some key unknown parameters about:

- Incidence (new cases per annum)
- Mortality rate at each of mild, moderate and severe
- (note that mortality for those in the mild and moderate stages is not from dementia, as such, but deaths from other conditions of people who also happen to have dementia. At the severe stage, it is possible that some deaths are a direct result of dementia/brain degeneration, and many deaths are from other, probably multiple causes)
- For those who do not die at the mild and moderate stage
  - The average length of time spent with mild dementia, from onset to progression to moderate
  - The average length of time spent with moderate dementia, from progression to moderate to progression to severe.

As an example, consider the model diagram shown in Fig. 13.2. All incidence is to the mild state, out of which people either die (from some other condition) or progress to the next stage. The graphs within each of the stocks show the expected growth in the prevalence of dementia over a ten-year period. These data were calibrated from the Dementia Prevalence Calculator, an on-line tool developed by

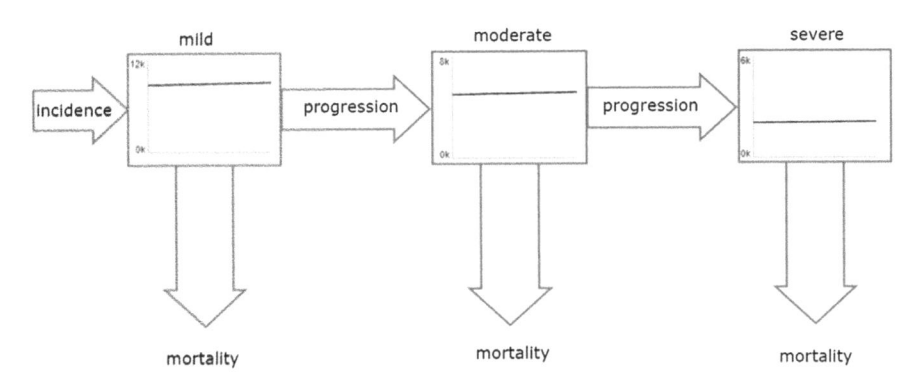

Fig. 13.2 Simple dynamics of dementia

NHS England. The numbers represent the prevalence of dementia in a local authority with a population that grows from 870 to 900 k over ten years.

Given that we are uncertain about the incidence, and that mortality rates of people with mild, moderate or severe dementia are also hard to estimate, what assumptions might we make about the parameters we listed earlier (incidence, mortality rates and progression rates)?

The solution offered here is that we should estimate our parameter values using a dynamic model. In every case, we want to make best use of whatever data might be available.

The interface screen in Fig. 13.3 shows how using a model can help. We have added the following parameters to the diagram:

(a) Incidence (shown as new cases pa)
(b) Mortality rates per thousand per annum for each of mild, moderate, and severe, values shown on each mortality flow, numbers are set on the vertical sliders positioned within the flows
(c) Average duration in mild and moderate, shown in months.

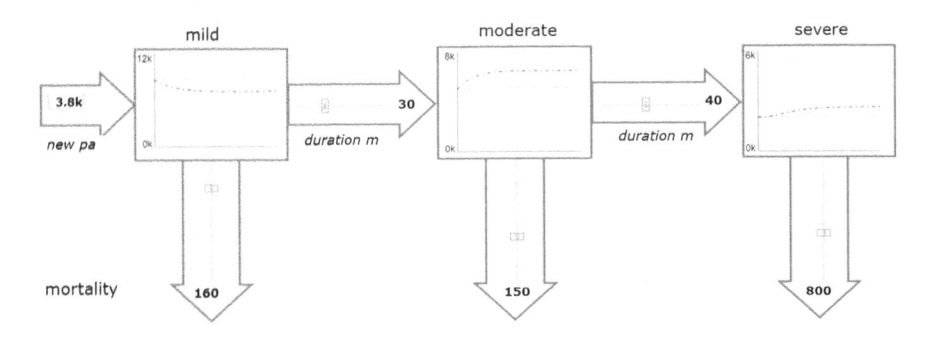

Fig. 13.3 Parameter estimation using a model

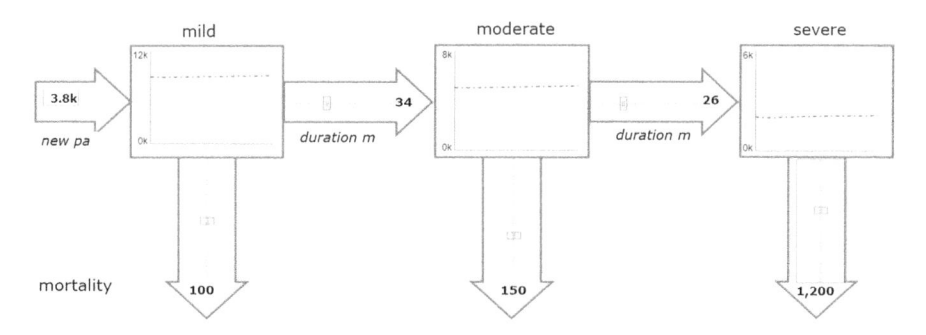

13.3 Developing the 'Condition Flow Chain' and Triangulating Missing Data   235

Fig. 13.4 Example of parameters yielding a good fit

The dashed lines on each graph show what would happen to prevalence, if we initialise the model stocks (mild, moderate, severe) with the same prevalence values as the 'expected prevalence' (shown as the solid lines on each graph), and run the model using the inputs shown for incidence, deterioration time and mortality. If we assume that the expected stock values are correct, our estimated parameters produce fewer people in the mild state, and more in the moderate and severe states. The challenge is, using the slider controls shown, manipulate the mortality and progression rates until the modelled prevalence matches the expected prevalence.

Of course, there are multiple combinations of parameters that will produce this outcome. One such is shown in Fig. 13.4, where the modelled prevalence line now tracks the expected line.

Clearly, we do not know whether this set of parameters is correct, but we can at least claim that they are internally consistent and therefore plausible.

13.4 Diagnosis and Diagnostic Capacity

Given that we can set up models with different combinations of incidence, mortality and duration to give the same prevalence, our key question for commissioners is 'how does this understanding affect the diagnostic capacity required?'

To try to answer this question we set up two instances of the model within the same model file with exactly the same prevalence but very different incidence rates and explore how much diagnostic capacity we would need in order to achieve a certain 'target'.

This model dashboard is shown in Fig. 13.5.

Here, in effect, we run two models with identical structure, labelled a and b.

Each flow contains input devices, mostly sliders. Condition b has a different incidence rate from condition a (2,200 new cases per annum, compared with 3,800

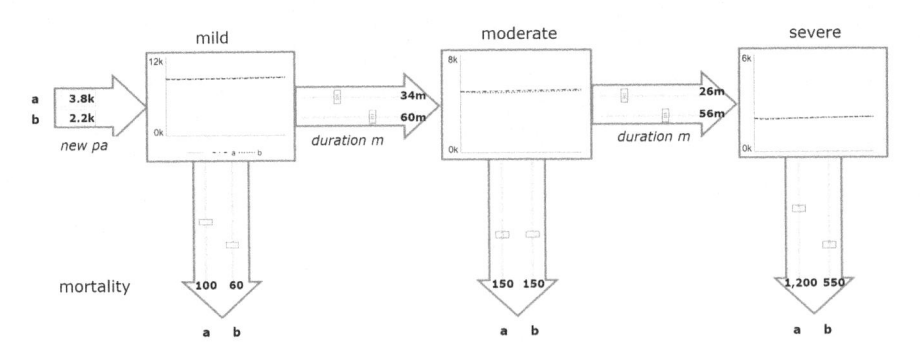

Fig. 13.5 Model dashboard for comparing two sets of parameters, a and b

new cases[2]), and we have set the various sliders to values that produce exactly the same prevalence. Although not obviously visible because they are at the same value, there are now three lines on each graph, representing the expected prevalence and the prevalence for population a and population b.

In this case, we have two very different incidence rates. And, obviously, for the lower incidence model (b) we need to set longer progression rates (for example, average time at mild stage is 34 months and mortality rate is 100 per thousand pa, compared with 60 months and 60 per thousand respectively). We now have two versions of reality, producing the same prevalence at each level of severity. We are still not claiming that either is 'correct'.

We have argued throughout this book that knowing about prevalence (stock) is not enough; we also need to understand incidence and duration (flow). To illustrate that point, the next step is to use this model to explore how much capacity it will take in order to achieve a target percentage of 'people diagnosed. The target is always expressed as a 'percentage of prevalence', where the prevalence constitutes both the diagnosed and undiagnosed. In England, the target was set at two-thirds (67%).

Figure 13.6 expands the model diagram shown earlier to show the diagnostic process. People can become diagnosed at any stage of the illness. In the early stages, diagnosis is less likely because memory-loss symptoms are less obvious and less frequently noticed.

In this version, the same diagnostic capacity is used (but in differing amounts) at all levels of severity. There are various possible service configurations, of course. The typical diagnostic service is known as a 'memory service or clinic', provided by a multi-disciplinary team. In the case of people with severe dementia, the existence of the condition is more obvious/noticeable, and therefore diagnosis might be made by a general practitioner.

In the model experiments that we show below, we make the following assumptions about diagnostic capacity and referrals for diagnosis, but the numbers

---

[2]This is the base incidence. Over the ten-year period, we increase incidence in line with the rise in the general population.

13.4 Diagnosis and Diagnostic Capacity

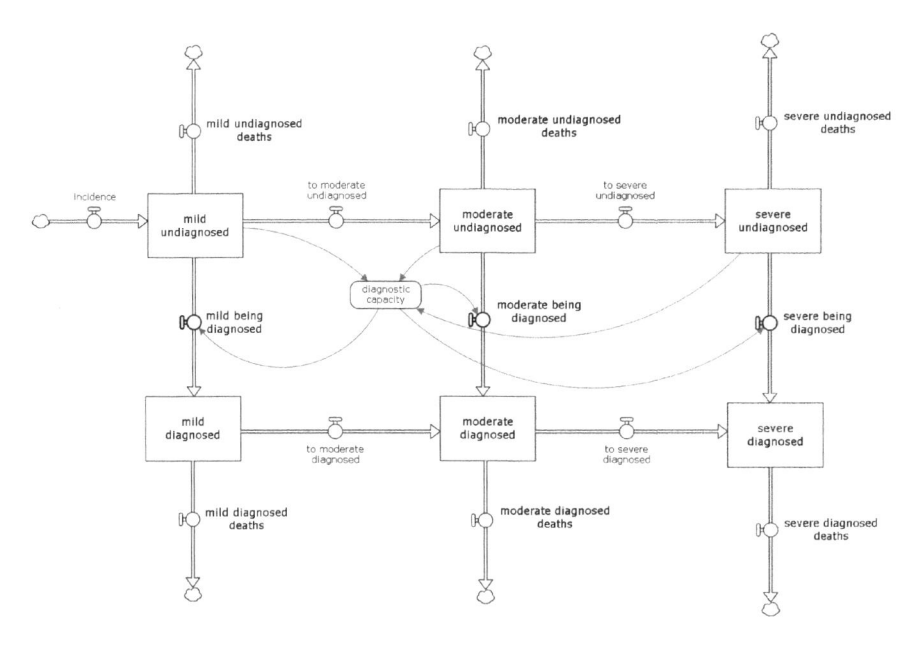

Fig. 13.6 Dementia model diagram showing diagnosed status

can be varied. And, as we have seen in relation to other models, with system dynamics we can represent different types of capacity (appointments, beds, clinic slots provided by multi-disciplinary teams, caseloads, etc.).

- **Capacity** is given in the currency 'clinic appointments provided per month' (this is an elaboration of the 'slot-based' capacity formulation we described in Chap. 2)
- **Number of appointments needed** to diagnose (mild, moderate, severe) dementia, where we assume that it takes more appointments, because the condition is less apparent, therefore more tests may be needed, to diagnose the less severe states of the condition (here, 4 appointments for mild, 3 for moderate and 1 for severe)
- **Months between appointments** (to give a realistic representation of the amount of time that people spend in the 'being diagnosed' stage)[3]
- **Referrals**: in order to be diagnosed, people need to be referred to the memory service—we express that in terms of the 'probability that an undiagnosed person will be diagnosed per month'—in the example shown here we probably

---

[3]The state 'being diagnosed' is a subset of the 'undiagnosed' stock, and is not shown in the simple model diagrams included here—we also take account of various other factors such as people waiting for a diagnosis, and if there is a backlog we also factor in that some people will move from mild to moderate or moderate to severe during the time that they are waiting for and being diagnosed.

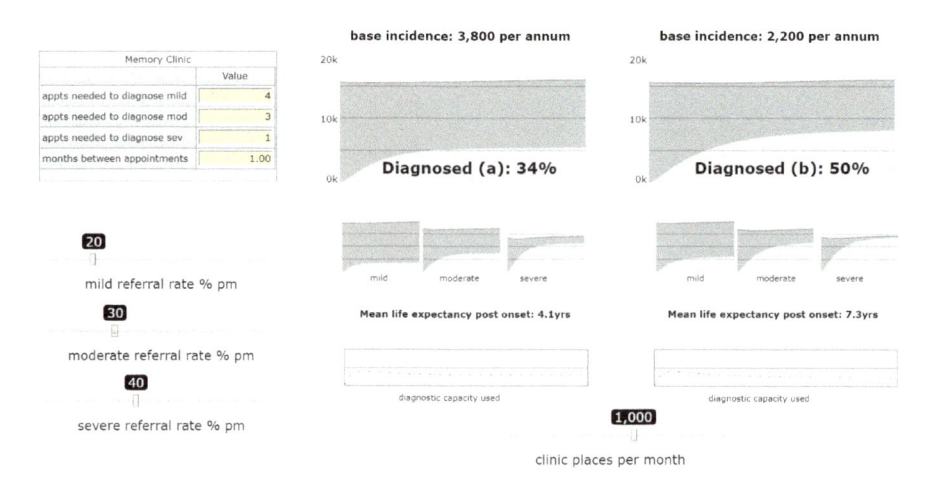

Fig. 13.7 Percentage diagnosed applying same capacity to populations with same prevalence and different incidence

over-estimate the probability of referral (20% of mild, 30% of moderate, and 60% of severe undiagnosed people will be referred per month). Obviously all of the above inputs/assumptions can be varied.

The results are reported in Fig. 13.7.

The diagram shows, on the left, the main inputs described above. 'Clinic places per month' can be varied on the slider at the bottom of the screen, here set at 1,000 appointments per month.

The two large graphs show the whole population of people with dementia over the ten-year period. The lighter area is 'people diagnosed', and, in this case, the model starts with 0 people diagnosed. The '% diagnosed' figure towards the bottom of the graph shows the percentage that are diagnosed at the end of a model run.[4] The smaller graphs disaggregate the number diagnosed into each of mild, moderate and severe. As one might expect, the percentage diagnosed increases with severity, because the higher the severity the more likely someone is to be diagnosed, and people who were diagnosed at a lower level are already diagnosed when they progress to the next stage.

The 'diagnostic capacity used' graph is included to show how many of the 1,000 appointments per month are actually used. In this case, with both populations, there is spare capacity.

However, the most important finding is that the percentage diagnosed in population b (50%) is greater than the percentage diagnosed in population a (34%). Remember that incidence is higher (and duration of condition lower) in population a. Although the prevalence is the same as population b, the rate of new arrivals is

---

[4]In fact, that number updates as the model runs, but this screen-shot shows the model at the end of a 10 year run.

13.4 Diagnosis and Diagnostic Capacity

higher, and the number of deaths per annum is also greater. More people develop dementia, but for a shorter period. Therefore, the same diagnostic capacity will have less impact on the population with the greater underlying churn.

We also report a value for 'mean life expectancy post onset', which is 4.1 years for population a and 7.3 years for population b. This value is calculated from the model as follows. Although our model has six stocks (three levels of dementia by diagnosed/undiagnosed) and six outflows (mortality from each stock, the flows between stocks are not 'outflows' from the model), the sum of the stocks divided by the sum of the mortality flows gives us a mean measure for 'the average length of time that people spend with dementia'.

It is clear that the dynamics of the whole system militate against the aspiration to reach a diagnostic target, for the following reasons:

- At all times (every day) new undiagnosed people are entering the prevalence stock (if we wanted to achieve 100% diagnosed, we would require a way of identifying people precisely at the point of transition from pre-dementia or 'mild cognitive impairment' to 'mild dementia', which is obviously impossible)
- At all times, people who are diagnosed are exiting the prevalence state through death
- The probability of people being referred for diagnosis is lowest for the mild and lower for the moderate states, which also include the majority of people with dementia
- It takes time (perhaps a few months), a series of appointments/diagnostic tests, to make a diagnosis. Diagnostic capacity constraints might mean that there is a waiting time to commence the diagnostic process, during which time a person might die.

All of these factors are represented in the model by flows. It should be obvious that the faster the rate of flow (the higher the incidence, progression and mortality) the more the underpinning dynamics of the system work against an aspiration to assess all of the people in the undiagnosed stocks.

The more dynamic the chain, the harder it is to diagnose everyone. And the best proxy measure for how 'dynamic the system is', is the ratio of incidence to prevalence.

To illustrate the importance of knowing the incidence, Fig. 13.8 compares two model runs where there is a relatively small difference in incidence. Clearly, the % diagnosed reached is slightly higher in the example where incidence was smaller (b).

But we already noted that the same prevalence can result from the same incidence, even where different assumptions are made about progression rates and mortality. Figure 13.9 gives a model comparing two scenarios where incidence is identical, as is prevalence (all the lines match the 'expected' prevalence), but there are some differences in the combinations of progression rates and mortality rates.

How does this affect the number diagnosed?

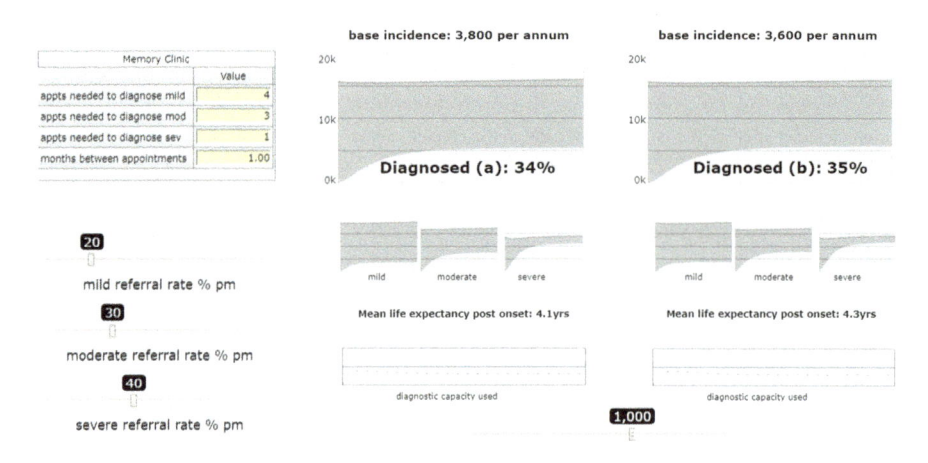

Fig. 13.8 Results of comparing runs with a small difference in incidence

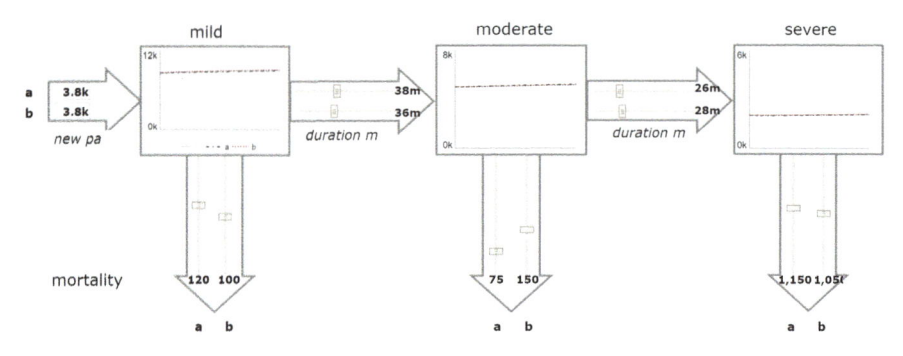

Fig. 13.9 Same incidence and prevalence, different progression and mortality rates

The results are shown in Fig. 13.10, when, not unexpectedly, the % diagnosed Figure (34%) is the same for both populations.

We have experimented with different combinations of referral rates and clinic places per month, but, although the % diagnosed figure varies (obviously, if there is insufficient capacity or lower referral rates, fewer people are diagnosed), the results are almost invariably the same, or only one percentage apart, when we simulate identical incidence and prevalence resulting from different transition and mortality rates.

Finally, given that the NHS England target is that two thirds (67%) of cases of dementia should be diagnosed, the model gives us some idea of the referral rates and diagnostic capacity that would be needed if that target is to be reached. Results are shown in Fig. 13.11 (which is a model run based on an incidence rate that is consistent with the 4-year life-expectancy discussed earlier).

To achieve that target, the referral rates needed would be upwards of 80% of the prevalence being referred for diagnosis PER MONTH, which seems incredibly

13.4 Diagnosis and Diagnostic Capacity

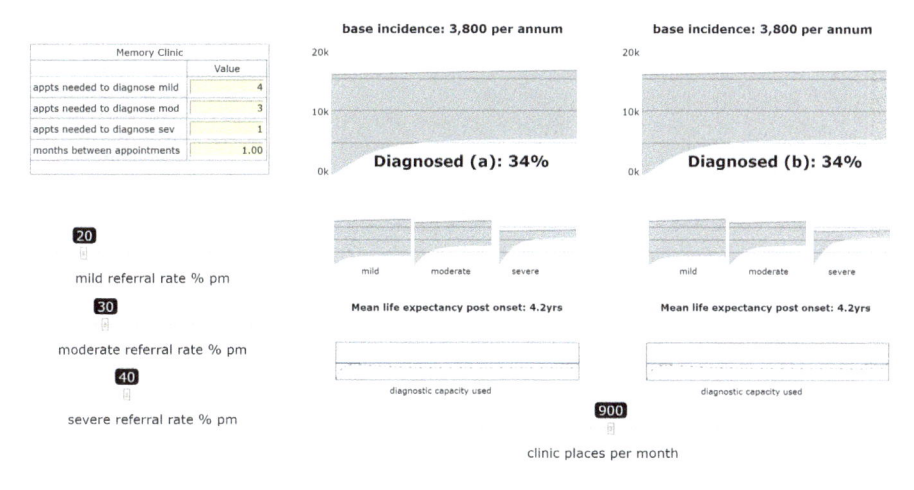

Fig. 13.10 Same incidence and prevalence runs, diagnostic % achieved

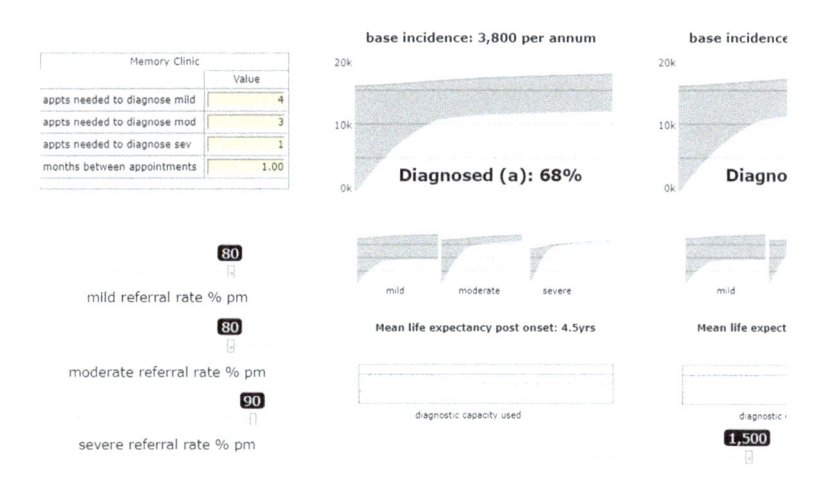

Fig. 13.11 Example of referral rates needed to achieve 67% diagnosed

high, especially for the mild and moderate groups. Nevertheless, the NHS England website[5] reports most regions as achieving this, with one, Greater Manchester, reaching 77%.

In a further run of the model (not shown), with reduced incidence and recalibrated progression and mortality rates which give a mean life expectancy of 8 years, the diagnostic target can be reached with referral rates of 40% per month.

---

[5]https://digital.nhs.uk/data-and-information/data-tools-and-services/data-services/general-practice-data-hub/dementia-diagnosis-rate-and-prescription-of-antipsychotic-medication-to-people-with-dementia (link active at the time of writing).

This still feels (intuitively, to the authors) a very high referral rate; is it really likely that the chances of someone having undiagnosed mild dementia being referred for memory assessment are 0.4 per month?

This makes us wonder whether, going back to the original estimates for incidence and prevalence (where prevalence was just over four times annual incidence), the 'real' figures for incidence should be lower, with an average life expectancy of eight years. Note that we are basing that estimate on our simulation and not on clinical data.

13.5 Broader Impact on the Social Care System

A subtle experiment that some clients have wanted to explore is what the impact of increasing diagnosis rates would be on the social care system. The causal links here are that earlier diagnosis means that people get access to medication at an earlier stage, and the most commonly used drugs have greater impact on people in the earlier stages of dementia. Although the underlying brain deterioration cannot be halted, it is reasonable to suppose that people on medication, whose day-to-day function has improved, are less likely to experience harm from related factors, such as having a fall at home (hospital admission for a person with dementia is typically a serious setback), or eating food that is not properly cooked or out of date.

This might mean that for those diagnosed:

- Morbidity and mortality rates resulting from the consequences of dementia might fall (people live for longer)
- People can manage to live at home for longer (with or without home care)
- Therefore, people move into a care home at a later stage in their life.

It is therefore plausible that better diagnosis combined with prescription of appropriate medication can lead to a reduction in the number of older people in care homes, while, at the same time, leading to an increase in the number requiring care at home, essentially a change in the balance of care.

At this point, a further issue arises which is, from a service-planning perspective, how fruitful it is to focus attention on dementia, rather than ageing, frailty or 'end of life' care more generally. Where people with dementia are the sole users of services (diagnostic services such as memory clinics), modelling 'dementia' makes sense. Where people with dementia use services that are also used by people who are frail or old but do not have dementia, perhaps it is better to explore these 'balance of care' and 'health and social care integration' issues more broadly.

13.6 Conclusions

In this chapter, we have focused on how prevalence, incidence, progression and mortality rates affect the demand for diagnostic capacity, and how to use modelling to estimate sustainable, feasible targets for numbers diagnosed.

We have built various extensions of this model in a variety of contexts, typically focusing on the demand for various treatment services that might be offered following a diagnosis of dementia, including home care and case management approaches.

A key insight is that estimating the need for diagnostic capacity requires paying more attention to the dynamics (flow through, which varies with incidence) of the system, whereas some kind of case-holding service capacity can be based more readily on knowledge of prevalence alone (albeit that 'diagnosed prevalence' depends on diagnostic capacity). To put it another way, diagnostic interventions are based more on flow, and case-holding is based more on stock (with the caveat that processing referrals to any service, including case-holding, takes us back into the realms of flow).

As in Chap. 3, the work challenges again how some performance targets are set. It is suggested that to achieve the current target would require unrealistic referral rates which has implications for the broader social care system.

13.7 Footnote

It is worth noting that in the time since we last worked on the kind of model shown in this chapter, a substantial new research programme, MODEM, which includes micro-simulation modelling, was established in England.

References

Alzheimers UK (2014) *Dementia UK: Update*. King's College London and London School of Economics.

Matthews, F. E., Arthur, A., Barnes, L. E., Bond, J., Jagger, C., Robinson, L., et al. (2013). A two-decade comparison of prevalence of dementia in individuals aged 65 years and older from three geographical areas of England: Results of the cognitive function and ageing study I and II. *Lancet, 382*(9902), 1405–1412.

Matthews, F. E., Stephen, B. C. M., Robinson, L., Jagger, C., Barnes, L. E., Arthur, A., et al. (2016). A two decade dementia incidence comparison from the cognitive function and ageing studies I and II. *Nature Communications, 7,* 11398. https://doi.org/10.1038/ncomms11398.

Chapter 14
Making Predictive Risk Assessment 'Dynamic': The Underlying Churn Effect

Chapter Summary
This chapter applies dynamic impact assessment (as described in the introduction to Part III) to 'risk stratification'. People at high risk of being admitted to hospital were to be identified to receive a case management approach based on interrogating a 'patient at risk of readmission' database (a 'risk stratification' tool). The project arose as an attempt to explain disappointing early results of the case-management service. A comprehensive two-dimensional model was constructed to simulate the dynamic behaviour of the stratification pyramid. This representation was capable of utilising both *stock* and *flow* data from the database and hence capable of changing assumptions about the churn of the underlying population, both between and within risk categories. The project identified that population churn was significant and that the factor weightings in the existing toolset were perhaps set too much towards fast recovery from episodic events, whereas those who designed the case management service had believed that the risk stratification tool was mostly capturing long-term degeneration dynamics. Further modelling showed that the impact of risk assessment would have had much greater financial impact under that (long term degeneration) assumption. This whole different thinking was made possible by marrying up the comprehensiveness of big data to hold (but rarely report on) flow data and the capability of system dynamics models to make use of that data. We believe that those using population risk stratification tools should more-rigorously explore these flow dynamics.

14.1 Introduction

If we can identify people at high risk of being admitted to hospital, can we also design interventions[1] that will reduce the hospital admission rate? And how could system dynamics modelling contribute to a greater understanding of what is involved?

---

[1]The term 'intervention' is mostly synonymous with the idea of a 'service' and we tend to use them interchangeably.

In an innovative example of an attempt to do this at scale, an English local authority (social care) and its coterminous NHS (healthcare) commissioning body, jointly designed a preventive service, based on a population-level 'risk stratification' approach (Lewis et al. 2011, NHS England 2013) aimed at reducing the number of older people being admitted to hospital.

Six months after going live, there was little evidence of impact. To explore why, the local authority turned to system dynamics modelling using 'group model building' (see Chap. 6). The resulting small study diagnosed the problem: the 'risk stratification' tool could identify the 'stock' of people 'at high risk' at any time, but did not factor in the 'flows' of people through that stock. We call these flows the 'underlying churn'. 'Risk stratification' is a major issue, not just in the UK, and we think that this tendency to 'focus on stocks but not flows' might be common,[2] which makes this a significant insight.

The systems literature comments widely on the problem of 'misperception of stock behaviour', typically using a 'pen and paper' exercise where people are given perfect information about the inflow and outflow to a stock but most struggle to deduce what is going on in the stock (Sterman 2002). This will be apparent for those who undertook the Chap. 2 exercise in this book. This model inverts that discussion; in this example a great deal was known about a stock value (the number of people in each risk group over time), but nothing was known about the underlying flow behaviour.

To use the language of public health, when planning services, it is not enough to know about the 'prevalence' (stock) of a problem; one must also factor in its 'incidence' (inflow) and 'duration' (outflow). Moreover, if flow rates were known and understood, System Dynamic simulation would provide arguably the best means of understanding the probable impact of intervening in that stock/flow system. Service commissioners are expected to have a realistic idea of what it would be reasonable to expect when intervening in a complex system, but how can they do that without using simulation?

It is our experience that, in general, databases in health and social care tend to be strongest on stock information and weakest on flow information and it can be misleading to know stock levels without knowledge of the associated rates. Flow data may be more fragmented (for example, hospital admissions or discharges) and not referenced against/triangulated with relevant stocks. 'Big Data' provides databases which contain a repository of dynamic information (about changes in status over time) but we speculate that little of this is currently analysed or understood.

---

[2] Just our hypothesis at the moment, we would be interested to hear about risk stratification approaches that take account of flow.

14.1 Introduction

This chapter:

- Introduces the idea of case finding services based on predictive risk approaches, and how these approaches have not been sufficiently informed by flow-thinking
- Outlines the main 'modules'[3] of a system dynamics model, developed using group model building
- Presents the main findings and reflects on how the modelling work highlighted important learning about the risk assessment tool being used.

14.2 The Problem—Lack of Impact of Local Implementation of Case Management to Identify Those at Risk of Hospital Readmission

In an English metropolitan area, the local authority (responsible for social care) collaborated with its coterminous NHS commissioning body to design a service to be offered to older people identified as at 'high risk' of readmission to hospital. 'High risk' is the second-highest of four categories[4]; the sound rationale for targeting this group was that those most at risk (very high) were probably already known to local services and receiving appropriate support packages.

Such a service was imaginable only because the NHS organisation maintained a comprehensive database of almost the entire population[5] in terms of their 'risk of rehospitalisation'. The technical term for this is 'risk stratification'. The particular risk stratification tool in this project used a factor analysis of elements of each individual's current health record, with risk-level being updated in real-time (for example, as soon as a hospital admission or a new diagnosis is entered on a patient's electronic record, their risk-score is recalculated).

The new service was a version of 'case management'. As the term implies, case management seeks to be proactive, enabling individuals to manage their health conditions, rather than simply reacting to changes in their condition (such as onset of an acute phase). Here, case management would be carried out by the local authority, which would contact people identified as being at 'high risk' of hospital readmission offering them a needs assessment. If it worked well, this would result in people being linked to various community services that they should already have

---

[3]To be consistent with other chapters, we use the term 'module' here to describe a model's sub-models: technically, in this model, these are represented as Stella 'sectors'—nowadays we mostly use Stella 'modules'.

[4](low, moderate, high, very high).

[5]In England, most people are registered with a primary care doctor.

been getting. The hope was that if people are properly supported at home, they should be less likely to be admitted to hospital; the economic case was that the cost of assessing and supporting people at home would be outweighed by the savings resulting from a reduction in the hospital population.

A case-management approach linked to an 'invest to save' aspiration is common. What was innovative here was to base case-finding on the 'patients at risk of readmission' (PARR)[6] database, believed to be comprehensive and current with good data quality. At aggregate level, the database could provide a summary measure of the state of health of the whole population at any time.

However, six months after introducing the service there was no identifiable impact on hospital admissions. Staff reported that many of the people they were contacting appeared to be in better health than their risk score suggested, and the local authority, which was already engaged in a system dynamics modelling project in a related service, decided to explore/explain this by using system dynamics in a 'group model building' approach.

14.3 The Model

The system dynamics model was commissioned a few months after the service started. The service provider had noted that the level of need encountered in the 'high risk' contacts was somewhat lower than had been expected. Modelling would be useful to diagnose why this might be.

From a modelling perspective, this issue presented the exciting and rare possibility of using good quality, readily available, regularly updated whole population data, using a database whose structure could validly be represented in terms of stocks and flows. From the client's perspective, the problem was that the new service might not be targeting exactly the right people. The generic structure of the proposed model is shown in Fig. 14.1.

The main focus of the model was on the 'population' (demand) and 'case finding' (supply) modules, which will be described in more detail.

14.4 Population Module

The Patients at Risk of Readmission (PARR) tool allocates everyone in a population to one of four states described in terms of their risk of admission to hospital. This is commonly presented as a pyramid, such as developed by Kaiser in the USA (Goodwin 2006). *Low risk* people form the base of the pyramid, *moderate risk* people form the next highest segment, *high risk* people the next segment and *very*

---

[6]The specific risk management tool being used here is known as 'combined PARR'.

14.4 Population Module

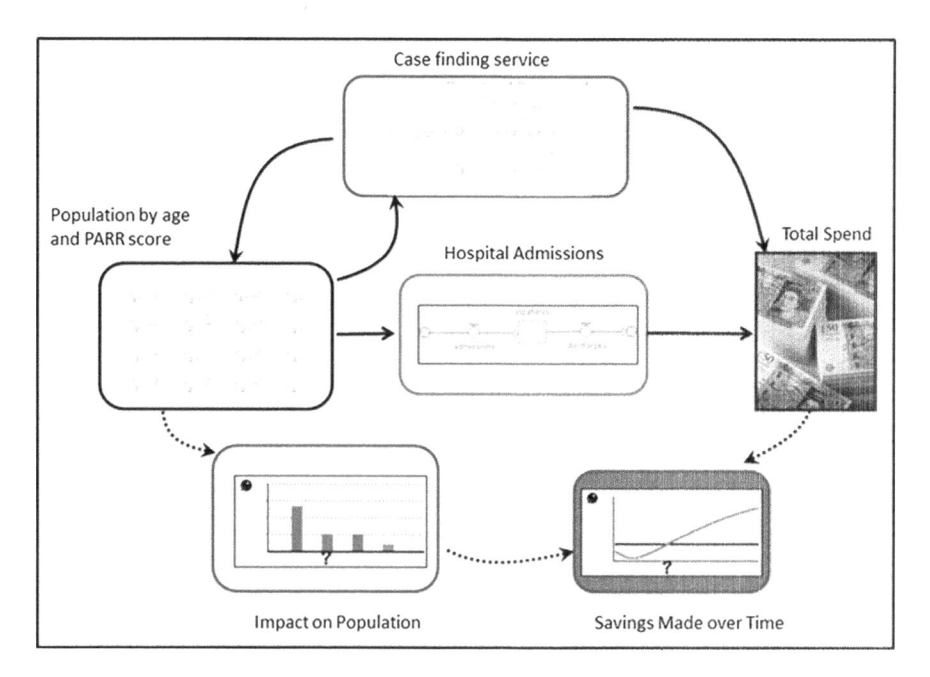

Fig. 14.1 Patients at risk of readmission case-finding model

high-risk people form the apex of the pyramid. In the example modelled, a local authority targeted the second highest group based on their high utilisation of services in relation to population size, and also in the belief that people in the highest group would more likely already be known to services.

The pyramid is a compelling metaphor but not a dynamic one although there is some movement recognised upward though the pyramid with inflow of new cases to the lowest level and exits (mortality) from the highest. Readers who have absorbed our earlier references in the book to dynamic equilibrium will well pre-empt what we will say next. Each segment of the pyramid is essentially a 'stock' of people and may appear static but is actually changing in repose to the net flows in and out.

Figure 14.2 shows that the same pyramid distribution (numbers of each people in each segment at any point in time) may arise from many different dynamic possibilities.

In dynamic equilibrium where the numbers in each segment remain the same the inflows and outflows could be big or small (cases a and b) or just unidirectional where the inflow equals the mortality rate (case c).

Even assuming that the general trend in flow is upwards towards deterioration, as one would expect of a growing population getting older, the amount of churn in each segment could be significant.

In system dynamics we would define these segments as stocks in a two-dimensional matrix having the dimensions of:

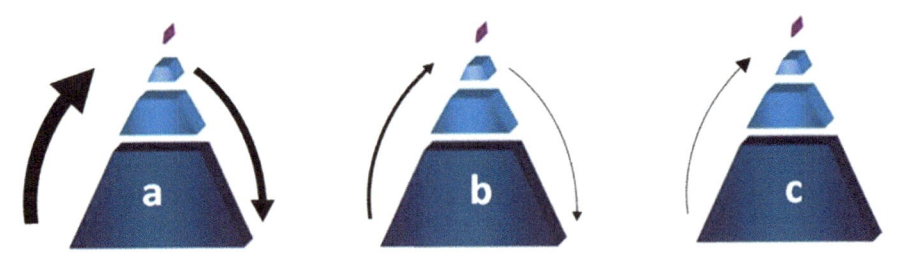

Fig. 14.2 Same pyramid, different dynamics

- Chronological ageing
- Moving between health or dependency (risk) states.

Reconfiguring the pyramid as a matrix of risk and ageing produces the representation of the adult (18 and over) population shown in Fig. 14.3. (It is not intended that the individual stock and flow labels be decipherable here, as just the shape of this configuration is sufficient to demonstrate that it represents the numbers of people in each risk/age category together with the flow between them.)

As drawn, Fig. 14.3 represents the pyramid on its side. The inflows (at the top) are people becoming adults on their 18th birthday distributed across the four PARR levels. People then flow:

- between PARR levels within an age band
- to the next age band
- or die.

The main data source was the PARR database. In essence, the service system described here is a good example of a (Big) Data driven initiative. The state of the population is known at any point in time. Obtaining values for initial stock conditions was straightforward.

What was new here, and what proved to be crucial in diagnosing what was happening in the new service, was that we also needed to know flow rates. From a limited[7] study of the literature, risk assessment tools focus firmly on stocks and case-identification. System Dynamics forces the question: 'what dynamics underpin this phenomenon and how will your proposed intervention affect these dynamics?' because it is by affecting flow that change happens. And so an additional question was asked of the database, which it appeared had never been asked before and is absent from the literature, which we posed this way: 'if people are in this stock in month 1, in which stock will they be in six months?' We chose six months for that query having assumed that the rate of movements between categories was relatively slow, and mostly in the direction of deterioration/degeneration.

---

[7]The model being described in this paper emerged from a 20-day consultancy engagement; there is scope for much more research on risk assessment tools.

14.4 Population Module

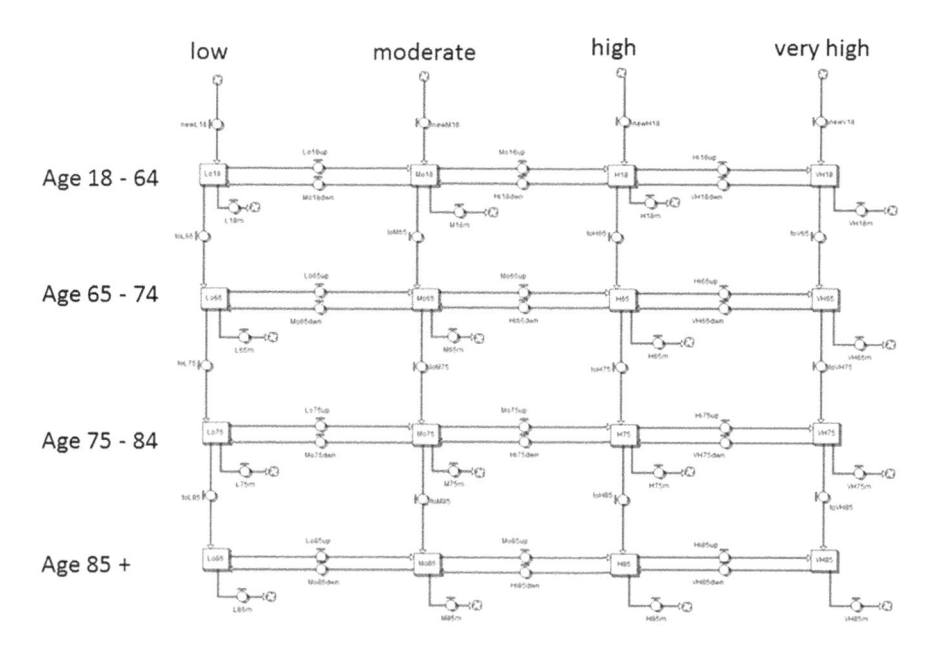

Fig. 14.3 Combined risk and ageing chain

The unexpected answer was that the degree of churn around the system was

- higher than expected
- in both directions (deterioration and improvement), even for the oldest and most disabled group, as shown in Table 14.1.

This in itself is a significant finding. Within the modelling group, there had been an assumption that PARR might be a composite measure of a range of indicators of degeneration, including prevalence of long-term conditions. In fact, it turned out to be measuring more transient states, something borne out by the experience of those running the case-finding service.

When modelled and run over five years, the population chain for each risk category produced the very plausible and stable set of projections shown in Fig. 14.4.

Table 14.1 *People* aged 85 and over—movements (%) from one group to another over six months (columns add to 100)

To	From			
	Low	Moderate	High	V High
Low	*70*	25	10	10
Moderate	20	*52*	31	12
High	10	15	*43*	25
V High	0	8	16	*53*

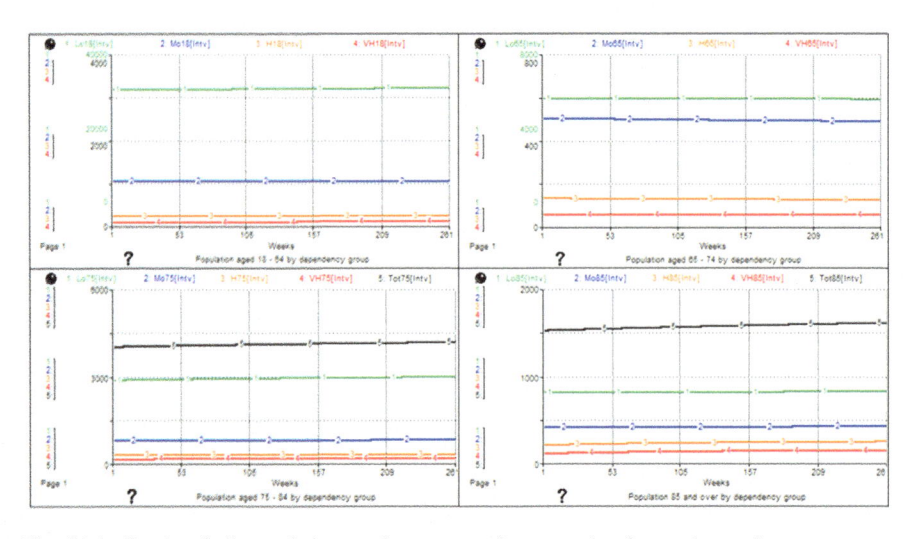

Fig. 14.4 Graphs of all population stocks run over five years (totals not shown for younger two age bands)

This underlying churn-rate phenomenon proved to be the most revealing learning-point, which will be obvious when the results are presented.

14.5 Service Module 1—Use of Hospital

The other modules are more straightforward.

The hospital admissions module is not a complex model of flows through hospital, but a simple in/out structure based on admission rates and duration. As part of the dataset produced by the client, hospital admission rates (elective and emergency) and lengths of stay were produced for each of the sixteen population stocks (risk/age dependency category).

The data confirmed that people in the highest dependency group did, in fact, generate the highest number of admissions and occupied bed days (confirming that the risk assessment tool made intuitive sense). Figure 14.5 shows population size, admissions per annum and occupied bed days for one age band.

The hospital admission rates for each group are strikingly different. The average length of stay (which can be deduced from the ratio of the occupied bed days to admissions (OBD/Admissions) did not vary much between groups. This analysis, a good example of a non-routine data query prompted by a system dynamics model, also highlighted some of the limits to what might be achieved by the case finding service targeted only on the 'high' group.

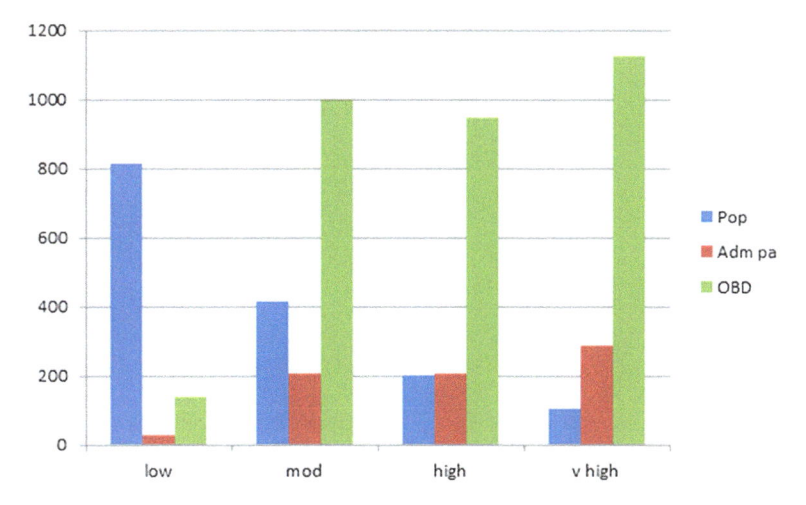

Fig. 14.5 Population size, admissions per year, occupied bed days by dependency group, for one age band

14.6 Service Module 2—New Case Management Service

This part of the model comprised a typical service capacity structure, being a high-level view of the service supply chain, arrayed by the two dimensions of age and dependency in the main chain. 'Arrayed' means that there is an instance of the Fig. 14.6 diagram for each population group. For readers unfamiliar with this terminology, imagine that each 'stock' in Fig. 14.3 contains its own version of the sub-model shown in Fig. 14.6. In the 'using service' stock people's levels of need will change, but perhaps at a different rate to the general population because of the service impact, and they age or die. As needs change, so people move out of the service, stepping up (to a higher tariff service, not modelled here) or down (service no longer needed).

There are two capacities in this service:

- case management, consisting of a short-term engagement with a case manager for initial needs assessment and thereafter for periodic reviews; reviews are annual for those who remain in the service that long, or triggered by a crisis. The capacity is the 'maximum caseload per whole time worker x case managers'; people can only enter the 'being assessed' or 'being reviewed' stocks if there is space on a case manager's caseload, otherwise there will be a backlog of people 'due for review' and/or a limitation on the inflow 'referrals accepted'.
- Support—which is not limited in the model because the idea is that service users are linked with a wide range of services that they should have been getting.

Relating this service chain to the population chain posed some questions for the service provider about what impact they considered it might have on hospital admissions. Three possible impacts can be modelled:-

- people using the service remain in the same dependency stock as before, but because of the additional support they get they are less likely to be admitted to hospital and/or if admitted perhaps they have a shorter length of stay

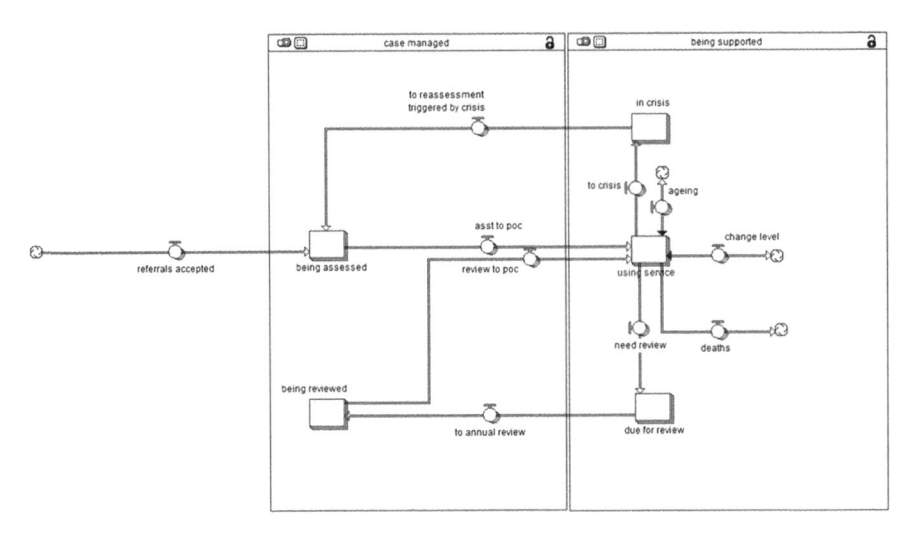

Fig. 14.6 Service structure

- people using the service step down to a lower level of need at a faster rate than if they were not using it (speedier recovery)
- people using the service step up to a higher level of need at a slower rate than if they were not using it (slower deterioration).

At the service design phase, there were no data to support these hypothesised impacts, the model providing a testing ground to explore 'what would happen if we achieved (a, b, c)?'

This simple module was probably the full 'model' that the client expected to get at the outset of the enquiry.

14.7 Finance Module

The Finance module tracks the costs of the two service systems modelled:-

- hospital admissions, costed on a simple 'cost per occupied bed day'[8]
- case finding service, based mostly on cost of staff plus overheads, and an assumed average cost per service user generated by greater uptake of some mainstream services.[9]

---

[8] A useful measure, but requiring caution if assumptions are to be made about savings; for real savings to be generated, wards, or parts of wards, would need to be decommissioned.

[9] Difficult to estimate because the client also assumed that this impact would not be costly, being based on uptake of spare capacity, rather than generating a need for more capacity.

14.8 Model Findings

The purpose of the model is to test management assumptions about service utilisation and impact on dependency, against likely reductions in hospital use, and compare costs over time. Users can vary assumptions about the target group for the intervention (typically people in the second highest need group), referral rates from that group, numbers of case managers employed and impact on dependency/hospital admissions.

In models of this type (invest to save), simulating a new intervention and comparing against a base run without the intervention, typical behaviour is that in the initial period costs rise, because we are paying for a new service but its impact on the population, and hence the demand for hospital, is unchanged. As the model runs, the cumulative impact of the intervention means fewer hospital admissions. The hope is that the increased spend on the new service is outweighed in time by a reduction in hospital spend. It can be several years before savings are realised.

The authors remain cautious about the ethics of 'invest to save'. The justification for taking an action should be that someone benefits, even although this might cost more. In health economics, such calculations typically calculate the additional cost of generating one 'quality adjusted life year'. In a local cost-comparison study like the one described here, where managers are under pressure to demonstrate that they can generate savings, one should not lose sight of the bigger picture, as explained in Fig. 14.7.

The model shows the scale of the reduction in hospital admissions that might be expected. Line 1 is the base run, and Line 2 a run with the case finding service deployed.

The top graph shows the expected stock of inpatients at any time. The impact of the service is to reduce acute occupancy from 75 to 70 at any point in time, achieved within just over one year.

But the impact on costs is disappointing. The 'change in spend £k' graph plots the difference in spending (base line obviously zero, no change). In fact, there is no 'invest to save'; the cost of the new service is greater than the saving in hospital occupancy.

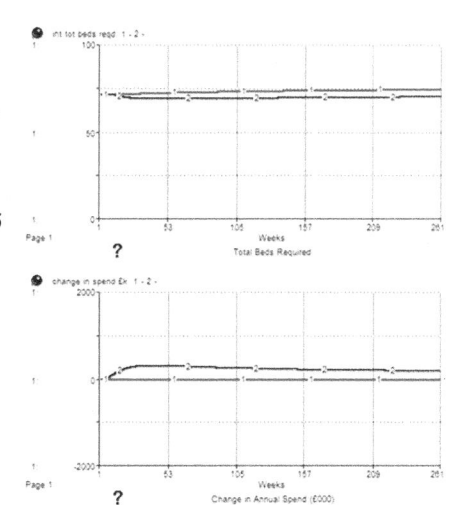

Fig. 14.7 Impact of new service on hospital occupancy and total cost

This client had hoped for a more optimistic finding, whilst acknowledging that the model findings were consistent with their early experience of implementing the new service, which had been running for about six months when the modelling took place.

However, this initially disappointing finding pointed to the key learning point from the modelling project. As Table 14.1 showed, there is a considerable churn rate between PARR categories, meaning that people in the higher risk groups return to a lower risk group in greater numbers than one would expect. The PARR database had initially appeared to be a godsend, to the client because it 'predicted risk' at the individual level, and to the modellers because the 'holy grail' of modelling degeneration/ageing would be a single indicator reliably counted in a real-time, comprehensive database.

Figure 14.8 gives a glimpse of an animation we developed to illustrate the difference between the client's mental model and what the SD model revealed. We have converted the pyramid into a stock—flow diagram. This makes it clear that the stock-levels, which do not change much over time apart from gradually increasing, are the same in both parts of the diagram. We also know that stocks are driven by, and only by, their inflows and outflows. However, the same stock level over time can result from very different flow rates, as long as the net difference is the same. If I remove 10 beans from a bowl and replace them with 11 new beans, the stock rises by one. But if I remove no beans and add one bean, the stock also rises by one.

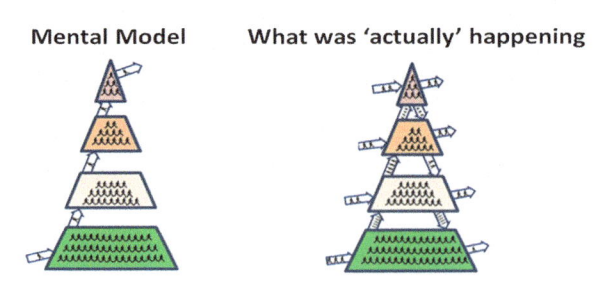

Fig. 14.8 The underlying churn: same stocks result from very different flow patterns

The Mental Model interprets the changes in stock levels as if they were describing a generic, degenerative, 'long term condition' where: • Incidence is always at the mildest state • People move slowly to ever-increasing levels of ill-health • Deaths come from the 'very high' risk group only (the outflow to the right coming only from the highest risk group)	'What was actually happening' was quite different. What is actually happening is: • People enter the pyramid at all levels of severity • There is considerable movement between levels, up a down • Also, less clear from the diagram, people might move more than one step at a time (e.g. going from well to acutely-ill, as in the sudden onset of a serious illness) • People may die (suddenly) from any level of ill-health Whatever composite phenomena the database summarises, the result is not analogous to a 'long term conditions' view

14.8 Model Findings

This raises two key questions:

1. Does the difference between the mental model and 'what is actually happening' help to explain why the initial results from the service were disappointing? If so, the lessons might be that
   a. It is not worth persevering with this approach
   b. Having recalibrated our expectations, we should persist with the service but with more realistic expectations about what would result

2. If PARR does not, as was thought, describe long-term degeneration as a summary measure, should we find a tool that does, and continue with our idea of case management?

In this case, the interests of service providers and modellers coincided. Good population-level data, such as a database that links dependency with acute service use, increases the potential for accurately modelling the important processes of ageing and degeneration. Such models have been achieved for specific long-term conditions (such as diabetes or dementia). As the population ages, so multi-morbidity becomes a feature. A measure of need that is not condition-specific reflects the reality of 'social care', rather than health care, service commissioning and planning.

It seemed, therefore, that the multivariate factor analysis underpinning the PARR database was probably too weighted towards recent events in an individual's life - including acute, episodic ill health - to be a useful case finding tool for a social care intervention. This is a positive finding. What it means is that a system dynamics study of a Big Data implementation drew attention to dynamics that could be deduced from the database, but only if the right kind of longitudinal queries were made of it. From initial reading of the literature on 'risk assessment tools' (Lewis et al. 2011; King's Fund 2006), these appear to be describing a static population stratified and shaped as a pyramid of need. The question of flows between the needs groups is not mentioned, but, we believe, merits attention.

Nevertheless, the phenomenon of long-term degeneration as people age is real, and this is the reality encountered daily by our social care providers. Their aspiration to identify people in need and proactively offer a new service seemed sound. Perhaps it was simply a case of using the wrong database to identify those at risk? To test this hypothesis, we ran some further scenarios, loading the model with a postulated composite indicator based on long-term degeneration. ***That is, a reduced rate of flow in the direction of deterioration and no flow in the direction of improvement***. In this case, for example, instead of the figures shown in Table 14.1, we imagined the figures shown in Table 14.2.

Table 14.2 Inputs for an imagined 'generic' long term conditions measure (85 plus age band shown). For comparison, the clients inputs, shown earlier in the chapter as Table 14.1 are included in the table below

To	From			
	Low	Moderate	High	V High
Low	84.0	0.0	0.0	0.0
Moderate	10.0	96.0	0.0	0.0
High	5.0	2.5	90.0	0.0
V High	1.0	1.5	10.0	100.0
Table 14.1 as shown earlier, for comparison				
Low	70	25	10	10
Moderate	20	52	31	12
High	10	15	43	25
V High	0	8	16	53

Now, if we run the model using the Table 14.2 values instead of those in Table 14.1, we get the outcomes described in Fig. 14.9.

Run 3 is the same as run 2 but using the 'long term conditions' inputs shown in Table 14.2 (the same needs pyramid but with different dynamics).

There are further reductions in bed occupancy.

The 'change in spend' shows a reduction, whereas with higher churn reduction in spend on beds was less than increased spend on case management. (Note, too, fine margins.)

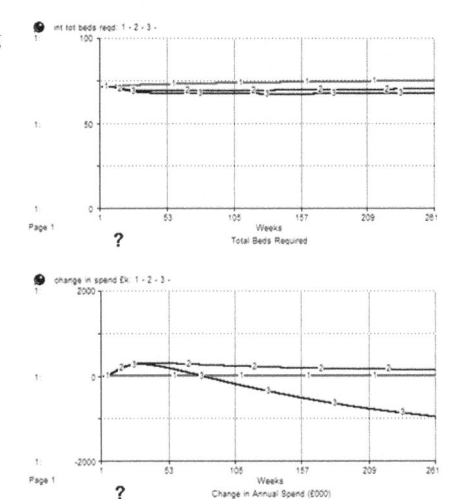

Fig. 14.9 Impact of new service with 'long term conditions' hypothesis

14.8 Model Findings

So, the main learning points from the modelling were that:

- the idea of a case management service targeted on individuals identified through a Big Data risk stratification tool has some merit, though savings might be modest
- the PARR tool itself might usefully be reviewed, because it appears to give too much weight to recent, episodic events, and many people identified as at 'high risk' using the tool might move to a lower risk group quite rapidly even without the case management service
- we should not throw the baby out with the bathwater; the model does not in any way undermine the notion of a case-managed service but it does point to the need for a different proxy measure of long-term degeneration, which could perhaps be achieved by changing the factor weighting in the PARR tool.

14.9 Conclusions/Summary

This chapter has presented a project to help understanding of why the impact of using a risk stratification tool to identify people at risk of hospital admission was disappointing. Rather than assuming the problem lay with just the case management aspects, attention was focused on the stratification thinking associated with the underlying data base. A comprehensive two-dimensional model of risk stratification was constructed to represent the stratification pyramid. This was capable of utilising both stock and flow data and hence capable of changing assumptions about the churn of the underlying population, both between and within age and risk categories.

The project identified that population churn was significant and that the factor weightings in the database toolset were perhaps set too much towards recovery from acute episodic events. The impact of risk assessment was shown to have much greater financial impact under the assumption that people with long term conditions could only move up the risk scale (albeit at a lower rate).

This whole different thinking was made possible by marrying up the comprehensiveness of big data to hold flow data and the capability of system dynamics models to make use of that data. An important contribution of the project was to show that the same distribution of people in stocks over time can result from different underlying churn (flow) rates. This is something that may not be detected by database tools.[10] The same intervention introduced to two populations with identical stock over time values, but different underlying flow rates, will have significantly different impacts, including the impact on cost. To understand the dynamics of interventions we must understand flow. To understand flow, we often require the kind of data that has not hitherto been routinely collected or, if collected, analysed with flow in mind.

---

[10]Perhaps because nobody thinks to look.

References

Goodwin, J. (2006). *Long-term conditions: How to manage them?* Midlife and Beyond, Geriatric Medicine.

King's Fund, Health Dialog UK and New York University (2006). *Combined predictive model final report*. King's Fund London.

Lewis, G., Curry, N., & Bardsley, M. (2011). *Choosing a predictive risk model*. Nuffield Trust London.

NHS England. (2013). *Information governance and risk stratification: Advice and options for CCGs and GPs*. NHS England, Leeds.

Sterman, J. (2002). All models are wrong: Reflections on becoming a systems scientist' Jay wright forrester prize lecture. *System Dynamics Review, 18,* 501–531.

Part IV
Health and Social Care Workforce Projects

Chapters 15–17

Overview of Part IV

Workforce is a major component of capacity in health care and social care, and we have undertaken numerous studies to understand the dynamics of workforce recruitment and staffing levels. Part IV of the book describes five example projects to assist workforce planning. The common theme of these models is that the workforce is represented as a stock–flow chain linking the states of training, junior and senior staff and that they account for recruitment and training delays, target staff in posts, dropouts and leaving and retirement rates.

Chapter 15 covers what might be described as 'classic' workforce issues. The first model involved developing a new profession from scratch. The second model involved establishing a trainer workforce from existing employees to train new recruits and the third the strategies for maintaining a workforce of paediatric consultants in the light of implementation of the European Working Time Directive.

Chapter 16 describes a control theory model to design recruitment policies for workforce planning and comments in general on the idea of using control theory solutions in healthcare and social care modelling.

Chapter 17 covers workforce projects to assist healthcare and social care integration. The first model here focusses on examining alternative strategies for adapting the mix of skills and qualifications necessary to create a more flexible workforce. The second examines the relationship between the home care workforce and the people who need and get care. This is a comprehensive model aimed at understanding the impact of care workers on the dynamics of the service, particularly their effect on reducing delayed hospital discharges. In 'workforce planning' terms, because there is no required qualification for home care staff, employers are competing for staff within the labour market as a whole, highlighting the interesting relationship between rates of pay offered and overall cost of the service, defrayed by improvements in hospital flow.

Chapter 15
Classic Workforce Projects

Chapter Summary

This chapter provides a brief history of workforce planning and outlines why system dynamics provides a natural approach to the major challenges of such planning. It describes three modelling projects as what we describe as 'classical' workforce planning problems. The first model involved developing a new profession from scratch. The second model involved establishing a trainer workforce from existing employees to train new recruits and the third the development of strategies for maintaining a workforce of paediatricians in the light of the implementation of the European Working Time Directive. The common theme of these models is that the workforce is represented as a stock-flow chain linking the states of training and categories of staff. Further, they account for the classical dynamic issues of planning in the face of complexities arising from recruitment and training delays, meeting targets for staff in posts and coping with drop outs, leaving and retirement flows.

15.1 Introduction (UK Perspective)

Workforce planning has a chequered history. Once incorrectly known as 'manpower' planning, it emerged in post-war UK to support the effort to grow a skilled workforce in key industries, happily coinciding with the early days of mainframe computers and the emergence of management science/operations research. In that context, the question of the extent to which any aspect of the economy could or should be planned was not straightforward. By the 1980s, with the prevailing view that 'market forces' would solve complex supply/demand problems, the idea of 'workforce planning' using mainframe computers had gone out of fashion.

However, from the 1990s onwards, as desktop computers and spreadsheets became ubiquitous, the idea emerged that we should use these new tools to tackle problems such as 'skills shortages', or determine how many students to train for specific professions. In the UK, there was an increasing dialogue between employers and education providers, including about the content of national qualifications, based on national occupational standards and workforce development generally.

Various iterations of industrial training boards, employer lead bodies and national training organisations matured, in the new century, into a framework of 'sector skills councils', employer-led bodies, licensed by government, covering about 80% of the UK workforce. Their remit includes 'to reduce skills gaps and shortages and increase productivity'.

At the same time, central government began to take a more explicit role in developing workforce strategies for sectors such as health, social care or school teachers, and there is once again a presumption that something called 'workforce planning' is actually possible. Enter 'workforce planning' and any profession you can think of (especially if its practitioners are mostly employed in the public sector) into a search engine for evidence of this. Sadly, your search will probably uncover more bad news than good about how well workforce planning is going.

> Anecdotally, one author recalls working as a regulator of social work and social care qualifications in the 1990s: during that decade, attitudes among employers shifted from
>
> 'workforce planning, that's impossible isn't it?' or
>
> 'we tried that before and it did not work' to
>
> 'it should be possible to do this better'.

Clearly, those charged with the task of 'workforce planning' already use some kind of model, most likely, based on spreadsheet calculations. We would argue with others (Cave et al. 2016; NHS 2016) that for workforce modelling, system dynamics software offers advantages because of its:

- Recognition of the complex, dynamic interactions resulting from training delays, drop-out rates, vacancies, promotions, target numbers in post and turnover (recruitment/leaving)
- Level of aggregation (if we are concerned with strategic questions about the 'workforce as a whole' rather than, for example, scheduling or rota patterns)
- Ability to cope with long time horizons
- Diagrammatic approach (we maintain that SD models are easier to follow than rows of spreadsheet calculations, precisely because of their explicit representation of the flow through education, into employment, to promotion, and ultimately retirement, with people dropping out along the way, see Fig. 15.1)
- User-friendly interface (graphs, sliders and buttons, see Fig. 15.6)
- Modular capabilities that make it straightforward to represent the demand as well as supply side of the problem, which in any case are not independent because of feedback effects

15.1 Introduction (UK Perspective)

- Representation of feedback effects (for example the interplay between what is currently happening in the workforce and whether students will be attracted to training courses, or the possibility that a shortage of staff will lead to more pressure on the existing workforce, increasing turnover, exacerbating the shortage, and perhaps demotivating potential recruits)
- Capacity to stimulate discussion and promote learning, and play out a range of scenarios rather than provide 'one right answer', however much the commissioners of models want simple answers
- Ability to address workforce planning from the perspective of a single employer or the 'sector' as a whole
- Capability to incorporate layers-upon-layers, such as who trains the trainers? We include a workforce model covering the workforce that is delivering training
- Flexibility to design workforce systems from new or transform existing ones and deal with skill-mix problems; important in the context of health and social care integration (integrated care agenda)
- Ability to test new regulatory requirements (for example, reducing the number of hours for which a junior doctor can work)
- Ability to encompass the labour market and the challenges of securing <u>unqualified</u> employees in essential services, where the care sector must compete with other industries to recruit and retain staff (for the same level of pay, a frontline carer might prefer to work in a supermarket), or where there is seasonal competition for staff (e.g. it becomes harder to recruit carers during the tourist season).

15.2 Basic Workforce Model

Figure 15.1 shows a very simple version of a workforce model for a single occupation, with only one (pre-entry) qualification, and a straightforward career path. Most models in this chapter and the next will resemble this but with different levels of disaggregation, career progression possibilities, and workforce mixes. Some will go into more detail about the 'on courses' part; others will characterise the qualified workforce differently (for example, by age bands).

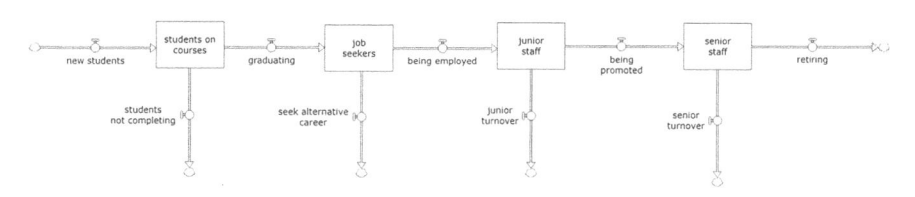

Fig. 15.1 Simple workforce stock—flow chain

The obvious challenge in workforce planning (and hence modelling) is how to take account of long time-delays,[1] such as the length of time (several years) it takes to achieve a qualification, the length of time people spend in post, and the various drop-out rates.

To figure out the appropriate size of intake to courses involves taking into account:

- How long it takes to train (in other words, how many job vacancies are there likely to be when people starting courses this year graduate?)
- The drop-out rate from training.

To work out how many vacancies there will be for junior staff involves calculating:

- The current level of vacancies (if any)
- The rates at which people are promoted to senior positions
- The rates at which people turnover (leave the workforce altogether)
- The availability of newly-qualified.

And the rate of movement from junior to senior positions depends on

- The current level of senior vacancies
- The rates at which people are retiring (so, it would be good to have some kind of age breakdown of the workforce, as we shall see)
- Turnover rates (in addition to retirements) from senior positions
- The availability of junior staff who are ready for promotion.

And, obviously, the workforce dynamics (change over time) will be influenced by various feedback loops, because people's decisions to apply to courses, to seek promotion, or to leave the workforce, will depend on various perceptions. For example:

- If, currently, there are few vacancies, perhaps fewer people will apply to courses because they expect it will be difficult to get a job on qualifying. In any case, how might people currently applying for training forecast the likely chances of employment several years later? Perhaps currently there are few vacancies but workforce demographics might mean that there is an expected bulge in retirements coming, or perhaps the numbers of people already on courses will mop up the current surplus of vacancies
- Also, if there are few vacancies, on qualifying, people are likely to spend more time in the 'job-seeking' stock, and the longer that people spend there the greater the possibility that they will give up and seek an alternative career elsewhere

---

[1] In this book, 'delay' does not necessarily imply something bad, or something that has gone wrong; we often use 'delay' to mean 'the time it takes' to do something, such as complete a qualification, or be promoted.

- If there are many vacancies, meaning that there are fewer people employed than are needed, that might also mean that fewer people apply for courses, because they perceive that this profession will be characterised by the stress of workload pressure
- And if such workload pressures exist, that might well mean that turnover rates from the existing workforce increase, making for a vicious circle (a reinforcing feedback loop)
- And all of the above might be affected by advertised rates of pay and other conditions of employment
- In some cases, training places can be made more attractive by offering students bursaries, or reduced fees, to train for jobs where there are currently staffing shortages.

These various feedback loops are not shown in the simple stock-flow diagram but can easily be envisaged.

Another challenge facing workforce planners, even given the existence of an accurate model, is to decide on a policy for filling training places. It is possible in simple situations to use control theory policies within models to derive ideal and robust recruitment profiles over time to deal with changes in the workplace. However, such solutions often involve widely oscillating number of students as a consequence of the various feedback loops and delays. Perhaps the 'ideal' intake number from the perspective of the workforce requirement would prove to be unattractive to a provider of education and training (most will prefer not to have much variation in student numbers from year to year), and so intakes cannot be finely-titrated from year-to-year.

15.3 Elaborations on the Simple Workforce Model

The rest of this chapter comprises descriptions of various workforce models undertaken to explore specific client issues. Each model represents an adaptation of the basic structure in Fig. 15.1. Sometimes the focus is on providing more detail about the 'students on courses' (or equivalent) parts. In other examples, we expand the career stages/deployment of qualified staff, sometimes into distinct branches and (as would commonly be needed) by representing these as part of an explicit ageing chain.

We explore what we observed that the model added to the client's thinking, which was not always the immediate insight that was requested. This reinforces our view that, especially in a sector as diverse as health and social care, there are few standard template models that will apply in all circumstances, and also that a model is usually best encountered as part of a group learning experience rather than being some kind of back-office generator of simple answers.

15.4 Developing a New Profession

In 2010, we developed a model for the then Children's Workforce Development Council (CWDC), part of a 'sector skills council', to simulate the introduction of a new qualification for managers of early years and childcare centres in England, effectively creating a new profession to be called the 'early years professional'. This involved modelling various pathways to qualification, each with a two-stage assessment process, including a portfolio pathway for staff already in post.

The unusual thing about this model was that it described the creation of a new profession, the 'early years professional', being a person in charge of, or in a senior position within a childcare facility. Childcare in this context covers a range of facilities for pre-school children. This was part of a deliberate attempt by government to raise the profile and status of these services, within the context of an expansion of childcare provision.

The challenge, therefore, was to grow a stock of 'early years professionals' from a starting point of 0.

The main outputs from the model, from the client's perspective, were to be financial, to enable it to provide funding to the course providers based on the numbers of people at three different stages of the training course (starting, mid-point, completion). Therefore, the stock-flow structure of the model breaks the 'students on courses' stock in Fig. 15.1 into three stocks, as shown in Fig. 15.2 (in Part 1, in Part 2, 'with a shortfall' which represents students undertaking remediation in order to pass the course), where payments are triggered based on flow numbers.

The model also had to represent various different modes of training delivery (different versions of the course were delivered to experienced and currently employed staff, who simply lacked a qualification). This aspect is less obvious in the Fig. 15.2 diagram but note that the three in -training stocks are arrayed[2] (they appear as somewhat three-dimensional representing different versions of the course), merging into one final stock (Early Years Professionals—EYP) which appears flat.

Figure 15.3 shows a key model output, the number of EYPs over time plotted alongside the target number (starting from 0, a period of growth, then maintaining a target number).

In our view, although the main 'deliverable' from the model was a tool to support financial planning, this graph captures a key, simple dynamic insight. An interesting challenge is:

> can you estimate what the annual intake to training courses would need to be in order to achieve a workforce that grew to that target number?

---

[2]Using Stella software terminology.

15.4 Developing a New Profession

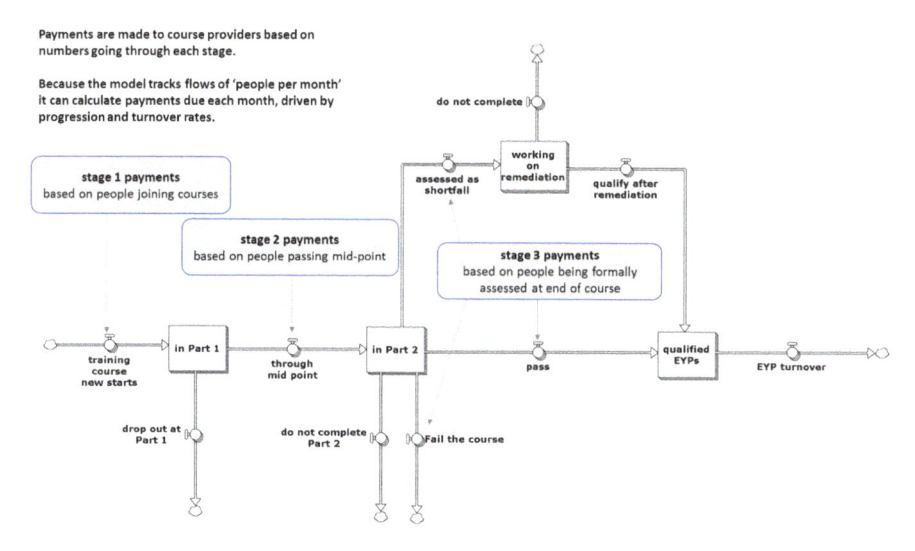

Fig. 15.2 The stock/flow structure of the EYP model which emphasises payments to courses based on student-flow

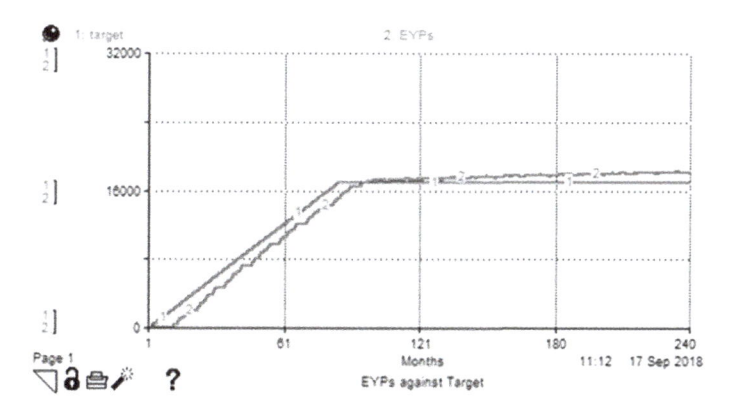

Fig. 15.3 Model run with a successful output (EYP number tracks target)

The answer (shown in Fig. 15.4, line called 'annual intake') surprised some, because it bears no relation to the shape of the Fig. 15.3 graph. In fact, it is quite simple. The intake figure only has to change once.

Initially, a large number of training places is required to grow the new workforce. Once the target level is reached, a much smaller number of training places will, other things being equal, keep the workforce at that level. Note the delay between the reduction in intakes and the flattening out of the number of staff (obviously, because of the time spent taking the course).

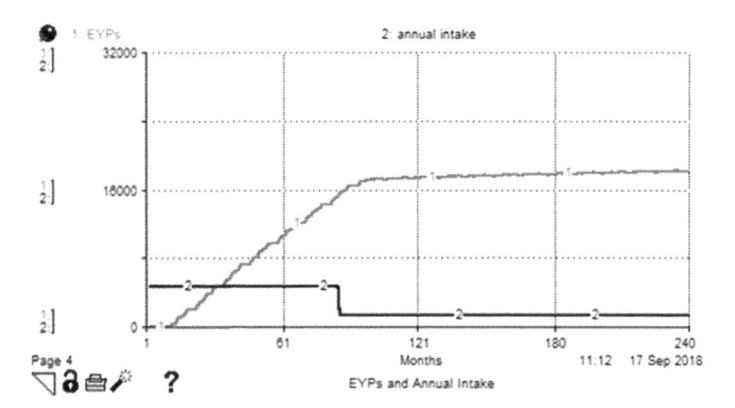

Fig. 15.4 Intakes (model inputs) over time to achieve target as shown in previous Figure

By simulating over a longer time horizon, the model prompted the CWDC to consider how many places would be required when the training moved into a maintenance rather than growth mode. This raised further questions. Would any training provider (such as a college) be prepared to cut back its intakes so severely? Would lecturers teach a course knowing that it would be seriously scaled-back after five years? In stock/flow terms, these phenomena are easy to demonstrate, the relatively simple model stimulated a new, and much needed, discussion for those charged with implementing the policy.

Another way of expressing the dynamics of growing this workforce is to concentrate on the various flows as shown in Fig. 15.2. If the inflow ('to training') is greater than the net outflows, the workforce will be growing. If the inflow is equal to the net outflows, then the workforce will maintain a stable level. However, at the planning stage, the main outflow (people leaving the EYP workforce) was not known, because the EYP workforce did not exist. The model could be run using various estimates of turnover. Clearly, as the training programme (and the workforce) became more established, a realistic figure for turnover could be estimated and a realistic intake figure derived.

15.5 Modelling a Trainer Workforce

At the heart of most workforce models is a representation of training (number of places, time taken to train, drop-out/completion rates). The model described below concerns professional training of social workers in Scotland, but the purpose of the model was to tackle the demand for trainers of social workers, rather than the demand for social workers. Workforce planning at one step removed, perhaps.

The demand for the model arose from a change in the structure of social work education and, in particular, the 'practice placement' element within training. Note

15.5 Modelling a Trainer Workforce

that in the Figures, the term PLO (practice learning opportunity) is used to describe 'one student placed'. Practice placements (PLOs) are an important part of any professional training system; in the case of social work, placements are supervised by accredited 'practice teachers' (drawn from the social worker workforce), and the route to accreditation itself involves training, which includes supervising a social work student.

As Fig. 15.5 shows, there are three types of practice teacher, who form part of the same workforce stock-flow chain:

- trainees (social workers who are supervising their first-ever student)
- singletons (people whose main job is 'social worker' but who provide learning experiences for students, usually one student at a time, often with a considerable gap between students)
- full-time practice teachers (a small number, recruited from the pool of 'singletons', who take on a full-time job of providing practice placements, normally because an employer has determined that this is a good model to follow, sometimes supported by some kind of external funding).

The demand for the model had arisen because of a change in programme funding that would mean fewer full-time practice teacher posts being supported, but some kind of financial support being offered to agencies based on placements being provided, mostly by singletons. The big question was whether such a proposal was sustainable. In general, funding full-time practice teacher posts is more expensive; but they can supervise several students at a time, and are guaranteed to provide a certain number of placements each year. Placements with singletons might cost less, but their availability is unpredictable given the other demands on their working time (a full caseload, normally), most have no contractual obligation to supervise students, may get no workload relief when supervising a student, and hence spend much of their time in a 'fallow'[3] state (between students but not yet ready to take another one).

Therefore, if the whole system was to rely more on singleton practice teachers, that would mean constantly running courses for new trainee practice teachers, as the sole source of supply of practice opportunities. From a professional development perspective, supervising students is a good thing for a professional to do, so that might be a good thing. But is it sustainable?

Note also in Fig. 15.5, the demand for placements is derived from students undertaking the four-year[4] social work degree, who must undergo placements of varying lengths (and degrees of intensity) at each stage of their training.

Characteristic behaviour of the model is shown in Fig. 15.6.

Figure 15.6 shows the number of placements provided against the capacity of the whole system over a period of eight years. Note that the uneven-ness of the

---

[3]Fallow in relation to taking students; they are typically fully, or over, employed (personal experience of author).

[4]Normal for a Scottish undergraduate degree.

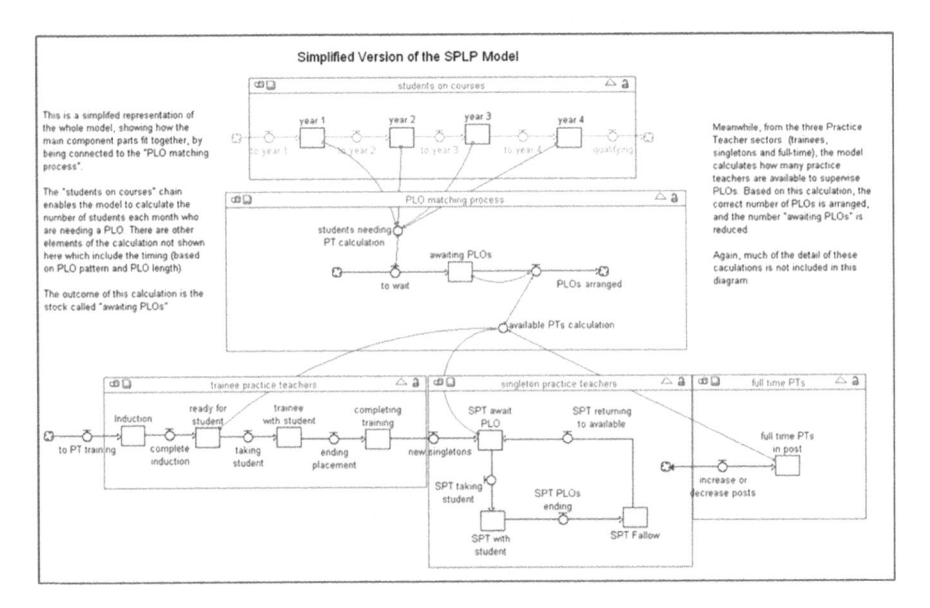

Fig. 15.5 Simplified (the simplified diagram does not show every flow in the model, for example, the turnover of singletons or non-completions of trainees (but they are definitely in the model)) diagram of the social work practice learning model

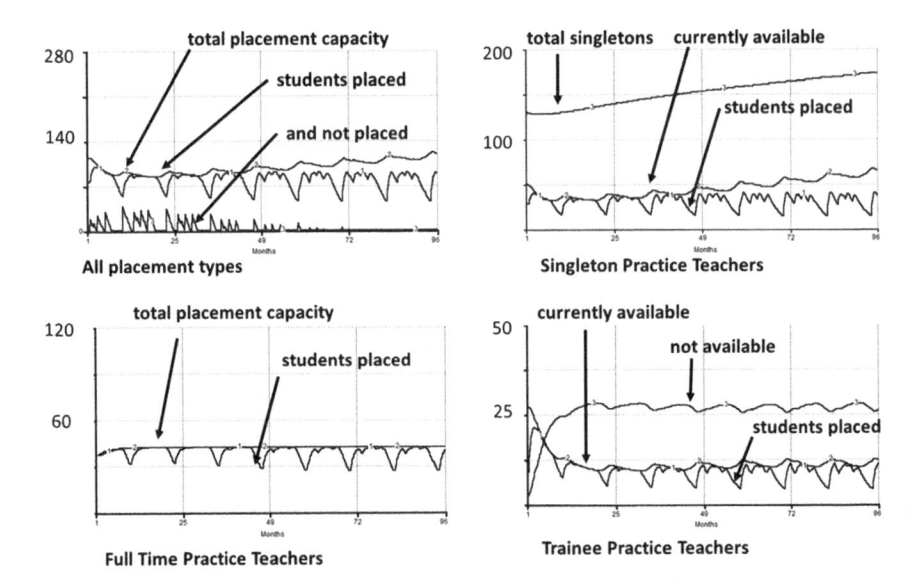

Fig. 15.6 Main dashboard screen from practice teacher model

15.5 Modelling a Trainer Workforce

occupancy lines results from the 'placement pattern' whereby students are only out on placement at various times during the academic year. To smooth this out, students from different academic institutions tend to have a different placement pattern, but nevertheless some times of year are inevitably busier than others (fewer students are placed during the summer, for example). The graphs show the 'capacity' figure, being the maximum number of students that could be placed at any time (a growing number in this example). The top left graph represents effectively the sums of the other three graphs (being the three types of practice teacher). Note also the policy that both full-time practice teacher and trainee practice teacher capacity should always be fully utilised (when student demand exists), because that is the actual job of full-timers, and it is a course requirement of those undergoing practice teacher training.

Therefore, having that capacity fully stretched is not an indicator of a problem. In the case of singletons, it is not a problem if there appears to be spare capacity (these staff have many other demands on their time). Note also that there is a line above the capacity line in the singletons graph, representing the total number of singletons. The gap between that line and the capacity line represents the total number of singletons in the 'fallow' state (not currently available to take a student). Unsurprisingly, at any given time, most accredited singletons are either not taking a student, or not available to take a student.

The desirable state is therefore as shown in this model run. There is always spare capacity in the singleton sector, and that spare capacity is growing (as the new trainee practice teachers complete their first student placement and move on to the 'accredited singleton' status). In fact, in this run, one might conclude that too many new practice teachers are being trained (but in many agencies training as a practice teacher is a normal first step on a career pathway to management).

Finally, returning to the summary graph (top left) note the line that sometimes appears at the bottom of this graph. That line merely represents the number of students currently unplaced. Given that in the model, it takes one month (time step) for a student to be placed, the existence of a small number at any point is only a cause for concern if, at the same time, there is no spare capacity in the system.

Various iterations of this model were developed, most recently to support the Scotland professors of social work group to co-ordinate plans for practice teacher training during a period of restructuring.

15.6 Workforce Model for One Type of Occupation Including Progression and Ageing

This model is probably our best example of a 'classic' workforce model because physicians represent the pure case of:

- A one-to-one correspondence between qualifications and jobs because
  - To do this job you need precisely this qualification
  - Almost everyone with this qualification does this type of job

- A career where there is very little leakage—qualified medical consultants rarely move into other types of job and are rewarded for remaining in practice.

The model was commissioned in 2009 by the England Department of Health along with the Royal College of Paediatrics and Child Health (covering UK) and Skills for Health, to support decision-making about intakes to specialist training in the light of the implementation of the European Working Time Directive (EWTD).

> The EWTD had produced a *step increase in the demand for junior doctors, but with fewer implications for consultants*.

The clients had rich, spreadsheet-based data analysis but recognised that this did not adequately capture 'behaviour over time'. The striking feature of consultant training is the length of time taken, in addition to qualifying training, with new responsibilities taken on at various mileposts. The model covered the junior/middle grade pathway in detail, modelling the specialist workforce as an ageing chain. The model represents both the Supply of consultants/trainees, and the Demand side (which sets out various scenarios).

Modelling the Supply of Specialists

Figure 15.7 shows that, compared with the basic structure outlined in Fig. 15.1, this model is much more disaggregated, both in its representation of the 'stock' of people in training (trainees) and the qualified workforce (consultants).

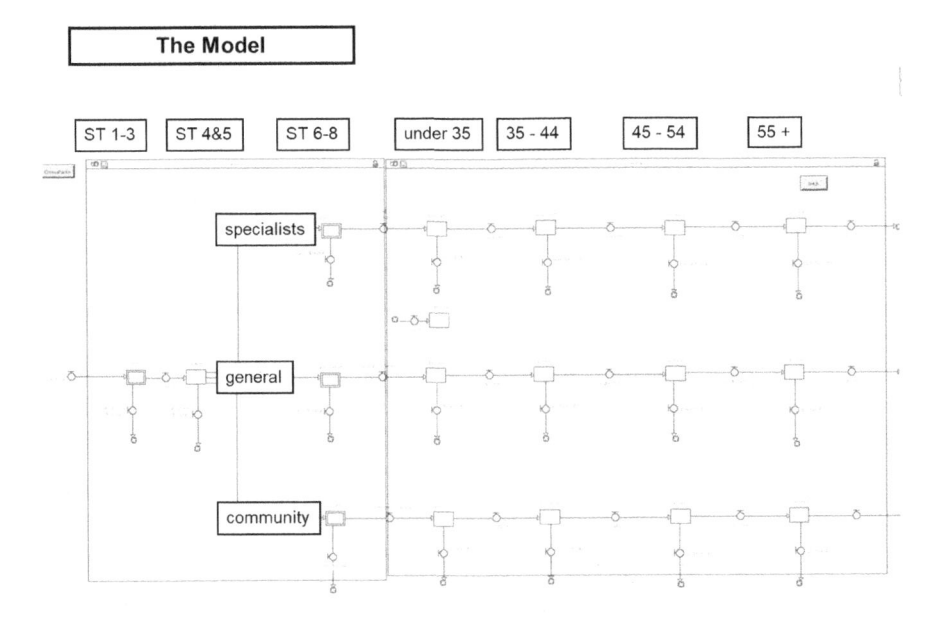

Fig. 15.7 Stock flow structure of paediatrician workforce (individual stock and flow labels are illegible but meanings are obvious)

There is one inflow to the 'trainees' sector. Doctors enter specialist training having completed two 'foundation' years immediately after qualifying; after these foundation years, many doctors delay applying for a specialism. The decision to apply for a particular specialism (or general practice) will normally set the course for a lifetime of work; few doctors change specialism, not least because the time involved to train as a specialist is so long. Specialist training is divided into three periods (labelled ST 1–3 etc. in the diagram):

- Years 1–3
- Years 4 and 5, at which point paediatricians choose between three pathways (generalists, community paediatricians, or one of many specialisms, reflecting many of the specialisms that exist in adult medicine)
- Years 6–8 (by pathway).

Although set out as an 8-year programme, this is actually the MINIMUM time it takes; for many, the training takes longer. And, at all stages, some drop out of training (the vertical flows, one for each stock).

The 'consultants' workforce is set out as an ageing chain, again with drop-out flows at each stage. Unlike the basic model (Fig. 15.1), this stock-flow chain does not show staff moving in and out of employment. The structure represents all consultants, whether employed or not. It makes sense to represent doctors as an ageing chain because, as noted above, they are likely to remain in the same occupation (with small losses through turnover and mortality) until they retire. The consultant workforce in Fig. 15.7 therefore represents a pool of people from which consultants are recruited, on a separate demand side of the model.

Modelling Demand for Consultants and Middle Grade Doctors

The model is set up to explore a range of scenarios, being different assumptions about how consultants and trainees are to be employed and deployed, attached to switches in the model. Without going into detail, the different scenarios include:

- Different future configurations of hospitals within which paediatricians might be employed
- Different ways of running staffing rotas to ensure that
  - Enough staff are employed
  - European Working Time Directive compliance (especially for middle grade doctors, in this model being ST 4–8, although other definitions are possible)
  - A 'gold standard' rota is achieved, above the minimum set out in EWTD
- Different ways of supporting consultants (such that fewer actually need to be on-site or on-call)

- Deployment of consultants who are qualified but not employed to a permanent consultant position (sometimes known as 'staff grades')
- Recruitment of staff from abroad.

We used 'group model building' with a combination of senior paediatricians, policy makers and data analysts to explore these scenarios, for example as shown in Fig. 15.8. This scenario shows the demand for and supply of consultants and middle grade doctors over a period of 20 years (the model runs in days).

The lessons are that with an (at least) eight-year lead-time, it is impossible to effect immediate change in this highly qualified workforce. Some flexibility can be built into the system by deploying surplus consultants in middle grade positions. And, once both targets (consultant and middle grade) are reached, it is difficult to bring about a levelling out, because the middle grades already in the pipeline (to meet the middle grade target) inevitably progress and become consultants.

This, of course, is only one of many scenarios we could have shown and remains hypothetical, probably bearing little resemblance to what happened next. A simpler

For both consultants and middle grades, demand, or 'required', increases in a single step early in the run, resulting from new restrictions on working hours.

Because it takes a minimum of eight years to train a consultant, even increasing training intake at the start run, the rise in middle grade doctors is insufficient during the first eight years. From year 10, note the over-supply of consultants. In the scenario shown, surplus consultants are employed to cover the middle grade rota; the consultant 'surplus' is therefore added to the middle grade complement, and by year 15 the target number of middle grades is reached. Thereafter, the bottom line on the consultant graph, showing qualified consultants who are not employed (surplus to requirements) grows. Note also, that at no time in the 20-year period does the 'not employed' line appear on the middle-grade graph.

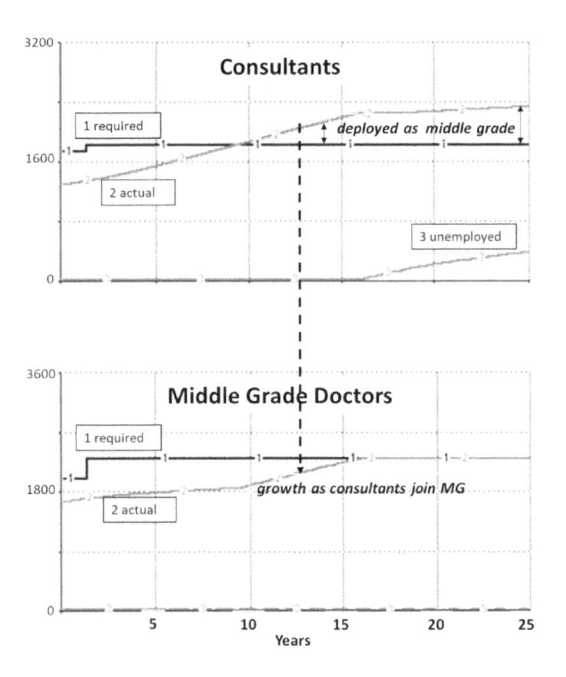

Fig. 15.8 Outputs from a model run—consultants and middle-grades

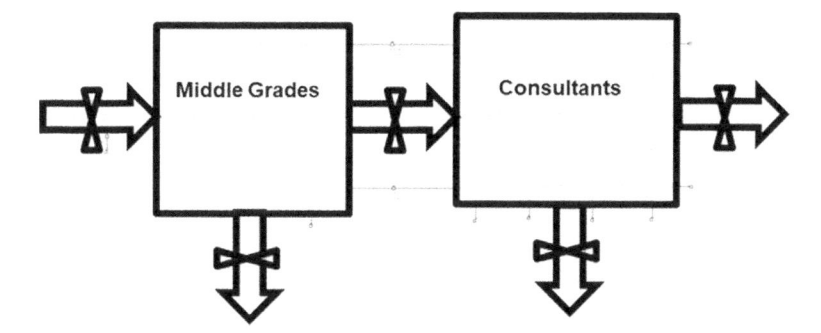

15.6 Workforce Model for One Type of Occupation Including ...

Fig. 15.9 A more-aggregated (two stock) view of the middle grade → consultant workforce

version of this model was developed and used in training courses for health workforce planners.

The final report included an options-appraisal outlining more than 20 scenarios. But from the modelling team's perspective, the **main learning point was simple**, and might possibly have been missed given the level of detail in the model. The key and relatively simple dynamic that the spreadsheet calculations had not uncovered was that increasing the numbers in one part of the pipeline (middle-grade doctors) would in time inevitably produce a surplus of consultants. This becomes more obvious if we superimpose a very simple two-stock structure on top of the detailed stock-flow structure in the actual model, as shown in Fig. 15.9.

Because of the focus on the EWTD, which would affect the demands for middle grade doctors and consultants differently, the modelling group had focused on these two targets as if they were independent variables. In fact, to change the number of consultants means first changing the number of middle grades (the main source of consultants), and to change the number of middle grades, we inevitably, after a time delay, change the number of consultants. It makes no logical sense to set targets for consultants and middle-grades as if they are independent variables, but the looming deadline of the EWTD had generated its own version of silo-thinking, from which this model provided an escape.

15.7 Conclusions

The chapter has described the use of system dynamics models to address three workforce planning issues.

In the first model an important counter-intuitive insight centred on the recruitment profile required to build a new workforce up to a target level. The second model confirmed the importance of singletons (people whose main job is 'social worker' but who provide learning experiences for students) in the training of social workers due to the flexible capacity this provides. The third model which examined the dynamics of balancing a long paediatric workforce chain, involving 8 years of training, highlighted the relatively simple but very important insights that it takes a long time to change staff numbers and that target numbers of staff in each section of a single chain need to be balanced. Increasing the numbers of staff in one part of the pipeline (middle-grade doctors) will in time inevitably produce a surplus of staff (consultants) downstream.

References

Cave, S. R., Willis, G., & Woodward, A. (2016). A retrospective of system dynamics based workforce modelling at the centre for workforce intelligence. In *Conference: 34th International Conference of the System Dynamics Society* (www.cfwi.org.uk).

NHS. (2016). *Building workforce models: A brief introduction December.* https://www.healthylondon.org/.

Chapter 16
Using a Control Theory Approach to Workforce Planning

Chapter Summary
This short Chapter is included to comment on the idea of using control theory solutions in health and social care modelling. Such thinking was introduced in Chaps. 2 and 3 and is applied here to classic workforce recruitment. A small model is introduced to demonstrate the thinking. The conclusion is that such an approach might in some circumstances complement the process of modelling as learning but users should be mindful of the impracticalities sometimes associated with 'solution' thinking of this type.

16.1 A Control Theory Workforce Model

The simple hospital model in Chap. 2 which underpins a lot of our treatment models is effectively a feedback control model, where we used spare beds plus discharges to control admissions. We demonstrated in Chap. 2 that it was essential to include discharges in admission policies. Of course, this is now standard practice in hospitals but perhaps few hospital managers realise the origins of this thinking and how generic and transferrable it is to other systems.

In Chap. 3 we introduced the idea that sometimes it can be informative to examine classical control theory solutions to other issues. In that case we were looking at a two-stock hospital model and trying to see if there was any way we might be able to control hospital capacity to give us a desired waiting time for patients. We concluded that this was entirely impractical since large and fast changes to bed and staff capacities would be involved.

Here we demonstrate the application of a control engineering feedback approach to workforce planning where it perhaps has more merit.

Figure 16.1 shows a simplified version of a classical workforce situation where we wish to design a recruitment policy which would be robust to changes in length of service, training and promotion times, information delays and drop-outs in training and junior grades.

As in the simple hospital model of Chap. 2, the control theory approach would suggest that the recruitment policy be based on several balancing information feedback loops to control recruitment to targets for each grade. The desired recruitment for our first experiment is therefore defined as the spare posts (vacancies) in both junior and senior jobs plus retirements. (Note that the recruitment variable appears twice in Fig. 16.1, the second dotted icon being a 'ghost' of the first to reduce the number of connectors shown).

However, as shown in Fig. 16.2 (here against a scenario of declining lengths of service and hence increasing retirements) the application of this thinking appears to be less than successful. Actual numbers of staff in training, junior positions and senior positions fluctuate significantly and target senior staff is not met.

These graphs reflect the classical mode of behaviour of 'balancing feedback loops with delays', which is oscillation caused by recruitment always being based on information lagging behind the real situation due to, in this case, to the training delay.

An additional component which must be taken into consideration, is the staff in training.

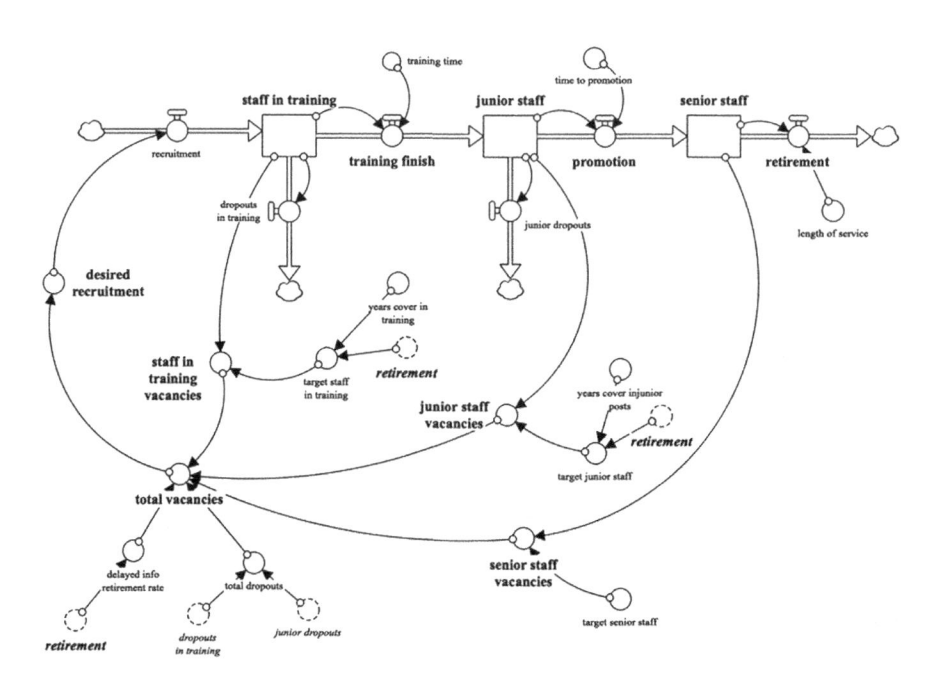

Fig. 16.1 A simple control theory model for planning workforce recruitment

16.1 A Control Theory Workforce Model

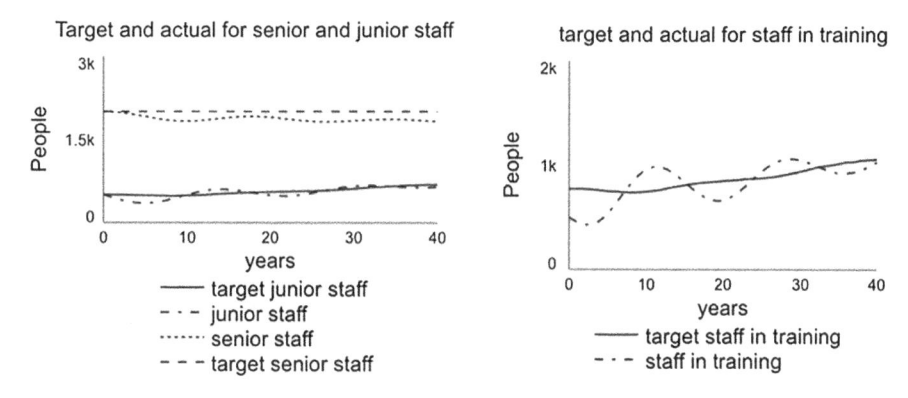

Fig. 16.2 Initial results from the simple workforce control model

In order to take the staff in training into consideration it is necessary to define a target for this number. The gap in training places between the target and actual can then be fed into the recruitment policy. However, the definition of this target needs careful thought.

A good way to define the target staff in training is as a number of years of cover of retirements, and a first starting point for finding this time period is the training time (Note in Fig. 16.1 that such thinking had already been applied to the target for junior staff.).

Including this third element (training vacancies) in the recruitment policy gives the results shown in Fig. 16.3.

It will be seen that this additional element in the recruitment policy reduces the oscillations of Fig. 16.2. However, the target for senior staff is still not quite met and further refinement of the policy is needed.

The final missing factor to also include in the recruitment policy is the drop-outs in each grade since these are additional outflows from the system. This is just the

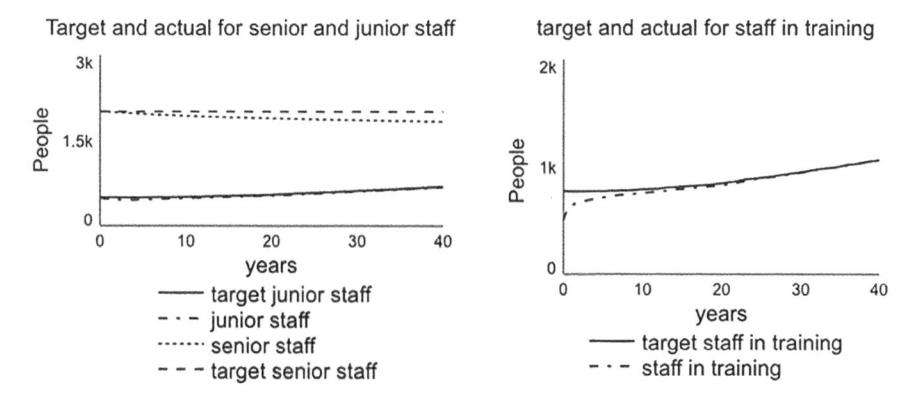

Fig. 16.3 The results of additionally including training vacancies in the recruitment policy

same thinking as taking discharges into consideration when determining admissions to hospital.

Figure 16.4 shows the improved performance resulting from building the average drop-outs into the recruitment policy.

It should also be pointed out that a big assumption in the formulation of the training is that there will be a variability in the number of people finishing training with some people needing a relative short time and others more as encountered in on-the job- training. If everyone needed the same training time as in academic courses, then it would be considerably more difficult to meet targets in post since drop outs in training could not be replaced as quickly.

Figure 16.1 incorporates the five separate elements (training vacancies, junior and senior staff vacancies, retirement and drop-out rates) to be taken into consideration in defining a robust recruitment policy.

One of the most important insights from applying this approach to workforce planning concerns the definition of target staff in each grade and in training. It will be seen from the graphs here that the target number of senior staff is constant, but that the target numbers for junior staff and staff in training are rising (since they are a function of retirements). This reflects the fact that under the scenario modelled the time senior staff spend in post is reducing hence retirement is increasing and there is a need to pull more and more staff though the system to replace these.

In most workforce planning, targets for staff in each grade are usually constant and possibly chosen arbitrarily, rather than related to what is happening in other parts of the system. This was the case in the paediatric workforce planning also reported in Chap. 14 and a major insight there was the need to understand that changing those targets for junior staff would automatically lead to more senior staff eventually.

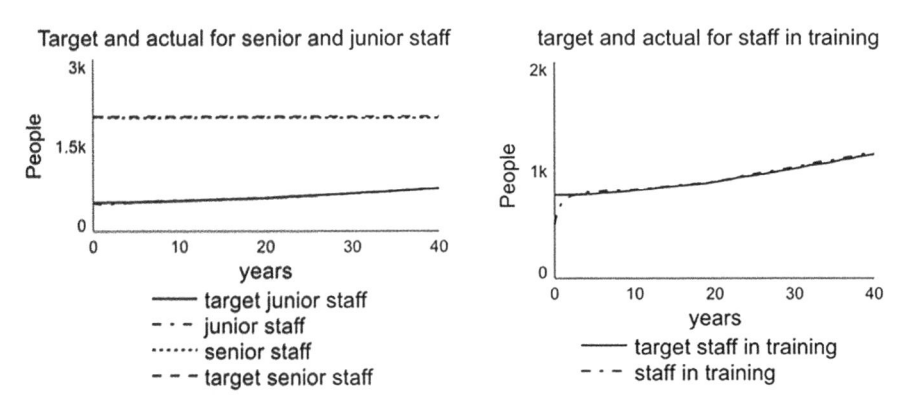

Fig. 16.4 The results of additionally including drop outs in the recruitment policy

16.2 Staffing a Start-up Organisation

In Chap. 14 we described a project concerning starting up a large workforce from scratch (Early Years Professionals) and it is interesting to use the control model of this chapter to do the same thing. The model of Fig. 16.1 has been configured in this way with recruiting starting at year 10 and Fig. 16.5 shows the results of doing this.

It was pointed out in Chap. 14 that starting up a new workforce requires a somewhat counter intuitive boost in training initially to establish the process. Figure 16.5 shows exactly the same effect generated for the model here, but even more dramatically. A very exaggerated start-up peak in recruitment occurs, due to the large initial gaps between all targets and actual staff numbers in each grade. As mentioned in Chap. 14 such a solution would be impossible to implement in practice due to the vast demands on training establishments and a slower build up would in practice be required, tailored to any training constraints.

Another impracticality of this result is the sheer time it takes to establish a new workforce by training them all and the process would need to be expedited by the recruitment of as many ready trained staff as possible from outside sources, which is

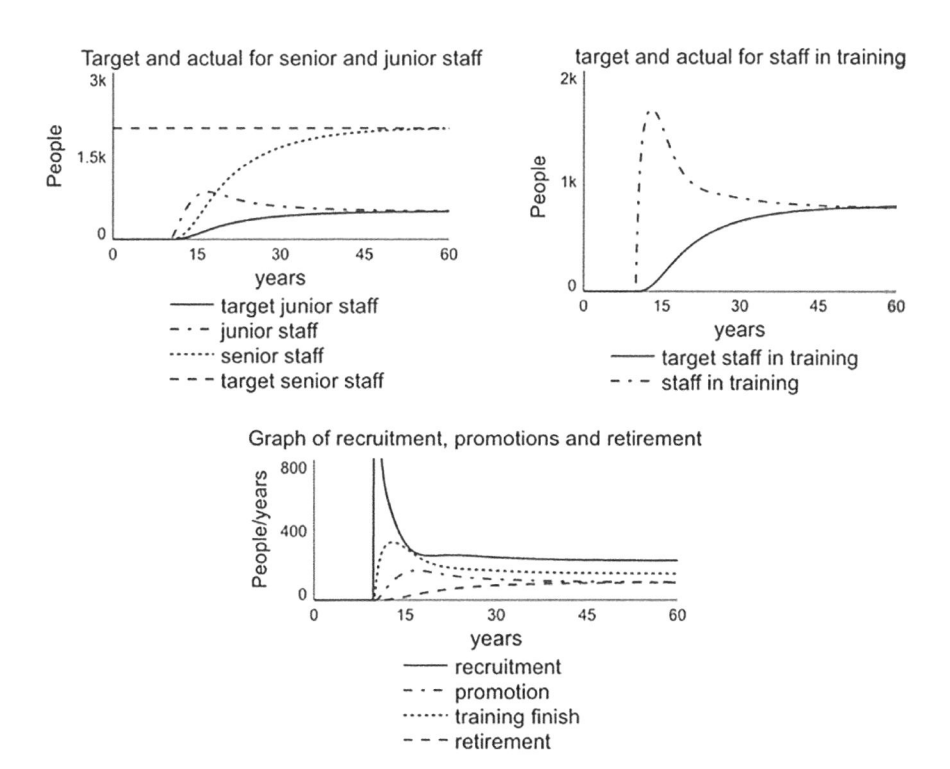

Fig. 16.5 The recruitment profile resulting from a workforce start-up

common practice in heath. It would however be possible to use such a model to determine the level of outside recruitment necessary to achieve target numbers in post within a given timescale.

16.3 Conclusions

The general rule which emerges here is that the input to any flow chain (such as admissions and recruitment) should be planned on a basis of:

1. closing any gaps between the targets (or capacity) and current levels of each *controllable* stock (for example, spare beds, staff vacancies) (i.e. not *buffer* stocks).
2. **AND** replacing the average outflows from *each* stock in the chain (for example, hospital discharges and retirements and drop-outs).
3. **AND** linking targets for stocks to changes in downstream trends. This obviously relates only to targets which can be chosen (i.e. not capacities).

These rules obviously become quite complicated when used in flow chains containing many stocks and are dependent on the availability of good information systems. However, it is suggested that, although sometime impractical, robust control engineering policies can offer interesting ideal possibilities on which to base the design of policies in many managerial situations. It is not suggested that there is any substitute for allowing management teams to experience the development of models as a learning process, but rather to complement the approach.

Chapter 17
Workforce Projects to Assist Health and Social Care Integration

Chapter Summary
This second chapter on dynamic workforce planning builds on the Integrated Care (Ham 2018) project work of Chap. 8 where system dynamics modelling was used to help stakeholders think about the consequences of changing the 'balance of care' between health and social care. Obviously, to implement any rebalancing might involve a change in the profile (or skills/qualifications mix) of the workforce. This might mean recruiting different numbers of specific types of professional, or perhaps simply relocating professionals in different settings; most likely, a bit of both. Two models are presented. The first model here focuses on examining alternative strategies for adapting the mix of skills and qualifications necessary to create a more flexible workforce. The second examines the relationship between the home care workforce and the people who need and get care. This is a comprehensive model aimed at understanding the impact of care workers on the dynamics of the service, particularly their effect on reducing delayed hospital discharges.

17.1 Model 1—Modelling Health and Social Care Integration Workforce Change

Individual employers clearly have an interest in national-level workforce planning, but the workforce challenge they typically face is more about whether it is possible to recruit and deploy a sufficient skill-mix of staff in order to provide a particular service or set of services.

The model developed here enabled those charged with implementing health and social care integration within one locality (a town and its surrounding area) to engage in a more strategic approach to workforce planning. We focused only on some key job roles, selected because either there was evidence of difficulty recruiting, or because they were most likely to be subject to change as a result of service reconfiguration. A model template was developed to represent the dynamics of each individual job-type, as shown in Fig. 17.1.

In the diagram, for each (arrayed) job type there is a given number of posts to be filled (a number that might be changing over time).

In the *employees* sector, most people are in the 'in post' stock, representing people currently employed. Many job-types recruit only people who are qualified. For some jobs, training and a qualification are provided on-the-job (as shown in the 'qualify on job' stock), and it is also possible that people in this stock should be counted as working only a fraction of their time (which is captured in a participation ratio). The stock labelled 'transition' represents, in a small number of cases, people in transition from one job type to another, either as a result of a move to another setting (e.g. from a hospital to a community-based position), or as a complete change of job.

There is one instance of this structure for every job-type, and the structure is 'arrayed' with each array-level representing one job-type. As a technical note, this explains why the transition process is represented by flows that appear to be unconnected; effectively this structure moves people from one array-level to another. And some of the people making a transition will move to the 'qualify on job' stock in the new position. This means that some variables must have the 'job type' arrayed twice (see variable marked 2d in diagram), being (from this job, to that job). And most of these will take a value of 0 because most transitions are not possible or feasible.

The simpler *recruitment* sector shows the recruitment process as being subject to delays (new staff rarely arrive on the same day that their predecessors leave, and for

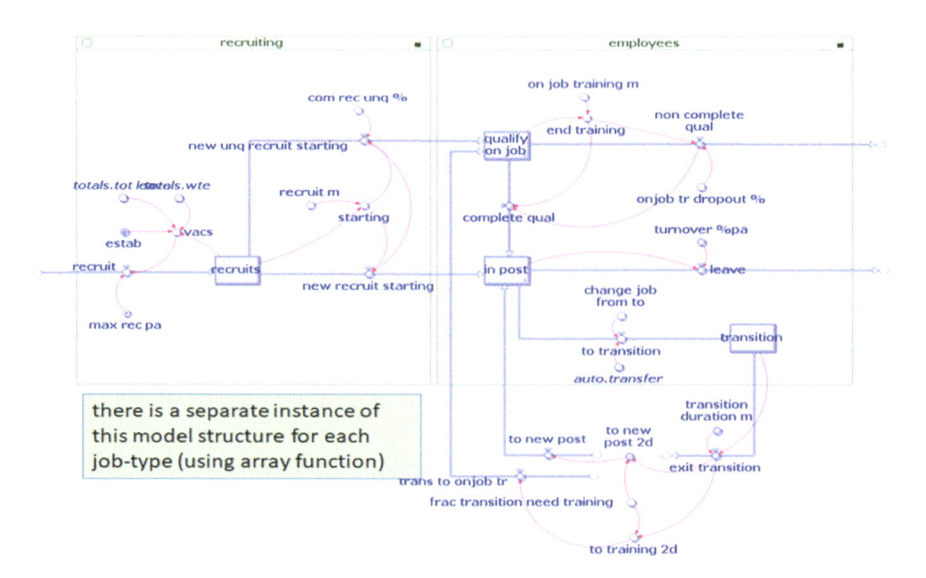

Fig. 17.1 Workforce model: same for each job-type

some types of job in more remote areas, recruitment takes months). The model also represents the reality that it is hard to recruit to some job-types. In a national workforce model, of the type we have already seen, that phenomenon is endogenous (newly-qualified staff are a stock in the model supply-chain). From the perspective of an individual employer, that phenomenon is experienced exogenously (there appears to be a limit on how many employees can be recruited, but this may be due to various factors, not just the number of new graduates but also whether or not people want to move to this area, and it is also possible to recruit from other employers). There is therefore a degree of uncertainty about just how many people it will be possible for any employer to recruit.

A management team could spend a great deal of time on this, but the purpose of this model was to support a group of managers operating at a fairly local level. The main issues they faced were an aspiration to create, from nothing, a new type of 'generic worker' job-role, so that more complex packages of care could be provided to people living at home. In considering where these new workers would come from, it became clear that there was a particular cluster of jobs that were particularly interconnected, and where movements might take place:

- Qualified nurses in hospital moving to community
- Unqualified nurses in hospital moving to community
- Unqualified nurses in community moving to 'generic worker'
- Home care staff moving to 'generic worker'
- New recruits from outside to 'generic worker'.

Therefore, to meet the demand for more 'generic workers', the home care workforce might be depleted, especially given that an early version of this model covered an area with a high level of tourism, meaning home care staff are hard to recruit/retain during the summer season. The model successfully facilitated a qualitatively different conversation within a locality management group. Effectively, staff were supported to tackle a strategic planning challenge whilst retaining an operational focus on 'what might actually happen if we did x?'

The model dashboard is the main screen on which users engage with this model. It is designed to facilitate group conversations where a wide variety of scenarios can be explored in a single session. This version runs for three years.[1] The small graphs plot the target number of people in post (solid line) and the actual number (dotted line) in this scenario. Note that some reduction is envisaged for some job types (e.g. home care) and a significant increase is desired in others (e.g. generic worker). The numbers represent working assumptions about the maximum number who can be recruited externally per annum, and the dials represent annual turnover rates. There are buttons (not shown in this screen-shot) representing three possible patterns of movement between job types that have been specifically identified as being possible career pathways.

- **Redeploy** means that people move from one job to another only if there are more people in post in the job of origin (push)

---

[1] We would normally recommend considering a longer time horizon.

- **Development** means (more likely) that a position in a new post is likely to attract people, and they will seek a move whether or not they are still 'needed' in their old position
- **Neither** means that nobody will move between jobs, and any increase in the workforce must be achieved by external recruitment.

The particular scenario in Fig. 17.2 shows that an aspiration to recruit a large number of new 'generic workers' has been achieved, but at the expense of creating a persistent shortage of home care workers, and a temporary shortage (a sharper reduction than had been hoped) of unregistered nurses in hospital.

Finally, the graph in the bottom right shows the overall skill mix (in this particular scenario, there is an ever-growing workforce. Job types are ordered on this graph so that closely related jobs appear side by side—therefore managers can quickly judge 'we have more of these but fewer of these, and it is probably ok… (or not)'.

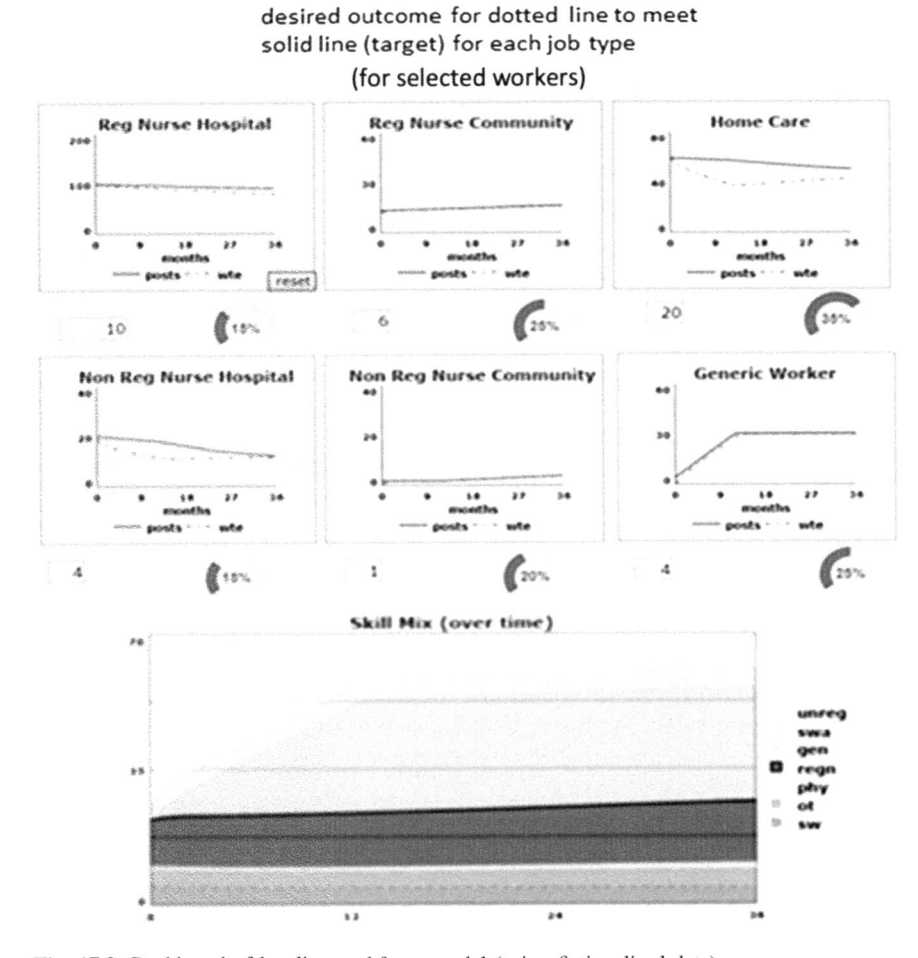

Fig. 17.2 Dashboard of locality workforce model (using fictionalised data)

The main purpose of this kind of model is not so much to provide a fixed set of figures to go into a workforce plan, but more to provide a group of managers with a tool that can facilitate a different kind of conversation, and quickly flags up 'unintended consequences'. The model also provides a rich list of performance indicators that will enable the management to monitor progress over time. Very likely, some of these data items will either not be routinely collected, or reported on management dashboards.

17.2 Model 2—Care Workforce in the Context of the Wider Economy

Every modelling project brings out the question of where the boundaries lie. For example

- A workforce model might be just a representation of the workforce chain, with a focus on intakes to training courses and staff turnover
- Often, the workforce model is embedded within a model of service capacity and service user flow showing the consequences of not having enough staff on service pressures, including waiting lists
- A further dimension in workforce modelling is to factor in the wider economy because the care sector competes with several other sectors to employ staff, especially unqualified staff.

Work currently in progress includes an exploratory model of the home care workforce in Northern Ireland (mostly applicable in the rest of the UK and beyond). The model has four components:

- Home care workforce (recruitment, training and turnover) and the wider labour market (including employment rates, pay rates)
- Service user demand for home care, including unmet demand from
  - People who need home care but are not yet referred
  - People referred and awaiting package at home
  - People referred and awaiting package in hospital (delayed discharges)
- Service description (in terms of how many hours per week per service user are needed, models of home care delivery—'time and task' versus 'guaranteed hours employment', rurality)
- Finance (mostly covering costs of employing staff, costs of delayed discharge, and contract price to be paid to providers).

This model is perhaps the most comprehensive project we have undertaken. It represents the interconnected reality of the labour market, the workforce, service demand and service use in social care and health. By linking workforce capacity to the delivery of service it provides an additional dimension to the models of service use described earlier in the book, which have been largely based on summary capacities such as beds and care packages.

As Fig. 17.3 shows, the model has three main parts.

People who need and get care represents the population of people who need care, coming from the general population. Initially, people crossing the threshold of being 'in need of home care' are not known to care services, and it may be some time, if ever, before they are referred. Once referred, they may have to wait (at home) some time to be assessed and then to get a care package (depending on the capacity of the care system). So, there are three categories of people in need: people who need care but are not known to relevant services, people who have been referred but do not yet have a care package, and people who receive the care they need. Being vulnerable, these people are all at risk of being admitted to hospital, and various feedback effects might exist. For example, the longer that people wait for a package, the more likely they are to experience a hospital admission. If admitted to hospital (here shown as two stocks, but the actual model is a bit more granular), people will have a spell of being in hospital because that is where they need to be (frail and in hospital), then, if a care package is not yet available, they may have to wait in hospital (also known as 'delayed discharge'). This poses the question of how spare home care places are prioritised.

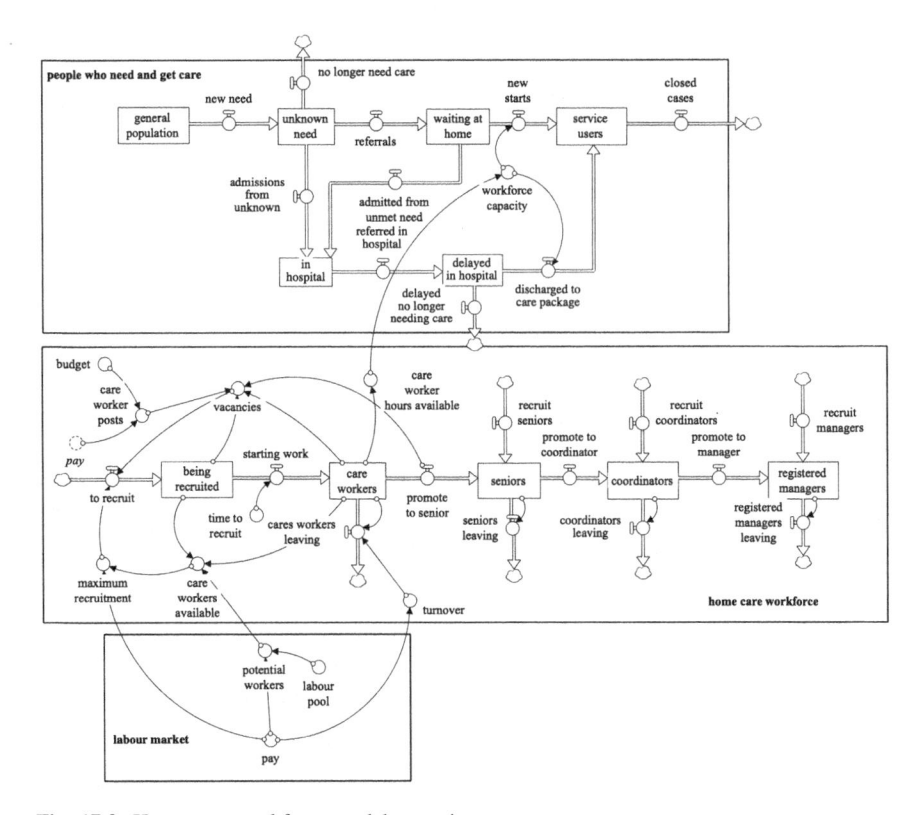

Fig. 17.3 Home care workforce model emerging structure

17.2 Model 2—Care Workforce in the Context of the Wider Economy

Should they go more to people who are currently waiting at home, because at least people delayed in hospital are being looked after, or should they go to people waiting in hospital, because that is a very expensive, and potentially dangerous because of the risks of infection or institutionalisation, place for people to be, and nobody should be in hospital if they do not need to be there. A further dilemma (not in diagram, but in the client model) concerns people admitted to hospital from the 'service users' stock. Should they retain their home care package, so that they can be discharged as soon as they are 'fit for discharge', even if it means keeping some home care capacity in reserve.

Clearly, showing this as a stock/flow diagram, even at this high level of aggregation, provides a means for exploring a range of dilemmas about how scarce capacity should be managed. It also makes sense to include this 'service user chain' in a workforce model, because the model can then show, for example, that by spending more on carers (people who are, wrongly in our view, mostly low-paid), significant savings might be realised in the hospital system (where the 'delayed discharge' phenomenon persists).

The *home care workforce* part of the diagram models four categories of staff: care workers, senior care workers, coordinators (who do the day-to-day operational management of the service, involving rapid decision-making about how to manage day-to-day crises, including staff absences and service user emergencies) and 'registered managers' (a statutory role governed by the regulator). In this iteration of the model, most of the focus is on the care worker stock. Further iterations will explore the implications and benefits of growing the senior social care worker stock which enables a wider range of people to be looked after at home (rather than be admitted to a care home, for example). The striking thing about the care worker part is that to recruit and retain staff, the sector must compete against other employment sectors, such as retail and hospitality, that draw on the same pool of 'unskilled', under-qualified people doing insecure, low-paid work.

This is captured in the variables shown in the *labour market* sector of the diagram. In this iteration, we assume the following relationships, whilst seeking economic data that would enable the model to be parameterised.

- With an ageing population, we need more care staff to look after people at home
- With almost full employment, it is difficult to recruit care staff—in the model, by increasing the hourly rate of pay we assume that a higher percentage of the unskilled workforce will be attracted to a career in home care
- Without staff, people who need care may need to be looked after by family members (informal carers) who might otherwise have been economically active
- If fewer people are economically active (available for work) the problems of full-employment (labour shortages) are exacerbated.

Beyond that loop:

- Without enough capacity in the care system, hospital pathways become blocked by people who need care but cannot access it
- Depending on the level of care required it is normally much more expensive to look after someone in a hospital bed than care for them at home.

In running the model, we can explore the extent to which increasing hourly pay for care workers would help solve the problem. By increasing pay, but without increasing the overall budget, we can afford to employ fewer people, but we are more likely to be able to fill all vacancies. Whereas, with a lower pay rate, we perhaps can afford to employ more people, but fewer people will want to work in the sector and many vacancies are unfilled. At a certain point this leads to many more people delayed in hospital (because the under-staffed home care system lacks the capacity to look after them). Therefore, under certain conditions, paying home care staff more actually makes the 'whole system' more affordable because fewer people will be in hospital.

To illustrate some of the model's behaviour, the letters superimposed on the model diagram Fig. 17.4 highlight how various connections affect model behaviour. In this case, we are exploring the impact of increasing the pay of home care staff on 'whole system costs'.

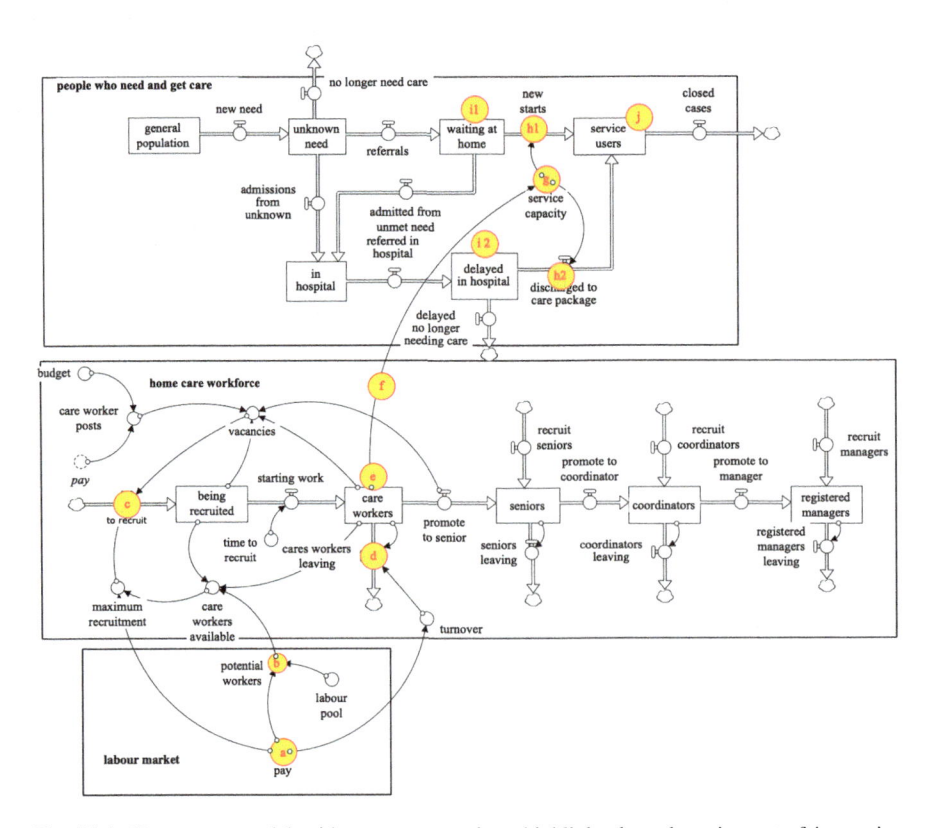

Fig. 17.4 Home care model with some connections highlighted to show impact of increasing home care staff hourly pay

17.2 Model 2—Care Workforce in the Context of the Wider Economy

(a) The rate of pay is increased
(b) This increases the number of people who might want to work in home care
(c) Which increases the inflow of new recruits (if there are vacancies)
(d) And REDUCES the turnover rate, therefore fewer people leave
(e) Increased inflow (c) and reduced outflow (d) result in more people in the care worker stock
(f) This increases the capacity of the system
(g) Which translates into an increase in the number of people who can be looked after at home
(h) The flows from both hospital (delayed discharges) and people waiting at home increase, leading to
(i) Fewer people, possibly almost none, on waiting lists, including people in the delayed discharge stock (which costs several hundred pounds per day per hospital bed)
(j) More people receiving care at home.

As Fig. 17.4 shows, a complicated chain of events follows when we change just one variable (pay rates). And, although it cannot be repeated indefinitely, this chain of cause and effect is in essence a virtuous feedback loop.

The model is capable of producing a wide range of outputs, mostly as dashboard graphs, but here we show just one thing, the impact of these changes on the 'whole system cost', being the combined costs of providing home care and the cost of delayed discharges (paying for hospital beds) as shown in Fig. 17.5.

In this scenario, the model is run for 10 years and there is a growing problem of delayed discharges, the cost of which rises steadily.

Five years into the run, **home care pay is increased**[2]. This leads to more carers being recruited (and paid more). The costs of home care go up, but the costs of delayed discharges reduce.

Most importantly, there is an overall cost reduction AND more people receive the care they need.

Fig. 17.5 Impact of increasing home care pay rates on whole system costs

17.3 Conclusions

This chapter has described two workforce models to assist with health and social care integration. The first demonstrated how a well-constructed model dashboard can provide a very visual management decision aid, in this case demonstrating the effect of creating 'generic' workers from different sources on the staffing of those sources over time. The second created a comprehensive representation of the interconnectedness between the labour market, the home care workforce and care users—both in the community, receiving service and in hospital. This provided a platform to explore the financial trade-offs between health and social care. The main insight so far was that a smaller but more highly rewarded social care workforce could more than pay for itself by reducing delayed hospital discharges.

Reference

Ham, C. (2018). *Making sense of integrated care systems, integrated care partnerships and accountable care organisations in the NHS in England.*

Chapter 18
A Summary of Systems Messages and Insights

Chapter Summary

This chapter summarises the book and draws together important patterns and themes from the project work. These are presented as a series of general systems messages and their equivalents in health and social care. A graphic is first presented which captures and summarises the approach of system dynamics to health and social care on one page. This is used to help understanding of the messages.

18.1 Summary of the Book

Overview

This book has presented examples from the work of the authors in using system dynamics modelling with management teams to study many different types of patient flows in health and social care. In particular to develop insights into persistent problems in this area. The work is wide ranging, but there are many common insights.

Figure 18.1 is a schematic view of the interconnectedness of the health and social care system. It represents a summary on one-page of what our approach and work has been about. It forms the basis of our computer simulations to examine the behaviour of flows of different health conditions under different treatments and constraints over time. This figure will be used here to help ground and consolidate the messages.

© Springer Nature Switzerland AG 2019
E. Wolstenholme and D. McKelvie, *The Dynamics of Care*,
https://doi.org/10.1007/978-3-030-21878-2_18

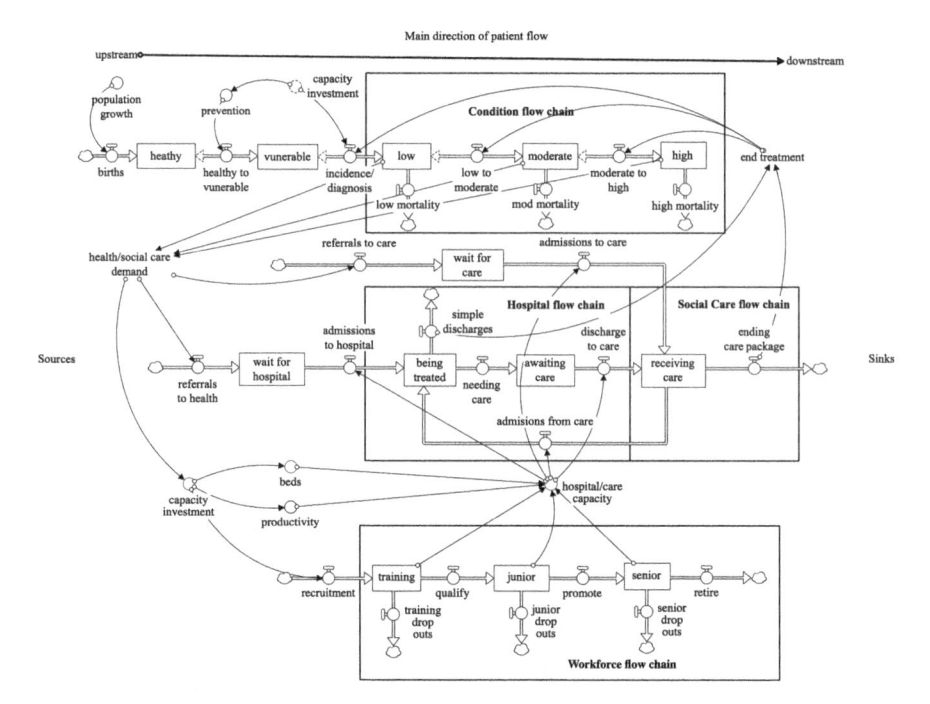

Fig. 18.1 A stock-flow and feedback perspective of health and social care conditions and service delivery

There are three types of flow chains in Fig. 18.1:

- condition flow chains,
- health and social care treatment flow chains
- capacity and workforce flow chains.

Each are described in the language of stocks and flows. A stock is a measurable accumulation of a flow and a flow the way in which stocks are filled and drained. Flow variables provide the levers by which we can try to control the flows, perhaps towards desirable performance targets.

It should be noted in Fig. 18.1 that the main direction of patient flow is from left to right and that variables towards the left are hence referred to as upstream variables and those to the right as downstream variables.

Condition Flow Chains

The demand for health and social care arises from people flowing through many different health conditions. These are largely *natural* flows due to condition incidence and degeneration and are uni-directional for degenerative conditions and bi-directional for non-degenerative conditions. The whole purpose of health and social care can be described as an attempt to slow down and where possible reverse progression along these chains. This is mainly achieved by trying to use public health to raise awareness of factors which lead to vulnerabilities and by the diagnosis of conditions which can be referred for treatment.

Health and Social Care Treatment Flow Chains

When prevention fails and primary interventions are exhausted, the alternative is to refer patients with different states of conditions for further diagnosis or for different forms of treatment, direct to health or social care. The hospital flow chain in Fig. 18.1 is applicable to both day care and inpatients. One of the major problems is that some older people often require both health and social care in that order whilst others require episodic admissions to hospital whilst in care (sometime referred to as a revolving door). These effects lead to hospital congestion if health and social care capacities are imbalanced. Treatment flow chains are not natural flow chains but chains built by people which can be designed, configured and controlled.

Capacity and Workforce Flow Chains

Diagnosis and treatment obviously depend on capacity which can take the form of facilities, beds and workforce, all of which can be improved by productivity and technology. These capacities act to limit the treatment flows in health and social care flow chains. Figure 18.1 focuses on workforce, the effectiveness of which relies on recruitment, retirement and leaving policies.

This book has described many projects both within and between different forms and sub-divisions of the flow chains captured in Fig. 18.1. The emphasis throughout has been on designing and testing policies which might improve efficacy and performance and hopefully lead to people retuning to less severe states of their condition flow chains.

18.2 Concluding Messages

For ease of reference the insights are presented as a set of systems messages applicable to any flow chain, together with how these relate to health and social care. The messages are classified as:

- general stock and flow chain messages,
- treatment flow chain messages,
- treatment bottleneck messages,

- health condition messages,
- workforce flow chain messages
- others messages.

General Stock-Flow Messages

- It is important to recognise the difference between *stocks* and *flows* in flow chains. Stocks are accumulations of resources and flows are changes over time of resource flows into and out of stocks. By distinguishing between *stocks* and *flows* we are effectively distinguishing between *static pictures of systems*, (point-in-time data) and *dynamic moving pictures of systems* (change over time data).

    'being treated', 'awaiting care' and 'receiving care' are examples of stocks, whereas 'admissions', 'discharges' and 'referrals' are examples of flows. Prevalence of a condition is a stock and incidence of a condition is a flow, as are movements between low, moderate and high states of a condition

- stocks can be of two kinds
    - *time-dependent stocks* where a resource passes through the stock over a time period (here the outflow is dependent on the stock level)
    - *buffer stocks* where the inflows and the outflows do not directly relate to the size of the stock and can only be changed indirectly through other parts of the chain in which they reside, such as changing upstream gatekeeping rules or downstream capacities. Buffers act as a means of delaying and dampening a fluctuating inflow into a smoother outflow.

    'patients being treated', 'receiving care' and in 'health condition states' are time-dependent stocks

    patients on waiting lists for treatment are in a buffer type stock separating fluctuating referrals from steady, perhaps capacity constrained treatment starts

    patients in a state of delayed hospital discharge are in a buffer between steady treatment finishes and fluctuating social care constrained discharge

    in hospital systems the only real and safe holding buffer is the elective wait list

18.2 Concluding Messages

Treatment Flow Chain Messages

- to increase throughput in a flow chain, it is generally much cheaper and more sustainable to change flow variables, rather than stock variables.

    *THROUGHPUT is the dominant key to improving the performance
    of HEALTH treatments*

    *to increase throughput in a patient pathway it is cheaper and more
    sustainable to change admission and discharge flows rather than bed capacities
    which will quickly fill up again*

    *CAPACITY is the dominant key to improving the performance
    of SOCIAL CARE since this keeps people safe and out of hospital*

- input to any flow chain should be planned on a basis of closing any gaps between the capacity and current levels of each stock AND replacing the average outflows from *each* stock in the chain.

    *hospital admissions must be planned on a basis of spare beds (capacity-beds
    in use) AND average discharges*

- if any stock in a flow chain leaks, as in drop outs, then this leakage must be also recognised as a stock outflow and allowed for in designing treatment capacity.

    *admissions to treatment programmes should also allow for drop outs
    at each stage of treatment*

- dynamic equilibrium is a good starting point for understanding flows. When a flow chain is in dynamic equilibrium all its flows are equal and the levels of all its stocks are constant. Dynamic equilibrium defines sustainability.

    *when hospitals are operating at capacity, admissions and discharges
    are in dynamic equilibrium and admissions can only be increased by increasing
    discharges. If referrals are greater than admissions and admissions cannot
    be increased, wait times will rise relentlessly because the waiting list will grow
    at each time step but its outflow (admissions) will not.*

    *hence treatment managers have no control over waiting lists and waiting times
    and to set targets for these waits is futile*

    *another way to say this is that buffer stocks cannot be controlled within the
    practical limits of capacity*

Balancing Capacity Messages

- bottlenecks determine the throughput of any flow chain—the overall capacity of any flow system is equal to the maximum flow capacity of its most severe bottleneck.

    in many countries where health and social care are state provided services, hospital performance is limited by social care capacity

- bottlenecks often occur in the section of the flow chain with the least power to do anything about it.

    in health and social care systems bottlenecks are predominately in social care

- downstream blockages have significant implications for upstream agencies. They feedback to provoke the use of coping strategies, all of which can have costly unintended consequences which can be more expensive than reducing the bottleneck.

    a lack of social care capacity results in delayed discharges in hospitals which in turn provokes the use of coping strategies to maintain patient flows. For example, the use of boarders, early discharge, demand management, emergency overspill areas and the spot purchase of both health and social care. All of these have unintended consequences for patients, staff and costs. For example, cancelled elective procedures, increased time in hospital, infections, additional unmet need, inefficient treatment and reduced staff productivity. Many of these consequences exacerbate the situation by reducing capacities, causing readmissions and increased future demand

- downstream blockages stifle and negate upstream innovation and investment to increase throughput.

    lack of social care capacity can nullify elements of both capacity investment AND efficiency and productivity gains in hospitals

- blaming and applying sanctions to the owners of the bottleneck is counter-productive.

    blaming social care for hospital delayed discharges does not solve the problem

18.2 Concluding Messages

- it is in the interests of any upstream agency to invest in expanding any limiting downstream capacity. This can be cheaper than the costs of coping with the constraint.

  hospitals should invest in social care provision
  (this does not mean buying social care on the spot market.)

- unblocking a flow system requires unblocking all bottlenecks together. The cost of opening a bottleneck is small compared with the volume of throughput enabled.

  health and social care investment should be proportionally balanced
  and such balance is a win-win scenario for both agencies, patients
  and staff

- investments in flow chains in the aftermath of periods of bottlenecks should allow for the additional spending necessary to return the chain to its normal mode of operation. Otherwise the investment will simply be used for the reestablishment of normality and not show the benefits it was intended for.

  investment in health and social care must recognise accrued financial
  debts incurred during periods of coping

- some elements of integrating health and social care can result in small changes in the right place and can lever large effects.

  placing nursing staff in care homes can significantly lower hospital
  occupancy levels, reducing the need for informal coping strategies

  a flexible workforce is vital to integrating care

  paying care agencies and care staff appropriately can increase care quality
  and more than pay for itself in reducing delayed hospital discharges

  integrating elements of health and social care can save money but is not a
  substitute for balancing investment between the two

- when introducing new services into a treatment flow chain it is important to manage the transition to those services.

when moving to stepped care services by balancing resources across a flow chain, it is necessary to progressively transfer resources from the specialised end of the services to the less specialised end or reallocate cases in order to deal with outstanding cases

Health Condition Messages

- planning capacities in a flow chain requires an understanding of the flow chains which drive it.

    the success of capacity planning in the supply of health and social care services depends on understanding the dynamics of population ageing and the dynamics of health conditions, both of which create the demand for treatment services. In particular, it is necessary to recognise net flows of people between condition states to design appropriate diagnostic and treatment capacity

- supply flow chains should be designed to be appropriate to their demand flow chains.

    maximising the effectiveness of health treatment (maximum numbers treated with minimum waits and minimum cost) requires segregating conditions and applying treatment appropriate to each segment

- it is often helpful to examine more than one dimension of flow chains.

    deriving matrices of age and health condition is useful to understanding treatment demand

- it is important to recognise bi-directional movement in some flow chains.

    in alcohol dependency flow chains people can quickly move up and down the chain and treatment capacity can be saved by recognising this effect

- whereas in a service pathway chain, often the most powerful interventions are downstream, in a health condition flow chain, where possible, upstream (stocks and flows) should be targeted for reduction. Because flows are connected, lowering upstream stocks will automatically reduce downstream stocks.

    reducing the level of vulnerable people by health prevention will reduce the level of those needing treatment and cure

18.2 Concluding Messages

diagnosing and treating conditions at an early stage has greater efficacy than doing it at a later stage. (However, this depends on whether earlier but lengthier low intensity treatment is less costly than later but shorter high intensity treatment, which in turn depends on the condition considered)

reducing the level of short-term incapacitated will automatically reduce the level of the long-term incapacitated

- success to the successful.

  a successful health service will reduce degeneration and increase longevity and must plan extra capacity to cope with its success

- when stocks have multiple inputs and outputs there are infinite permutations of parameters for these flows which will produce the same stock level.

  the same level of prevalence (stock) of a long-term condition can arise through many different permutations of condition incidence, progression and mortality (flows)

  the faster people flow through long-term conditions the greater the mortality and the more difficult it is to achieve high levels of diagnosis

Workforce Flow Chain Messages

- ideally, input to any workforce flow chain should be planned in a similar way to treatment flow chains. Recruitment of new staff must allow for:
  - closing any gaps between the target and actual staff in each grade
  - closing any gaps between the target and actual staff in training
  - replacing people retiring
  - replacing people dropping out in each grade
  - allowing for recruitment and training delays and workforce availability
  - flexibility in the provision of training places.

Other Messages

- good, integrated information systems and data are vital to the effective operation of flow chains, but what we often find are information systems whose purpose is 'performance reporting' rather than management 'decision support'; they reflect some historical, often external, view about what was important about a service rather than the need to describe 'what actually happens'.

the relationships inherent in dynamic models can be used to test data-bases for consistency and to triangulate missing data

health and social care information systems should record and extract data on flows, going beyond the routinely-collected admissions and discharges; the kind of flows that are often not counted may include transfers of people between different departments or service types, especially when crossing the health/social care boundary, or flows associated with joining and leaving waiting lists (we have often found that hospitals can give a number for quite obscure transfers of patients, whilst being unable to tell us 'the number of people per month who are discharged to a package of care at home' which goes to the heart of health and social care integration)

similarly, stock information can be hidden by the imperative to count 'key performance indicators' that may be composite measures of stock and flow data, such as 'number of people seen in past year' being the stock at the start of the year plus the new admissions during the year

not recognising data 'churn' can result in underachievement of risk assessment, or over-estimation of/unwarranted optimism about the likely impact of a new treatment

- system dynamics should be used as a strategic precursor to other operational methods of performance improvement. It is vital to analyse vulnerabilities across whole flow chains before carrying out detailed analysis of any one sector of the chain.

    It is essential to analyse whole patient pathways prior to detailed improvement initiatives in any one sector such as hospitals, as these may be negated by problems in other parts of the chain such as social care

- all too often much more effort is focused in cost benefit analysis on the determination of per unit or per capita costs and benefits and less on the number of units achievable. Understanding the flow of resources over time is fundamental to improving cost benefit studies and converting them into 'dynamic impact studies'.

    System dynamics in health and social care provides a means of assessing where patients come from and go to, the numbers accessing treatments, the numbers dropping out and the numbers benefiting.

18.3 A Final Word

This book has sought to demonstrate the power of dynamic models in providing insights into the pressing problems faced in health and social care. Recent years have seen how developments in computers have transformed our abilities to map and model complex issues in many fields and it is hoped that the work here will encourage clinicians, managers and analysts to recognise what such approaches can offer. We reiterate that the value comes from trying to see beyond conventional organisational or departmental boundaries and from communicating, sharing and testing mental models altruistically in a timely and cost-effective manner, to the benefit of all agencies, staff and, not least, patients.

Glossary

Terms Related to System Dynamics
(A combination of adaptations from the System Dynamics Society website, system dynamics software and personal views)

A System	A collection of elements working together as parts of a complex whole whose behaviour is greater than the sum of the parts. The word systems is often used to refer to complex phenomena existing in the world (such as, financial systems, health systems and computer systems) but the true meaning of systems refers more to an abstract or model of such phenomena existing only in a conceptual world we construct to think about systems.
Agent Based Modelling	A style of computer simulation based on the actions and interactions of autonomous agents. This type of modelling can be thought of as a combination of continuous and discrete simulation methods.
Bottleneck	A point of congestion in a flow chain usually caused by restricted capacity.
Causal Loop Maps	Causal Loop maps are a means of exposing and articulating the causal feedback processes at work in a complex system.
Complexity	Having a large number of interconnected elements which allow systems to be self-organising and adaptive, especially where the connections themselves form feedback loops (a influences b, b influences c, and c influences a).

Connectors	Information or influence links in stock flow maps connecting stocks or external sources to flows which feed policies to drive flows.
Convertors	Intermediate stages in connectors, often used to convert the dimensions of variables between flow chains of different resources. For example, price (cost per person) converts people per day to cost per day.
Delays	Lags in information or action or effects in flow chains which give rise to counterintuitive behaviour of flow chains.
Detailed Complexity	The number of elements contained in a system
Discrete Event Simulation Modelling	A method of computer simulation based on the movement of individual entities through systems over time represented as activities, sampled from statistical distributions, and queues.
Dynamic Complexity	The number of interconnections contained in a system.
Dynamic Equilibrium	A particular important behaviour of a system where inflows and outflows of stocks have the same value and hence the stock levels remain the same even though there is flow through them. Dynamic equilibrium can be thought of as a definition of sustainability. Dynamic equilibrium is the best way to set up the initial conditions of a system dynamics model for experimentation since any subsequent policy changes can then be seen as real effects.
Dynamical Systems	Systems where movement and flow is important and where evolution is as a result of internal (endogenous) rules based on feedback within and between sub-organisations.
Expert Groups and Group Model Building	A working group constituted to oversee the construction and validation of a system dynamics model and consisting of all representatives of all organisations and departments impacting on and responsible for a particular issue. Any model needs primarily to be a combination of the mental models of the group and to be owned by the group.
Feedback Loops	Feedback loops exists when information resulting from some action travels through a system and eventually returns in some form to its point of origin, potentially influencing future action.

Glossary

	If the tendency in the loop is to reinforce the initial action, the loop is called a positive or reinforcing feedback loop; if the tendency is to oppose the initial action, the loop is called a negative or balancing feedback loop. The sign of the loop is called its polarity which is derived from the polarities of its individual causal links. Balancing loops are goal-seeking loops which tend to stabilise systems, whereas reinforcing loops are growth or collapse loops which tend to destabilise systems.
Flow Chain	A sequence of stocks and flows in parallel or series through which a resource, such as people, is passing,
High Leverage Interventions	Small changes to a system which produce big effects.
Homeostatis	The internal feedback capacity of an organism to sustain stillness.
Microworld	A free-standing form of a model to facilitate experimentation by participants either privately or in workshops, possibly using their own data.
Model Dashboards	Model interfaces containing major inputs and outputs and performance measures of a model to facilitate experiments without recourse to the detail of a model.
Modelling as Learning	The process of experimenting with virtual models in a risk-free environment to learn about the behaviour of the real system.
Reference Modes of Behaviour	An observed past trend and future projected trends over time used to assist in defining the scope, time frame and validation of a system dynamics model.
Sources/Sinks	An infinite origin/destination of a flow chain.
STELLA Architect	A particular version of system dynamics software used in this book.
Stocks and Flows	A language by which to visualise and map the structure of a system in terms of accumulations and flows.
System Archetypes	System archetypes are generic combinations of reinforcing and balancing feedback loops which give rise to specific dynamic patterns of behaviour over time. Since there are only two types of feedback loops there are only four basic types of system archetypes. System archetypes are a concise means of articulating the problems

	caused by ***unintended consequences*** arising from ***well-intended*** actions and designing solutions necessary to mitigate these.
System Behaviour	The term used in system dynamics to refer to the behaviour over time of a particular system structure.
System Dynamics	System Dynamics is a systems-based computer simulation approach to policy analysis and design based on a language of stocks and flows. The approach can be considered as a continuous, aggregate simulation method analogous to water flows through bathtubs and pipes and combines elements of fluid dynamics and control engineering. It applies to dynamic problems arising in complex social, managerial, economic, or ecological systems–any dynamic systems characterized by interdependence, mutual interaction, information feedback, and circular causality. It facilitates the emulation of such systems for the purpose of communication, sharing and redesign.
System Dynamics Software	Purpose built simulation software used to model in system dynamics.
System Structure	The term used in system dynamics to refer to the total structure of a system (composing processes, organisational boundaries, information feedback, policy, and delays).
Systems Messages	Messages which are generic to any system.
Systems Thinking	Generally, the interpretation of the world as a complex, self-regulating and adaptive system based on taking a holistic, as distinct from a reductionist, perspective. Specifically, in system dynamics a way of using the feedback structures at the heart of system dynamics to hypothesise system behaviour over time without using formal simulation (or to help the conceptualisation of a system dynamics model or to explain its behaviour).
Unintended Consequences	The side effects of well-intended policies.
Upstream/Downstream	Stocks that are located towards the origin of a flow chain/towards the destination of a flow chain.
Wicked Problems	Long-standing problems that are resistant to solution.

Terms Related to Health and Social Care

Acute Hospitals	Hospital dealing with short-term conditions requiring mainly one-off treatments.
Adult Social Care	The provision of care services in Residential Care Homes and At Home (Domiciliary Care).
Better Care Fund	A pooled budget between Local Authorities and the NHS in England to better integrate health and social care services.
Clinical Commissioning Groups (CCGs) [Formerly Primary Care Trusts (PCTs)]	The local operating agencies of the NHS in England, which both commission (buy) and deliver health services.
Cognitive Behavioural Therapy (CBT)	A type of Psychological Therapy used to treat mental health patients.
Co-Morbidity	Patients having more than one serious health condition.
Coping Strategies	The strategies employed by service providers to attempt to maintain patient flow when faced with excessive demand beyond their delivery capacity.
General Practitioners (GPs)	Locally based general clinicians who deliver primary care services and control access to specialist secondary health and social care services.
Health Conditions	States or stages of an illness such as mild, moderate and severe.
Health Treatment	The application of drugs, therapies, and medical/surgical interventions to treat illness.
Hospital Delayed Transfers of Care—Delayed Hospital Discharges	Patients in hospital who have finished treatment and are fit for discharge but cannot be discharged, usually as a result of needing continuing heath or social care packages.
Incapacity Benefit (IB)	A state benefit in the UK paid to people who are unable to work for a period of more than 28 consecutive weeks because of illness or disability. Now replaced by Employment and Support Allowance (ESA).
Incidence	The onset of a condition, therefore the number of people per unit of time becoming unwell.
Increasing Access to Psychological Therapies (IAPT)	A set of NHS initiatives in England to provide increased access to psychological therapies.

Integrated Care	A means of co-ordinating the delivery of diverse health and social care services to the same person, based on the belief that services should be centred on the person, not the provider.
Intermediate Care	Short-term care between primary and secondary care, takes various forms, including 'admission avoidance' and 'discharge support'.
Local Government Association (LGA)	The Body in England responsible for representing Local Government and hence Social Care.
National Health Service (NHS)	The organisation in the UK responsible for the delivery of health care. It takes different forms (and names) in each of the countries of the UK.
NHS Confederation	The body in England responsible for representing individual NHS organisations.
NHS Continuing Care	The provision of health services inside and outside hospitals and in nursing homes.
NICE	The National Institute for Health and Care Excellence (covering mostly England).
Nursing Homes	Private and public residential establishments providing care for older people.
Outliers/Boarders	Patients located in hospital wards not related to their condition, due to bed shortages.
PARR	People at risk of readmission to hospital ("rehospitalisation").
Prevalence	The number or percentage of people in a population having a particular condition of an illness.
QOL	Quality of Life Index.
Risk Stratification	A means of classifying patients at risk of readmission to hospital.
Scheduled or Elective Care	Medical or surgical procedures where treatment is chosen by the patient.
Social Services	In the UK, services which provide non-health-related care, mainly for children and older people, located within local government (except in Northern Ireland).
Spot Purchase of Services	Purchase of care services outside existing framework agreements.

State Provided Health Services	Health services provided by the state through taxation as distinct from private health care funded through insurance.
Step Up and Step Down	The movement of patients between different levels of a health or care service.
Unscheduled or Emergency Care	Medical or surgical procedures arising from accidents or emergencies.
Well-Being	The state of being comfortable, fortunate, healthy or happy.

Terms Related to Health and Social Care Workforce

CWDC	Children's Workforce Development Council.
EWTD	European Working Time Directive.
EYPs	Early Years Professionals.
PLO	Practice Learning Opportunity.

Printed by Printforce, the Netherlands